COUNT BASIE
AND HIS ORCHESTRA

COUNT BASIE
AND HIS ORCHESTRA
Its Music and its Musicians

by

RAYMOND HORRICKS

With discography by
ALUN MORGAN

NEGRO UNIVERSITIES PRESS
WESTPORT, CONNECTICUT

The Library of Congress cataloged this book as follows:

Horricks, Raymond, 1933–
    Count Basie and his orchestra, its music and its musi-
cians. With discography by Alun Morgan. Westport,
Conn., Negro Universities Press ₁1971₁

   320 p. ports. 23 cm.

   Reprint of the 1957 ed.

1. Basie, Count, 1906– I. Title.	2. Jazz music.	3. Jazz musicians.
ML422.B25H6 1971 ISBN 0–8371–5656–4	785.4'2	79–138009 MARC
Library of Congress	72 ₁4₁	MN

Originally published in 1957 by Victor Gollancz Ltd., London

Reprinted with the permission of Victor Gollancz Ltd.

Reprinted in 1971 by Negro Universities Press, A Division of
Greenwood Press, Inc., 51 Riverside Avenue, Westport, Conn.

Library of Congress catalog card number 79-138009
ISBN 0-8371-5656-4

Printed in the United States of America

10 9 8 7 6 5 4

PREFACE

THE AMERICAN JAZZ scene in the 1950's has produced several significant small musical units: Gerry Mulligan's piano-less Quartet, a John Lewis-inspired Modern Jazz Quartet, Art Blakey and The Jazz Messengers, the Jay Jay Johnson-Kai Winding Quintet, the Max Roach-Clifford Brown Quintet, the Duke Jordan and Hank Jones Trios, Chico Hamilton's Workshop Quintet with flautist Buddy Collette, not least the Vanguard mainstream unit built around Edmond Hall, Vic Dickenson and Sir Charles Thompson. Each of these groups may be said to have acted as a lever in the evolution and development of collective jazz playing. And just as these groups of musicians have gradually widened the boundaries of ensemble construction and unit rapport, so a small number of new soloists have emerged—Joe Wilder and Randy Weston are two who spring immediately to mind—capable of expanding the music's improvisation.

Operating alongside these smaller units and soloists in the 1950's, the Count Basie Orchestra (at times in the face of opposition from the Duke Ellington and Stan Kenton bands) has slowly but surely re-established itself as the major force in the forward progression of the big band in jazz.

Basie's present domination of orchestral jazz cannot be argued against. He prospers economically and artistically, drawing capacity crowds to each and every "live" performance, supporting an expensive collection of jazz soloists within the band's framework, and carrying off the principal award in the *Downbeat* critics' poll almost automatically each year. In the main, musicians and critics are for once unanimous in their praise for the band's aesthetic qualities; audiences have been registering their appreciation even more ecstatically. Moreover, Basie's musical ideals, so expertly incorporated into the band's unique jazz style, are spreading their way into the musical policies of other bands and units, even into the individual styles of soloists, linking together

5

otherwise diverse schools of thought in jazz and indicating the path jazz invention is likely to follow within the next few years.

André Hodeir's despairing cry (and it is indeed a rarity for the dispassionate M. Hodeir to make so emotional an utterance), in his book, "Jazz: Its Evolution And Essence", that the big band form is now bankrupt has not reached all the heartstrings for which it was intended. His neat, pigeon-holing statement, "the fact that the world's foremost critics chose the band Count Basie had just reorganized as the best large orchestra of 1954 shows pretty well how stagnate this form of language remains", has misfired on him. It is the body of musicians, and not any one critic, which decides ultimately when a particular musical form has become bankrupt for jazz—when it is no longer navigable as a means for expressing fresh ideas. The fact that the vast majority of jazz musicians actively creating at the present time (and here I am speaking of arrangers as different in approach as Shorty Rogers, Quincy Jones, John Lewis and Johnny Mandel, and to soloists as varying in character as Lee Konitz and Milton Jackson) are revising their policies for the further progression of jazz so as to take in elements of the Basie band's approach provides sufficient proof that the Count's stylistic methods are still a suitable springboard for the innovator. For better or for worse, the jazz *avant garde* has re-associated itself with the Count Basie band and has upheld the band's style as an official means of ensuring a healthy development in the future.

It is the objective of this book to provide a survey of the Count Basie Orchestra's twenty years or more of existence, examining not only the personal fortunes of the leader but also something of the band's highly-individual style of playing and of the important musicians who have passed through its ranks and aided the Count in making such a style of expression possible. For remember, though the contemporary Basie band has achieved this rarity which we describe as security, financially as well as artistically, this band is but one link in a chain of important musical groups forged over the years by the Count. Basie has always led significant collections of jazz musicians even if he hasn't always achieved the widest popular appeal with them; from the unit which in 1936 left its native Kansas City and burst with the force of a tornado upon the New York jazz scene, through to the present-day group, this shy, amiable pianist has persevered with a sequence of bands, holding on tenaciously to his musical ideals

6

the whole time and enlisting as his allies an outstanding set of improvising musicians. Many of the most influential soloists in jazz have worked their passage with the band—men who have nevertheless respected Basie's ensemble decisions in addition to expressing their own solo styles.

I have constructed this book to the best of my ability without prejudice against any one band that Basie has led. The Count Basie Orchestra for me represents one complete entity, spread over the course of two decades; it is impossible to discuss one band without mentioning the others; no one, I believe, can satisfactorily understand the ideals of the contemporary group without first analysing the groups which have preceded it *and anticipated it.*

The thoroughness of Alun Morgan's accompanying discography precludes me from designing the main body of the book as a systematic progression from one recording session to the next, detailing every change in the group's personnel, and so on; nor would I have wished to approach the subject in this way. It is pointless becoming a glorified programme-seller (like certain academicians now writing about jazz that I know), carefully noting such facts as: "The band has appeared exactly twenty-seven times in Boston and three times in Portland." Every subject has its academicians, its critics whose chief aim is to reduce everything, quite impersonally, to a mass of diagrams, decipherable only by their own little club; like old ladies at a tea-party, fussily percolating tea through silver-plated strainers, they listen only to dissect. No, due to Alun Morgan's discographical spade-work (and in Basie's case a sound discography has recorded pretty accurately the changes within the band's ranks over the years) I have been free to examine the band's music and a number of its interesting musicians rather more closely.

As the book progresses, after two rather lengthy chapters (the first dealing with the more human side of Basie as a leader, the second describing how the band's musical style was gradually achieved and how it has since developed and influenced others over the years) the reader comes upon a series of essays, all of which stress the importance of the individual within the workings of the band. Headed by a chapter on Basie's piano playing, the series attempts a coverage of the various inventive solo minds and arrangers who have been responsible for much of the sustained artistic success of the band, with longer analytical essays on the musicians I consider to have been of the greatest importance, and shorter features on the others. I have not included biographical material on every one of the scores of musicians to pass through the band during its extensive existence, but I have striven to include every musician who has lent a definite character to the band's musical outflow, either by their individual playing or by their arranging. Though the Count Basie band has never evidenced the versatility and the profundity of mood, nor the delicate textures and tone colourings of its chief adversary over the years, the legendary Duke Ellington Orchestra, purely as an instrumental unit, despite the dissimilarities in style, it has proved a worthy contestant. Very rugged in its swing and generally more extrovert emotionally, it has nevertheless displayed in its looser ensemble patterns a collective musicianship, and during its passages of improvisation a series of individual solos, which Duke Ellington has been hard put to at times to contest.

For convenience I have divided the essays dealing with the soloists, arrangers, singers, etc., into two distinct sections, relating to two phases of the Basie band's existence, which the reader will note I refer to as "the old band" and "the new band".

Such terms as "old" and "new" are naturally only superficial in their application to a series of band personnels linked over a period of two decades by the same identifiable musical style. Yet although Count Basie has been a bandleader continuously since 1935, at one point in his career, on account of economic difficulties, he was forced to break up his large group and for a period of more than a year become the leader of an all-star septet. This septet was in existence during the years 1950–1951. Once the depression within the band business had safely passed, the Count reorganized his big band, a group he has led through to the present day. I have made use of this break in the existence of the full-sized band to identify the sidemen with their respective phases of the band's life. For, while the sidemen of the band's earlier period were generally of the same age group as Basie, those of the contemporary band are, in the main, of a younger generation than their leader. The reader should not be misled at the outset into believing that "old" and "new" denote revolutionary changes in musical policy between one group and another; certain changes have occurred, but the bands remain firmly linked musically.

In collecting biographical information, human anecdotes, notes from recording sessions and other details for the book, I have been either assisted or encouraged at different stages by a number of people, and I would like to express my gratitude to them all for their unselfish efforts which have so improved this introduction to Count Basie.

My friend Alun Morgan's handling of the gargantuan discography speaks for itself. Collaboration with Alun over this project has been as pleasant as it was for our previous book "Modern Jazz". The statements by Basie's present arranger, Ernie Wilkins (my "inside man"), which frequently garnish the course of the book also make their value obvious. Despite a heavy programme of work, Ernie found time to answer all my questions.

I have to thank Ernie Mills of Vogue Records Ltd. for permission to reprint, with suitable additions and amendments, the liner notes I had written for his company on Harry Edison and Thad Jones; also to Albert J. McCarthy, the editor of "Jazz Monthly", for permission to reprint articles I had earlier contributed to his magazine on Lester Young, Joe Newman and Joe Williams. Nat Hentoff and Nat Shapiro, and their publishers, Rinehart & Co. of New York, have assisted my work by allowing the incorporation of a number of quotations from their book, "Hear Me Talkin' To Ya", into my text.

Conversations with visiting American pianists Jimmy Jones, Marty Paich and Gene Di Novi have yielded interesting facts and points of view; so has a correspondence with arranger Quincy Jones.

Of the British critics, Stanley Dance displayed an interest in the book when it was only in the embryo stage, and he subsequently provided me with useful information and certain obscure magazine articles. From time to time I have also consulted Max Jones, Charles Fox, Vic Bellerby, John Forrester and Norman Jenkinson—and I have made use of the latter's enormous record collection. Carlo Krahmer of Esquire Records has supplied me with dubbings of several rare recorded items, while of equal importance, Derek Coller of "The Discophile" and Jorgen G. Jepsen have supplied Alun Morgan with information about rare recordings.

My thanks go to all these people, and finally to my wife Sheila, who has supplemented my own work by easing the secretarial duties, and who has provided, at the right moments, the right amounts of coffee and alcohol.

Ashford, Middlesex　　　　　　　　　RAYMOND HORRICKS
December 1956

ACKNOWLEDGMENTS

The words of the lyric on page 148, *Sent For You Yesterday*, are copyright by Bregman, Vocco and Conn, Inc., and are printed by their permission in Canada and by kind permission of Messrs. Chappell and Co. Ltd. throughout the rest of the British Commonwealth.

All the photographs are reproduced by kind permission of the "Melody Maker". Where it has been possible to ascertain individual photographers, credit has been given in the text. The author wishes to thank all concerned.

CONTENTS

ILLUSTRATIONS

between pages 160-161

Benny Goodman with Count Basie in the late 1930's

Count Basie, Artie Shaw and Duke Ellington at The Bandbox in New York

Harry Edison

Freddie Greene

Joe Sullivan, Dicky Wells, George Wettling and Walter Page

Count Basie and Jimmy Rushing at Basie's twentieth anniversary dinner

Joe Williams

Lester Young

Thad Jones and Joe Newman

Frank Wess and Frank Foster

Frank Wess, Ernie Wilkins and Marshall Royal

Charlie Fowlkes and Henry Coker

The saxophone section: (*l. to r.*) Frank Wess, Ernie Wilkins, Marshall Royal, Frank Foster and Charlie Fowlkes. *Behind:* Gus Johnson (*drums*) and Freddie Greene (*guitar*)

CHAPTER I

BASIE THE LEADER

In his casual travel discourse "The Colossus of Maroussi", the singular Henry Miller, caught up in his familiar fantasia of thought, waxes grandiloquent on the subject of Bill Basie, describing the pianist and bandleader in such terms as: "Count Basie (*sent for you yesterday here you come today*), long lost brother of Isidore Ducasse and last direct descendant of the great and only Rimbaud." Later on in the book he heaps still further complexities upon Basie's character and playing. We read of how: "On a certain day it became the Fourth of July, which is Dipsy-Doodle day in Walla Walla. Louis had by this time made a few friends as he went riffin' his way through the new land. One was a Count and another was a Duke. They carried little white rats on their finger-tips and when they couldn't stand it any longer, the sad, white gut bucket of the world, they bit with the ends of their fingers and where they bit it was like a laboratory of guinea pigs going crazy with experimentation. The Count, was a two-fingered specialist, built small and round like a rotunda, with a little moustache. He always began—*bink-bink*! Bink for poison, bink for arson. He was quiet and steady like, a sort of introverted gorilla who, when he got bogged in the depths of the gerundive, would speak French like a marquis or babble in Polish or Lithuanian. He never started twice the same way. And when he came to the end, unlike other poison and arson men, he always stopped. He always stopped sudden like, and the piano sank with him and the little white rats too. Until the next time. . ."
To approach Basie via Miller's thinking is surely to be confronted by an enigmatic figure, a man torn betwixt inspirational heights, at times raising his creation to the same level as that of the giants of other artistic fields, and the fashionable couch of the psychologist.
In reality Count Basie has led a private life *and a musical one* remarkably free from complication, earning the esteem not only of the musicians who have passed under his command but also

of the many more who have made only slight contact with him as an essentially simple, honest and forthright personality.

It has been rather the tradition in the past three decades or more for bandleaders—as figures constantly before the impressionable public eye—to effect poses or to allow certain eccentric manners to become firmly attached to their reputations. Ellington has his enormous collection of suits, shirts and other splendid accoutrements; Shaw and Barnet a liberal tally of wives; Calloway his balloon-like trousers; Kenton his spasmodic medical studies; Armstrong a pile of white handkerchiefs almost as high as the Empire State building; Hampton a perpetual lather of perspiration. Compared with these exaggerations of manner, dress, etc., Basie's personal habits must appear very ordinary. If one were to analyse deliberately his life for eccentricity it would be difficult to press the case very much beyond his healthy appetite for food, his rarely-disturbed high spirits, his predilection for soft felt hats—on the smallish side—worn with the brim upturned and a determination (yet to achieve fruition) to master the subtle game of golf. The writer of the gossip column and the seeker of sensationalism, the cynic and the moral reformer; these people would not find easy cannon fodder if they directed their literary guns at Count Basie's way of life, though they might be personally impressed as they looked through their sights at him on account of his freedom from inhibition, his modesty, his physical and mental stamina, not least his simple belief that what he has to say in his music is a sincere expression and that he will continue to say it in spite of the rapid fluctuations of fashion in the dog-eat-dog environment of the musical profession.

Simplicity is perhaps the surest keyword to his personality —as indeed it is to his singular musical style. His is a balanced simplicity. Just as his piano playing is devoid of glamorous cascades of notes and superfluous runs, and his orchestra free from unnecessary technical displays, so his life has escaped being cluttered up to choking point with intrigues, enormous affectations of manner and even the shoulder chips of tree-like proportions which so many artistic figures deliberately make a part of their daily burden.

The Count is a balanced, integrated personality, who suffers from the same passions and sorrows and disappointments as the next man but who has never allowed such feelings to become the bane of his existence. Many years spent in leading a band have not successfully bogged down his normal jovial high spirits, and if these have been unable to depress him, then very little else has stood much chance. He has been too industrious playing *and actually living* his music to ever become soured by the many pitfalls which have disrupted his path. In the lean times he has always struggled on, firmly fixing his eyes and mind upon his immediate task, inwardly composed and certain that the milk-and-honey days will have their turn too. He has given so much of himself to his playing and leading. So much of his life has been engaged in the cause of music, in thinking about its creation, in discussing it and experimenting with it; so much of his time has been spent on the concert platform, or in the rehearsal room, or jamming backstage after the show, or in travelling between musical locations, living the music still above the pounding, screaming wheels of the railway coach or the scudding rubber tyres of the band-bus. Living his music and really becoming a part of it has kept him so busy that the time allotted for sitting down and brooding and lamenting over misfortunes has been practically nil. He's taken his share of the rough times, but even when the slumps have hit the band business he's kept playing—though it might have been for only a dollar a night in some disagreeable cellar club! And he's remained fresh and constantly enthusiastic for what he has to say in jazz. As Stanley Dance has attested: "No witness of his constantly alert interest would credit Basie with thirty-odd years in the music business—twenty of them as a leader. These have been years of keen listening and enthusiastic reaction: 100 per cent immersed in the music, digging it and enjoying it."

A lack of complication and of nervous tension, an avoidance of the elaborate and the abstruse; these qualities have branded Basie's wholesome personality and its application to everything in life, in work and in play. They have identified themselves with his music. To hear his sparse, economical piano notes, or to hear the band swing easily, elliptically, yet with a naked spirit into an arrangement of the blues, rendering unison riffs cleanly, precisely, always zestfully, the rhythmic pattern steady and sure and never finical, is to gain a strong insight into the vital man of whom this music is a part. To hear the band play is to sense Basie himself feeling and thinking and speaking, shaping its overall style according to his own nature, giving its policy his own ideals. And these same qualities have identified themselves with even his personal habits, emphasizing the integrated, balanced simplicity of his life.

Basie's appetite for food, for instance, is an expansive one, yet it calls for quantities of solid "home-cooking" rather than making up its bulk with mounds of delicate *petits fours* and other titbits. On one occasion during the band's 1954 tour of Europe, Basie quite distressed one of the notable French journalists by this desire for a simple and wholesome diet. The Frenchman, a connoisseur of his native land's cooking, had invited the bandleader to dine with him at one of the most exclusive restaurants in Dijon. With infinite care he had planned the choice of food, skilfully including numerous local delicacies in the list of courses; his final order called for quite a dazzling array of exotic preparations. The Count consumed the early courses with relish; they were light and had served to whet his appetite. When the main course arrived, however, instead of being confronted by a thick steak or something of similar proportions to satisfy his pangs of hunger, the musician was faced with a dish concocted from many obscure sources, arresting to the eye, but abstract and varied to the palate, the type of dish one carefully dissects but not the type to be waded through lustily. Basie seemed nonplussed. Here there wasn't anything to satisfyingly attack. He toyed with it a little, while waiters hovered in the vicinity, suggesting such-and-such a sauce—"A local speciality, you know, sir." Finally, in despair, the Count directed his big brown eyes towards the nearest waiter and entreated, "Say, have you any ketchup?" Once supplied, he proceeded (to the horror of the waiter, the journalist and several other Frenchmen seated close by) to splash the thick tomato sauce all over his food, and then, having applied this common denominator which he knew and trusted, he proceeded to eat the course with gusto!

As the hazards and the pitfalls of the musical profession (particularly the many obstacles placed in the path of his early career) have failed to sour Count Basie or to turn him into a complex, neurotic personality, so an ultimate and sustained personal success has been unable to inflate his ego. Born into a modest family in the district of Red Bank, New Jersey (a district which was later to recognize his talents by proposing to rename one of its busiest thoroughfares "Basie Street"), on 21st August 1904, Basie has remained modest to the present day. Even the title "Count" is not a self-imposed honour, but an accolade awarded to him by a Kansas City radio man in 1936 and which has since crept into common use with musicians. Despite a dramatic reversal of fortune, a change from the youthful pianist scuffling around New York in search of work with inferior vaudeville acts to the position of an established bandleader controlling a highly-priced collection of jazz musicians, he has not developed a fashionable king-sized temperament. Diffident and reserved before the poised pencil of the newspaper reporter or the radio commentator's bright microphone, still apt to be boyishly excited whenever an audience roars its acclaim for his band, unstinted in his praise for other musicians he admires, the Count is at once affable and lovable.

In appearance he has shown little change over the years. A few less hairs may now adorn his crown, and a few more at his temples have turned grey, but otherwise he registers scarcely an alteration. Essentially he is the same jovial personage, wide of smile and hearty of laugh; his face and figure are plump and rounded, his jowls heavy, his upper lip lightly covered with moustache, his eyes big and wide and frequently dancing with merriment, his gestures indicative and tireless. He is easily identifiable, with his portly figure, whether in his double-breasted lounge suit or else swathed in the musician's robes of office, the tuxedo or the dinner-jacket. He incites friendship with his ready humour and warm sympathy, and there are few who upon entering his company do not fall under the spell of his high spirits just as they do on making contact with Louis Armstrong; he has a warm wit, without being a clown, and it is noticeable that people laugh with him rather than at him. Yet this is still the same man who in the 1930's lived safely through the Pendergast era in Kansas City, and who, when forced to go under the protection of the gangsters, would crack jokes at their expense and then have to tame their wrath with his smile and with his nimble fingers at the keyboard; the same man who later presented a broad back to the audience when his band opened at the Roseland Ballroom in New York, asserting that the musicians and not the listeners had the first call upon his attention; later again, the man who broke through a rigid colour bar by playing to white audiences in the plush New York hotels. He is the same imposing, yet liberal and friendly man today as he was then.

The musicians who have worked for Basie, and those who still do work for him, are the first to chant out praises for him. In them he inspires a mixture of friendship, freedom of expression, admiration and obedience. As Ernie Wilkins, who has spent the greater part of the 1950's playing and arranging for Basie, and who has proved a valuable fountain of information for this book, has explained: "Basie is a vibrant, modest and unassuming man who is hardly aware of his greatness and his contribution to the world of jazz. He's an easy guy to work for and is not a disciplinarian, yet he seems to be a born leader, and all the men in the band and those people that come in contact with him respect him. He doesn't demand anything from the men in his band except that they do the job right, and that they certainly are glad to do!"

Basie steadfastly believes in his musicians. To use again the words of Stanley Dance, he "hears everything and engages musicians he has heard and knows, unlike those who engage on the strength of second-hand recommendations". Like the ant he has a sixth sense, allowing him to judge at first hearing just how well a musician will fit in with the singular jazz style of the band. He pins his faith on the men he has chosen, treating them as individuals rather than as chattels, letting each have his full say in the musical expression of the band. He respects feelings, and while he will never stand in a prominent soloist's way if the man wants to branch out with his own group, he likes the sidemen to stay in the band as long as possible. Harry Edison has confirmed how Basie stood by his musicians whenever a depression hit the music business. Recalling his days with the band for the benefit of Marty Paich, the trumpeter mentioned how little money the sidemen earned when the Basie band was in its struggling days in the late 1930's, but he endorsed the fact that the moment the band began to prosper Basie raised salaries; he always paid the men the highest wages he could afford, and even in the depressions, when the band business slumped badly, Basie never lowered salaries like so many of the other leaders in the United States. Edison recounted that to his own knowledge Basie's personal bank account went broke at least three times through his refusal to lower wages, but he preferred to hold on to good musicians by paying them what he thought they were worth.

Ernie Wilkins feels that it is because Basie is such a warmhearted, healthy and co-ordinated person, little affected by success, free from all snobbery and distinctions, that he establishes such close ties with his musicians. As the arranger says, "The Count is a man of such modest habits. He likes to take his drink, and to get out on the town like anybody else, and after concerts, if there is a party for the musicians, he likes to be just one of the boys in the band. He's happily married, and his wife Catherine is just as modest a person. They have a daughter, and like any other married couple they have their troubles and their joys. You know, the Count seems to be loved by everyone wherever he goes; he's just mobbed by his friends, old and new. I often wonder when he gets a chance to rest!'"

Wilkins has presented an illuminating commentary on the life (on-stage and off) of the pianist/bandleader, a life he has been able to view at close quarters for a number of years now, and I think it is interesting at this point to allow his store of knowledge on the subject of Basie the man a free rein.

I have already hinted at the Count's considerable appetite. This is just one item which the arranger effectively confirms.

"The Count loves to eat," he says. "For instance, for breakfast he'll have ham and eggs, a stack of pancakes, and then top that off with a large T-bone steak with fried potatoes. And he loves 'Southern cooking' too, with its fried chicken, red beans and rice, ham and turnip greens, and big slabs of corn bread.

"Basie tries to diet every once in a while, but I'm afraid that on this score he doesn't have much will power! It's a funny thing, though, he used to come on the band-bus, whenever we took to the road, with a huge paper bag filled with fried chicken, cakes, cookies, fruit, etc., and give it to the band boy to keep for him so that he wouldn't be tempted to stick his hand in the bag too often. It wasn't any good, though, for every five or ten minutes he'd call the band boy from the back of the bus for his bag!

"Eating seems to be a full-scale operation with the Count once he's off the stand; not that he's off it very often these days. His life is so intensive that he doesn't have much time to pursue any hobbies, though he has a Hammond organ installed in his house, and spends as much spare time as he can playing it. Shortly after I came to know him he bought a set of golf clubs, but he still hasn't learnt to play the game. The funniest sight I ever saw was Basie one day, taking cuts at the ball—with his big, round belly getting in the way—and missing it *every time*! Another delight he has, of course, is listening to jazz musicians play. Billy Eckstine made him a present of a tape recorder at the end of a tour we made together, and the Count loves to use it, though again I don't think he's had so much time as he'd like with it."

The fact that Basie, since his early youth, has been thoroughly monopolized by his music should not, however, mislead the reader into supposing that his life has been set in a pattern, that it has become nothing more than a monotony, a tedious tale of 100 per cent labour, devoid of any incidents of human and humorous interest. On the contrary, it has been peppered with anecdotes, some of them worthy of providing autobiographers as diverse in character as Benvenuto Cellini and James Thurber with quite sensational copy.

Who, for example, can lay a claim (as Basie justly does) that he was given impromptu lessons in his youth by the legendary Fats Waller? When the youngster from Red Bank first became interested in music he used to insinuate himself into Fats' apartment. There, he would often sit for hours, cross-legged on the floor, while Fats—his equal in years but already a musical Titan —would wistfully doodle at the organ. Listening to Waller was the first training Basie ever received as an organist.

As a youth Basie learnt to steel himself against the multitudinous rackets attached to the music business pretty quickly— he had to or he wouldn't have kept himself alive in the profession. He knew when to fight for his rights and when to remain tactfully quiet. By the time he went into Kansas City in the late 1920's he was already wide awake and hardened to the vices interlaced with the business, and in Kansas City he ran up against one of the toughest of all the vice scenes. Kansas City at this time was under the control of Tom Pendergast, one of the most notorious racketeers, and, aided by the laws of prohibition, the town was an active place for gambling, illegal spirit drinking, narcotics and other vice forms. Basie received one sharp shock soon after his arrival in Kaycee, one which threw him on his guard for the rest of his stay in the town. After taking a job in a saloon run by a nationally-feared gang leader, he unwisely made a slight criticism of the management's methods one evening. He was offered the alternative of working two weeks without pay or of a long ride in a sleek black car. The Count worked his two weeks, and thereafter conducted his business affairs very carefully. Later, when he formed his own band, he became the favourite of a big saloon manager known in Kaycee as "The Chief", a generous man who supplied many of the musicians with free food and drink when they were out of funds. "The Chief" helped Basie to avoid any more serious trouble with the racketeers.

Once the Count began to make some headway as a bandleader, and in 1936 transplanted his operational base from Kansas City to New York, the tension of a gang-dominated scene gave way to the worries of making the band pay its way in the face of enormous competition from other known and respected groups, yet though life became perhaps less dramatic it did not cease to have its out-of-the-ordinary incidents.

One night in 1942, when the band was performing a dance-date at Millburo, Delaware, the Count's urbanity as a performer was temporarily placed in jeopardy. Apparently in the afternoon prior to the date, trombonist Dicky Wells and three other members of the band had gone off on a lobster-catching trip. Spending rather longer than they had intended in the pursuit of this sport, they hurried back to the ballroom, and had to dash on to the stage in order to be seated when the curtain arose. In their haste the afternoon's catch was deposited—still alive—in a bucket behind the piano.

Half an hour later the Count felt a twitch at his trouser leg, and, casually glancing down, beheld to his horror a huge and decidedly active lobster crawling up it. For several seconds the rhythm section's perfect tempo went beserk. Basie gave a desperate kick and successfully cleared his leg of the thing, but this only added to the confusion, for the lobster, disengaged, sailed high in the air and then plopped down right in the middle of the saxophone section. Disorder reigned! It was a good fifteen minutes before the dangerous sea-food was finally removed and the dance resumed!

"So many things happen on the band's tours—some funny, some sad—that I often thought of keeping a diary of them," Ernie Wilkins relates. The arranger has been able to chronicle some of the more memorable events of the tours which he personally undertook with the band between 1951 and 1955.

"One time," he recalls, "we travelled all the way from Dallas, Texas, to Lake Charles, Louisiana, to make a date—the distance was over two hundred miles—only to get there exactly *one week* too soon. Was Basie disgusted! He had to pay all that transportation out of his own pocket, and besides, we had to go back to Texas that night because we had more dates there. The booking office had certainly messed up that programme!

"Then when the new Basie band was just getting on its feet, so to speak, we used to play quite a few one-night stands where hardly anyone would show up for the dance. Now that's the most disheartening thing that can happen to a musician, and especially to the bandleader. I don't see how Basie managed to pay our salaries most weeks. [This remark unconsciously seconds Harry Edison's statement about salaries.] But do you know—even when the audience was small—the men would get on the stand and blow like mad anyway! This had some effect apparently, because the next time we played at these places the crowds would be bigger. I think that those people who were at our dances before had passed on the word—you know the line, 'Count Basie has a hell of a band—don't miss him.' We found good musicianship brought better results than any amount of placard advertising.

"We also had to play many one-night stands—especially in the Deep South—in towns that thrived on the so-called Rhythm-and-Blues stuff. Towns that rarely had a chance to hear good straight jazz. Well anyway, we'd get on the stand, start tuning up and getting our music together. In the meantime the people would crowd around the bandstand, seemingly full of resentment, and they'd cast sarcastic and insulting remarks at us. We'd get mad, of course, but we'd ignore them and start wailing away. Before the night was over they would usually change their opinions, and many would actually fall in love with us. Whenever we played in that town again everyone would have a ball! Surely this is ample proof that good jazz can win anyone over.

"Once, we went to play in a town in New England, and on arriving we found that we were set to have a battle-of-the-bands with the great Duke Ellington. Basie nearly fainted! The Count has all the respect in the world for the Ellington band—and who hasn't?—and he was sitting in his dressing-room before the dance started, worrying his head off. We in the band were not so worried, though, and we all went to him and assured him that we'd be at our best. I never heard the band sound greater than on that night! At the end of the evening Basie was almost in tears as he thanked all the musicians one by one for the way they had played. Let me get this straight though—Ellington's band was great too. We played another battle with him on the next night in a nearby town and had another ball. Later we did two weeks opposite the Duke at the Bandbox on Broadway, and everybody said that it was the greatest musical event that happened in New York in years. One other date I knew to almost equal it—that was when we shared the bill with the Modern Jazz Quartet at Birdland in New York.

"On another occasion we got to a town—after a long road journey—and when we found the dance-hall all the people were standing around outside; there were police in front of the place, and the door was padlocked. It didn't take us long to find out that the local promoter didn't have a licence to give a dance—and there was *no* dance. We all crawled back into the bus and made for the next town. 'There must have been about a thousand people standing out there!' Basie cried as we pulled away. He had a fifth of Scotch whisky with him so we all got drunk as we rolled down the highway."

Travel, travel, travel. The journey is an endless one for Basie and the band musicians.

Nowadays the facilities are much improved, unlike the early days when the Count was struggling to keep his musicians together, and often was barely able to scrape the price of transport together. Today, the band travels most of the time by chartered bus. Basie makes use of a bus company in Newark, New Jersey; one which specializes in transporting bands and understands the needs and problems of the musicians. The same driver stays with the band, whether the tour is one or six months long, and usually becomes part of the family. Naturally to most of the musicians "the road" is a tough deal, but, as Ernie Wilkins has affirmed, it can be made so much easier when all the fellows are like brothers and try to help one another. Basie makes it easier too by only using buses with reclining seats so that the men can sleep on the journey, and in the summer months he usually has a bus which is air-conditioned.

The musicians in the Basie band divide off the bus into two sections. People can sit or sleep in the front section. The rear section they call their "lounge", and here they frequently get together for impromptu parties. When Billy Eckstine was travelling with the band he persuaded the sidemen to form a club, making everyone on the trip "Lounge Members". The club has its rules, and even a treasury. The funds from the latter are used to buy gin, whisky and beer, and the members meet in the "lounge" to sing, tell jokes and, in Ernie Wilkins words, "to raise hell in general". "Didn't we have fun, though," the arranger recalls. "You should have been to some of our meetings. On second thoughts, perhaps one would have been enough! Oh yes, and the Count himself was a club member in good standing.

"The hardest thing anywhere to get though is good food,"

Ernie adds, swift to dispel any impression that life on tour is easy. "And although it's not too difficult to obtain decent hotel accommodation in the northern states, it's very hard to find a place in the South on account of conditions there, as you most likely know. During my last two years or so with the band I found some slight improvements in the South, but it still has a long way to go."

Note well the pointed reference to Jim Crow in this last statement by the arranger; it is well founded. Just as soon as a tour takes a coloured band below the Mason-Dixon line racial prejudice openly dogs the heels of the musicians for every inch of the way. It seems that a civil war, the sustained efforts of Sinclair Lewis, Carson McCullers, William Faulkner and the main twentieth-century American literary movement, and even the Senate rulings of the 1950's cannot banish Jim Crow from Southern minds and hearts; changes come but slowly there. And while the conflict is prolonged, Negroes are subjected to the full Southern social treatment: separate travelling services, separate hotels, separate restaurants, separate educational institutions, even separate toilet facilities, and, naturally, inferior jobs and frequent tongue lashings, at times leading to physical violence. Coloured bands have one further insult to endure, though one which the white Southerners tell them they should consider an honour: they are allowed to play to all-white audiences in clubs where their own people are refused entry. Every coloured band has been faced with ugly scenes whenever it has toured the South, and frequently such appearances there have led to physical violence. Bassist Milton Hinton has recalled an occasion when the entire band he was with had to be escorted from an all-white dancehall by police patrols in order to escape an angry mob of hoodlums; and there have been times when the police have sided with the mob.

Basie has had to face his share of the problems in the South, not the least of them being the difficulty of finding suitable eating and hotel accommodation. Little wonder that the band always travels by coach in the South to avoid the segregated railways.

Even outside the South, though physical violence is less frequent, Jim Crow still rears his ugly head at times. One night in the autumn of 1943, when Basie was working along the Californian coast, two of the band's trumpet section—Harry Edison and Snooky Young—were invited by the Count's friend and rival, the late Jimmie Lunceford, to come over and hear the Lunceford band at a club named Trianon's in Los Angeles. The band was playing to an all-white audience there. Edison and Young were refused entry by the doorman at the club, and again by the club manager when he came on the scene. Then Lunceford appeared, and a witness reported that he ranted and raved at the manager and "did everything but break somebody's jaw", but the musicians didn't get in. Later the Negro press took up the crusade against the club without achieving any satisfaction, and Lunceford, while furious at the insult, was still forced to fulfil his legal contract there.

The New York writer Nat Hentoff has similarly implied that while the South contains the most flagrant and lamentable instances of racial prejudice, Jim Crow still flourishes elsewhere in the United States, if not in people's physical action then in their attitude and in their hearts, and that touring is never really easy for the coloured bands. As he says: "The Basie men . . . relax in Birdland [the leading New York jazz club in the 1950's] for two weeks, confident in the reciprocal warmth of their own blowing and the reaction of their audience. But then they go on a bus for a one-nighter tour. A tour not in the South, mind you, but through New England and upper New York state. There are suddenly reservations that have not been 'confirmed'; there are gas station owners who look at the bus and announce that there are no washroom facilities while they carefully lock the door to the men's room. How many Basie admirers in towns like these are aware of this kind of reception not only to the Basie band but to the many Negroes of all vocations passing through?"

It is typical of Basie's warm humanity, and yet a thing which gives him dignity as a man, that while forced to accept the various snubs and insults over a period of many years, he has not descended to the same degenerate intellectual level as his assailants by matching spite with spite. Instead of bearing malice—almost a justifiable action considering the full circumstances—he has, by employing white musicians in his own band from time to time—Buddy De Franco, Serge Chaloff and Johnny Mandel—placed his music above the level of racial prejudice. His refusal to trade blows with an essentially nervous and fearful section of the community on this biased issue, thereby immunizing his music, is the soundest philosophy on the subject. As trumpeter Miles Davis, speaking to journalist Allan Morrison, has explained, "Music has no colour: it's a raceless art. I don't care if a musician is green as long as he's talented."

I think that with Count Basie every question, large or small, and the question of racial prejudice is a good instance, is debated in the light of how it aligns itself with his musical reasoning—that to the Count everything eventually translates itself into musical terms. He has been, and still is, a perfectionist in his attitude to jazz. He has been a spirited, energetic, and continually swinging improvising musician whenever he has sat down at the piano, in whom a feeling for the blues has been deeply ingrained, and he has been the leader of an equally swing-conscious band, one which displays a rugged collective emotion—a band with a way of thinking together and dreaming up spontaneous arrangements as if it were one man, yet still with channels of freedom between the bursts of unison playing for the soloists to speak without reserve. And Basie has welded these ideals as a pianist and these mannerisms of his band into a working jazz style, and has sponsored its projection for over twenty years. New elements have crept in from time to time, while new soloists and arranging minds have taken up the cudgels on the band's behalf, yet Basie's personal style and the style of his band are as easily identifiable today as they were when the band made its first broadcasts over the Kansas City radio in the mid-1930's. It has been the Count's task to maintain these original ideals of musical style over the years, to maintain playing standards, to find suitable replacements for departing sidemen, most of all to preserve the band's individual musical sound and feeling expression. In performing these tasks he has been a perfectionist, and he has registered a notable success, despite a number of setbacks, with this policy, unlike many of his fellow bandleaders who have become musically anonymous through chasing one elusive new sound after another. Basie has stuck to his guns and supported the style he believes in through the lean times and the alternative years of plenty. Few other musicians in jazz can lay claim to such a resolute idealism.

On examining Basie's own personal creation, it is remarkable the extent to which he has allowed the musical style of the band to be his supreme advocate. As a pianist, for example, he has admired quite a number of jazz keyboard exponents over the years: Ellington, Waller, Wilson, Hines, Tatum, Stacy, Sullivan, Mary Lou Williams, Powell and others, yet he has never lost faith in his own employment of the piano as an additional voice

28

to the jazz ensemble, though such a usage is far removed from the dazzling flights of the majority of these very piano soloists he admires. While he admires them he has not allowed this admiration to sway him away from his policy of playing typical ensemble phrases at the piano. Likewise he has respected many jazz orchestral minds, varying from Duke Ellington to Gerry Mulligan ("He's a strange one—but to me he's wonderful!"), yet he has resisted the attempts of any arranger to hustle his own band away from its logically-built and accepted methods—he has allowed his arrangers to introduce new ideas and devices of phrasing, but only if they have maintained the avowed fire of the ensemble, the strong and uncomplicated section voicings and the unfettered rhythm pattern.

Even the original themes which Basie himself has conceived and which have later been stabilized into orchestrations for the band (and there have been many of them: *Roseland Shuffle, Every Tub, John's Idea, Sent For You Yesterday, Shorty George, Swingin' The Blues, Swinging At The Daisy Chain, Jumpin' At The Woodside, Topsy*, and, of course, the band's signature tune, *One O'clock Jump*) have in turn been fashioned with the band in mind, with simple, melodic, swinging riff figures, usually based upon the harmonic structure of the blues. These themes too have been servants to Basie's perfectionist sense, helping to preserve the band's individual character. His determination to nourish this singular orchestral style has been a revelation.

It would be foolish to pretend that, while Count Basie has been a perfectionist in his aims for the band, everything that he has accomplished with it has been perfect. Human nature is still imperfect, and so far, praises be, the scientists have been unsuccessful in their attempts to convert music to an automatic production though they have made several daring attempts. Basie has had his musical flounders, and it does no good to disguise them; occasions when either the band was simply off form or some bright-eyed A. and R. manager broke through Basie's guard and forced him to do something quite out of character with the band's style. There was the ill-fated Columbia recording session of February 1945, as one instance of the latter cause, when twelve strings from the studio orchestra were linked up with the band; another session, a year later, again for Columbia, found Bob Bailey singing a naïve *Danny Boy* backed by a Basie band so fidgety and ill-at-ease that the whole orchestration had become quite muddy. In recent years, Norman Granz had the band record a mambo feature for his Clef label; the musicians performed the score competently, but the material sounds alien to a band of this type, with its tendency to swing at a moment's notice. Also there have been the odd occasions when a soloist has fluffed a note on record, or sounded less-inspired than normally, or when one of the sidemen arrived late at a concert and had to slip into his seat during the second number of the programme. Yet for a band which has made many score recordings and several thousand concert appearances, spread over more than two decades, the lapses in artistic consistency have been so rare that each has been conspicuous. In the same way Duke Ellington's band has made a number of recordings which have been below the normal standard set by the leader's orchestration, yet because they are inferior the value of the remaining masterpieces hailing from the leader's pen has not been lessened.

The Count Basie Orchestra has maintained a truly remarkable consistency of inspiration, taste and technique over the years, and the preservation of its individually-fashioned style has rarely shown evidence of giving way before the high-pressure assaults of the commercial men. By analysing the course of big-band jazz since the mid-1930's, it will be realized that only Duke Ellington's various bands, and Lunceford's band of the late 1930's and early 1940's have been capable of doing battle with the Basie band in top form with regard to rhythmic impulse, emotional ensemble strength, and the stamina and artistic inspiration of their soloists' improvisation. And it has been Basie's personal guidance which has been the final determining factor in forging *and sustaining* the band's unique jazz expression; with him at the helm, the band has overcome all its teething problems and the various difficulties which have beset it in subsequent years, so that today its reputation stands higher than ever.

CHAPTER II

THE KANSAS CITY MELTING POT
AND ITS AFTERMATH

ONE NIGHT IN the autumn of 1954 the Starlight Roof of the Waldorf Astoria Hotel in New York was the scene of a great festive celebration. Lights blazed down on a glittering throng— upon important names from every conceivable branch of the entertainment world. Nat "King" Cole, Dr. Marshall Stearns, Hazel Scott, Rocky Marciano, Benny Goodman, Lena Horne, John Hammond; these and many others had collected to pay tribute to a giant of entertainment. The speeches were legion; excitement mounted as, one after the other, stars vied to outpace their fellows in reminiscing over their personal contacts with the man whose health they were there to toast. Sentiment flowed almost as freely as the wine.

At length, a little, frail old man, bent with age, rose to speak. He brought tears to many eyes with his simple, dignified words, searching with obvious sincerity through a memory which went back further than any other in the room. Concluding, he turned to the smiling, portly figure by his side and said with considerable emotion: "This is my son, whom I am well pleased with."

Eyes swivelled round to take in the object of his moving ending; people were applauding, and it is doubtful whether there was a single man or woman in the room who didn't clap with all sincerity. They all registered their warm feelings for William Basie, the pianist from Red Bank, New Jersey, the leader of America's most virile jazz orchestra, the man they all affectionately knew as "The Count".

The occasion was a special dinner organized by journalist Allan Morrison of *Ebony* and a group of friends to celebrate Count Basie's twentieth anniversary as a bandleader.

After the speeches came the music. Curtains parted at either end of the room to reveal, on one dais the contemporary Basie band, and on the other, as near as possible, the original Basie band of twenty years previously. Many members of the old band had not been fully active for some years. Ed Lewis, renowned years ago for his lead trumpet work, had been employed as a taxi-driver for some time in New York City; trombonist Dan Minor was working in a factory and playing with a calypso band for two nights a week; Earl Warren was a house musician at the Apollo Theatre; Jack Washington was an airport employee in Oklahoma City. All, however, wanted to register their affection for their former boss. Tenorman Lester Young had flown in at the eleventh hour from Chicago; right after the party he had to fly back, but he wasn't going to miss the historic occasion. The only exception from the band was the tragic trumpeter Oran Page, who lay dying in a Harlem hospital.

Both bands took their turn to play the jazz numbers associated with Basie over the years, and the honoured guest, like the genial, informal, fullhearted man he is, jumped down from his position at the top table and sat in with the musicians. He moved from one stand to the other and then back again; he accompanied the ebullient singing of Jimmy Rushing with all the precision and the relaxed swing of which only he is capable at the piano; he jammed with Lester, Emmett Berry and others; he spent the remainder of the evening doing what he has been used to for most of his life—the entertaining of people with jazz music of a uniformly high order. It was a fitting climax to a deserved celebration.

Perhaps the most noticeable feature of this significant evening, however, even ahead of the incredible musical reunion between the old Basie musicians and the new, was the fact that one honoured guest (and easily the most important one after the Count at this particular party) was not provided with a knife and fork at the table. He wasn't even given a seat. Yet in spite of this apparent breach of etiquette the party did not make him an unhappy man. He wandered at will amongst the other guests, he listened to the speeches, he mixed with the highest and the lowest. And when the bands began to play he got his own chance to make a speech. It was the most moving and expressive speech of the entire evening.

That guest was the blues.

For certainly, if the party represented a triumph for Count Basie, then the blues was entitled to share the triumph, and the Count himself would have been the first to admit the fact. To think of Basie in connection with music necessitates thinking of the blues as well; the two names are synonymous. Each has been adviser, sculptor, interpreter, advertising agent and custodian for the other ever since the day, a good quarter century ago, when a little-known New York pianist, stranded without work or money due to the folding up of the show he'd been touring with, first went into Kansas City. They have been comrades-in-arms through the subsequent years; today there is still no obvious slackening of their friendship.

The esteemed position of Count Basie in the 1950's—at a time when jazz has been split into many diverse paths and schools of thought regarding its evolution and development—elicits praise for the durability (and the versatility) of the blues as a source of material for instrumental jazz. Basie's widespread acclaim after twenty years as a leader (in the face of a public renowned for its fickle attitude towards musicians) provides an impressive climax to an important chapter in jazz history; the unfolding story of the instrumental blues style which grew from a small sapling in Kansas City in the early 1930's. A style quite different from the blues expressed in dirge form by unknown Negro singers in the cotton fields of the Deep South, different from the "classic" interpretations of Bessie Smith and Ma Rainey, different too from the blues improvisations played by Louis Armstrong and the New Orleans jazz musicians. A style, in fact, which has even changed the original emotional and spiritual motivation of the form. Nevertheless, a style which has contributed enormously to the strengthening of jazz as an instrumental form in the years which have followed. For while certain of the original essential elements of the blues were cut away by the experiments which took place in Kansas City and were later broadcast in a more matured state by Count Basie and the members of his school, they were replaced by other qualities—qualities which when mixed with the remaining ingredients made up a still satisfying whole. In short, a musical form worthy to grace the same Olympian heights as a Bessie Smith song or an Armstrong solo.

To a person who has not studied the various evolutionary changes in the history of the blues, it may at first seem odd perhaps that Kansas City, and not one of the major American cities like New Orleans or Chicago or New York, should be the scene for such vital developments. After all, these developments have subsequently influenced all instrumental jazz in one way or another. Why did they emerge from Kansas City? If they were to come from just an average-sized American city why was the backdrop not Seattle, or Boston or Pittsburgh? In actual fact, the reasons soon present themselves once the United States map has been scrutinized a little.

It is interesting to study the geographical location of Kansas City, and to link up its position with its economic status in the early 1930's. A city depends upon its position very much for its trade; and if trade booms then the city has plenty of money; and money encourages many things, including entertainment. Kansas City was rich beyond its size. Situated close to the western boundary of the State of Missouri, by the 1930's the place had grown wealthy from the trading benefits brought by a good position. It was a port of call for riverboat traffic, being at the junction of the Kansas and Missouri Rivers. It had also become an important railway junction, where many arterial routes running east and west converged, and with direct links to Chicago and St. Louis. Usually it was the half-way house for the transcontinental express trains. Important highways also converged there.

The location was a distinct encouragement to jazz in Kansas City. In the first place, the influx of trade and money increased the demand for entertainment and allowed a large local jazz scene to be maintained. Yet even more important, the many routes which passed through the city caused hosts of musicians and singers to visit the place. Jazz music and blues singing had both become national entertainments by the 1930's, and the people who propagated them spent a great deal of their time touring from place to place, plying their talents from San Francisco to New York and back again, stopping *en route* at Kansas City for a meal and an intended night's rest.

The Negro section of the city became a familiar calling place for singers and for musicians passing through with the big touring bands, many of whom had only a few hours to spare before catching the train for the next leg of their journey, yet who wanted to play at a private jam session with the core of resident musicians there. Some of them liked the music that they heard so much that they came back and settled, swelling a local jazz school which in size was already out of all proportion to the population of the coloured quarter.

As the early 1930's unfolded, the Negro section had become a

34

musicians' town, and tales of its colourful jam sessions and high standards of musicianship regularly percolated through to the larger American cities, passed on by word of mouth from the men who had been there and who had been astounded by the jazz activities in the place. Such was the fame of these jam sessions within the ranks of the musical profession that almost every important jazz soloist felt that somehow he had to go there and pit his strength against the local school, every blues singer to go and sing there, in order to prove themselves to their contemporaries. Many reputations were made with the Kansas City sessions; many were broken. Crowned heads of the jazz world toppled on numerous occasions.

During these years it didn't matter what time of the night or the morning one arrived in Kansas City, there was sure to be a jam session going on somewhere; usually a large, exciting affair, the residents augmented by a handful of important jazz soloists from the larger touring bands, either blowing for their own pleasure or determined to match their talents against the local talents. Sleeping was a drudgery to everyone.

Pianist Sammy Price, recalling the situation for the purposes of the book "Hear Me Talkin' To Ya", exclaimed: "Jam sessions in Kansas City? I remember once at the Subway Club, on Eighteenth Street, I came by a session at about ten o'clock and then went home to clean up and change my clothes. I came back a little after one o'clock and they were still playing the same song!"

And drummer Jo Jones, whose loquacity was surely the most impressive feature of that whole fine book, has enlarged upon the story even further, explaining: "Some places in Kansas City never closed. You could be sleeping one morning at 6 a.m., and a travelling band would come into town for a few hours, and they would wake you up to make a couple of hours' session with them until eight in the morning. You never knew what time in the morning someone would knock on the door and say they were jamming down the street."

Mary Lou Williams remembers once being woken up around 4 a.m. by Ben Webster. Apparently Ben, Coleman Hawkins, Herschel Evans, Lester Young and several other tenor-saxophone players were jamming down at The Cherry Blossom night-club, all trying to carve one another and not one would back down. They had been playing for hours and had tired out all the piano

35

players, and Ben wanted Mary Lou to come down and help out at the keyboard.

"In those years around 1930, Kaycee was really jumping," Mary Lou recalls. "So many great bands had sprung up there or had moved in from over the river. I should explain that Kansas City, Missouri, wasn't too prejudiced for a mid-western town. It was a ballin' town, and it attracted musicians from all over the south and south-west, and especially from Kansas. Kansas City, Kansas, was right across the viaduct, just about five or six miles distant. But on the Kansas side they were much snootier. A lot of their musicians were from good families who frowned on jazz, so the musicians and kids would come across to Kaycee to blast. In Kaycee, nothing mattered.

"I've known musicians so enthused about playing that they would walk all the way from the Kansas side to attend a jam session. Even bass players, caught without streetcar fare, would hump their bass on their back and come running. That was how music stood in Kansas City."

In consequence, one may visualize Kansas City in the early 1930's as a kind of enormous melting-pot, into which large quantities of music were constantly being poured; soloists from the Fletcher Henderson and Duke Ellington bands rubbing shoulders with born-and-bred New Orleans jazzmen, urban blues singers breathing the same air as jazz musicians who had learnt their jazz not from the sunny South but from the bands playing in Harlem.

Such an intermingling was not without its repercussions as the various styles congregated and strove to fashion a musical common denominator in Kansas City. An enormous smelting process took place, and the music which ultimately emerged was without precedent in jazz. A new form of instrumental jazz was evolved, of which the blues was the most important single component— and in turn a new form of blues singing developed, a style of singing containing a greater proportion of jazz material and much more closely linked in its conception and expression with the jazz group. This Kansas City revolution was to have a snowball effect on jazz, gradually taking shape, broadcasting its essential changes to other musicians, and ultimately becoming responsible for the swing age of the late 1930's. Indirectly, certain vital characteristics of the style were to aid a further revolution in New York in the early 1940's, resulting in the creation of the musical school now known as the modern jazz school.

36

The use of the blues in the new Kansas City instrumental style represented a radical change of concept. Previously, a New Orleans jazz musician playing a blues had with all sincerity attempted to convert to his instrument the stylistic approach and the moving sentiments of the blues singer. He re-created the words of the singer in his musical phrases, playing to relieve his depressed feelings, his solo becoming a thing of melancholy. With the new style of the Kansas City musician all this was swept away. The Kaycee man harnessed the structure of the blues as an aid to his technical expression, approaching the form in the same way as an industrialist approaches a river and builds a dam in order to obtain the water's potential hydro-electric power.

In Kansas City by the 1930's the approach to collective jazz itself had changed drastically from the approach which musicians had adopted in New Orleans towards primitive jazz in the early years of the century. The new high standards of musicianship at the free-wheeling balls in Kaycee had encouraged the virtuoso soloist to transcend the beauties of the entirely improved New Orleans ensemble, so that the city's jam sessions, instead of featuring contrapuntal designs from the ensemble for the greater part of their duration, now tended to become a string of solo choruses sandwiched between two very brief ensemble statements. Ensembles, in fact, came to be regarded merely as a base, a kind of rock-like foundation, allowing men to get a firm grip of the melody, the harmonies and the rhythmic pattern before launching forth upon the paths of their individual solos. The whole approach to jazz became more contrived, placing greater emphasis upon virtuoso musicianship than ever before.

This new type of jam session, however, in order to allow often large numbers of musicians from travelling bands to sit in and take turns at improvising upon chosen themes, required as its basis certain forms and constructions familiar to as many musicians as possible. Many of the men in the touring bands had only a few hours to spare so they had no time to sit down and study masses of manuscripts before the session. On the other hand they felt the inner desire for freshness, having grown tired of continually replaying the more hackneyed New Orleans tunes. They wanted musical satisfaction, something which would provide them with an artistic outlet, yet with material not so complicated that they couldn't walk into a room where men were playing and join in immediately.

One source of material consisted of the popular songs and show tunes of the day. In the 1930's Jerome Kern and several other song-writers had elevated their musical idiom to fresh heights (heights far above the bowls of slush which the Tin Pan Alley publishers now serve up each year) with tunes of strong melodic and harmonic substance, the type of substance which cried out for the jazz musician's caress. They were writing tunes which all America—from the newsboy upwards—was whistling; tunes that jazz musicians who were only in Kansas City for a few hours could improvise upon from memory.

Yet there was one fountain-head of inspiration which even outclassed the use of show tunes: and that was the twelve-bar form of the blues.

Although musicians had grown tired of some of the New Orleans melodies, the twelve-bar blues could be treated purely as a construction; something to build new things upon. Every musician in jazz knew the chords and the form of the blues. Here then was something that they could remould, dreaming up their own melodic ideas to sit upon it, ringing the changes with tempo and degrees of attack. Therefore the blues—or rather a series of variations upon the original blues form—became the new primary source of material for the active Kansas City jazz scene.

Let us examine briefly how they handled the blues as an instrumental form.

First of all, they began to exploit the fact that the blues did not of necessity have to portray sadness or an outcry against some act of injustice. They found that the technical form of the blues—the simple, twelve-bar chord progression—could be used to express any mood or emotion, that it was just as pliable when taken at a faster tempo to fit a happy, spirited jazz expression as the stomps and rags of New Orleans jazz had been. When regarded purely on its constructional merits there was not a tempo or a mood that the blues harmonic progression would not fit.

Once this new facet of the blues had been unearthed the Kansas City men lost no time in co-ordinating the form with their also freshly-developed approach to jazz rhythm. Rhythm has always been a vital component of all jazz music, and a new concept of rhythm was one of the most distinctive features of the Kansas City revolt against the traditional ideals of New Orleans jazz. For whereas the New Orleans musicians had been content to play a two-beat rhythm, perhaps emphasizing, say, the first and third beats, in Kansas City the men began to experiment and search for something new. Bass player Walter Page first tried accenting the alternate two beats, the second and fourth. Then with the formation of the Count Basie rhythm section the various experiments suddenly clicked into place. The rhythm men began filling in the remaining two beats to the bar, accenting all four beats equally, promoting an even flow: one, two, three, four. This new, smoothly-flowing beat brought a feeling of relaxation to the music no matter what tempo or degree of attack the men might employ, and it became one of the most easily-recognized characteristics of Kansas City jazz, ultimately being adopted by all the important bands to emerge from the city's music scene like Andy Kirk's, Jay McShann's and Count Basie's and being used at all the informal sessions. From the moment of its inception the new beat was to be a constant in the city, and of course the twelve-bar chord progression of the blues was made to merge in with it. Thus was completed a further stage in the industrial revolution that had overtaken the blues.

Next came the building of new melodic designs upon the blues. No more copying the phrases of singers; the new regime wanted something more suited to its singular jam sessions, something simple which would serve as a suitable launching base for a string of improvised solos. As a result the use of riffs became a common practice, the riff meaning a short, simple melodic phrase which would be repeated, staccato-fashion, through the twelve bars. Combined with the rugged, swinging attack evidenced by the Kansas City men, these short, direct riffs became vehicles for great excitement and drive, particularly when the musicians were playing an ensemble in unison, repeating the same phrase again and again but with increasing force and intensity. In fact, though in the first place instituted for its simple strength as an aid to musicians at jam sessions, the idea of instruments playing riffs in unison was to grow, ultimately graduating from the jam session to usage by larger groups and stamping the ensemble style of every big band which Kansas City produced. By the late 1930's riffs were being played by just about every large swing band in the United States.

Many of these riffs were just melodic phrases dreamed up by musicians on the days that the bands recorded; a musician might create some appealing phrase in the course of a solo, someone else would pick it up, replay it, then it would be tossed around the band until everyone was blowing it. This way half a dozen new themes might be born in the course of one night's playing. It wasn't very difficult to superimpose such "head" arrangements upon the twelve-bar pattern of the blues. Count Basie, whose band was to become the most significant exponent of the Kansas City jazz style, has estimated that at most times half the arrangements in his book were "head" arrangements developed from little riff ideas which members of the band had expressed in their solos to fit the form of the blues. Sidemen like Harry Edison, Earl Warren and Freddie Greene, who have made no pretence to being trained arrangers, have provided Basie's band with some of its finest themes in this way.

So grew up the familiar instrumental blues style of Kansas City, with loosely swinging ensemble sounds, the use of simple ensemble phrases and brass riffs delivered with great precision and drive, the distinctive rhythm pattern with its four clear beats to the bar, the reliance upon the twelve-bar progression as a technical basis for improvisation and for composition, and finally, the relegation of the original blues mood, allowing musicians to use the structure for all occasions. And it is noticeable that even today, more than twenty years afterwards, almost all the musicians who grew up in Kansas City play with these same characteristics. The contemporary Basie band still has them, even though it has also absorbed elements of the modern jazz movement which grew up in New York in the 1940's. In fact, two of the men who were to spark the modern jazz school came from Kansas City groups, tenorman Lester Young from Count Basie's Orchestra and altoist Charlie Parker from Jay McShann's large unit; and despite the new medium of expression which they chose, the Kansas City desire to improvise upon the chord sequence of the blues remained deeply ingrained in their work.

The style of the blues singer, meanwhile, had been developing along parallel lines. Singers came into Kansas City, discovered the resident musicians treating the blues in a revolutionary fashion, and, if they wanted to sing there for their own pleasure, they were forced to change their own approach accordingly. Singers who stayed in Kaycee found themselves treating the blues with the same bold ideals as the musicians, and just as the musicians had broken with previous standards of jazz playing, so the great singers that the city produced—Jimmy Rushing, Joe Turner, Pha Terrell, Helen Humes, Walter Brown and a few others—

caused a revolt against previous blues singing styles, both classic and country varieties.

The singing became suddenly more superficially energetic, more prone to aggression in its delivery, and so in keeping with the rhythmic excitement and attacking swing evidenced by the town's jazz groups. The blues song became more catholic in outlook, embracing all moods and all spirits, therefore suitable for the expression of excitement as well as depression. The dramatic, heart-searching dirge of Bessie Smith was replaced by the volatile driving song of Jimmy Rushing. Lyrics retained their message of outcry against a lost lover or against some oppressive action by the authorities, yet the phrases which propagated the stories took on a rhythmic force, edging closer than ever to the moulded, decorative phrases of a jazz instrumental solo. Make no mistake, the blues songs didn't lose their sincerity or their intensity. If anything, pushing the approach closer to the alive, swinging style of the Kansas City jazz unit served as a precautionary measure against undue elements of sophistication creeping in. Jimmy Rushing singing a blues at medium tempo above the emphatic beat of the Count Basie rhythm section didn't represent a dilution of the lament-type blues brought to perfection by performers such as Bessie Smith, Ma Rainey, Ida Cox and Leroy Carr. If one considers the linking of the plaintive lyric with the force and delivery methods of a jazz group a crime, then Rushing could be adjudged guilty. Yet while he and others took on the spirit of jazz musicians, of the men with whom they worked, they still retained all the old intensity and feeling in their singing. If Rushing felt sad he sang a slow blues; but if he felt gay he didn't just stop singing, for fear of desecrating the blues form. Like the musician he used the blues for every mood and he worked constantly with jazz groups.

If Rushing committed a crime by shifting part of the musical emphasis of the blues, then surely Bessie Smith must have injured the form by using it as a commercial proposition and elevating it from the cotton fields to the concert platform, and Billie Holiday must have committed crimes innumerable by co-ordinating the intensity of the blues singer with the lyrics and melodies of popular song-writers like Kern, Gershwin, Porter and Youmans. Rushing and the other singers in Kansas City felt the blues in the same way as every blues singer felt them, that is, as a vehicle for the expression of feeling. They were not wrong because jazz musicians instead of a solitary guitar accompanied them. They were not wrong for singing about city life, for those were the troubles which they lived with and knew. They would have been insincere if they had sung lyrics about the cotton fields and the chain gangs (things which they did not know at first hand) purely to carry on the early traditions of blues singing.

Without doubt, in the musical style which Kansas City evolved for itself, such terms as "blues" and "jazz" appeared to be inseparable. The jazz musician became greatly dependent upon the blues form, and, in turn, the blues singer became dependent upon the concept and methods of jazz. As the new school of thought grew in stature, so one musical form gave strength to the other.

Kansas City donated so many important musicians to jazz in the 1930's that it would be too enormous a task to catalogue all the names here. Certainly, if one examines the Negro side of "mainstream" or "middle period" jazz (the nominal descriptions with which critics have sought to pigeon-hole the swing era of the 1930's), then the bulk of its leading musicians could trace their education in jazz back to the style of the Kaycee school, and many of them could even trace their place of birth to the city. And, after all, it was the Negro side of swing which was the significant one; the white side was so much the prerogative of smart commercial agents trying to cash in on the style.

The Negro section of Kansas City was brim-full of great musicians in those years, each and every one of them steeped in the influence of the blues.

There were the pianists, Sammy Price and Pete Johnson, men who even at that time managed to earn their living in the city as solo performers, by playing the blues. Johnson, of course, was also developing fast as an interpreter of another derivation of the blues: boogie-woogie. In Kansas City he usually teamed up with the blues shouter, Joe Turner, and, in 1938, when these two were playing at the Sunset Café, critic John Hammond heard them and took them to New York to play in the "Spirituals To Swing" concert at Carnegie Hall and later to become stars at Café Society.

Then there were the tenor-saxophone players of repute: Ben Webster, Dick Wilson, Herman Walder, Herschel Evans and Lester Young, the first four disciples of Coleman Hawkins, the last-named man already a revolutionary in the stylistic approach to his instrument. Buster Smith was there too, the altoist so frequently cited as being the foremost influence upon the development of the young Charlie Parker, and also Eddie Durham whose fine trombone and guitar playing made him one of the busiest men in the place. Pianist Art Tatum played for quite a while in the city, and so did Clyde Hart. Somehow there always seemed to be a number of fine improvising jazzmen for every instrument of the jazz ensemble. Standards of playing were so high that even the redoubtable Jo Jones later admitted that for a long time he wouldn't go near Kaycee through fear that his drumming would be shown up by the local boys!

By the early 'thirties, the years of real fruition for Kansas City jazz, most of the big names were making a living with regular bands.

Actually, should one care to delve back that far, it is possible to trace the existence of well-organized jazz groups in the place at a much earlier date, right back, in fact, to the early 1920's. The riverboat bands of Marable and Celestin often stopped off to play engagements there; Bennie Moten led a band in the city as early as 1922; and yet another largish group at that same time was the Jesse Stone outfit, fronted by one George E. Lee and later re-titled George E. Lee and His Novelty Singing Orchestra. This latter group contained a fine altoist, Harlan Leonard, and recorded for the old American Brunswick and rare Merritt labels. In 1924 Leonard left Stone to join Bennie Moten, and from then onwards the Moten band outstripped all its rivals.

However, it was not until the 1930's, after Basie and several other great soloists had joined, that the Moten band began to impress a lot of people outside Kansas City. Basie, after arriving in Kansas City, had for a time played with The Blue Devils, a small group led by bass player Walter Page, and featuring the singing of Jimmy Rushing and the trumpet playing of Oran "Lips" Page. Only with the opening of the 1930's, after The Blue Devils broke up and the men joined Moten, did the larger band don its mantle of true greatness.

There were several other large units too by the 1930's which had grown up alongside Moten, all playing well enough to keep Bennie's men on their toes even if they were unable to surpass his group. Andy Kirk had taken a band from Kansas City to play in the Roseland and Savoy Ballrooms in New York as early as 1929. In the decade which followed he continued to interpret the Kaycee jazz style at a consistently high musical level, featuring arrangements by May Lou Williams and also the fine tenor-saxophone playing of Dick Wilson and the underrated singing of Pha Terrell. Pianist Jay McShann built up a fine band at about the same time, featuring the blues predominantly. Walter Brown sang with McShann; altoist Charlie Parker, a Kaycee man by birth, had his first chance with the band; and Paul Quinichette, Gene Ramey and Gus Johnson (all three of whom were to join Count Basie's reorganized orchestra in the 1950's) played long terms with the band. Other outfits came into being just a little after these two. Harlan Leonard formed his own band, and was the first important leader to give a job to the modern arranger Tadd Dameron when the latter arrived in Kaycee. George E. Lee formed another group, and there were units led by Woodie Walder and Everett Johnson (the younger brother of pianist Pete Johnson).

Yet although music of quality came from these various groups, it is still true to say that the instrumental blues style of Kansas City reached its most significant stages of development with the formation of Count Basie's band in 1935. Moten helped the sap up through the stem, but it was under Basie that the style burst into its full, luxuriant growth. To trace the Basie fortunes through, from the date of his arrival in Kansas City to the present day, is also largely to trace the history of the Kaycee blues in its most exalted state.

Count Basie started playing the piano in New York, where he picked up the rudiments of ragtime and early jazz piano playing from the Harlem school of Johnson and Waller. (In fact, it was only after playing for a while afterwards in Kansas City that he developed his own unique style as a soloist.) His first professional experience in New York came through working as an accompanist to vaudeville acts. He took Fats Waller's place with an act called "Katie Crippen and Her Kids", earning about forty dollars a week—the pay made him seem as rich as Croesus in those days.

His first taste of Kansas City music came when he got a job travelling around as pianist with the "Gonzel White" show, playing one-night stands on the Keith circuit. He was staying in a large hotel in Tulsa, Oklahoma, when one morning he woke up to hear "music that sounded like Louis Armstrong and the gang". Basie went from room to room to see who had those records in the hotel, and then he discovered that the sounds were coming from the street. Out there, on a wagon advertising a dance that night, was the most wonderful trumpeter and band Basie had heard since leaving New York. It was "Lips" and Walter Page and The Blue Devils. The pianist followed that wagon all over town, and when he got into conversation with the musicians they told him about all the things happening at that time in Kansas City. Before he left Tulsa, Basie got the chance to play with the group for a breakfast dance, and the sensation of playing with such men fired him with excitement.

A little after that the "Gonzel White" show was suddenly stranded without any money in Kansas City and the whole outfit broke up, leaving every man to fend for himself. Basie landed a job at the cinema called The Eblon playing the musical supports for silent films. While working as a single he wrote to Walter Page and was overjoyed when quite out of the blue Walter wrote back and offered him the piano job with The Blue Devils. For about a year he was to work with that group—"the happiest band I've ever been in", he says. Jimmy Rushing was singing with the group by this time.

Then in 1929 The Blue Devils broke up, and some of the men went over to the powerful Bennie Moten Orchestra, their addition just about giving Bennie the cream of the entire Kaycee scene in his band. He had Harlan Leonard, Woodie Walder and Jack Washington (saxophones), "Lips" Page, Ed Lewis and Booker Washington (trumpets), Thamon Hayes and Eddie Durham (trombones), Basie (piano), Leroy Berry (guitar), Walter Page (bass) and Willie McWashington (drums), with Jimmy Rushing, of course, singing. This personnel held together pretty well for several years, making a number of fine recordings for the Victor label. There wasn't another band in Kansas City which relished a battle with it.

In 1935, however, Basie's circumstances changed dramatically with the sudden death of Bennie Moten. Bennie's brother, Bus Moten, took over the leadership of the band, but Basie left and took a combo composed of local youngsters into the Reno Club. When he had the job nicely set he called in Walter Page, Jack Washington and Carl Smith (a trumpeter who had been with The Blue Devils); the Moten band was left as but a shadow of its former self. Word had spread around Kansas City at this time about a drummer from Chicago who was really "playing like the wind" (to use one man's apt description), so Basie sent for

45

the man in question, this legendary Jo Jones. "Jo just came in and *took* the job," Count remembers. Then the leader added Buster Smith on alto, and Lester Young came in on tenor-saxophone. Musicians soon began to recognize the group as the best in Kansas City.

Piece by piece the size of the band crept up to three brass, three reeds and three rhythm. "Lips" Page would act as compere at the Reno Club, and sometimes he would sing with the band or sit in with the trumpet section. The group broadcast regularly over a local station and got twenty-one dollars a week for seven nights' work, starting each evening at 10 p.m. and going on until 4 or 5 o'clock in the morning. Sometimes the Sunday breakfast dances lasted until 8, 9 and 10 o'clock in the morning. "Yeah, two dollars fifty a night. You were happy when you got one of those *good* four-dollar gigs at a club!" Basie recalls.

This was the band critic John Hammond heard on the radio and which so excited him that he determined to bring the musicians east to New York.

"John said we had to enlarge the group," Basie remembers, so they added Herschel Evans as a second tenor for a start. Herschel had been with Basie in the Moten band and came on from Los Angeles to join. Three trombones—George Hunt, Dan Minor and Eddie Durham—were employed, and Jimmy Rushing was the band's featured blues singer. When the band was preparing for its journey east, trumpeter Buck Clayton caught the main party and expressed his willingness to join. And after the band had been in New York for only a little while, Basie discovered a fine guitarist, Freddie Greene, playing in an obscure Greenwich Village club. The pianist persuaded Freddie to join the band, so completing with himself, Walter Page and Jo Jones what, at least to my mind, has been the finest rhythm section jazz has ever known.

Strange to say, when Basie first brought the band to New York in 1936 to play at the Roseland, the reception by the general public was not so enthusiastic as Hammond and other critics had imagined it would be. Musicians went to hear the band in action and were literally stunned by its dynamic power, its almost intoxicating swing and the freshness of ideas evidenced by the leading soloists. The New York public, however, showed a preference for the music of the Andy Kirk band which had arrived in town at almost the same time, and which had benefited from a good publicity campaign. It was not until the band moved to The Famous Door that things really began to look up for them. Determined to sink or swim with the band, John Hammond and agent Willard Alexander took over the club for the Basie début. They sponsored a wide-spread publicity campaign, knowing full well that if they could only get the public into the club then the music would take care of itself. Thanks to their slogans and advertising the club was packed for the opening night, and the band, sensing that the audience expected big things, blew like a raging gale. Stacked in tiers at the end of the elongated club-room, the musicians blasted away, rocking the blues just as the men had done in the Kaycee jam sessions, inciting the listeners to a riot of enthusiasm. After that night the band's reputation was assured.

By the late 1930's and early 1940's, when the call for big-band jazz had increased competition immeasurably for bandleaders of the top flight who claimed to combine musical artistry with the power to attract audiences, Basie was indeed a force to be reckoned with. Of the mighty Negro bands of the day, only Duke Ellington's and Jimmie Lunceford's dared to do battle with it. The white swing bands of Goodman and Shaw, though often interesting for their arrangements, could not nearly equal the Basie group's virile swing and enormous ensemble drive, and their soloists seemed pale by comparison with the Count's wholesome set of individualists.

The band in 1940 had elevated the Kansas City style to new heights, swinging the blues with a verve and inherent spirit the envy of every other group in the country, yet always tempering the magnitude of the direct ensemble attack with the qualities of precision, taste and sensitivity. The band played with an obvious fire, yet its music never bordered upon exhibitionism.

Every man in the ensemble would be on his toes, blowing into the wave of attack, yet the swing was always facile, never taut or contrived or the act of men moving mechanically with the beat. The overall sound of the band took on the compact strength of a single voice, mellowed by an inbred relaxation. The men were capable of building up incredible "head" arrangements, riffing in unison as one man, gradually increasing the ensemble sound in intensity and volume to create an essay in climax with each and every number they played. Sections would often come together behind a soloist, picking up a simple blues riff and punching it out to form a strong cushion behind the improvised line, in this

47

way urging on the soloist to greater inspirational heights. "Head" arrangements constructed on the Kansas City blues formula still constituted the bulk of the band's repertoire; trombonist Eddie Durham had contributed several arrangements of a more complex nature, yet the blues riff remained the stock item of material, the greatest single source of inspiration for the soloists and for the ensemble. Harry Edison's *Jive At Five*, Earl Warren's *Rocking The Blues* and Basie's own *Jump For Me* and *One O'Clock Jump* are typical examples of where slight melodic phrases occurring in the course of solos by these men were picked up by the entire band and moulded immediately into riff tunes.

Solo talent abounded in the band; indeed, it seemed as though Basie had hired a press-gang to go around Kansas City, to listen in at all the jam sessions and then kidnap the most important soloists and pack them off to New York to join the band. Judging by the enthusiasm of the men in the band, however, it seems more likely that the great Kaycee men actually queued up to be bound and gagged for the first available train east!

Basie himself at the piano was like a complete additional section to the orchestra, of course, alternating riffs with the ensemble, cleaving open theme statements and inserting solitary piano chords where another band might have scored a unison voicing for the brass, leading the whole unit with confidence from the keyboard until it seemed that every note he executed held some secret signal to urge on the rest of the musicians. He had developed a unique solo style at the piano. With simple melodic phrases, an economical use of notes and a delicate gradation of touch, he succeeded in portraying more swing in four bars of piano than a great many other musicians were able to project in several choruses of over-elaborate, note-cluttered improvisation. With Basie's approach the maxim appeared to be to use technical efficiency for the precision, the perfect sense of timing and the delicacy of touch which it could bring, instead of employing it to produce an ornate, yet cold and automatic display. Basie placed each note so carefully in relation to the rhythmic pattern of the theme that the solo would swing from first to last. And when accompanying another soloist the Count seemed to have a sixth sense for feeding the right supporting chords, so exciting the man to give of his best. In all, he was, alongside Duke Ellington, the supreme band pianist.

In the rhythm section behind the pianist, drummer Jo Jones

restrained from indulging in any over-long percussion displays, concentrating instead upon the maintenance of a sure, steady beat. He knew perfectly how his rhythmic power was best distributed, and he was equally adept at brushing a sensitive accompaniment to a solo and at dropping bombs behind the full ensemble. Jo set the pattern with a shimmering cymbal beat, emphasizing the four clear beats to the bar with immaculate articulation to give a kind of "bouncing ball" effect, just occasionally pulling out an aggressive roll to urge on a solo at up-tempo or to climax a theme statement.

Playing this same steady, swinging 4/4 time, Freddie Greene's guitar allied with Walter Page's rich, booming bass tone gave the overall sound of the rhythm section a lightness and relaxation.

Among the trumpets Ed Lewis played a powerful, far-reaching lead part, while Buck Clayton with his sharp, glassy, incisive tone and Armstrong-inspired phrasing took the major share of solo parts. What solos remained after Buck had taken his share usually fell to Harry Edison, the "enfant terrible" of the section, a trumpeter whose extrovert, explosive phrases were completely without precedent in jazz, yet who played with such tonal force and uninhibited swing that his surprising improvised phrases gave every other man in the band a fillip. Edison was an orator outspoken beyond his time; the phrases he created were already pointing towards the formation of modern jazz. Basie was probably the only bandleader who fully understood the significance of the things pouring from his horn at this time.

The band's other radical, tenorman Lester Young, was also given complete freedom of expression for his revolutionary approach, and one of the most distinctive features of the band was the sound of his soft, pure tone and subtle, devious phrases improvising over the united drive of the ensemble. In contrast, Buddy Tate, who replaced Herschel Evans as the band's other tenor, played with a richer, fuller tone in the older tradition. Earl Warren's alto proved a brilliant lead for the section, while he also acted as deputy leader of the band, taking charge of much of the organization and rehearsing.

Head man among the trombones, of course, was the ubiquitous Dicky Wells, one of the great personalities of "middle-period" jazz, a soloist gifted with humour, imagination, a spirited, slashing attack when he cared to use it, and, not least, a superb rhythmic facility.

In all, it was a band crammed with vivid, and in some cases contrasting solo styles, yet every man also fully realized the importance of the ensemble, and the fact that he wasn't in the band merely to project his own individual character.

The Basie band's musical policy hasn't varied in its basic ideals very much since its salad days. The "old" band, as we have now come to call it, kept together right up to the year 1950. Even then the break-up was not the wish of the musicians; in actual fact the leader was forced to disband on account of the slump which had hit the jazz scene at the time and which caused the break-up of most of the large groups in the United States. That slump was like a ball knocking down skittles. The Dizzy Gillespie band was another to go down before it. The strange thing was that even up to the dissolution Basie never compromised his musical policy, and his ranks had been overflowing with solo talent right through to the end. After Lester Young had left, the Count had a series of brilliant tenor players—men like Don Byas, Illinois Jacquet, Lucky Thompson, Paul Gonsalves and Wardell Gray. Buck Clayton had left the trumpet section, but the indomitable Edison stayed through to the end, and other gifted brassmen like Emmett Berry and Joe Newman had been brought in. Even when Jo Jones, the principal generating force behind the band, had grown sick of travelling and left to freelance in New York, Basie wasn't easily crippled. Somehow he managed to entice Gus Johnson, the propulsive rhythm man from the Jay McShann band, to move over and fill the drum stool. With Buster Harding writing arrangements of enormous impact and ensemble force for the band, and with the usual quota of "head" scores, the Count never once lost his reputation for swinging the blues or his lead on the other Kansas City graduates.

Most surprising of all, however, the Count's faithful adherence to the fundamentals of Kansas City jazz even continued when he reorganized and started out with another big band at the end of 1951. For about a year after the break-up of his "old" band he led an all-star septet, but this was purely a stop-gap group while he was building up his resources for another crack with a large orchestra. When in 1951 he announced his intentions of taking another big band on the road, even the most optimistic observers in the music profession felt that he would have to make enormous concessions with his style and policy if he were to succeed to any great extent. Obviously they had reckoned without the man's musical tenacity!

Certainly Basie took in the later jazz developments with his new band—the new methods of improvisation, the new writing techniques, and so on. Yet in the overall sound of the band the Kansas City style was still uppermost. When the Count was preparing his new band his maxim was that no scrap of manuscript offered to him would be passed over, and no musician denied a hearing as long as they had that emphatic swing (a naturally relaxed swing) which recalled immediately the great music of past Basie bands. If they did not swing then to the Count they were just not jazz musicians. The soundness of such a maxim is proved by the fact that the policy of the new band has paid off. In the mid-fifties the band is in a stronger position with the American public than it has ever been.

The Count now has one out-and-out modernist in his trumpet section; one of his tenormen takes solos quite frequently on flute, while the other is one of the most respected of the younger New York modernists; several of his arrangers are fully accepted by the present *avant garde* of jazz. Yet all these people, despite their modern overtones, fit the Basie style. They have absorbed the devices of modern jazz and successfully aligned them with the fundamentals of the Kansas City style. The swing, the direct statements of emotion, the feeling for the blues; such things are precious to them. Every man in the orchestra is ready to swing at the drop of a hat.

As one might expect with such a man as leader, the blues form is still as important as ever to the band's style. The jumping, twelve-bar chord progression is still the stock item in the repertoire. Of the men now writing for the band, Buster Harding and Ernie Wilkins have proved the most adept at handling the blues structure, co-ordinating it with the modern devices, yet losing nothing of its rhythmic potential and its attacking impact.

Ernie Wilkins has also, together with one of the band's two young tenor-saxophone players, Frank Foster, been penning arrangements to feature the blues singing of Joe Williams, the Count's replacement for Jimmy Rushing—that is, if anyone can be considered a "replacement" for the great Rushing.

Although Williams is quite clearly a descendant of Jimmy Rushing and the school of urban blues shouters who emerged with the Kansas City jam sessions, he is a much more extrovert singer than the great Jimmy. An exhibitionist performer, both in his physical movements and in the verbal delivery of his material, he is certainly a tremendous asset to the band as a stage performer, for he has the knack of whipping up the excitement of an audience, punching out each word so forcefully above the unison riffing of the ensemble. His voice is rounder than Rushing's, and he has a sense for dramatic touches, like the sustaining of notes in the higher octave of his voice in order to heighten the climax of a song. What he lacks, however, and what undoubtedly denies him the greatness that is Rushing's, is the intensity of voice, the sincere emotional ring which Jimmy succeeds in projecting through each song no matter how maudlin its lyric. Rushing's environment for singing is the "mainstream" jam session; he is like an additional instrument to a jazz group in both his rhythmic sense and the spirited impetus of his delivery. Yet Rushing is also connected with the "classic" blues singers of an earlier period in that he has their intensity of voice, a heart-dominated intensity, with a raw, yet singularly truthful edge to his voice. Joe Williams is essentially a more sophisticated artist, meriting attention as a good derivation of Kansas City jazz, but without being a great consummate artist on the same level as Rushing.

Count Basie's position today is akin to that of the one-time revolutionary, who, with the passage of time and the emergence of new revolutionary material from other sources, has been turned into something of a conservative.

He bears comparison with certain other figures in greater artistic fields. With Claude Debussy, whose delicate, impressionist music was in its time a defiance against the then fashionable excessive romanticism of Wagner, yet whose creation is now quite normally accepted while the precocious young ladies with pony-tail hair-styles and dark-rimmed spectacles go into raptures over the twelve-tone building of Arnold Shönberg. Or with the impressionist painters who also lived in Paris at the end of the last century: men like Manet, Pissarro, Sisley and Cezanne, who were laughed at by the National Academy in their day, yet who in later times have been called masters while extremists in art now discuss the work of Matisse or Klee. With Swinburne, who gave the Victorian poets a kick in the pants, yet who is now studied in grammar schools while more avid disciples and students of poetry delve into Ezra Pound and Dylan Thomas. With Eugene O'Neill too, whose plays startled the smugness of American society in the earlier part of this century, yet whose ideas are now accorded the reverence of "classics", with the more out-on-the-limb critics already chanting the praises for the increased psychological searchings of more contemporary playwrights.

Count Basie, and the other Kansas City men who grouped themselves around him in the 1930's, undermined previous standards of jazz playing and of blues singing, only to discover that by the 1950's the Kaycee revolution was fully accepted and that other experimentalists had been busily at work developing even more new things. However, in common with the important innovators I have mentioned belonging to other creative fields, Basie's work, though in itself a revolt against the things which had gone before, was possessed of intrinsic qualities—certain vital qualities which allowed his style to stand upon its own merits when in subsequent years the actual revolution was considered a thing of the past. Like Debussy and Cezanne and Swinburne and the others, Basie in his field represented a style of substance; a style so mature and complete in itself that no intelligent critic or listener in later days has dared to sneer at it, or call it "Uncle Tom".

It is true that Basie and his henchmen were revolutionaries in their use of the blues, and even in their whole approach to jazz, yet they were not merely sensation seekers. The things which the Kaycee musicians achieved with the blues form were so powerful that critics and musicians respect them even today when the explosive effect of the revolution has largely subsided. Their theories are still being felt within the schools which have followed in jazz.

In the mid-1950's there has been a headlong rush by musicians from all schools in jazz to reassociate themselves with Basie's musical style. Critics of both purist and extreme modern tendencies have sought to claim him for their own, thereby admitting recognition of his style's power. We are faced with a reawakening of appreciation for "middle-period" jazz, it seems, and Basie and the Kansas City musicians are riding on the crest of the wave once more.

The renewed success of Count Basie's own orchestra in the 1950's, and also the growing trend on the part of today's more gifted modern jazz arrangers like Johnny Mandel, Ernie Wilkins, Al Cohn, Manny Albam, Quincy Jones and Neal Hefti to nestle closer to the rhythmic and ensemble impact evidenced by Basie, instead of attempting to further the cold, mechanical writing

53

experiments of extremists like Russo, Tristano and Graas, provide healthy signs for the jazz of tomorrow. That the Basie band, a simple instrument of swing, should so fire the imagination of a younger generation of orchestral minds in jazz with its insistence upon a direct, attacking beat, its expression of open emotion in the work both of the individual and the ensemble, and the overall impression of virility in its music is heartening at a time when too many jazz musicians are seeking to divert jazz away from its emotional and rhythmic basis.

It is a sobering thought, of course, that the Basie band cannot stay with us permanently, yet the fact that a younger school of jazz musicians has taken up the cudgels on behalf of the Count's style holds promise that the future development of jazz will not fall completely into the hands of the formalists now actively engaged upon testing the endurance of jazz within their row of test tubes known as music conservatoires on the west coast of America.

Should it happen that the formalists do gain power in the future, however, there is one aspect of Basie's music which even they cannot prove to have been at fault. When the Basie band is no more, when all the men who partook in the Kansas City experiments in the 1930's have passed away, even if it so happens that the actual characteristics of their style are abolished by succeeding generations in jazz, there is one thing which they established which cannot be dissembled. This concerns the elasticity of the blues form.

The Kansas City men proved that the structure of the blues is capable of nourishing jazz improvisation and jazz composing indefinitely. I don't wish to claim that their discovery has brought nothing but good to jazz. At its worst it has allowed men like George Handy and Pete Rugolo to reshape the form beyond all recognition. Yet I do claim that the good it has brought outweighs the evil. The men who have worked seriously to enhance the jazz form by their handling of the instrumental blues structure easily outnumber the black sheep who have tried to sabotage it. Basie and the Kaycee men proved that the feeling for improvisation upon the blues is deep in the soul of every sincere jazz musician, and that it will always find its own outlet. They showed that the blues could be remoulded to suit different moods and rhythmic patterns, and that it provides the source of inspiration behind many varying styles of technical make-up.

54

Of all the achievements of the Kansas City musicians, their greatest lies in the fact that their style provides a direct link between the poor, unknown singer in the cotton fields of the Deep South and the brilliant instrumental creations of a modernist like Charlie Parker. They fashioned that link through the blues; and, by examining it, one can understand with greater clarity why Parker and other modernists in jazz are but a continuation (though produced by a different set of circumstances, of course) of the branch of folk music which the Negro has donated to America and to the artistic world. The blues has undergone many revolutions; it has taken on many shapes, many forms, many complexities. Despite all the changes, however, it still finds a place of rest in the soul of every sincere jazz musician.

CHAPTER III

BASIE THE PIANIST

"WE WHITE MUSICIANS are always striving to achieve the swing so essential to all jazz. The Negro jazzmen are fortunate—they swing naturally. They just can't play any other way. They don't have to worry about the swing, and they can go on to the next stage of jazz creation and innovate interesting musical ideas, knowing that the beat will always be there."

So announced pianist and composer Marty Paich when he was in London in the spring of 1956.

Marty, a close friend of Harry Edison, and an unabashed admirer of the Basie band and its leader's piano style, was swift to seize upon one of his favourite topics of discussion when I met him. It wasn't long before he was expounding upon the band's merits in detail.

"Why, that Basie group plays just like it was one man," he hammered at me. "The men work together like brothers. They all have the feel of the music so well, half the time they don't even need any manuscripts in front of them. You know, 'Sweets' [Harry Edison] told me that when he was first with the band in New York they used so few written arrangements that he used to cram the manuscripts for the whole band into his own little music case. That was how the band was. Practically everything the sections played was in the form of 'head' arrangements. No wonder the band always sounds like one long improvisation."

Clearly he was warming up on the subject.

"And I can tell you something else about Basie," he went on, delving deeper into his memories; "something that Johnny Mandel told me."

Mandel, one of the most brilliant of the younger school of jazz arrangers, left the Basie band at the end of 1953 after several months of playing in the trombone section and penning scores for the group's repertoire. Sick of the constant touring, he'd settled on the Pacific coast of America, merging his talents

56

with the modern jazzmen there, and becoming a considerable influence upon the formalists and the experimentalists of the coast school.

Comments from such a penetrating mind were not to be missed. I held my pen in readiness for Marty to relay the story.

"After Johnny Mandel came out to the coast," he continued, "I became very friendly with him. If you remember, I'd played piano on the Shorty Rogers' Victor sessions, the ones where we recorded all those Basie tunes. Having to imitate the Count's piano parts in the arrangements I'd been fascinated by the man's easy, effortless swing and the simplicity of the phrasing. I'd enjoyed playing over those parts. Anyway, one day I tackled Johnny about the matter, asking him just what he thought was the sum total of Basie's influence *as a pianist* on the band. I said to him: 'If another pianist sat in with the orchestra and played an imitation of Basie's style, would the band still sound the same?'

"Well you know, Johnny's answer came straight back in the form of an emphatic 'No'. He said that the moment the Count stepped down from the piano the band was somehow no longer the same. Yet when he was there he always made the men feel like they wanted to play. When Basie led from the piano, every man would be on his toes, just itching to blow. Enthusiasm shot through the band like an electric current. And no other pianist, no matter how good he was, could imitate Basie's phrasing at the piano, or ever had that same effect on the band. No, there was just no substitute."

I think that Johnny Mandel's feelings speak as well as any on the subject of Basie's piano work; about the vital job which his keyboard work fulfils in the projection of the band's musical style. Where another leader gets up and waves a baton in front of the musicians, Basie actually directs operations from the piano. The cushion on the piano-stool becomes his rostrum, and the notes he plays are like levers in a signal box. The keyboard under his touch might well be termed the "control panel" or "nerve-centre" for the band, so well does he govern the other musicians' output from it.

Basie represents the complete band pianist: a musician equally adept at feeding the best supporting chords (one might almost say: "instinctive" supporting chords) to another improvising soloist and at leading an entire ensemble.

He will signal the band with a chord to be ready, lead off with a delicate descending run, and then, when the entire band has swung into motion, he'll be urging both sections and soloists along with confident, emphatic chords. He'll trade melodic ideas with the ensemble, setting a riff phrase which the men will pick up and repeat with rising intensity, setting off a chain reaction with almost every musical thought which enters his head. His piano is the equivalent of a complete additional section to the orchestra, a kind of roving ambassador that always manages to pop up in the right places. Quite often during one of the band's scores, with perfect timing, Basie will cleave open an ensemble passage and insert perhaps just a single chord or phrase, something trivial in itself, yet sufficient in the place of its insertion to provide a neat variation in sound from the full-blooded orchestral unison. Used this way the piano's voice makes possible a remarkable range of light and shade within an arrangement; the degrees of orchestral sound are extended considerably.

Nor is his ability to play this role of band pianist restricted merely to the confines of his own orchestra. With the personality of a chameleon he will alternate between the full orchestra, a small unit of leading sidemen drawn from the orchestra or with a group of leading solo performers at an extended jam session, some of whom he may never have worked with before; he can play the part of band pianist with equal facility at any time, anywhere, and with any number of musicians. The rhythm sections of both the old Basie band and the new one have been, without doubt, the most swinging and yet the most relaxed in the whole of jazz.

Guitarist Freddie Greene, who has played with both these rhythm sections, and who perhaps knows the Count's piano playing better than anyone else, has been moved to say of it:

"Basie's piano certainly contributes to making the rhythm smooth. He contributes the missing things. I feel very comfortable working with him because he always seems to know the right things for rhythm. Count is also just about the best piano player I know for pushing a band and for comping soloists, I mean the way he makes different preparations for each soloist and the way, at the end of one of *his* solos, he prepares an entrance for the next man. He leaves the way open."

Leading jazz soloists jostle with one another to get into the recording studios when they know Basie is scheduled for a date there, breathless to work with him, knowing full well that their own improvisation will receive the utmost support if he's sitting at the keyboard. A good illustration of his sensitive accompaniment can be heard with the Clef extended jam sessions on which he plays. These numbers—often lasting for twenty minutes or more—find him teamed with such diverse stylists as Harry Edison, Stan Getz, Buddy De Franco, Willie Smith, Benny Carter and Wardell Gray, yet with patience and systematic thoroughness he carves a different support for each soloist in turn, and he succeeds in bringing out the best in each musician.

Yet although Basie gives so much to his band and to the improvising soloists he accompanies, no ill effects have been caused upon his individuality as a pianist. In conjunction with the roles of band pianist and accompanist he has also succeeded in developing a unique solo style for himself at the keyboard—an improvising approach which makes him easily distinguishable on the instrument.

Quite naturally, contributing so much to the overall style of a band and to other musicians has had its say in the formation of this solo style. At times the things which he improvises seem to be a logical expansion upon the methods he has built up for use with a band, the methods which grew from his contact with the Kansas City jam sessions in the 1930's. Nevertheless, analysed purely on its own intrinsic merits, his solo style is one of the most complete and satisfying things in jazz—a style which has served him well over the years, and which, even today, with so many new things happening in jazz, still appears fresh and exciting *and* interesting to the listener.

Few piano styles in jazz can have undergone such a dramatic change of face as Basie's did after he allowed himself to become entangled in the golden web of the Kaycee music scene. Prior to entering Kansas City he'd been a very ordinary disciple of the Harlem piano school, listening with admiration to the work of James P. Johnson and Fats Waller, playing his solos competently in a style strongly influenced by ragtime, but not particularly impressing his fellow musicians. In the mid-1930's, however, when he returned to New York with his own band, his revolutionary piano playing bowled all the musicians over.

Incredible as it may seem to us now, when Basie first became interested in music he didn't have any time for the piano. Instead his eyes were all for the glamours of the drum kit; he was fascinated by the variety of attack and the stylish showmanship exhibited by the men he'd seen playing drums in his home town. He even played a few semi-professional jobs as a drummer.

It wasn't until he met up with drummer Sonny Greer, another native of New Jersey and later to become famous with Duke Ellington's Orchestra, that Basie was to effect a change of instruments. Basie watched the spectacular Greer in action and his heart sank. "Sonny's playing on drums discouraged me," he recalls; "his work was too, too much on those tubs. So I got off them and onto piano."

He set to work with a will to conquer the intricacies of the different instrument. His mother played a little piano and knew a little theory—enough to teach the boy his scales and simple finger exercises. After that, as he became more deeply engrossed in piano playing, he started taking lessons with a Red Bank teacher —"a wonderful German lady named Holloway"—at the price of a quarter of a dollar a lesson. Once he'd mastered sufficient theory and technique he set out to improvise as best he could upon the elements of ragtime he'd heard being played by the New York pianists. He admired Waller particularly at this time for his spirited, boisterous swing, infectious humour and fine sense of melody. A little later, as his knowledge and experience grew, he came to admire the glittering tracery of Earl Hines, with its flashing runs and clusters of sharp, treble notes. There was no question of Basie being a singular pianist at this period; he was just a young and very impressionable musician, an easy prey to the stylistic devices of the great pianists of the day. He was to continue his attempts to copy the methods of such men until he entered Kansas City.

Apart from several gigs in his home town, Basie's first work as a pianist was with vaudeville acts around New York. He replaced Fats Waller in one show, "Katie Crippen and Her Kids", an occasion of great pride for someone who had not yet learnt the value of individuality. Later he joined a show called "Hippity Hop". In this latter job he was working with a tenorman called Elmer Williams and a trumpeter by the name of Freddy Douglas. When the show was due to go out on the road, the musicians presented an ultimatum to their agent to the effect that they wouldn't travel for less than forty dollars a week. The agent gave them this wage for a whole season. When the time came for the renewal of their contract, however, this same agent (kind-hearted

60

to the last) told them they really should get their rightful salary: eighty dollars a week. With the syrupy charm universally associated with his profession he explained that the men could have had this wage in the first place if they hadn't insisted on taking forty dollars!

After that Basie joined the "Gonzel White" act, and it was when this show got stranded and broke up in Kansas City, of course, that Basie joined the local jazz scene there and his whole attitude to playing changed radically. Once with the Kaycee men he found his feet as a pianist, discovering for the first time his own latent power and how best to express it through an individual style. Gone was the attachment to ragtime in the fully formed Basie; gone too the desire to copy the devices of Waller and Hines. Instead Basie reached for and clutched securely a personal maturity with a new and singular piano style—a style destined in subsequent years to be the greatest single influence upon the keyboard men of "mainstream" jazz. What he created in Kansas City was a piano style completely his own, something free from all contrived devices, a style perfectly balanced and beautifully moulded yet completely without precedence in jazz.

What are these characteristics of the matured Basie, then, these peculiar qualities which make his style of playing at the piano so easily distinguishable? What was it that came over the personal creation of the man who entered Kansas City as an impressionable and still, to a certain extent, raw musician?

Well, when listening to his matured piano playing, the first feature of the singularity that is Basie's to become obvious is the surface simplicity of everything he expresses. No matter how many thousands of ideas are buzzing around in his brain as he sits improvising at the piano, all awaiting their turn to be unscrambled from the general throng and receive an airing, Basie always selects carefully from them and then proceeds to state only in the simplest terms—with a most economical use of notes.

He certainly has never believed in undue embroidery when improvising. Rather, his motto appears to be: If one has a melodic idea strong enough to warrant expression, then express it directly; don't fuss with it, don't hide its melodic strength beneath a surfeit of bizarre, yet basically worthless technical embellishment. When Basie translates one of the multitude of melodic phrases from his mind, through his fingers to the piano, how direct, how clear and true, how uncluttered it always is! He won't use a single note more than he needs to express an idea. Nor will he go on improvising for chorus after empty chorus, merely for the purpose of impressing his listeners with his powers of durability or to show off his technical mastery of the keyboard. "I don't want to run my piano into the ground," he says. "This idea of one man taking one chorus after another is not wise. I prefer to feed people in small doses." And feed in small doses he does.

Yet don't be led by this mention of the essential simplicity in his playing into believing that the Count only plays skeleton phrases at the piano; such a belief would be very far from the truth. No, when I say that "he won't use a single note more than he needs", it is the last word of my phrase which one should dwell upon. The Count plays *as much as is needed* to accurately project his thoughts through to the listener. He is always to the point when speaking through his piano, always simple, yet decisive and complete; each phrase is finished and satisfying in itself.

Like another pianist in a very different school of jazz whose playing knows the value of a simple, direct expression—the esoteric Thelonious Monk—Basie arrived at this style of expression through the process of trial and error. He had to learn by experience the pitfalls which lie in wait for the pianist who overstates his mind. He had once tried to be a spectacular pianist, to emulate the glittering fantasy of Earl Hines' playing. Only after falling into the trap did he realize that something which was a natural gift in Hines became but an empty shell of a style for those contriving to imitate him. Because Hines was fashionable it didn't mean it was right to copy him. It only created something pretentious, like some massive, ornate palace which had no monarch to reside upon its throne. Basie in Kansas City discovered his own natural gift: the power of delivering everything he had to say simply and directly. He discovered too that musicians admired the clarity of those neat, emphatic melodic statements; that they liked him to play that way with them. After that he determined to be himself—to play what was natural to him.

Naturally, when Basie brought such a pianistic attitude to New York in the mid-1930's he aroused a great deal of interest. Both audiences and musicians debated his values at length, and their decisions were not always in his favour. To an east coast public which had heard the rich, dazzling flights of Earl Hines and Billy

Kyle, the intricate harmonic variations of Art Tatum, the classical patterns of Teddy Wilson, Basie's utter simplicity came as quite a shock. People who heard him, particularly the musicians, realized that what he was playing openly criticized the florid piano techniques which were very much the vogue in those days— techniques which only a very few men were capable of employing to good purpose. They were amazed too at the way he worked with the band, playing simple, melodic riffs on his piano which everyone had expected the ensemble to be playing, and the way he dared to alternate piano phrases so boldly with the mighty voicings of the ensemble.

At the time a number of voices were raised in disapproval of his approach, but he made an impression upon the younger musicians of that period. Bit by bit his influence grew. It is still growing even today. Talk to musicians today about who they admire in "mainstream" jazz. When discussing pianists the odds are that Basie's style is the first to spring to their lips. Even ask the believers in extremist experiments in modern jazz who they care for from the jazz musicians to emerge in the 1930's. If they care for anyone at all, there's a very strong chance that Basie will head the group. His simple, direct, decisive piano has succeeded in making a deep impression upon many memories.

However, simplicity is only one feature. There are the others to be taken into consideration when discussing his piano playing.

If the various components of Basie's style were all runners in the same race, with the prize at the end being a silver cup bearing the words "I am the most prominent feature of the Count's piano playing", then the runner to next breast the tape after simplicity would be rhythm.

Rhythm, one of the three important elements of music, has, of course, many forms and many uses. In Basie's case it has come to mean a propensity to swing on all occasions, no matter what the tempo, no matter what the musical setting. So deeply inbred in Basie's piano style is the ability to swing, that I have no hesitation whatsoever in saying that if a piece of musical material ever came to light which defeated his efforts to exert a supple, relaxed, swinging beat upon it, then no other jazz musician would stand even a reasonable chance of conquering it and converting it to his idiom. When Basie sets his piano playing in motion, he swings automatically—like a man giving the first push to a pendulum, and knowing that thereafter it can take care of itself.

Swing causes Basie no trouble. It's always there. No matter how short the solo, how small the dose he decides to feed to the listener, even if it is only one chord or short run of notes between two ensemble passages or just a four-bar introduction, it is never without its emphatic, swinging beat.

It is always a relaxed swing too. There is never any sign of tautness or strain about Basie's playing. Even when he's pushing the band or a particular soloist as hard as he can, he never reaches beyond himself, never loses his grip so that the easy, effortless swing is replaced by a rhythm which is fast and furious and inclined to be ragged. His swing is never brittle. It is always steady and sure.

Basie's simplicity is a very distinct aid to this relaxed swing which he is wont to project. Not having to tussle with the restless weavings which so frequently grow as a result of attempting to express too many elaborate ideas in too short a time, Basie has been able to distribute his ideas so that they will emphasize his sense of swing all the more. He has developed an acute sense of timing, being able to poise every single note perfectly in relation to the rhythmic pattern, so that the easy, flowing beat—four clear beats to the bar, like a "bouncing ball"—is never ruffled by the melody being improvised above it.

It is noticeable that he likes a strong background behind his playing; indeed, he has hardly ever been known to work without a rhythm section. Yet I would stress the fact here that he does not use a rhythm section in the way that many pianists of the modern jazz school have used supporting sections, namely, to let the section play the direct, unvarying beat, so leaving the pianist with both hands free to weave around the main tempo, doubling it and alternately relaxing it. No, Basie's swing never varies in this way. He uses a rhythm section because he likes to feel those four clear beats to the bar with him all the way, emphasizing his own four. He leads the section but he is also part of it, and when he and his section set that easy, swinging 4/4 time, there's no musician that can edge them off it.

However, to return to our imaginary race again. After simplicity and the ability to swing easily, one discovers that a number of remaining features of Basie's piano playing rush across the finishing line so close together that they all tie for the next place.

There's his considerable gradation of touch, for one. He can be playing hard, percussive chords one moment, employing a strong,

64

two-handed attack, pushing along a full ensemble, and the next he will be stroking light, delicate touches in the treble, sensitively filling in the gaps which a soloist has left in the melodic line. After striking a note or a chord with ferocity he will suddenly change his approach and caress it as if it were some family pet. He knows the power that is vested in his two hands; he knows when to smash and when to practise the art of restraint; and through this gradation of touch, this knowlege of the power of touch, he succeeds in giving both his solos and his band piano parts a wide range of light and shade.

Then there's his sense of taste. Just as he will not play merely to show off his technical prowess, so he is just as stringent about never playing anything which smacks of vulgarity. Were he a saxophone player, then one could describe him as a man who will "never overblow, or direct his creation towards those who sit in the gallery and hanker after sensationalism". At all times Basie is elegant, poised, selective in only playing the most apt and clear phrases, and generally a model of consistently good taste. Even if he has a piece of banal material to improvise upon he will exert his own dignity upon it.

Basie's ideas are always freshly conceived too. Though he believes in simplicity, his imagination has never become stifled and so gradually sterile. Nor is he like several of the established names in jazz, who have built up a collection of clichés over the years and who reshuffle these stock phrases and tricks into different orders of presentation, somehow managing to work them all into every solo they play. Basie doesn't rest upon his laurels; one never catches him using his reputation to cover any faking or his experience to pull a series of tricks upon the listener. Originality is a constant with him. He always manages to say something new and interesting when he improvises. To give an illustration of this point, let me cite the separate versions he has recorded of the theme *How Long Blues*. The Columbia solo which he recorded of it in 1942 is quite different again from the Decca version which he made four years earlier, the improvised phrases telling an entirely different story, and even the tempo being different, although the style of expression in both is unmistakably Basie's.

The lack of monotony in his piano playing has been a decisive factor in maintaining the admiration which so many fellow musicians feel for Basie, in spite of the fact that he has been playing for so long.

Co

In all, then, Basie is an artist of consummate skill at the piano. Very simple and melodic; always the producer of an easy, flowing rhythmic pattern; always a confident technician, clean in phrasing, very assured in everything he delivers, yet never glib; and always tasteful and imaginative, no matter what the musical setting.

It is doubtful whether there is a recording in existence by a Basie group—from the first small group date, the quintet which recorded under the title "Jones-Smith Incorporated" for the Vocalion label in 1936, right through to his more recent Clef albums—on which his piano has not made its presence felt very definitely. Even if the record features an arrangement scored throughout for the ensemble, in which Basie has been allocated no space for a piano improvisation, he's sure to put in an appearance at some point, either by phrasing a four-bar introduction to the arrangement, by plugging the gaps left by the sections, or by striking a single chord to fill a split-second opening left by two bursts of the full ensemble. Even on a recording where the unison ensemble is featured from first to last, one can invariably feel his support behind the sections, just as one can always sense the presence of Jess Stacy's piano on so many 1930 recordings with Benny Goodman's Orchestra. To all the small groups drawn from the band (the Kansas City Sevens, the 1942 Sextets with Buck Clayton and Don Byas, the 1947 nine-piece units with Emmett Berry, Jack Washington and Paul Gonsalves, the groups from the recent band with Newman, Henry Coker, Marshall Royal and others) his contribution is so vital.

In addition, of course, Basie has contrived to donate to posterity a superb set of piano solos, accompanied only by the rhythm section of his band. In 1938 and 1939 he recorded ten such solos for Decca—every one an artistic gem. Basie's deep love and feeling for the blues has never been better demonstrated than with these. When playing with the band he naturally plays on the blues structure more than any other, but in keeping with the true tradition of the Kansas City school he always swings the blues then, and proceeds to construct riffs and other melodic figures on the chord sequence of the form. A number of his solo features, admittedly, adopt this same approach: records he made as solos during this period with Decca, for example, like *The Fives, Dupree Blues* and *Red Wagon* (this latter theme incidentally was to be stolen and wretchedly abused in the 1950's under the new title of a Rock'n Roll tune), all find him swinging the blues in the best

Kansas City style. However, there were also the moments when Basie felt the melancholy of the blues, and improvised accordingly. He could still play with a "lowdown" feeling when he wanted to express the sadder aspects of the blues form. For Decca he revealed his sensitivity for the slow, plaintive blues piano solo with *When The Sun Goes Down, Hey Lawdy Mama* and, best of all, *How Long Blues*. With these solos it seems as if one enters the very soul of the man.

In 1942 he recorded four solos for Columbia, including the second *How Long Blues*, and his gay *Cafe Society Blues*. And since these sides there have been other, occasional solo items. He has not recorded prolifically away from his orchestra. On the other hand, as with his band piano, he says so much in so concise a way that his score or so of solo recordings make an interesting and valuable document.

Mention must also be made, in this chapter dealing with Count Basie's powers as an instrumentalist, of his use of the organ. For although subordinate to his piano playing, he has used the organ both on record and at concerts, and there have been signs in recent years that his use of the instrument is on the increase. It is a facet of the Count as an instrumentalist which cannot be overlooked.

Despite many attempts to utilize the organ as an instrument for jazz improvisation—the majority in exceedingly bad taste—success with the venture has been denied all but a handful of musicians. Either through lack of control or lack of organ technique, or perhaps just on account of insufficient taste, the instrument so often tends to "run amok" when used in a jazz group, swamping the sounds of the front-line soloists and shattering the normal poise of the other members of the rhythm section. It seems a difficult instrument to swing quietly and with relaxation; rarely has it been sufficiently tamed to support another soloist with sensitivity. As I have mentioned, just a few pianists have controlled the organ well enough for use in jazz. Marlowe Morris is one. He has the swing, and when he accompanies his work is always a monument in the cause of good taste. Bill Davis has an enormous swing, though at times his control of the "big sounding" notes slips and his listeners suffer from a bombardment. (Davis, by the way, is the man responsible for one of the arrangements being used by the present Basie Orchestra, a score of *April In Paris*.) Bill Doggett has made good use of the organ, which performed when he accompanied Ella Fitzgerald on record. Then there's Fats Waller, of course, who possessed a deep love for organ music, though the people who knew him intimately have said that he really preferred to use the instrument for the playing of more serious concert works.

Even above these men, however, it is Basie who must be given an accolade for bringing the organ as near as it will ever be to acceptance in a jazz group. All the features which so distinguish his piano playing reappear when his hands descend upon the keys of the organ: the quiet swing, so relaxed, the melodic simplicity, the taste, the ability to carve strong supports for another soloist, and so on. If the organ has a place in jazz then it owes more to the Count than to anyone else.

I have already mentioned that Basie's use of the organ seems to have been on the increase of late. In 1947, when recording a small-group session for Victor with Emmett Berry, George Matthews, Paul Gonsalves and his usual rhythm section, he used the organ for one number, a theme entitled *Basie's Basement*. Since the formation of his new band his appearances on record playing organ have been more numerous. He used the instrument to accompany tenor-saxophone player Illinois Jacquet for Clef, recording features such as *Port Of Rico* and *Cool Rage*. Behind another tenor player, Eddie Davis, he made one of his own favourite records while using organ: the lively *Paradise Squat*. Then there was the sextet session for Clef, the one with Joe Newman, Paul Quinichette and a rhythm section including Buddy Rich on drums; Basie was very busy with the organ that day for numbers like *Basie Beat* and *K.C. Organ Blues*. And one must not forget the long jam session features with Edison, De Franco, Getz and the other stars. His organ acted as a lintel for the other soloists throughout the twenty-minute version of *Blues For The Count*.

Wherever possible he has been using the instrument for all his recent concert tours with his orchestra. A fine illustration of the sensitive way he has moulded it into the pattern of the orchestral style may be heard on the recording of the Neal Hefti arrangement, *Softly With Feeling*, again for Clef. How subtly with this score Hefti, after allocating Basie sixteen bars of improvisation at the organ, moulds the leader's sound on the instrument into the succeeding voicing by the reed section. Certainly Basie's contribution to jazz with the organ, though less vital than his contribution as a pianist, is such that it cannot be ignored.

68

As a pianist Basie has been much more than just an outstanding soloist of the mainstream or middle period in jazz; his approach to the piano has even percolated through to the later forms which have evolved with the musical form. In the modern jazz school, which grew out of the swing period of the 1930's, evolution has been even more prolific. Even within the confines of the modern movement there are already several musical approaches engaged in active warfare. Yet elements of Basie's piano methods are still active within the modern school, and it is frequently the case that one unearths in modern jazz two pianists who hold diverse beliefs in the main, yet who both admire Basie and will openly admit being influenced by him. Modern pianists like Hank Jones, Marty Paich and Johnny Williams all show traces of Basie's phrasing and sense of touch, though in most other matters they are quite individual and little-related stylists. Clearly the influence of a piano style with the same proportions as Basie's doesn't die overnight.

In the late 1930's, when he first achieved critical recognition, and now again in the 1950's, when a revival of interest in mainstream jazz has developed, Basie's piano style has motivated numerous attempts at imitation. On this score, however, he has been kept comparatively free from plagiarism, for his deceptively-simple style has proved tougher to master than most of the would-be copyists imagined before they tried it. One cannot copy something which is a natural product, something that is so highly personal that it is unique, and still hope to portray depth of feeling with the imitation. To play over every musical phrase which Basie has expressed over the years is not to play like Basie; to be successful at such a game one would need also the same sense of timing and precision, the same swing, and so on, all the qualities, in fact, which are peculiar to him. To copy parrot-fashion in any artistic form has never enabled the disciple to attain the same creative level as the original influence.

On the other hand, where a pianist belonging to mainstream jazz (to Basie's own school) has followed merely the Count's attitude to his instrument, and allowed his own already rich imagination to take over from there, it is then that he has been known to benefit from following the same path. Basie's approach to the piano is soundly-constructed, and, by adopting his ideals, such as aiming for simplicity and directness and an easy, flowing beat, several pianists with imagination as improvisers have found

69

a wider doorway to self-expression. Such men have not copied Basie in a child-like manner; they have their own minds, their own ideas. Rather it is that they have been helped in the projection of their personal creation by Basie's methods of delivery.

Three such pianists spring to mind immediately: Jimmy Jones, Nat Pierce and Sir Charles Thompson.

All three are very much their own masters as regards what they create, with their own stylistic devices, and so on. And, despite their strong mainstream sympathies, all three have obviously listened to and absorbed some of the better elements of modern jazz. Yet each has gained something from following Basie's example of never forgetting the importance of an easy, effortless, but still decisive beat, and also the effectiveness of melodic simplicity and the corresponding beauties of a clean, uncluttered statement. Having been set on the path by Basie regarding such matters, they have then been able to let their own productive selves take over and have all made important contributions to jazz.

I have deliberately mentioned these three men, not because they are the only ones to learn from Basie, but on account of the way (while still retaining their individuality) they have all contrived to sit in at recording sessions featuring sidemen from the Basie band which contractual difficulties prevented the Count himself from making. Moreover, they have all been successful in performing the difficult task of substitute, neatly fitting their talents into the environment and unique atmosphere which a session with Basie man always creates.

Jimmy Jones (who with his frequent use of block chords would belong to an entirely different school of piano players from Basie if he didn't display the symptoms mentioned above) has deputised on the Frank Wess Commodore sessions, a Vanguard date with Buck Clayton and Ruby Braff and also on one of the Buck Clayton Columbia jam sessions. On one track of the first Commodore LP. under Wess's leadership he deliberately played a humorous imitation of the Count's style (on a piece safely entitled *Basie Ain't Here*).

Nat Pierce, the white pianist for a long time with the Herman band, has deputised on the Joe Newman Victor sessions and on the Jo Jones Vanguard LP. with Lucky Thompson and Emmett Berry. Nat has also contributed arrangements to the new Basie band's repertoire, including *Basie's Kick* and *New Basie Blues*.

Sir Charles Thompson has played on most of the remaining Vanguard sessions (he has made one album of his own solos accompanied by the rhythm section of the old Basie band for the label too) and on the Buck Clayton Columbia sessions. It was through his work on one of these Clayton jam sessions that Sir Charles actually received one of the greatest compliments (though unconsciously delivered) of his musical career. Shortly after the records had been taped, critic John Hammond was entertaining the Basies at his home, and he casually slipped one of the tests from the session on the turntable. So well did Sir Charles urge on Buck and the other musicians in the first ensemble passage that Katherine Basie turned to her husband and said: "Bill, when did you make this record?" Despite the individual nature of the solos, Thompson had clearly learnt much from Basie concerning the way to best support an ensemble.

Perhaps the most significant point about this little story, however, is the fact that when Buck and the other musicians had gathered together to make the recordings and the question of a pianist cropped up, the man that everyone automatically thought of to give them the best support had been Basie. Knowing that his services would not be available, they had then chosen for the session a pianist who they all knew held roughly the same musical beliefs as Basie, a man who would try to support them in the same way. They knew what style of accompaniment they all needed most, and even if the Count couldn't be there, then they were determined that only someone with a similar approach would suffice.

Basie affects musicians that way. Musicians who have experienced the cushioning effect of his piano support develop a need for its sensitive spur—almost like some narcotic. He instils this need into practically every man he works with. In order to capture that elusive atmosphere which is at once relaxing and conducive to the drawing out of a deep inspiration, his piano, or the nearest thing to it in the same style, becomes vital.

This brings to mind again Johnny Mandel's feelings about Basie: "When he was there he always made the men feel like they wanted to play . . . every man would be on his toes, just itching to blow."

CHAPTER IV

THE PRINCIPAL SIDEMEN OF THE
OLD BASIE BAND (1936-1950)

BUCK CLAYTON

"On hearing him [*Buck Clayton*] one gets the impression that he plays without the least effort. His inspiration is amazingly 'even'; it seems that he always *feels* like playing and always has an abundance of ideas."

HUGUES PANASSIÉ

It sometimes happens that the vicissitudes marking the life of an artist cause him to adopt fresh approaches to his work without his essential inspiration being disturbed or the value of what he has to say lessened. James Joyce, though his heart never strayed far from the Liffey, allowed his mind to enter into the life of his native Dublin by various gates; the aestheticism of "Portrait Of The Artist" followed the anti-romantic realism of "Dubliners", and in turn was replaced by the conversational expressiveness, the beautiful word sounds and the impressive form of "Ulysses", and finally by the linguistic complexity of "Finnegan's Wake", and these remarkable transitions were effected without any hesitation in the writer's outflow or any wear and tear upon his creative ability. Joyce's sustained genius, however, has been a rarity in the course of writing. For every important writer who has maintained a similar steady creative output in the face of changing ideals and circumstances, one can name ten who have crammed their all-important work into a particular period of their writing career (as a result of a sudden increased sensitivity or a brilliant though fleeting insight). Frequently within the space of three or four years a man will produce a work which eclipses everything else he has ever done or ever will do. It does sometimes happen that a writer's muse hovers about him throughout his working life—but not often. And this rule I would apply to all artistic forms: to literature, painting, sculpture and music, and to jazz, which is a developing branch of music.

The trumpet playing of Wilbur "Buck" Clayton has been subjected to several alterations in style during his lifetime, and has been placed in a variety of musical settings, yet it has maintained a strong individuality at all times and has expressed a highly-inventive flow of ideas as well as a profound feeling for jazz music.

Unlike the trumpet playing of Louis Armstrong, which in more recent years has declined as a creative force on account of its contact with unsympathetic supporting musicians and of Louis' own increased exploits dressed in the cap and bells of a court jester, Buck's has proved remarkably durable. Though best known perhaps for his solo work of the late 1930's and early 1940's with Count Basie's Orchestra and for his subsequent recordings with small mainstream jazz units, Clayton has worked intermittently with traditional, middle-period and modern styled jazz groups without ever once losing his ability to improvise with purpose and imagination. There have been occasions when his inspiration has grafted distinction on to otherwise musically inferior groups. Buck's recent work, as explained by his recordings, is a logical development, and no less vivid in its thought and expressiveness, of the playing style he originally evidenced with Count Basie. He has weathered the passage of time, and the storming innovations time has brought with it, better than the majority of musicians who were active in the 1930's.

"I began playing trumpet when I was sixteen," Buck remembers. "My father played the trumpet, and my mother played piano, so I had a good musical foundation." His first instrument was the piano which he used to play at parties and socials in and around Parsons, Kansas, where he was born on 12th November 1911. It was mainly at his father's suggestion that he began to pay some attention to the trumpet, and he stammered out his first notes with the instrument as a member of the local church orchestra. At the age of eighteen Buck left home and travelled to California, to Los Angeles, where he met the famous New Orleans trumpet stylist Papa Mutt Carey, who generously gave him some training in how to handle his horn and how to phrase with it. Under the guidance of Papa Mutt he played his first jazz solos with the instrument.

When he could perform confidently in public, Buck worked

with several bands on the west coast, including Charles Echols (where he first met trombonist Russell Moore), LaVern Floyd and Earl Dancer, and then, at the age of twenty-two, he formed his own band, a fourteen-piece unit which included Baby Lewis on drums. Teddy Weatherford, who had been working in China as a solo pianist, and who had briefly returned to California to find some musicians who would play with him in a band in Shanghai, listened carefully to Clayton's group and decided that all the musicians in it would suit his purpose. So Buck and his musicians went to Shanghai to play at the Canidrome, a club owned by an English couple. The trumpeter remained in China for two years (1934–1936).

Upon his return to America, Buck played at the Cotton Club in Los Angeles with the early band of Lionel Hampton for several months. Tenorman Herschel Evans was in the same band. It was a period of depression in America and well-paid engagements were few and far between for jazz musicians. Buck and Herschel received tempting offers from Willie Bryant to join his band in New York. Both musicians cabled their acceptance, but on the way they broke their journey in Kansas City and heard the Count Basie band which was also about to leave for New York. Basie wanted Herschel, and he also wanted Buck as a replacement for "Hot Lips" Page, so he persuaded the two men to make the trip east with his band. Buck stayed with the Count for seven years in all from that date, and upon the band's arrival in New York began to make his first real recordings.

Buck's solos on record from the period of his life which followed his entry into the Basie band, some of them performed with the full band, others with smaller units drawn from the band or with accompanying units to Billie Holiday, reveal a style of trumpet playing that, while essentially personal in its stress of emotion and its imaginative flow, had been influenced by Louis Armstrong and by Joe Smith, the trumpeter who achieved some prominence with Fletcher Henderson's Orchestra of the 1920's. From Armstrong it had inherited the property of melodic structure in the linking of notes and the shaping of its phrases; from Joe Smith a certain delicacy and refinement of delivery.

These elements, in association with the stylistic mannerisms which were unmistakably Clayton's own, enabled the trumpeter to fashion a strong and distinctive solo voice.

With Count Basie, aided by the undeviating swing of the band's rhythm section, Buck manufactured solos which were lyrical, graceful and flowing in their construction, full of phrases that seemed to sing with melody, and he delivered them with considerable warmth and sensitivity. His execution was already clean and facile, and his range appreciably developed, by the time he entered the Basie trumpet section, allowing him to speak his mind clearly and concisely, while skilful adaptations of his tone made it possible for him to stress the moods and emotional motives of his solos most emphatically. Buck's tone was essentially smaller in sound than that of his colleague in the Basie trumpet section, the hard-blowing, volatile Harry Edison, but no less expressive. Sometimes he would state his thoughts very directly by playing in the upper register of his trumpet with a warm, open tone, producing a clean, pure, well-modulated sound, practically devoid of vibrato—a method which proved ideally suited to the musical attack of the Basie band. When the occasion demanded it, however, Buck could also play a moving slow blues improvisation, reaching down into the lower register of his instrument and blowing with a somewhat rounder, deeper tone to accentuate the solemn nature of his melodic phrases. Frequently too he would insert a cup-mute in his trumpet—particularly when he was improvising the accompaniments to singers—and emit a tight, stinging tone, so that his phrase designs appeared unusually tense and brittle, stabbing out their melodic message with the sharp definition of so many slivers of broken glass. With his trumpet muted in this way he achieved a remarkable clarity of sound even when only lightly embroidering a blues shouted out by Jimmy Rushing or a popular melody of the 1930's hauntingly expressed by Billie Holiday.

Buck's individual personality as a jazz soloist, together with his immense musicality and taste, his wealth of ideas, and the greater rhythmic sense he developed as a result of working with Basie established him as one of the outstanding trumpet stylists of the swing era—a man whose intense feeling for jazz was enhanced by his freedom of expression.

On 21st January 1937, at the Count Basie band's initial recording session in New York City, Buck was prominently featured as a soloist by the arrangement of *Swinging At The Daisy Chain*. This proved to be the first of a series of authoritative and inventive improvisations recorded by Clayton with the band; of the numerous ones which followed a survey of the trumpeter's finest work would have to include: *Boo Hoo* (an obbligato to Rushing's vocal chorus), *Smarty, Good Morning Blues, Topsy* (an outstanding instance of his muted work), *Jumpin' At The Woodside, One O'Clock Jump, Swinging The Blues, Blues In The Dark* (obbligato to Rushing), *Out Of The Window, Sent For You Yesterday And Here You Come Today* (solo and obbligato to Rushing), *Miss Thing* (trumpet-piano duet with Basie), *Fiesta In Blue* (a rather more contrived display piece) and *It's Square But It Rocks*. (While the facets of Clayton's style which earlier I have sought to describe are aptly demonstrated throughout his solos on these records, I would like to take this opportunity of pointing out that his obbligato to Rushing during the sinister *Blues In The Dark* perhaps best reveals the melodic influence of Louis Armstrong upon him, while *Smarty* portrays much of the refinement inherited from Joe Smith.)

During the years 1937, 1938, and 1939, Buck sat in on almost as many recording sessions with singer Billie Holiday as he did with Basie. The inimitable "Lady Day" was working with pianist Teddy Wilson during these years, and whenever she entered the studios, either to record under Teddy's name for Brunswick or under her own for Vocalion, her first plea was to have Buck Clayton and Lester Young from the Basie band to accompany her. It became a specific task for Buck's poignant, intense trumpet to cushion the jazz singer's voice or to weave an instrumental embroidery about her words, a task he performed outstandingly on *This Year's Kisses, I Must Have That Man, Mean To Me, Back In Your Own Backyard* and many other titles, but most particularly on *Without Your Love* and *Why Was I Born?*, which both contain superlative Clayton solo choruses. In 1938 Buck also figured importantly at the Commodore sessions of the Kansas City Five and Kansas City Six, groups organized mainly by the Basie trombonist-cum-electric guitarist Eddie Durham. The eight sides resulting from these sessions serve to illustrate the diverse moods and emotional attitudes that Clayton's trumpet playing is capable of expressing. It is interesting to compare the sprightliness of his muted solo on *Way Down Yonder In New Orleans* with the bitterness and frustration of his vindictive, Louis Armstrong-influenced open solo on *Pagin' The Devil*, or the wistful, sentimental nature of his playing on *I Want A Little Girl* with the quick-witted humour he evidences on *Countless Blues*. When listening to them for the first time I was overawed by the man's lucid portrayal of feeling.

On 24th July 1942 Count Basie entered the Columbia studios with a contingent from his band with the express purpose of recording three or four small-group features. It so happened, however, that the musicians were in such fine fettle that the engineers let them play into a period of overtime, and by the time they eventually packed away their instruments no less than eight sides were on wax. Basie had played four piano solos accompanied by the rhythm section, while Buck and tenorman Don Byas were added to the group for the remaining items. Buck's solo work from this session is curiously unorthodox in that his style of improvisation occasionally strays away from its normal methods. With *St. Louis Blues* he indulges in a bout of aggressive growling, employing a harsh vibrato, while he plays a chorus during *Royal Garden Blues* in which his volatile, extrovert phrasing and huge tone openly imitate the playing methods of Harry Edison. *Sugar Blues*, though, is a typical Clayton solo; improvising at a slow tempo, the trumpeter blows a series of melodic variations which are graceful, while full of lyric beauty.

Buck was compelled to vacate his position in the Basie brass section in 1943 on account of military service. He was kept in the U.S. Army until 1946. On 12th October 1944, during a period of leave in New York City, he recorded for Keynote with a quintet led by tenorman Coleman Hawkins, and, ably combining his technical mastery with his rich imagination, performed a dazzling solo on the up-tempo version of *A Shanty In Old Shanty Town*.

When the trumpeter was released from the army in 1946 he undertook two tours with an early edition of Norman Granz' "Jazz At The Philharmonic" show and his manner of playing changed perceptibly through contact with this, the most extrovert and brash of all jazz units. After only a few months of touring with "J.A.T.P.", without making any concessions to exhibitionism, Buck had developed a bigger and broader tone and was making better use of his considerable range to promote both glaring contrasts and increased subtleties in his attack. The melodic lines of the phrases in his solos became even more flowing, thereby accentuating the lyrical nature of his ideas. Such changes were effected without any loss of emotional warmth or any deterioration in Buck's sensitive, graceful construction and wealth of ideas; rather they served to enhance his already impressive style.

After leaving Granz' unit, Buck freelanced around New York City for some time, and his trumpet playing was heard in a wide variety of settings. In 1949 he toured France under the auspices of the Hot Club de France, along with trumpeter Merril Stepter and drummer Wallace Bishop. While in Paris he recorded under his own name for Vogue Records, and, though performing with an inferior rhythm section, produced two majestic and powerful slow blues improvisations, *Blues In First* and *Blues In Second*. Louis Armstrong's All-Stars were in Europe at this time, and Buck also deputised for the contract-bound Louis at a Vogue recording session built around Earl Hines and Barney Bigard.

Buck has never had any qualms about working with musicians from different schools of thought in jazz. He believes that technical developments will never fence in a true jazz feeling. Back from Europe, he worked with blues singer Jimmy Rushing at the Savoy Ballroom, then at Lou Terrasi's Club as leader of a small group playing traditional jazz (Buster Bailey played clarinet and Ken Kersey piano with this unit), and from 1951 to 1953 he was mainly at The Embers in New York City as a member of pianist Joe Bushkin's Quartet (with Milt Hinton on bass and Jo Jones on drums). The musical policy of the latter unit made distinct concessions to modern jazz, and, without endangering the essentials of his style, Buck consciously absorbed certain modern overtones and devices of phrasing into his trumpet.

For Columbia Records in 1953 Buck recorded eight sides accompanied by Marlowe Morris (organ), Herbert Brown (guitar) and Les Erskine (drums). These features included three improvisations upon standard melodies: *I Want A Little Girl*, *Blue Moon* and *S'Wonderful*; the remaining themes were conceived at the session and names were tagged on at a later date.

Later in 1953, when the Bushkin Quartet was dissolved, Buck received another invitation to very briefly tour Europe, this time as a member of clarinettist Mezz Mezzrow's group. The inevitable recording sessions were lined up for him in Paris. Of the various sides (*Patricia's Blues*, *Special B.C.*, *She's Funny That Way*, etc.) which Buck taped with Mezzrow or with other sidemen from the clarinettist's group, the outstanding recording for his trumpet solo work is *Wrap Your Troubles In Dreams*. A chorus of delicate muted trumpet countering Mezzrow's clarinet lines in the theme statement, and a nobly conceived and constructed open solo which

78

follows cause this record to be one of Clayton's finest excursions on record.

The years which have elapsed since Buck's return to the United States from his second European tour have witnessed the trumpeter leading various small jazz groups around New York City, making appearances at Basin Street and the majority of the city's leading clubs, and he has played and acted in the film of Benny Goodman's life story.

Even more important, however, Buck has been the central figure of a number of extended jam sessions, mainly instigated by John Hammond and George Avakian for recording by Columbia Records. These sessions, preserved for posterity in four 12-inch LP. albums, have given a lasting artistic value to the middle stages of Buck Clayton's career as a soloist comparable with that given to his early career by his recordings with Count Basie's Orchestra.

Though made in the Columbia studios, these Clayton albums have come closer than any other recordings I have heard to recreating the atmosphere of warmth and relaxation, as well as the unique musical rapport and the soloists' freedom of speech associated with the lengthy, "after hours" jam session which took place in Kansas City in the early 1930's.

When the musicians assembled and began to play there were no anxious glances at the clock by the engineers; after a tune, and a key and tempo for it, had been decided upon, it was left to the soloists to determine the length of a performance according to how they felt the music was shaping itself; some of the items run on for as long as twenty minutes or more. Individual soloists took advantage of this situation to express themselves fully with the various themes. If a man felt he could extend himself to three choruses without exhausting his ideas, then he was free to do so.

Some of the men had never even met before these sessions; others, like tenorman Julian Dash, who for years had worked in the semi-obscurity of the Erskine Hawkins band, and altoist Lem Davis, were entering the recording studios for the first time in several years. Modernists like Urbie Green and Al Cohn rubbed shoulders with such mainstream stalwarts as Henderson Chambers and Trummy Young. However, when supported by the sure swing of the old Basie rhythm section (Freddie Greene, Walter Page and Jo Jones) the men evidenced a rare compatibility in their work and stimulated one another so that many spirited solos resulted. Jo Jones and many other musicians have commented upon the unselfish attitude of the musicians at the Kansas City jam sessions; these Clayton sessions reveal a similar attitude. There are no carving contests; and no one blows in the direction of the gallery. The soloists never get in each other's way, and when they come together for a spontaneous head arrangement their unison is clean. The feeling and warmth existing between the soloists is never more obvious than when, in *The Hucklebuck*, Buck Clayton and the Harry Edison-influenced trumpet player, Joe Newman, come together for a lengthy improvised duet. Alternating four-bar phrases, the trumpeters, instead of battling their way through, delicately complement each other, and actually develop each other's melodic ideas so that the duet appears to be one logical solo.

The first of these jam sessions, held on 14th December 1953, produced *Sentimental Journey* and *Moten Swing*, performances running to over fourteen minutes and thirteen minutes respectively. On the former Buck buries a discreet, tightly-muted chorus, full of phrases which are extremely fragile in appearance, in between solos by Urbie Green and Julian Dash. On *Moten Swing*, though he is bolder in approach, improvising a chorus without the use of a mute that is fiery and outspoken in its phrasing.

A second session, held two days later and with only one change in personnel (Henderson Chambers replacing Benny Powell in the trombone team) extended the average length of the performances even further. *Christopher Columbus* runs for more than twenty-five minutes, and the soloists take thirty or more choruses of improvisation between them. Clayton is kept extremely busy during this performance. He plays the middle-eight of the thematic chorus with considerable dignity, but when the solo sequence gets under way his improvisation runs through almost the whole gamut of possible moods. His two muted choruses between the solos of Henderson Chambers and Lem Davis are somewhat coquettish as he flits between moments of seriousness and humour; his style of phrasing also varies here, alternating between flowing legato phrases and clipped, more rhythmic ones. A three-chorus duet with Joe Newman, however, firmly decides him to devote himself to the cause of humour, and when he next comes to the fore on his own for three choruses he is full of juicy witticisms. Later in the performance he plays a chorus of strident, forceful open above a unison figure from the ensemble, and he completes the cycle of moods by improvising a sad little duet with pianist Sir Charles Thompson.

The Hucklebuck and a leisurely version of Sir Charles Thompson's composition, *Robbins Nest*, both of them lengthy performances, must have cost the record company a small fortune in overtime fees for the musicians when added to the length of *Christopher Columbus*, but the men were creating so well that the engineers just left their tape spools running.

On 31st March 1954 a further session found veteran Joe Thomas (the man who played trumpet on Art Tatum's recording of *Lonesome Graveyard Blues*) replacing Joe Newman as Buck's partner. Jimmy Jones, just recovered from two years of ill-health, was at the piano; Urbie Green and Trummy Young were the trombones; Woody Herman, just passing through New York on his way to Europe, found time to sit in with his clarinet and produced the finest recorded solos of his career. At this session *How Hi The Fi* and *Blue Moon* were recorded. Buck's two choruses on the former title illustrate the immense power he is capable of unleashing, as well as the intelligent use he has made of modern jazz construction in his work. His solo on *Blue Moon* tends to vary in mood; at times he is inclined to be short and careful of what he says, while at one point he growls grumpily, but the solo still has its more lyrical moments when his phrases become shapely and flow more easily.

Buck maintained his highly-inventive solo work at the two remaining sessions held on 13th August 1954 and 15th March 1955. (In fact he contributed so many rich and varied solos at all these Columbia sessions that I feel it really requires a separate essay to fully evaluate his work in the four albums.)

Only one performance, the hybrid *Jumpin' At The Woodside*, falls below the level of the rest. The musicians had first attempted to jam with this theme at the end of the 31st March 1954 session, but, tired by their previous efforts of that day, had given it up part way through. The theme was tackled once more at the 13th August 1954 session, and later George Avakian spliced sections of tape from both versions together (with Buck extemporising out-of-tempo breaks with his trumpet to cover the joins). Unfortunately, the personnel had altered greatly for the second of these sessions, and Milt Hinton's bass tone in particular sounds so different to that of Walter Page, which is heard at the opening of the performance, that the whole thing sounds much too con-

81

trived. Yet this is a point of criticism aimed at the recording; in no way does it reflect upon Buck's trumpet work.

It has seemed only right and just that I should conclude my essay on Buck Clayton with a survey of his recent jam-session albums on Columbia. For these recordings, reuniting Buck with a musical atmosphere to which he is ideally suited, have enabled the trumpeter to confirm his position as one of the three or four outstanding soloists with this instrument in jazz—a position he first laid claim to almost twenty years ago when actually working with the Basie band. His solo playing has never been more highly esteemed than it is today.

HARRY EDISON

"Edison hardly ever looks for instrumental brilliance; he just wants to swing, and he swings as much as the great New Orleans trumpet players, even if he uses very different phrases."
HUGUES PANASSIÉ

Since 1950 it has been noticeable that the Californian coast (though in particular the cities of Los Angeles and San Francisco) has virtually become the focal point for the new sounds of the younger white modernist school in jazz. Leading soloists from the Kenton and Herman bands have invaded the clubs, the music colleges and the recording studios of the west coast. They have built up a large experimental centre, rich both in solo strength and writing ability. However, their music is of an isolationist nature, for it represents jazz in its most highly organized state; in a taut environment of technique and precision. Few of the Negro jazzmen have attempted to interfere with the west-coast scheme; while they may admire the advanced thought of the white modernists, they are hesitant to depart from the direct, emotional force of jazz. They prefer to bypass the futuristic sounds, seeking instead a more logical development which retains their ideals of vigour and natural feeling. As a result this lack of common beliefs regarding collective jazz has rendered the position of the white modernists almost sacrosanct in California.

The Negro jazzman can now only work along the west coast on his standing as a featured soloist, and even then the reaction is often doubtful. Benny Carter has succeeded in this role, though partially because he has discovered a profitable sideline in the film studios which helps to defray any losses he might incur with his jazz appearances. The late Wardell Gray managed to vanquish all opposition from the modern white tenor-saxophone players on the coast. Flautist Buddy Collette supplements his income as a jazz musician by teaching and by playing for commercial radio shows. Yet the man to repeatedly gatecrash the west coast clubs and elicit a genuine admiration has been the veteran trumpeter Harry Edison. Edison has played to the white modernists and also worked with them. His ability as an improvising soloist has never failed to make an impression. In fact, despite a refusal to accept the experimental theories now being employed by the majority of the west coast musicians, Edison has made the residents in the area very conscious of his presence. Arranger Bill Russo was even moved to dedicate one of his compositions to the trumpeter, though its musical substance had little in common with Edison's own style of expression.

Harry Edison is not a true modern stylist; he still belongs to the middle-period group of trumpet soloists. For though in the 1930's he acted (alongside Roy Eldridge) as a pointer towards modern jazz with his bold, adventurous phrases, he never evolved completely into a modernist with regard to the distribution of emotion and the manner of changing from a melodic to a harmonic source of improvisation. Even today his attack still shows all the fire and the surface intensity of the great trumpeters of the swing era.

Born in Ohio on 10th October 1915, Edison made his professional début in 1933 with the orchestra of Alphonso Trent. Prior to this he had never studied music formally. "With me playing jazz has always been a natural thing," he says. "I never had a lesson in my life. My mother bought me a horn when I was twelve, back in Columbus, Ohio, and I just picked up my music, learning a few fundamentals in the high-school band." Certainly Edison has been one of the great natural stylists in jazz, an unconscious, extrovert improviser, yet a musician who hardly knows the meaning of sensationalism. His style is one which cannot be tamed, so naturally gushing is it in its outflow, yet it fortunately contains an inherent sense of taste which saves the sheer emotional force of his style from turning the musician into an exhibitionist. The importance of Edison's solo power was

83

quickly realized in New York in 1937 when he was playing there with Lucky Millinder's Blue Rhythm Band. Musicians were astounded by the mighty attack, uninhibited swing and complete freshness of phrasing which distinguished Edison at the time.

The late 1930's was the great age for the large jazz group, and sidemen of Edison's calibre were scarce as gold. Basie badly wanted a stylist who would act as a foil to the playing of Buck Clayton; Edison was ideally suited to play the part. Early in 1938 he became a regular member of the Count Basie trumpet section, a position he was to hold until the old band's dissolution in 1950.

Originally Edison was influenced by the style of Roy Eldridge; an influence which was to gradually diminish after he became a part of the Basie organization and merged with the pianist's singular concept of jazz.

Just like Eldridge, the playing style of Edison—upon joining Basie—revealed its owner's tendency to break away from the simple melodic variations of Louis Armstrong, adopting an altogether more searching style of improvisation which contained bold, unusual intervals, intricate constructions upon the melody, volatile cascades of notes, and so on. (In this respect both Eldridge and Edison pointed towards the experiments which were to take place at Minton's Playhouse in New York in the 1940's.) Harry came to differ from Roy, however, in that he gradually took on the greater rhythmic relaxation which so distinguished the musical style of the Basie band. He still played with a direct attack as a result of his tremendous emotional feeling, yet the tautness which accompanied Eldridge's flurry of invention was gradually erased from his work. The waves of excitement still flowed liberally through every solo he took, but the tenseness, the almost breathless desire to rush on and on which so strikes one when listening to Eldridge was confidently replaced by a more supple, more relaxed attack.

While Edison pointed towards modern jazz with his daring phrase construction he was not a contrived creator in any of his work. He did not break away from Armstrong merely for the sake of doing something different, but rather in order to express himself in the only way he felt possible. Had he merely been striving for effect, then it would have been logical for him to enlarge upon his breakaway from Armstrong still further, pressing on with his advances, following up his adventurous phrase ideas by becoming a member of the modern jazz school in the 1940's. This event did

84

not take place. Having found a way to express himself he was fully satisfied. He did not seek to place himself in the vanguard of the modern jazz movement by adopting the devices which entered jazz playing as a result of the searchings of Charlie Christian and others at the Minton's Playhouse sessions.

Too many things stand in the way of classifying Edison as a modern jazz musician, even though he was one of the important revolutionaries of the late 1930's in jazz. In the first place, being essentially a musician who reached maturity with the swing era, Edison's jazz was founded on a strong rhythmic basis. He played with the beat, not around it. This has remained so even with his most recent work. He has not shown any great predilection for the modernist's device of using double-time, continually increasing and alternately relaxing the tempo of a solo. He likes a straight, direct rhythmic pattern. Even when improvising upon a tune which is normally treated by jazz musicians as a slow ballad he usually converts his improvisation upon it to an easy, riding tempo. Through this feeling for the direct beat he plays with an exceptionally powerful swing. He is possessed of a wide range and control, which he uses to good effect, fiercely punching home his melodic statements, only rarely playing with a lyrical approach. He feels jazz in the way that its notes can punch, in the way that emotion becomes the backbone of a soloist's strength. When Edison is playing he's oblivious to the solidity of his technical make-up. Technical artistry abounds, but for him it represents only a side issue when compared to the swing and the inspiration.

Perhaps Edison's most easily distinguishable characteristic, however, is the beauty of his tone. For a musician who exhibits so boldly the modern phrasing, Edison's tone has retained a remarkable purity and fire, a thing which has held him rigidly apart from the many out-and-out modernists who have sought in the past decade to exchange the surface intensity of jazz for something which is cold and lethargic. His tone has always possessed great depth; a rich, rounded sound which perfectly matches his finely-articulated notes. Edison has been nicknamed "Sweets" on account of the fullness and clean sound of his tone. "This name happened one day back in the 1930's," the trumpeter recalls, "when all of us in the Basie band were sitting around the lobby of the Woodside Hotel [the same place which inspired the Basie theme *Jumpin' At The Woodside*] in New York. It was snowing out-side, and we were waiting for the bus to go on a series of one-night stands. We were all like brothers in that band. I was the baby of the band at the time and I took a lot of ribbing. So this time Lester Young was joshing me about my sweet style and he said: 'We're going to call you "Sweetie-Pie".' They did too, for a few months. Then they shortened it to 'Sweets'. The nickname has lasted a long time." It has indeed lasted a long time, but it is a very apt way of describing the full, clear tone which is so vital to Edison's playing. Do not imagine that it is a lush, sugary tone, though; a pre-modern jazz hotness in it illustrates the intense feeling of its originator. Moreover, the full moulding of the tone lives in each register of the instrument when he is playing. It adds clarity to his high-note work, while to the middle and lower registers its roundness always gives the impression of a big, fat sound. Occasionally he will allow a little vibrato to wriggle through the normal purity of the tone, just a slight spasm but sufficient to relieve the huge sound, a delightful stress of light and shade.

Within the Basie trumpet section the fullness of Edison's tone and the forceful swing and daring phrases which he produced all combined to make his playing a perfect foil for the tight, stinging tone and delicate, melodic phrases of Buck Clayton. A number of critics even made the mistake of thinking that Edison's solos were actually by Buck Clayton playing in an open style! If this were so, then Buck would have been the most versatile trumpet player in jazz! Certainly Edison and Clayton between them gave Basie a fine range of ideas and a remarkable diversity of solo approaches in his trumpet section. At no time since has he possessed two trumpet players of the same calibre.

Edison's solo style, while indirectly pointing towards modern jazz, has also been an important *direct* influence upon a number of trumpet players. Amongst these one would include such men as Taft Jordan, Snooky Young, Ernie Royal, Emmett Berry and Joe Newman. All of these men are gifted improvising jazzmen in their own right, yet they have all been given a sense of direction by Edison, and, by adopting (in part or in whole) his stylistic approach, have been able to make an important contribution to jazz.

During his twelve years as a regular sideman with Basie the trumpeter recorded many solos with the full band, including *Panassié Stomp, Swinging The Blues, Texas Shuffle, Jive At Five, Miss Thing, Rocking The Blues, Louisiana, Blow Top,* and so on. In addition he made up quite a number of outstanding themes, either from melodic ideas appearing with his own improvised choruses or by piecing together "head" arrangements. Though usually orchestrated by someone else, Harry is actually the composer of such themes as *Beaver Junction*, *Jive At Five* and *H and J*. In more recent times Ernie Wilkins took the opening phrase of Edison's solo on *Miss Thing* and turned it into a strong theme.

Edison's might epitomized the general superiority of the Count's brass in the late 1930's and early 1940's. No jazzman, save perhaps the Count himself, ever harnessed the power of the Basie rhythm section to better effect. Harry also recorded a number of small-group features with the Basie sidemen. In 1939 Billie Holiday had used his support. In 1946 he made a historic recording session with blues singer Jimmy Rushing, and in the same year, strictly in contrast, led a six-man trumpet team for the annual Metronome All-Stars date. Also in the mid-1940's he appeared with Lester Young, Jo Jones and several other musicians in the Gjon Mili film "Jammin' The Blues".

Although Count Basie regained his position and prestige as a bandleader in the 1950's, Harry Edison didn't join the new band. After the 1950 break-up he played for a while with Buddy Rich's group, and he recorded a number of items for Clef with this unit, including his own composition *Sportin' Life*. Later he worked in turn with Norman Granz' "Jazz At The Philharmonic" unit, with trombonist Bill Harris and in an orchestra touring with singer Josephine Baker. During 1953 he settled on the west coast of America, freelancing around the clubs. Apart from another tour with "J.A.T.P." towards the end of 1954 he has been on the coast ever since.

Most of Edison's recent recordings have been with Norman Granz' various jazz groups on Clef. The settings with Granz have varied from an appearance on the Machito recording of Chico O'Farrill's *Afro-Cuban Jazz Suite* to a fine series of jam sessions in the company of Count Basie, Wardell Gray, Stan Getz *et al*. It was on one of the latter sessions that he recorded a rare and outstanding slow ballad performance, *If I Had You*.

To my mind, however, the finest records that Edison has made since leaving Basie are the ones issued in an album on Pacific Jazz entitled "Sweets At The Haig". Hardly can his ability to improvise extended solos have been so excitingly captured on record.

The album contains four long solos recorded "live" in July

1953, during one of the trumpeter's sets at The Haig, a small Hollywood club. The Haig had originally built up the reputation of the Gerry Mulligan Quartet and it was consequently a tribute to "Sweets" and his ability as a soloist that he conquered the "new sounds" complex of the audience. He was soundly supported on the occasion by pianist Arnold Ross, bassist Joe Comfort and drummer Alvin Stoller. Ross had actually first recorded with Harry as early as 1945 on a Red Callender session in Los Angeles. He also played on the trumpeter's "I Blowed And Gone" session on Aladdin. The decisive touch of his bass chords and the general attacking nature of his style conformed with the zest of Edison's own musical personality. Alvin Stoller, one of the most highly-valued west coast modernists, created a continual swing with his rhythmic patterns. Joe Comfort, who rose to fame while with King Cole, bound the section well together.

In accord with his normal desire to improvise upon strong melodic material, the four solos in the "Sweets At The Haig" album by Edison are all based upon well-tried standard compositions. The trumpeter plays well-extended versions of *September In The Rain, Indiana, Pennies From Heaven* and *These Foolish Things*. The last title only serves as a vehicle for a slow ballad performance.

Despite the quality of Arnold Ross as a soloist, the trumpeter remains very much the star of these recordings. He shoulders the weight of each performance, yet never once falters in the production of ideas. For example, on the nine-chorus *Pennies From Heaven* solo the pianist is only allocated chorus number six. Harry commences gently with the charming theme. Arriving at the second chorus he plays a typical Armstrong out-of-tempo break, and then launches forth with his own familiar, swinging attack. For the last three choruses he maintains a tremendous power of expression. He begins by building an ascending phrase from the main line of the melody, only to continue with some beautiful cascade work, at times with each note punctuated by Stoller's drums. Edison can also be a subtle humorist, as indeed he demonstrates with *September In The Rain* (a mere six choruses, again split by only one from Ross). With this solo he reshapes the middle-eight of the thematic chorus, and, in the second eight bars of the second chorus, he just can't resist *Swinging On A Star*.

Nowadays Harry has enough work on the west coast to make a living. He does quite a lot of studio work, mostly for Capitol under the baton of Nelson Riddle. He has recorded a whole host of things as an accompanist to Frank Sinatra, including the "Swing Easy" and "Songs For Swinging Lovers" LP.s, and the Capitol recordings of the themes from the film "The Man With The Golden Arm". He was the only trumpeter present in the thirty-piece orchestra which Capitol assembled to record the score of "Oklahoma". By doing these studio jobs during the day, Harry is left free to play in the west coast jazz clubs at night. And he seems determined to stick to his jazz playing by hook or by crook. He wants to play it because it has always been natural to him.

Harry Edison has been one of the outstanding jazz trumpeters of all time. One can listen to his recordings (from his early sides with the Basie band through to his recent west coast efforts with Ross, Barney Kessel and Cy Touff) and trace the high standard of his solo work over a period of twenty years. It is a remarkable fact that for a trumpet player with such an obvious power of expression he has received very little critical recognition for his singular talents. He was underrated as an innovator with Basie when his style was a direct pointer towards modern jazz. Today, though modern jazz is an established force, he still does not receive the credit for his important work. It is unfortunate that some of the people who go into such raptures over Louis Armstrong's current showboating cannot spare a little of their precious time to listen to the sincere and spirited jazz creations of Harry Edison.

DICKY WELLS

"When a man plays the blues he tells the truth about himself. Simplicity reveals the poverty as well as the richness of an artist's imagination. Every phrase Dicky Wells blows seems exactly poised; the unexpected suddenly becomes transformed into the inevitable."

CHARLES FOX

On one occasion in the autumn of 1954 (some time before I began marshalling information for a book concerning the musicians of the Count Basie band), I recall discussing the status of the trombone in jazz with my friend Albert McCarthy, who had just returned to London to pave the way for his magazine project, "Jazz Monthly", and concluding with him that the man to realize fully the expressiveness of the instrument had been Dicky Wells.

We had searched about in our debate, analysing first one musician and then another, and trying to give credit where it was obviously due. To the late Jimmy Harrison of the Fletcher Henderson band, and to the Chicagoans, Jack Teagarden and Floyd O'Brien, had gone the necessary acknowledgments for their roles in originally hoisting the trombone out of the collective improvised style of the New Orleans frontline; for transforming it into a real solo voice, largely by eliminating the exaggerated tailgate mannerisms, the rough slurring, and so on, from the New Orleans ensemble style, and developing instead the "formal" melodic shapes and phrase designs. A product of the later swing era, Vic Dickenson then called for praise as an assistant in making the trombone even more the property of the individual in jazz, a musician who became contemptuous of both purely formal design and exaggerated ornamentation, desiring instead a scrupulously honest confession of mood, be it sorrowful or gay, humorous or cynical; few trombonists have equalled the warmth, the truthfulness, or alternatively the acid wit of Dickenson. Subsequent years have introduced the sophistication of Lawrence Brown, the sensuousness of Tyree Glenn, the lyrical surges of Benny Green, and with Jay Jay Johnson, the facile, brilliant product of the modern jazz experiments, a reversion to formal construction and balance, though in association with a greatly enlarged concept of technique. Nor could the emotional intensity of the late Joe Nanton be overlooked, even though his isolated musical experiments were as much the brain child of Duke Ellington's orchestral writing as they were of his own creation.

Even when the contributions of all these men had been considered, however, the status of Dicky Wells' finest trombone improvisations was not undermined by comparison with them. Then, as now, I held the belief that Wells, during the 1930's and early 1940's when his powers as an innovator and interpreter were most pronounced, had given to the trombone an importance comparable to that given by Louis Armstrong to the trumpet in jazz, and by Earl Hines and Art Tatum to the piano. As with Armstrong and Hines and Tatum and their mediums of expression, Wells' importance as an improvising trombonist meant something more than mere musical virtuosity (though he too employed a

90

considerable degree of technique in his solo work); rather it symbolized the forging of a solo personality, one which combined an accomplished technique, an emotional inspiration susceptible to a wide range of moods and attitudes, and a vivid imagination continually urging fresh and even alarming musical thoughts through his instrument. Seldom has a jazz musician been so vital, so moving or so expressive as Dicky Wells was in the 1930's. His musical, emotional and creative flexibility when handling the trombone in that decade left him with no equal among his contemporaries.

Seldom, though, has a jazz musician been so disappointing as Wells has been since the 1930's in failing to sustain the flow of masterpieces. Since the mid-1940's his creative instinct and greater sensitivity have unfortunately worn blunt. Because I cannot dispute the intrinsic musical merits of his recorded solos from the period of the 1930's and early 1940's, I revere his playing, but I stress the fact that any artistic durability has belonged to the solos *and not to him*; in the later 1940's and 1950's, Vic Dickenson, for one, has been a superior improvising soloist to Wells with the trombone in jazz.

Andre Hodeir in "Jazz: Its Evolution And Essence" makes a penetrating study of Wells' style and output, and also arrives at the conclusion that the trombonist's recent work has been sadly inferior to his recorded solos dating from the 1930's.

Though I find myself at variance with the majority of M. Hodeir's theories in his critical book, it would be a dog-in-the-mangerish attitude on my part if I withheld my endorsement of his views when analysing Wells. This chapter impressed me as the highlight of his book, and I do not hesitate to echo what I hold to be a correct assessment. I feel grateful to the French critic for raising and examining in his essay so many points about the trombonist's methods of delivery, and also for stressing the importance of the recordings which Wells made in 1933 with the British arranger Spike Hughes; in the case of the Hughes' sessions, an official commendation, ranking them alongside the fine improvisations Wells created in Paris in 1937 and later with Count Basie's band, was long overdue. Most of all, however, Hodeir's overall reasoning assists me in dividing Wells' playing into two distinct periods of creativeness, namely the decade and a half dating from the year 1930 when he was at his finest, and the later period of famine as a creative artist. Having read his essay I feel justified in devoting the major portion of my own to Wells' truly productive years at the expense of what he has accomplished since. In view of the trombonist's previous distinction, to examine his recent work is not exactly an exhilarating experience.

Though Dicky Wells has been the most distinguished trombone soloist to perform with the Count Basie Orchestra (ahead of men like Vic Dickenson and the impressive Henry Coker) his individuality was not a product of the Kansas City jam sessions of the early 1930's. He was, in point of fact, one of the rare stylists to successfully fuse his talents with the Basie band without any definite previous contact with the Kaycee scene, having developed his style in New York while playing with a series of inferior bands. Born at Centerville, Tennessee, on 10th June 1909, Wells moved to Louisville, Kentucky, with his family as a boy and grew up there, attending the local high school, where he had his first music lessons. Another important jazz musician, trumpeter Jonah Jones, attended this school at the same time as Wells. Jonah, then playing a French horn, remembers Dicky Wells performing alongside him in the local municipal orchestra. Upon the completion of their studies they parted company, Jonah to play on the riverboats and later with several name bands, including Lunceford's, Fletcher Henderson's and Cab Calloway's, Wells departing immediately for New York City, where he arrived in 1927 and commenced working with the Charlie Johnson band.

From 1927 until 1932 the young trombonist played with a series of early east coast groups, including Johnson's, the Lloyd and Cecil Scott band, Elmer Snowden's and Luis Russell's, the majority of them typified by muddy ensemble work, partly the fault of only semi-articulate arrangements, partly through incompetent musicianship from certain sidemen. The signs are, though, that Wells merely used these inferior units as convenient bread-and-butter jobs while experimenting to mould an individual solo expression with his trombone. A handful of recordings he made for Victor in 1927 and 1929 with the Scott band show a trombonist already possessed of a bold attack, and capable of introducing surprising melodic shapes and ingenious rhythmic devices, while searching still for certain imaginative and musical improvements which would allow him to throw off the influence of Jimmy Harrison and become a completely individual stylist. Apart from Wells' contributions, the musical value of these Scott sessions now appears to be quite negative.

By 1932, however, when Dicky Wells joined the fourteen-piece band which Benny Carter was struggling to keep in existence in New York City, his search for a mature and individual style of self-expression was virtually at an end. From this date his recordings reveal that he had successfully cast off his more youthful influences as a jazz musician, and that he had finally reconciled the various radical elements occurring in his playing so as to form a strong, cohesive and highly-personal trombone style. When he joined the Carter band, Wells was on the threshold of greatness as a soloist, preparing to sally forth with a stream of improvisations destined to overshadow everything previously accomplished with the trombone in jazz.

This style, innovated by Wells for the trombone, and which he was to employ outstandingly as an outlet for his creative urge throughout the remainder of the 1930's, featured as its basic foundation the alliance of a fine sense of form and construction with a most vivid imagery. (Such a concept branded him immediately as a revolutionary, for the majority of jazz soloists have tended to be either strict formalists or passionate romantics, but rarely both together.)

As a formalist Wells appreciated the fact that phrase formation, carefully constructed and deployed with an intelligent amount of technique, could assist the emotions in building up the tension of a solo towards a dramatic climax. As a result, whenever the trombonist embarked upon a chorus of improvisation, he regarded his solo as a complete entity, as a framework to be logically built upon, rather than as a series of isolated, disjointed phrases. Thus, within his solos on record, each phrase appears to be shaped so as to pave the way for its successor, and it consequently steers Wells that much nearer to his elevated climax. At the outset of a solo he will normally blow a single introductory phrase, firmly marking the termination of the previous soloist's work and the commencement of his own. Having thereby announced himself, he will then proceed to improvise upon the theme, audaciously twisting the melodic lines into new shapes but taking care to mount successive phrases one upon the other so that the conclusion becomes the formal as well as the emotional climax.

As a romantic, as the inventor of passionate and vivid images, Wells also realized the value of musical contrasts within a solo, of balancing daring opposites within the design of phrases in order to give the solo the right amount of light and shade. With his creative thinking he learnt how to fashion an elastic, varying attack, making full use of his technical range, so that he might commence a phrase by growling out a deep, throaty low note only to complete it by surprisingly shooting, by means of an upward glissando, into the higher register of his instrument; also, how to vary the strength and size of his tone, one moment producing a light, smooth sound to create the impression of a natural shyness and reserve, the next swaggering forth in an aggressive and bombastic manner with a big, brassy tone, barely controlling a fierce vibrato.

I have already mentioned the remarkable expressiveness and sincerity of Wells as a trombonist. Perhaps more so than any other jazz musician, he appears (at least, on record) to give the instrument the power of articulate speech, at times a speech which is unnaturally close, emotionally, to the utterances of the human voice.

The range of emotional moods he brings to bear reveals the profound sensitivity inherent in his being. An immediate susceptibility to the the vein of feeling underlying a theme or an arrangement romantically colours the teeming phrases which he will improvise upon it. His outlay is always a truthful statement of the way he feels a piece of music at the time of playing, of the effect that each theme or particular orchestration has upon his personal spirits. When unfolding a solo upon a slow blues lament, if the underlying mood of the theme has so moved him, he will soulfully express a grief so immense, applying a tone of deep sonority, pleading, complaining, sounding so wretched and woe-begone with his phrases, that the sorrow of the theme becomes his own particular property. Of all the soloists upon that theme, his cry for certain will be the longest and the loudest. On the other hand, when Dicky Wells, in better spirits, encounters a composition with a mood of intense excitement (for example one of the Kansas City "head" arrangements from the repertoire of the Count Basie band), he obviously revels in the situation and unashamedly confesses his enthusiasm as he swings energetically through phrases which are bombastic and savagely outspoken in their construction, his tone becoming raw and fierce. Alternatively, he can feel happy and flash a radiant smile with his skilful handling of the trombone; then warmly humorous (without so much of Vic Dickenson's irony and cynicism),

94

crackling with wit, chuckling over a theme with delicate nuances of his slide, inserting tongue-in-the-cheek quotations which nevertheless snuggle exactly into place between the surrounding phrases. He can be wistful, poignant, downcast, hilarious, tragic, gay, sombre, furious and gently-disposed within the space of a single recording session. I know of no other jazz musician so subject to changes of mood. Certain attitudes, however, he never projects. He is never sulky or mean or aloof. He is always a warm, vibrant personality, an improvising musician who expresses a wonderful humanity through the voice of his trombone. And while he uses his technical assets, his wide range and his fine articulation, daringly, often startlingly, to effect his moods and to humanize the sound of his trombone, in the overall result such technical devices are made to appear integral parts of the solo. There is not a tonal inflexion, nor a hint at vibrato that is not vital to the solo wherein it occurs, just as in his phrase construction there is not a note too many.

Wells' emotional warmth and humanity, colouring his inventive flow of improvised thoughts so vividly, and expressed in conjunction with a rhythmic ingenuity and a sense of form and proportion, have made him at once the most individual and inimitable of jazz trombonists. Though his style is so easily identifiable, and so admired by other musicians, it has never been plagiarized; so personal has been his creation that exploitation of his methods and ideas by other soloists has been an impossibility.

The British arranger and composer Spike Hughes sailed for America towards the end of January 1933. Upon his arrival in New York he met critic John Hammond, who took him on a brief tour of the clubs and ballrooms devoted to jazz music in the city. He heard tenorman Choo Berry and trumpeter Henry "Red" Allen playing at Small's Paradise, a New York restaurant, and many other soloists playing in different parts of the city. Hammond also took him to a rehearsal of the Benny Carter band (containing Dicky Wells as its featured trombone soloist); after several months of touring, this band, though musically so fine, was very close to dissolution on economic grounds. The British composer was both amazed and inspired by what he heard from the Carter group; here was the jazz spirit he'd been attempting to inject into European bands for several years! Immediately he determined to carry out the next stage of his Decca recording contract in New York, using as a vehicle for his compositions a

95

large band of coloured jazzmen. The American Brunswick studios at No. 1776 Broadway were hired for three recording sessions; Benny Carter's band was engaged as the nucleus of the group, with "Red" Allen, Choo Berry and Coleman Hawkins added to it as featured soloists. Choo had actually been rehearsing with Carter, though he was not a regular member of the band.

Hughes, the most important figure connected with British orchestral jazz at this period, and perhaps the only one at any time whose thematic creations and subsequent orchestrations have been favourably compared with the musical writings of Duke Ellington, Don Redman and Fletcher Henderson, made a good decision in choosing the Benny Carter band, for the musicians in it were well versed in rendering advanced scores. Hughes' pieces of composition, freshly individual in substance, not only provided a sound launching base for the improvisation of the soloists, but also contained a remarkable beauty of form. They had shape and design, the melodic lines flowing with delicacy and charm, the harmonies clearly pronounced, the rhythmic patterns firm yet gifted with relaxation, while the orchestrations revealed tone painting of extraordinary skill. Carter's musicians were duly impressed by the textures and melodic strength of these themes. Where in his orchestrations Spike Hughes had deployed section against section he found that the band responded easily, achieving a fine clarity and definition. On the recordings which resulted it is noticeable that the brass sounds have firmness as well as power, while the reeds produce unusually delicate textures, full of swirling and eddying phrases which are as much a tribute to Benny Carter's ability to rehearse a band as they are to Hughes' orchestrations. No one else but Carter, doubtless as a result of his personal talent for playing every reed instrument, would have been capable of leading a saxophone section on to produce such a unique variety of tonal blends.

The three sessions produced, in all, fourteen recorded items, the majority of them scores of original themes by Hughes, though one or two arrangements of tunes which were jazz evergreens were included, as well as two small group features. (In 1955, when set to select twelve of the items for issue on an LP. in the United States by London Records, it grieved me considerably to have to omit even two of the arrangements, so high were the musical standards achieved by all the recordings.) Hughes' writing has never been so vividly expressed as it was by this band;

nor in turn has his writing ever inspired a stronger collection of improvised solos. Carter, Hawkins, Berry, Allen, Wayman Carver, Bill Dillard, Dicky Wells: all these musicians excelled themselves as soloists. Recording for the first time under ideal conditions, and surrounded by sympathetic musicians, Dicky Wells for his part advertised his powerful personality as a jazz soloist so effectively that not only did he eclipse his own previous recorded playing, but he also caused a revised estimation to be taken by critics and musicians of the trombone's potential expressiveness as an improvising medium. The issue of the recordings caused him to be regarded as a new pace-setter with the instrument.

On 18th April 1933 Hughes directed the recording of two of his compositions, *Nocturne* and *Pastoral*, and two arrangements of jazz standards, *Bugle Call Rag* and *Someone Stole Gabriel's Horn*. The theme of *Pastoral* has a quiet, almost plaintive air, and a main melodic line reminiscent of an Irish folk-song. Wells appears to have mixed feelings about this composition, for his improvised chorus contains quite startling variations of approach. As his solo commences he seems agreeable to continuing the mood set in the thematic chorus, sounding if anything a trifle subdued as he blows fairly simple, straightforward phrases which stay close to the melody of the theme. In the closing stages of the solo, however, the trombonist suddenly becomes quite animated, ardently setting loose a series of intricate phrases, his tone thickening with conviction. During *Bugle Call Rag*, which Hughes scored at a fast tempo, Wells' solo seems even less predictable. He opens his solo as though he intends to devote himself purely to a rhythmically-inspired style of phrasing, and indeed, for several bars, his lustily swinging improvisation hinges entirely upon one or two notes. Once into his full stride, though, his use of the trombone becomes increasingly audacious, and, taking advantage of his extensive range, he makes lightning jumps from one register to another, often in the middle of phrases. Only an inherent rhythmic sense allows him to engineer these moves without losing his grip upon the pattern of the beat.

A month later, with several personnel changes, the Carter band recorded three further originals by Hughes: *Arabesque*, *Fanfare* and *Music at Midnight*, plus an arrangement by him of the *Sweet Sorrow Blues* theme, with Wells taking solos on all four titles.

Do

On *Arabesque* the trombonist approaches his solo with a casual, curiously detached air, fashioning his phrases mainly in a legato style which he achieves by a subtle use of the slide of his instrument, submitting each thought with a "take-it-or-leave-it" attitude. With *Fanfare* and *Music At Midnight*, though, he returns to the attack, phrasing with great determination and power, stressing each image he portrays to the utmost. Then, as if two contrasts of mood at a session are not sufficient for him, Dicky concludes the afternoon's work by creating one of the most melancholy and moving solos of his career upon the theme of *Sweet Sorrow Blues*. Within the framework of this solo, Wells' playing becomes the essence of simplicity, sacrificing everything to the expression of grief. Economically sustaining his notes, his tone seemingly choked with emotion, he is considerably stirring to the senses with this, probably the most heartfelt speech he has ever made on record.

The third Hughes session on 19th May 1933, though artistically as successful as the preceding ones, in reality was a headache for all concerned. *Donegal Cradle Song* took two hours and a half to record. At the rehearsal several days before, Wells' section-mate, George Washington, had arrived at the studios carrying a baby as well as his trombone, under instructions from his wife to nurse it while she went to the cinema. Humour at this situation frequently disturbed the rehearsing as the infant lay cooing at Washington's feet. On the day of the recording, though the baby was missing, an unsure brass section persisted in playing cracked notes into the introduction to *Donegal Cradle Song*. Hughes tried everything to co-ordinate the men, including bootleg gin, coffee and frequent rests, without reward. After the fifth attempt at recording, the musicians' hats were removed. (Drummer Sid Catlett was playing in an overcoat, despite the glowing May afternoon!) Finally, Hughes suggested re-scoring the introduction passage for Wayman Carver's flute. This worked the trick. The trumpeters sat up and played the passage to perfection!

Despite all the trouble, however, Coleman Hawkins attained his highest inspiration with two solo passages of improvisation on this pseudo-Irish theme. As the composer wrote in his autobiographical work, "Second Movement": "Once having heard Hawkins' decoration of the melody, no other was possible or desirable."

Firebird caused further complications. Spike Hughes had scored a part in this exciting piece for Benny Carter to play on soprano-saxophone. On the day of the recording he discovered that Carter had pawned his soprano some time before, had lost the ticket, and had forgotten which pawnshop. While the other numbers were being recorded, the bandboy was hurriedly despatched to run the instrument to earth. Unruffled by the crisis, Dicky Wells proceeded to create, with considerable animation, a fine solo during the recording of *Air In D Flat*, happily bubbling forth with phrases of a richly-inventive nature, maintaining a perfect balance between his spirited attack and his formal construction. Upon the completion of the feature, a breathless bandboy returned, having chased practically all over Harlem before finding the right soprano-saxophone. The broker allowed it out on condition that it was returned immediately after the session. Carter didn't mind. He didn't think he'd ever need it again after the session. In the finished edition of *Firebird*, after Carter had satisfied himself that his soprano was in a fit condition to play after its neglect, Wells improvised a heated solo, his tone becoming thick and guttural, punching out his phrases with great determination.

To complete his New York recording programme, Spike Hughes decided to try two jam session features, using for themes the tunes *Sweet Sue* and *How Come You Do Me Like You Do?* These were recorded after the main sessions, when the majority of the musicians had departed from the studios. There were no orchestrations, beyond the selection of a key and a tempo for each theme; everything was freely improvised. A string of fine solos resulted from the concept. It must have looked a strange little group: Big Sid Catlett still wearing his overcoat, Wayman Carver fingering his gold-plated flute, Spike Hughes playing bass with his fingers encased in alabaster plaster. The music produced was of superb quality. *How Come You Do Me Like You Do?* reveals Wells, swinging easily at a medium tempo, projecting phrases in sharp, aggressive bursts, indulging in fresh contrasts of emphasis and technical deployment. During *Sweet Sue* he follows Wayman Carver's flute solo with delicate, probing phrases, then gradually builds up the tension, via several phrases of increasing complexity and a strengthening of attack, until he concludes with a most dramatic flourish. His solos with this small unit ably supplement his recorded work with the full band.

Benny Carter's band did not hold together for long after making these recordings. Upon its eventual dissolution, Wells joined Fletcher Henderson for a year, at the end of which time he moved into Teddy Hill's band. The trombonist spent three years altogether with Hill (1935–1938) and he recorded with the band in New York City for the Perfect and Vocalion labels, being featured importantly as a soloist by the scores of *Here Comes Cookie* and *When The Robin Sings His Song*, both on Perfect, and *Marie* and *A Study In Brown* on Vocalion.

The really vital months of Wells' association with Teddy Hill, however, at least when viewed from an artistic standpoint, actually occurred in 1937 when the leader undertook with his musicians a tour of England and France in support of the popular "Blackbirds" show. When the band arrived in Paris, Dicky Wells, in the course of a conversation with the critic Hugues Panassié, expressed a desire to make some recordings with the late Django Reinhardt, the legendary gypsy guitarist and one of the comparatively few outstanding musicians that Europe has contributed to the course of jazz music. Panassié was immediately enthusiastic over such a project, and set arrangements in motion for the trombonist to record two sessions for the French Swing label. Thus it was that Wells came to record a set of improvisations which matched, in their passionate emotional inspiration and formidable inventive flow, the work he had preserved on record with Spike Hughes.

Panassié so organized it that at the first session, on 7th July 1937, Wells was teamed with Reinhardt, bassist Dick Fulbright and drummer Bill Beason from the Teddy Hill band, and a trio of trumpet players. This latter section consisted of Bill Dillard and Shad Collins from the Hill brass section and the Paris resident, Bill Coleman; it was gravely decided that Hill's young third trumpeter, Dizzy Gillespie, a suspected musical anarchist bent upon altering jazz, would be too dangerous an inclusion. Despite the unorthodox construction of the unit, with its heavy brass contingent, the results undeniably justified the means. Wells' excitement at the instrumental concept is fully revealed in his solo choruses, while the trumpeters, playing as individuals or scored as a section, warmly offset his improvisation. *Between The Devil And The Deep Blue Sea* (on which all the trumpeters are present) and *Japanese Sandman, Sweet Sue* and *Hangin' Around Boudon* (with only Coleman complementing the trombone) are

100

all recordings employed by Wells to display his virility as a soloist; dramatically poised, heated and often violent in the way he thrusts his thoughts upon the listener, heightening the emotional tension seemingly at will by means of a bold application of tonal strength and phrasing, these improvisations allow this most human of jazz trombonists to evidence all his turbulent passion.

At the second Paris session, held on 12th July 1937, Wells was assisted by two trumpeters, Dillard and Collins, altoist Howard Johnson, and a rhythm section consisting of Sam Allen (piano), Roger Chaput (guitar) and Bill Beason (drums); note the absence of Reinhardt's emphatic rhythmic support, an unfortunate feature of the date. Much of the emotional fire, so conspicuous in Dicky's playing five days before, would seem to have subsided by the time he entered the studio for this session. The prevailing mood throughout the records from this later date appears to be one of extreme melancholy. Artistically such a change of attitude was not a detrimental factor to the making of records, however, for Dicky's feelings prompted him to blow three of the most moving slow-blues improvisations ever conceived by a trombonist: *Nobody's Blues But My Own, Dicky Wells' Blues* and *Hot Club Blues. Dicky Wells' Blues*, in particular, containing seven consecutive choruses of improvisation by the trombonist, is a masterly exposure of a man's depressed spirits. I can think of no other trombonist in jazz who has ever declared his mental state with quite so much honesty, describing in detail the worries which leave his feelings so downcast.

In 1938, back in the United States, Dicky Wells joined the trombone section of the Count Basie Orchestra, not as an aspiring soloist from the Count's normal recruitment centre in Kansas City, but as a musician with a reputation already established quite firmly in the minds of the critics, and with an individual style of improvisation forged during many years of playing with name bands. Nevertheless, from the time of the trombonist's entry into the Basie band, his recorded solos with it portray that temperamentally as well as musically he was ideally suited to the job of featured soloist within the band's jazz framework. With the well-regulated, though propulsive patterns of the Basie rhythm section underlying each and every passage of his improvisation, the stinging unison riffs of the ensemble acting as a backdrop to his expressive thoughts, and the presence of innovators of the calibre of Clayton and Edison (and, for a time, Vic Dickenson) to provide competitive solo invention, his mind and senses were obviously stimulated, and once more a stream of richly-conceived and emotionally stressed ideas flowed through his instrument.

During the years of his first long association with the band of Count Basie, dating from 1938 to 1945, the trombonist placed on record a collection of important improvisations: *Texas Shuffle*, *Panassié Stomp* and *London Bridge Is Falling Down* in 1938, *Taxi War Dance*, *Jive At Five* and *Miss Thing* in 1939, *Love Jumped Out* and *Dicky's Dream* in 1940, *Down for Double* and *Harvard Blues* in 1941 and *Jimmy's Blues* in 1944 are perhaps the best known of these features. Additional to recordings with the full band, in 1943 he recorded four titles for the Signature label under his own name—*I Got Rhythm*, *Linger Awhile*, *Hello Babe* and *I'm For It Too*—sharing a sequence of highly-inventive solos with Lester Young, Bill Coleman and pianist Ellis Larkins.

Comparisons between these various solos are not to be easily drawn, except where isolated technical devices appear (for example, during *Taxi War Dance*, when he blows a series of short notes—eighths actually—thereby duplicating one exploration of the modern jazz movement), for his remarkable inspiration fully enlivens each passage of improvisation he plays. One comparison does exist, however, between these solos which Wells made with Basie and all the recordings which preceded them of the trombonist with a variety of other bands, and that concerns the partial elimination of sorrowful blues improvisations caused by the association with Basie. On account of the musical policy set by the Count, and its particular use of the blues, Dicky's playing was rarely allowed to slip into moods of grief. Instead the band tended to boost his spirits, drawing out the vivacity, the boldness and the colourful humour inherent in his nature.

Texas Shuffle is perhaps one of the best examples of Wells' fine sense of form while performing with Count Basie. Here, while swinging lucidly at a fast tempo, and despite a sudden reversal of approach midway through the solo, when after a fierce opening he subsides into a more relaxed, reflective frame of mind, Dicky's phrases are logically linked together so that they tell a story, melodically as well as emotionally. This solo also illustrates the vital nature of Wells' outlay of thought when he is improvising: its phrases, each one of importance to the life of the solo, do not contain a single note that is of ornamental value only. Wells is never superfluous, though his ideas are often rich in musical substance. He hates the phrase which is inserted purely for ornament and does not assist him in revealing his passionate images, almost as much as he hates an empty display of technique. *Dicky's Dream*, an exquisite miniature, made with only Buck Clayton, Lester Young and the Basie rhythm section, I have admired since my initial acquaintance with this soloist. While *Texas Shuffle* tends to typify Dicky Wells' usual approach to improvisation while working with Basie, and in itself is a précis of the style of delivery he adopted on a score of the Count's records, this small-group feature is quite unique amongst a collection of the trombonist's recorded solos. It reveals meekness, and a gentle nature, whereas the majority of his recordings with the full band find him caught up with an intense theme and bent upon delivering a strong emotional message.

The recordings made during these first seven years with Basie really climax Dicky Wells' immensely creative period as an improvising mind. Since 1945, after firmly establishing himself beyond all doubt as the most individual and inventive of jazz trombone players, Dicky has gone into a decline as an expressive force. Though still an accomplished musician, and possessed of a facile technique, so much of the emotional fire and inventive zeal which once enlivened his lucid, audacious delivery has slowly but surely disappeared. The once rapidly flowing ideas dwindled to a mere trickle so that Wells today, far from being the doyen of middle-period trombonists, has degenerated into a musician unable to improvise with any enthusiasm or strength of purpose.

Wells was working with Count Basie's Orchestra again from 1947 to 1950, but in these three years his solo contributions to the band's recordings became fewer, and the inventive quality of those he did make became indifferent. Subsequently he has worked in jazz units led by Buck Clayton, Sy Oliver and Jimmy Rushing, has toured Europe with Bill Coleman, and for several months in 1954 played with the Earl Hines band. More recent reports come of him labouring with an unsympathetic Dixieland combo., performing in a style quite out of character with his previous work. Some recordings which the trombonist made in 1952 for the Mercury label with tenorman Paul Quinichette (*Shad Roe*, *Crew Cut*, etc.) portray a dispirited, disinterested musician, playing phrases which on account of their lack of inventive qualification appear glib and meaningless.

Wells' decline as a jazz soloist has been a tragic reversal of fate for one who was originally so gifted. It is indeed a strange fact that of the four main innovators to work with Count Basie in the late 1930's and early 1940's—Buck Clayton, Harry Edison, Lester Young and Dicky Wells—the two trumpeters, Clayton and Edison, have since progressed to even more exalted positions as improvising soloists, while Young and Wells appear to have lost the incentive to create.

LESTER YOUNG

"The sound of Lester on the old Basie records—real beautiful tenor-saxophone sound, pure sound. How many people he's influenced—how many lives!"

LEE KONITZ

The introduction to Gjon Mili's semi-documentary film "Jammin' The Blues" projects, as a background to the explanatory relay of titles, participants, director, etc., what appears to be a series of diminishing circles; ill-defined, and irregularly spaced, these circles have little symbolic significance, save perhaps to suggest a radar mechanic's pipe dream. As the reel unfolds, however, and the captions pass away, these circles finally resolve themselves into an aerial view of Lester Young's headgear, a hat of the pork-pie variety with an exaggerated brim inevitably upturned.

What then ensues is typical of this man, the most influential tenor-saxophone player to emerge in jazz since Coleman Hawkins' absolute domination of the instrument's development in the 1920's and early 1930's; if ever there has been one jazz musician whose personal actions and physical appearance have epitomized the superficial characteristics of his singular improvisation, *who has looked the part of his music*, then it has been Lester. As the camera passes from the hat, pulled so far down over the brow that it appears to have been screwed on, and views the face, it reveals an unmistakable expression of languor: eyes sleepy and heavily hooded, a slight downward curve of the lips, the flesh of the cheeks tending to sag. Slowly, so slowly a cigarette is placed to the lips. Taking a long pull, then inhaling deeply, Lester closes his eyes

104

fully as the smoke swirls about in the innermost recesses of his lungs. The camera then recedes, to take in a view of the full person. Slouched in his chair, with his jacket falling in crumpled folds about his waist, his legs twisted together, the ténorman oozes exhaustion—his attitude says that this could well be the end of a jam session rather than the beginning. When he lifts his instrument on high to play, the apparent drain on his reserves of energy gives the saxophone the semblance of a lead weight. As Lester blows it he inclines his head with the strain; when he has said his piece he slumps back into his original position.

After witnessing Lester's performance in the flesh it is almost possible to *feel* the surface methods of his improvisation whenever at a later date one hears an example of his solo work on record. Behind the disembodied sound emerges a vivid image of the man himself. Pick out any solo, from his years of bountiful invention, or from the years of comparative sterility, and listen to the more obvious features of his playing style: the soft, flattish-sounding tone, the slippery, pliable legato phrases, the shifting rhythmic emphasis with a tendency on his part to lag behind the beat, just as Billie Holiday's voice does; note how well these facets illustrate the person of their creator.

It is indeed unfortunate that Lester's personal lethargy, *and its similarity with the surface mannerisms of his improvisation,* have caused a number of critics and their camp-followers to pass over his work without appreciating the *underlying* qualities in his improvisation. His singular playing style has been one of the most subtly-inventive fountains of jazz material, and the roots of this style have wriggled their way deeply into the jazz explorations and developments of subsequent years. Beneath the tired physique, and the *apparently tired* stylistic devices, there has been a rich source of improvisation—a source (and I hereby freely admit that it has suffered from a drought in recent years) which at its finest has proved a significant inspiration to jazz music. Few musicians have been able to equal the ingenuity of a Lester playing at his best, with his ability to furnish prolonged runs of freshly-conceived phrases.

"A Lester Young playing at his best" hints at quite a limited subject—let me without further ado, therefore, qualify it and kick my intentions for this essay out into the open. I have long held an admiration for this highly-individual tenorman, and certainly, at his best, I believe that his stimulating line of thought bears worthy comparison with the best of Hawkins, Webster and the earlier tenor school. On the other hand, I do not deceive myself into thinking that Lester has remained at his best since his first precocious entry into jazz. In more than two decades of active participation in jazz his work has passed through varying phases of creativeness, and in recent years it has registered a definite decline in originality and sustained invention. Today Lester is but a shadow of his former self as a jazz soloist, even though his theories as an improvising mind are still influencing the younger school of jazz tenor-players. "A Lester Young playing at his best" has been virtually a closed book for several years now.

I state this view in the earlier stages of my essay, not as an attempted slight on the musician himself (after all, Rimbaud's creative vein was exhausted at the age of nineteen; T. S. Eliot has not produced a new book of poems in recent years; this has in no way undermined their literary distinction) but because I feel that the varying levels of Lester's inspiration have seldom been evaluated by those chroniclers of the events in his life. It is disturbing to witness the jazz critics who are Lester's fanatical supporters chanting his infallibility when ample evidence exists on record testifying to his recent relapse as an inventive mind. By tarring all his performances with the same eulogistic brush, they leave the way clear for any newcomer to jazz, *or for any classical critic already suspicious of jazz*, to approach Lester via one of his inferior Clef performances made in the past few years, and to condemn him for a lack of invention, thereby missing the fruits of his earlier playing career.

When analysed for changing levels in creativeness, Lester's musical history may be neatly sliced into three portions. First, a period from the late 1920's to the mid-1930's; these were years when Lester was developing an individual and revolutionary use of the tenor-saxophone, a style in advance of its time which caused him to be treated like a leper by many musicians and bandleaders. Then the golden middle period of his career, running from the mid-1930's to the mid-1940's, when a prolonged association with Count Basie's Orchestra offered his style a wide outlet of expression; he consolidated his playing during this period, perfecting his alliance of a new technical approach with his fertile sense of invention, and making the majority of his best recordings, some with the Basie band, others with small groups drawn either from the band or formed as the accompaniment to singer Billie Holiday.

Finally, in the third period, running from the mid-1940's to the present day, there is the evidence of a decline in spirit; his playing style, once so radical and full of fresh ideas, has become more of a routine, and the majority of his record dates seem to be treated with the "just another job" attitude. In this last phase of his career Lester has been financially successful while replaying the various phrases and devices which were once so revolutionary; frequently he has given to sensationalist audiences exactly what they wish to hear (namely, honking noises and other vulgar mannerisms). As a result he has become the victim of an increasing ennui, the tiredness of his appearance overflowing and spreading its way into the once so inventive mind. Nowadays Lester is seldom jogged out of his state of lethargy.

Having brandished my analytical measure of Lester's creative abilities first, I feel a little easier about plunging into a survey of the tenorman's varied playing career, for within this survey I intend to place the greater emphasis upon the events and the produce of his significant years as an associate of Count Basie rather than upon the dwindling harvests of his later period.

Lester was already an adept musician with a certain amount of jazz experience behind him when he made contact with the Kansas City music scene, and subsequently with Count Basie—he had to be, for second-rate musicians did not last for very long with the Kaycee jam sessions. Born within the city limits of New Orleans on 27th August 1909, into an extremely musical family, Lester's instrumental tuition commenced from the age of five. His father, a blacksmith by trade, but a skilled violinist and a teacher of various local choirs, determined that he would learn theory in addition to the tunes he was picking up by ear. At the age of ten the boy was playing in a carnival band, *as a drummer*, while his brother Lee was playing a saxophone; about a year later they exchanged instruments, and the arrangement hardened into permanence. (It is interesting to note here that Lee Young is now one of the most respected west coast percussion men.) Lester mastered the new instrument reasonably fast. At thirteen he was improvising confidently with it. Meanwhile, under his father, he continued his lessons in music theory. Ben Webster, who went to study theory under Mr. Young senior at the same time, has confirmed that Lester was a competent sight reader at quite an early age.

When eighteen, after shining shoes, selling papers and performing various other tasks which he found distasteful, Lester left home, without even a musical instrument. At Salina, Kansas, he met Art Bronson, the leader of a group known as The Bostonians, who supplied him with a baritone-saxophone, an instrument he was forced to play until Bronson could afford to buy a new tenor for him. Later he played for a year with the veteran trumpet player King Oliver.

Lester was actually working in Minneapolis when he heard (and was considerably excited by) a broadcast programme featuring Walter Page and his Thirteen Original Blue Devils; the unit was chiefly composed of musicians from Oklahoma City, but Lester discovered that Page took his group at various times into Kansas City and saw a possible chance to reach that reputed musical centre if he could join up with the band. He wired Page and offered his services in place of the rather sad tenorman then working with the band. Page accepted him, but on joining the tenorman discovered to his dismay that finances were so precarious that there was every evidence of the band breaking up. One day, when Page and the rest arrived in Cincinnati after, as Lester recalls, "grabbing a train like hobo men, making it with bruises, no loot, no horns, all raggedy and dirty", the musicians held a conference and decided it was "every tub" (every man for himself). Without the band, Lester rode like a hobo to Kansas City, where his fortunes improved slightly; he met Herschel Evans, who lent him a tenor and some clothes and secured a job for him with the Benny Moten band. Money was scarce in Kansas City, but as a working musician Lester found it easier to eat and drink on credit there, and he was playing in the company of good musicians all the time.

It was at this period of his career that Lester first began to build a reputation for himself as a revolutionary within the sensitive ranks of the musicians. Kansas City, when Lester moved his operational base there, contained a number of mighty tenor-saxophone personalities, all of them, however, disciples of Coleman Hawkins, the man who with Fletcher Henderson's Orchestra had elevated the tenor from a sluggish section instrument to a source of rich solo variations. Now Lester too was a strong admirer of Hawkins' style; in fact, one night, when Henderson was playing in K.C., he had deputised in the band for Hawkins, playing the clarinet and tenor parts and even using Coleman's own instruments. Yet as

Lester reached maturity as a soloist, as his individuality as an improvising musician progressed as a result of contact with the Kansas City music scene, it became apparent that his personal style was growing completely alien to everything that Hawkins stood for as a tenor player.

Coleman Hawkins' tenor style has an aggressive nature; one can well imagine him flexing his muscles before launching himself upon a course of improvisation. With his rich, ripe tone, barely controlling an excitable vibrato, his way of poising a melodic line firmly upon a strong rhythmic pattern and his tendency to produce a dramatic turn of phrase, the Hawk's expression is essentially very direct and forceful; his outpouring displays a turbulence reminiscent of Roy Campbell's verse. He has been one of the most productive of all jazz improvising minds, and his creamy variations have donated to the music many exalted and ageless moments, yet always his realization has been through strength. Emotional intensity has ranked equally with the inventive sense. He plays the tenor-saxophone with a grand flourish, and always has played it that way, even in the days when he was fumbling to express simple solo ideas through it.

The style of Lester Young, on the other hand, during his years of intensive productivity, gradually grew away from these ideals of Hawkins, allowing a cerebral creation to take slight precedence over the exterior emotionalism. The stylistic devices and phrases took on a greater relaxation: tone soft, smooth, rather flattish in sound, phrase designs more elastic and their delivery tending on occasions to lag behind the regulated accents of the beat, manner of attack restrained. Lester would play sensitively (emotional sincerity remaining a part of his outflow), yet his whole manner was lighter and more relaxed than Hawkins' strong attack.

Behind this surface relaxation there lurked an alert and nimble mind. A mind teeming with ideas of a less obvious nature than those disgorged so directly by Hawkins. It was a mind which searched around within itself for subtle melodic runs, avoiding the simple sequences, searching always for the devious and the unexpected. His playing became a prolonged exploration, as behind the seemingly sleepy characteristics of style he improvised fresh and surprising phrases, weaving subtly around the main melodic lines, taking the theme and bending it, twisting it, squeezing out its essence, then totally reshaping it—but never, never stating it directly. Naturally such an attitude to improvisation conspired to overthrow the regime of the robust Hawkins.

Ultimately Lester was to wrest the tenor-saxophone crown away from Hawkins, and in firmly establishing his own ideals was to act as a major source of inspiration to the development of modern jazz, lending to that movement his exterior relaxation and calm as a replacement for the open emotionalism of the New Orleans and the Swing Period soloists. However, such events as these were still some way off. The experiments with a new form of jazz improvisation were to take place at Minton's Playhouse and other New York clubs for musicians in the early 1940's. When Lester Young developed his radical approach in the Kansas City of the early 1930's, Hawkins was still the master, the pace-setter for the majority of tenor-players. Lester's inventive sense drew respect from the musicians who surrounded him in Kaycee, and he became a familiar figure at their jam sessions there, though for several years his singular style was to remain an isolated voice.

Mary Lou Williams, relating her Kansas City memories in the "Melody Maker", has described one legendary after-hours jam sessions there at which Lester surprisingly whipped Hawkins, and at which he encouraged several of the Hawk's own disciples to back him. Even in his prime Hawkins had to face some pretty stiff battles whenever he passed through Kansas City!

This session took place early in 1934, shortly before Coleman departed for Europe. "The word went round," Mary Lou remembered, "that Hawkins was in the Cherry Blossom, and within about half an hour there were Lester Young, Ben Webster, Herschel Evans, Herman Walder and one or two unknown tenors piling into the club to blow.

"Bean [*Hawkins*] didn't know the Kaycee tenormen were so terrific, and couldn't get himself together, though he played all morning. I happened to be nodding that night, and around 4 a.m. I awoke to hear someone pecking on my screen. I opened the window on Ben Webster. He was saying: 'Get up, pussy-cat, we're jammin' and all the pianists are tired out now. Hawkins has got his shirt off and is still blowing. You got to come down.' Sure enough, when we got there Hawkins was in his singlet taking turns with the Kaycee men. It seems he had run into something he didn't expect.

"Lester's style was light . . . and it took him maybe five

choruses to warm up. But then he would really blow; then you couldn't handle him on a cutting session.

"That was how Hawkins got hung up. The Henderson band was playing in St. Louis that evening, and Bean knew he ought to be on the way. But he kept trying to blow something to beat Ben and Herschel and Lester. When at last he gave up, he got in his car and drove to St. Louis. I heard he'd just bought a new Cadillac and that he burnt it out trying to make the job on time. Yes, Hawkins was king until he met those crazy Kansas City tenormen."

Jo Jones has confirmed that Lester was still playing at the session when all the other tenormen were finished.

Nevertheless, while this victory and other feats of durability enhanced Lester's reputation with the musicians close to him, he was still regarded as an outsider by the main body of jazz musicians. His radical style lost him an important job at one period in the 1930's. After Moten's death, Lester had thrown in his lot with Count Basie at the Reno Club, and one night a cable came through from Fletcher Henderson, the most flourishing bandleader of the early and mid-1930's, offering Lester the chair recently vacated by Hawkins, who had finally left for Europe. Henderson offered a salary far above what Basie could afford to pay, so Lester went on tour with the band—a decision he was to regret.

"They expected me to sound like Hawk," Lester later complained to Leonard Feather. "But why should I blow like someone else? We got to New York in 1934—feeling the draught all the way—and they rang the bell on me. Fletcher's wife gave me this 'Why don't you blow like Hawk?' line and took me down in the basement to listen to Hawkins' records. I asked Fletcher to give me a letter of release saying that he hadn't fired me, and that was it.'

Returning crestfallen to Kansas City, while Ben Webster, tonally a very close disciple of Hawkins, took his place in the Henderson band, Lester again found himself in a precarious economic position. He lived by the "coffee-and-cakes" routine for a while, and then he secured a job for several months with Andy Kirk's Orchestra. Eventually he succeeded in rejoining Basie at the Reno Club.

1936, the year when John Hammond's initial encouragement caused Basie to terminate his agreement at the Reno and take the band on the road, marked the beginning of Lester's real rise to power as a tenor stylist. At the Reno Club the tenorman had been earning two dollars fifty a night. Leaving this job to travel with the Count, he suffered a relapse in salary during the first few weeks, but as the tour gradually gained impetus wages grew higher and Lester's personality also gained a wider audience. The Count had faith in his tenorman's radical style (which contrasted so sharply with the Hawkins-inspired style of the band's other tenorman, Herschel Evans) and he featured it extensively at both dance dates and recording sessions, thereby stimulating public appreciation to an unprecedented degree.

When the band settled into a prolonged job at the Grand Terrace in Chicago, Lester made his recording début for the Vocalion label, cutting four sides: *Shoe Shine Swing, Evenin',* *Boogie Woogie* and *Lady Be Good,* together with trumpeter Carl Smith and the Basie-Page-Jones rhythm section. *Lady Be Good,* after a jaunty thematic statement by Basie at the piano, contains a chorus of Lester's tenor work which ably expresses his relaxed approach to improvisation. As he unfurls his thoughts concerning the melody, first dodging around the direct line, then crossing it, one feels that he must surely lose his hold on the rhythm pattern before long—yet just as he seems about to lag right behind the beat he swirls back into position. Though he seems at moments to weave right away from the regular beat, a light, airy swing is never absent from his playing. *Boogie Woogie,* though basically designed as a feature for singer Jimmy Rushing, actually proves to be equally a showcase for Lester. His tenor is heard in turn alternating phrases with Smith in the thematic exposition, blowing in obbligato manner behind Rushing, improvising a superb solo chorus, cushioning Smith's solo and finally phrasing a sinewy coda.

Early in 1937, after moving its work base to New York City, the enlarged Basie band signed a contract with American Decca, a move which brought Lester one of his busiest spells of work as a recording soloist. In the three years which followed, the tenorman hardly ever entered the Decca studios as a Basie sideman without being called upon as an improvising mind. And indeed, it was fortunate too that Decca should have preserved such a prolific output of solos by a Lester playing at his creative best. On *Roseland Shuffle, Shorty George, Smarty, Jumpin' At The Woodside, One O'Clock Jump, Lester Leaps In* (a septet feature), *John's Idea,*

Panassié Stomp, Honeysuckle Rose, Hollywood Jump, Broadway, I Never Knew, Louisiana, Blow Top, Tickle Toe (his own composition), *Taxi War Dance, The World Is Mad* and *You Can Depend On Me*, playing tenor with the band, and on *Blue And Sentimental* and *Texas Shuffle*, playing clarinet, he laid down a series of improvisations which were quite excellent in their invention and delivery. Audacious in construction, cool and relaxed in expression, pure in tone, suavely swinging, they confirmed Lester as perhaps the most assured and consistently creative jazz musician in operation at this period, a figure whose work formed a bridge between the gradually ailing swing school (already suffering from the interest of the white bands and their commercial traps) and the still-undeveloped modern trends. Lester has nominated his solo on *Taxi War Dance* as his favourite contribution to the band at this period. Personally, I feel that his strongly-designed, poised and musicianly output and supple swing, backed, of course, by a profound emotional sincerity (even if it is not pushed to the front) have seldom been so faithfully expressed as they are during *You Can Depend On Me*, which he made with only Jimmy Rushing, trumpeter Shad Collins and the band's rhythm section; such a comment here, however, is rather like grading gold into its various carats.

Concurrent with his industry in the Decca studios at this period, Lester was also in demand with the Vocalion people as a part of the regular accompanying group to singer Billie Holiday. Billie's memorable series of recording sessions made for that label between 1937 and 1939 invariably found Lester complementing Lady Day's intense, acrid, bitter-sweet voice, and on the occasions when the tenorman improvised transitional choruses (as on *Sailboat In The Moonlight, Back In Your Own Backyard*, etc.) his sympathy for the singer's feelings became evident. So accurately, in fact, did he continue her emotional mood, that Billie herself insisted that she would not make any records for Vocalion unless he also took part. "He played music I like," Billie recalls; "he didn't try to drown the singer."

How similar the musical expressions of Holiday and Young appear when one returns to these records! Note the way they both tend to lag behind the regular accents of the rhythm pattern; also the way their phrases continually slide away from the written melodic line; not least, the air of sadness which prevails when they are creating. Holiday sang for a time with

Basie's band at this period (though she never recorded with it) and Lester used to lodge at her home in New York. It was he who first called her "Lady", and in return she bestowed upon him the title of "President" or "Prez", a term which in later years was to be liberally cited by a school of younger white tenormen of the modern jazz movement, Stan Getz, Zoot Sims, Herbie Steward, Brew Moore, Allen Eager, and so on, who came to regard Lester as their stylistic idol.

Nor must I overlook at this juncture the several superior solos which Lester recorded in 1938 with a piano-less small group (actually drawn from the Basie band and led by trombonist-guitarist Eddie Durham) for the independent Commodore label. Lester, together with Durham (who used electric guitar for the sessions), Buck Clayton, Freddie Greene, Walter Page and Jo Jones, calling themselves The Kansas City Six, co-operated to produce slight, yet dignified and neatly-constructed ensemble statements, enclosing important solo sequences by Clayton, Young and Durham.

Lester's chorus of tenor during *Way Down Yonder In New Orleans* reveals an inspirational magnitude which equals that of his very best recorded work with the full Basie band; the phrases which he builds about the theme he makes appear so logical that they practically close the door in the face of any other tenorman seeking to extemporise upon the melody. And *Pagin' The Devil*, *Countless Blues* and *I Want A Little Girl* contain what are certainly Lester's finest recorded clarinet solos. Using an all-metal instrument, Lester's improvisations with the clarinet have always succeeded in pushing phrases through it very similar, in their lucidity and elasticity, to the weaving, searching phrases he blows (or has blown, rather) through the tenor. These constructive designs, together with a pellucid tone, so clean and pure and free from any vestige of vibrato, and again, an air of sadness which is difficult to define, have made Lester's improvisations with the clarinet some of the most individual in jazz. The recordings from The Kansas City Six sessions offer the fullest explanations of Lester's ideals as a clarinettist. Nowadays, he doesn't use the instrument on the job, complaining that he cannot lay his hands on a model to really suit him. A rather surprising thing, however, is that the only other jazz musician to *effect a sound* on the clarinet closely resembling Lester's has been Jimmy Giuffre, the west coast tenor player and arranger, who only turned to the instrument in

114

the 1950's, and who otherwise has little in common with Lester as a jazz soloist.

Lester's lengthy association with the Basie band terminated abruptly on 13th December 1940, resulting allegedly from the tenorman refusing to make a recording session arranged for a Friday the thirteenth. He'd pleaded superstitiously that all kinds of complications were destined to arise if the session took place. The session did take place, however, and Lester became a bandleader in his own right. He formed a small unit with Shad Collins on trumpet, the late Clyde Hart (piano), John Collins (guitar), Nick Fenton (bass) and the late Hal West (drums) to play at Kelly's Stable in New York City. Unluckily this group, though generally well received, failed to secure its own recording contract, though the musicians cut several sides for Bluebird as an accompanying group to Una Mae Carlisle—and Lester remembers taking solos on *Blitzkrieg Baby* and *Beautiful Eyes*. Also at this time, of course, Lester's stylistic approach to improvisation was being picked up by the modern experimentalists and employed as a lever in engineering the transition from the hot to the cool way of jazz playing; frequently Lester would join these experimentalists in jam sessions at Minton's Playhouse, Nick's, the Village Vanguard and other New York centres.

When the engagement at Kelly's Stable ended, the tenorman contracted to tour for the U.S.O. as a guest star with Al Sears little band, but the sudden deaths of both his parents caused him to leave this package show after only a few weeks on the road and return to Kansas City; and when the family's affairs had been settled satisfactorily, he continued travelling westwards to Los Angeles, there to form a band with his brother Lee. This latter unit held together for the best part of a year, actually making one trip east to play at New York's Café Society. It was dissolved mainly through Count Basie bringing his band to Los Angeles and persuading Lester to settle his differences and return to the cherished tenor chair—a job again destined to terminate abruptly, though not, on this occasion, due to ill-feelings between the leader and the soloist.

Lester actually rejoined Basie during December 1943, and that same month he recorded an important session for the Signature label with a small unit under the nominal leadership of trombonist Dicky Wells. Trumpeter Bill Coleman completed the front line; the rhythm section had Ellis Larkins at the piano, Freddie Greene (guitar), Al Hall (bass) and Jo Jones (drums). The four titles which Lester recorded with this group (*I Got Rhythm, Linger Awhile, Hello Babe* and *I'm Fer It Too*) contain several fine illustrations of his inventive thinking as a soloist—illustrations I've always felt that mark the culminating of his strongest period as an improvising soloist.

I well remember the occasion in 1955 when I played the *I Got Rhythm* feature during a recital at the Institute of Contemporary Arts in London. The framework of the piece allows the tenorman one chorus of improvisation prior to Wells' solo, and then four choruses immediately following the trombone part. During these latter choruses Lester really unleashes an avalanche of freshly-conceived ideas, which he develops systematically, weaving his way with dexterity through variation after variation, swinging fluently at a fastish tempo, all the while gradually increasing the tension and mounting his ideas towards a climax. As the climax to the record arrived, and the ensemble re-entered, I heard a collective gasp of incredulity from the audience! This has been the only instance I have witnessed personally of *a recorded solo* so moving a large audience.

Soon after this recording session the American military authorities displayed an interest in Lester's life. Again embarking upon his travels with Basie, this most easy-going of human beings either ignored or failed to receive several summonses to attend medical examination for the army. Eventually the Military Police took action. "The army wanted me so bad they took me right off the bandstand," the musician ruefully recalls. He was marched off, finally examined and absorbed into the services! One can well imagine the discomforts caused by military discipline to a man of Lester's physical and mental attitude to life. The subsequent fifteen months were the most miserable of his entire life; he could not be reconciled to the army's methods. When he finally obtained a release he had not changed one iota, though his complaints against the services were legion.

Since leaving the U.S. Forces, Lester's musical output has been principally associated with impresario Norman Granz, both for personal appearances and for recording purposes. Though from time to time he has spent intervals of several months duration leading his own quintet in New York City, he has normally been an attraction of Granz' annual "Jazz At The Philharmonic" tour, and has visited Europe with this expensive group of soloists.

Similarly with his recording sessions. Upon release from the army, he undertook a series of recordings, between December 1945 and December 1947, for the Aladdin label; some of the sessions were held on the west coast with Joe Albany at the piano, the others in New York with a rhythm section composed of Gene Di Novi (piano), Chuck Wayne (guitar), Curley Russell (bass) and the late Tiny Kahn (drums). (When Di Novi visited London in 1956 he told me that Lester was a sick man when he made these recordings. "It was still an honour to play with him, though," the pianist stated.) Apart from this Aladdin contract, however, Lester has been tied firmly to Granz Clef label for recordings.

This later period of his musical career has unquestionably brought Lester considerable financial remuneration, for at a time when jazz music generally has gained a stronger footing with the public, as an original pioneer of modern jazz development he has come to be regarded as a musical oracle; his very presence has successfully pulled in the crowds at Granz' circus-like jazz shows. Unfortunately, though, the inventive element of his musical output, when analysed and compared with his work of earlier years, has failed to match the magnetic powers of his name. His outflow of ideas, originally so fresh and audacious, has largely been replaced by a series of stock devices, i.e. the phrases he knows are expected by his less-discerning audiences. His once revolutionary style (a style, incidentally, which is still the basis of the tenor improvisation we are hearing today from Getz, Sims and a younger school of musicians) has degenerated into an audience-pleasing routine. The "live" "Jazz At The Philharmonic" concerts recorded by Norman Granz and issued via the Clef label illustrate this point; with them one hears Lester constantly exaggerating and repeating phrases, or making honking noises in the direction of the gallery. It seems that though the mannerisms of style remain, the inventive thought has not been replenished. Even the studio recordings by Lester which are available on Clef (and for several of these he has been furnished with adequate rhythm sections) reveal an absence of virile thinking. Conceived by a lesser-known tenorman than Lester Young, these performances would perhaps scrape by the reviewer without an open attack, but from a musician whose stature as an innovator and as an inventive improvising mind was firmly established as early as the 1930's they cause disappointment.

Lester Young's contemporary work, like that of his one-time

117

rival Coleman Hawkins, has been beset by a state of lethargy. There are fleeting moments of the old brilliance in his output, but generally it is a rarity nowadays for his heart, mind and fingers to combine to produce an improvised solo of the calibre with which he ably decorated Count Basie's recordings of the late 1930's. For some reason, perhaps the departure of the nervous energies of youth, the incentive to create has waned; of late he seems to have been churning out records rather mechanically, many of them completely devoid of creative thought. He might have been lying on his back in the studios, a feather pillow beneath his head, bored by the entire proceedings, for all the energy he displayed.*

As I have intimated earlier in this essay, however, an artist's period of creativeness need not necessarily begin in the later stages of his life; he may mature early, work intensively for several years and then abandon his calling, his creative streak completely burnt out. Lester Young is now a diminished force as a jazz tenor-saxophone player, yet this does not detract from his overall greatness. With the Basie band alone he has recorded sufficient improvised material of an inventive nature to assure him a permanent place in jazz. The paucity of ideas which harms his present playing cannot obliterate these past achievements, nor should it be confused in any way with them.

HERSCHEL EVANS

"Herschel Evans was a natural. He had a sound on tenor that perhaps you will never hear on a horn again."

JO JONES

Musicians who were present in Kansas City in 1934, on or about the date of the legendary carving contest at the Cherry Blossom between Coleman Hawkins, the hitherto undisputed pace-setter with the tenor-saxophone in jazz, and the

* I except from this judgment the Clef album entitled "Jazz Giants '56", which teams Lester with Roy Eldridge, Vic Dickenson, Teddy Wilson, Freddie Greene, Gene Ramey and Jo Jones. Playing in a style which is a logical development of Count Basie's Kansas City Seven, this group excites Lester so that he produces some of the most inspired and inventive solo work of his career, thus showing that he can still play well if he considers the occasion worthwhile.

prominent Kaycee tenormen, Ben Webster, Herschel Evans, Lester Young, Herman Walder and one or two others, have attested that the incident sparked off a certain musical animosity between Herschel Evans and Lester Young.

Let me explain here that Herschel and Lester obviously had different reasons for entering into the blowing session with Hawkins. Herschel was an ardent admirer of Hawkins' playing style; it had been through listening to the Hawk playing the tenor as a solo vehicle with Fletcher Henderson's Orchestra that he had in fact taken up the instrument, employing approximately the same methods of delivery. At that tenor battle in Kansas City, Herschel improvised upon his instrument like a man inspired; yet he was not blowing against his idol—he would never hear anything wrong said about Hawkins; rather he went into the session with the idea of showing Coleman just how much he'd personally improved and progressed since they had last met.

Lester Young, of course, a complete radical, was blowing in direct opposition to everything being said by Hawkins. Instead of merely trading ideas with the other tenormen at the session, Lester was improvising with a stronger object in view, namely to undermine the monopoly which Hawkins held upon the tenor's development in jazz by plausibly disagreeing with his stylistic methods. "I do not wish to destroy the monument, but merely to deface it" was his attitude. As witnesses have since told us, Lester had rather a rough time during the preliminary stages of this session. He always took a long time to warm up when improvising, and this gave the other tenormen several choruses start. Once into his stride, however, when his ideas were flowing freely, the others found they just couldn't handle him. He was still blowing when all the others were finished.

Now Herschel had previously held Lester in high regard as an improvising mind. Without actually endorsing Lester's revolutionary mannerisms of style, he'd shown an appreciation of his contemporary's inventive flow. He had even, at an earlier date, when Lester first arrived penniless in Kansas City after months of scuffling for work with bassist Walter Page, provided him with clothes and an instrument and had introduced him to Bennie Moten. The open aggression on Lester's part against Hawkins, however, touched off something within Herschel. Thereafter he set out to defend Hawkins' style, the style which he himself had adopted, on all occasions against further attacks by Lester. Though they remained on reasonably friendly terms as men, the two just could not enter a jam session in Kansas City without engaging in a battle of wits, each vying to outdistance the other in their expression of ideas through their respective mediums of style. This state of affairs continued even when both Lester and Herschel became members of the Count Basie band; there was not a dance date or a recording session performed by Basie's group when the contrasting tenor stylists were not at loggerheads. Only Herschel's premature death in 1939 terminated this healthy rivalry.

It was the opposition of Herschel Evans and Lester Young which originally set the tradition in the Count Basie band for having two tenor-saxophone soloists whose styles were noticeably in contrast. Since the days of the Evans-Young combat, and its resulting stimulation of the band's musical programme, the Count has persisted in employing tenor soloists with styles directly opposed, even through to more recent times with couplings like Paul Quinichette and Eddie Davis, and the two Franks, Wess and Foster. These contrasts, of course, are not to be confused with the tenor-saxophone battles innovated within Lionel Hampton's Orchestra of the mid-1940's, and later by Norman Granz' "Jazz At The Philharmonic" unit, which set the contestants off upon exhibitionist displays, seeking to outdo each other in the length and loudness of their musically-worthless screaming notes. Basie always insisted that his tenor players maintained a singular degree of good taste in their exchanges—that their playing brought out only sincere contrasts of expression and ideas.

Lester and Herschel, the pioneers of the contests, though continually searching for new ideas and fresh melodic variations to outstrip each other musically, nevertheless held each other's abilities in high esteem. They were never satisfied unless they were thinking up something with which to surprise the other. They kept their tones as different as their reeds made it physically possible. "Why don't you play alto, man? You got an alto tone," Herschel quipped at Lester. "There's things going on up there, man," Lester would reply, tapping his head. "I think some of you guys are all belly." Rivalry kept them on their toes while working together. Yet a high regard for each other's work did persist (though verbally they would never admit the fact); there was some form of feeling existing between them. Perhaps it was caused by the musical style of the Basie band acting as a basis for both their styles, promoting an underlying feeling which linked, though unconsciously, their playing. Jo Jones has said that since Herschel's death, he has frequently heard Lester replay some of Herschel's phrases in his solos, thereby giving recognition to their material worth.

Herschel Evans, one of the most gifted of all the improvising tenor-saxophone players belonging to the Coleman Hawkins school, was born at Denton, Texas in 1909. He grew up as a member of the Kansas City jazz scene, and appeared with Bennie Moten's Orchestra there in the late 1920's and early 1930's. Between periods of working in Kansas City, though, he travelled around and played in most of the surrounding states. There is discographical information to the effect that on 14th March 1928 he recorded four titles for the Okeh label in San Antonio as a member of the obscure Troy Floyd Shadowland Orchestra. For a time in the 1930's he also went to California to work with Lionel Hampton's early band, the one that the vibraphone player had organized to play at Sebastian's Cotton Club in Los Angeles. Buck Clayton returned from China to join this band. In 1936, however, he linked up with the band of Count Basie, then preparing to leave Kansas City for New York, and he remained a featured tenor soloist with the Count until only a short time before his death, which occurred in New York City on 9th February 1939.

As a soloist, Herschel, who never once betrayed his musical allegiance to the style of his idol, Coleman Hawkins, was capable of creating fresh, and well-extended improvisations. While a disciple of Coleman's in the way he handled the tenor, he relied solely upon his own mind as a source of melodic ideas, and the recordings still in existence of his work, particularly those made with Count Basie, reveal that he was everlastingly seeking to decorate the subject matter of his solos in a rich and inventive way.

He did not believe in ornament for ornament's sake. He liked to weave a romantic and colourful story about his theme, though he took good care to give everything he played a meaning so that it did not make the solo ponderous and top-heavy. Also, when improvising, his elaborate variations, as well as having a vital meaning, were never obscured by an inferior technique or an imperfect sense of form and proportion. When improvising, Herschel was a consummate artist, projecting ideas which were fresh, exciting and at times remarkably beautiful, in a fluent manner of speech and with a sensible build-up of emotional and formal power.

Employing the big, full, warm tone of Coleman Hawkins and its subsequent vibrato with telling effect; Herschel could be extremely vigorous, and even turbulent in his method of attack. When firmly attached to one of the faster rhythmic patterns of the Basie band, phrasing directly with the well-defined accents of the beat, he would generate a forceful drive with his outlay of phrases. It seemed that he carried his emotions in his bloodstream when improvising upon one of the jumping riffs from the Basie repertoire, for he was so easily excited as a soloist by such material, and with or without the support of the unison ensemble, his resulting improvisations were certain to heighten the tension of an arrangement quite considerably. He was so different in this respect from Lester Young, who was likely, despite a lucid swing, to assume the manner of an introvert when improvising with the band. Herschel never disguised any of the excitement he felt for the swing of the Kansas City jam sessions and, later, of the Count Basie band. Thus, when compared with the silken, subtle improvisations of Lester, his inventive flow, though finely carved and shaped, and perfectly balanced rhythmically, appears so much more impetuous in its attack. With Lester the affairs of the heart are surreptitiously withdrawn; Herschel Evans, however, could not speak through his instrument as a jazz soloist unless his words came directly from the heart.

The all-important remains of Herschel Evans' playing are to be found by listening to the recordings made by the Count Basie Orchestra in 1937 and 1938 for American Decca. *Swinging The Blues, Panassié Stomp, One O'clock Jump, John's Idea* and *Swinging At The Daisy Chain* all contain instances of his hard-hitting, energetically swinging tenor playing, while *Blue And Sentimental* is a rare and beautiful example of Herschel sensitively embroidering a slow ballad, rhapsodizing over the theme in the manner of a Coleman Hawkins solo, his tone breathy, his phrases soft and delicate.

Count Basie's success in the east in the late 1930's, and the wider appreciation shown to a number of his featured soloists, caused Herschel to have a brief secondary career in New York City as a sideman on a number of small-group recording sessions. On 29th June 1937 he joined Buck Clayton, clarinettist Edmond Hall and the Basie rhythm section in providing accompaniments to four songs recorded by Mildred Bailey for Vocalion. Then on 1st December 1937 and 5th January 1938 trumpeter Harry James, not yet advanced along the road to a more commercial exploitation of his instrument, used contingents from the Basie band, including Herschel, Buck Clayton, Eddie Durham, Earl Warren, Jack Washington, Walter Page, Jo Jones and singer Helen Humes (Jess Stacy replaced the Count at the piano) to record eight titles for Brunswick. Lionel Hampton, an old friend, used Herschel when he recorded *I'm In The Mood For Swing, Shoe Shiner's Drag, Any Time At All* and *Muskrat Ramble* for Victor on 21st July 1938, while pianist Teddy Wilson used both Herschel and Lester Young as part of the ten-piece orchestra with which he recorded six titles for Brunswick in the autumn of that same year.

Herschel Evans' joyous, spirited, aggressively shaped solo on *Panassié Stomp* (recorded with Basie on 16th November 1938) gives no indication that an illness was slowly consuming the tenor player. Only three months after this, however, Herschel was dead. It is likely that his last recordings with Basie were *Sing For Your Supper* and *My Heart Belongs To Daddy*, made on 5th January 1939. He is officially listed by some discographers as one of the musicians who participated at the Basie Decca session on 2nd February 1939, but Choo Berry certainly deputises for him on a number of the recordings from this session. His untimely passing came as a severe blow to the jazz scene, for he had been admired as a man as well as a musician. Basie, realizing the value of the contrast which his style had formed when ranged alongside Lester Young's, determined to continue the tradition thus set and replaced him with another disciple of Coleman Hawkins, Buddy Tate.

Though not an innovator of the same importance as Lester Young, and though his playing has been less developed by a later school of jazz tenormen than Lester's, Herschel Evans proved himself while working with Basie to be one of the two or three outstanding soloists of the Coleman Hawkins school of tenor-saxophone players. Examined, not as a prophet, but as a musically accomplished, imaginative and emotionally fired soloist, complete within himself, he bears worthy comparison with Ben Webster, Choo Berry, Don Byas and Buddy Tate, after Hawkins the giants of middle-period tenor-saxophone playing.

It was a fitting tribute to Herschel's expressive powers as a soloist that when, at one of Buck Clayton's Columbia jam sessions in 1954, Coleman Hawkins had the opportunity to improvise upon a theme from the old Basie band's repertoire he chose *Blue*

And Sentimental, the melody which Herschel had so enhanced, and dedicated his resulting solo to the memory of his pupil.

FREDDIE GREENE

"Basie's sense of tempo and Freddie Greene are responsible for the impact which typifies the band's style."

QUINCY JONES

One immediate outcome of the musical experiments which took place at Minton's Playhouse and other New York jazz clubs in the early 1940's—experiments which we now look back upon as being the embryonic stage in the gradual evolution of the modern jazz movement—was a revolutionary use of the guitar as a jazz instrument. For a decade or more prior to these experiments the guitar had been looked upon as an integral part of the jazz rhythm section, an instrument for relaying a steady, well-regulated pulse behind the ensemble or the soloists, normally merging its sound with the double-bass and drums to give a lightness and lift to the beat of the jazz group. True there had been several jazz guitarists, including Teddy Bunn, Eddie Durham and Danny Barker, who on occasions had been known to hoist the instrument out of the section and improvise solos, and the accompanists to blues singers still used it extensively in an individual role, but in the main in the 1930's the guitar was utilized as a spur within the rhythm sections of the larger orchestral groups of the day. Ellington, Lunceford, Calloway, Goodman, Basie; these and almost every other important bandleader during the decade employed the guitar in this way.

Primitive modern jazz brought radical changes to this concept. Mainly at the instigation of Charlie Christian, who dominated the New York experiments of the early 1940's, the guitar was cast away by the rhythm section. Christian, making use of the new amplified guitar, obtained a sound on the instrument not unlike a soft-toned saxophone; he commenced to improvise phrases with it similar to the saxophone, and before long, instead of supporting the wind instruments which comprised the front line of the jazz group, he was flying the guitar alongside the horns and gradually blending with their voicings. At the same

124

time, the experimentalists also broke down the hitherto regulated, unwavering jazz beat into a series of shifting patterns, with unusual accents and cross-rhythms. They employed the double-bass as the pivot of the rhythm section, thereby setting free the drums and guitar from their previous boundaries; the tendency became for the former to be devoted to producing accents and an assortment of cross-rhythms, while the latter, following Christian's teaching, attached itself firmly to the front line.

The effect of these changes upon orchestral jazz soon became apparent. As modern jazz gained a wider acceptance, a new generation of guitarists following in Christian's footsteps (men like Barney Kessel, Chuck Wayne, Tal Farlow and Jimmy Raney, and even several of the older men like John Collins) sprang into being; men who had matured principally as soloists on the new electric instruments, and who preferred to work with the ensemble of a small jazz group rather than as a rhythmic strut in the larger bands. One by one the big bands began to shed their guitarists. Some continued to use the instrument until its owner moved into a small group and then made no effort to replace him; others, even though they did not indulge in a game with broken rhythms, saw that the bass could act as a single pivot for the section, and for financial reasons dispensed with the guitar; even Ellington, though little impressed by the devices of modern jazz, did not bother to find a replacement for Fred Guy when the veteran banjo and guitar player retired from the band after many years and entered the agency business. By 1950 scarcely any large jazz group in the United States contained a guitarist as a rhythmic support.

Count Basie's Orchestra was the principal opponent of this casual dismissal of the guitar from the large jazz group. Though only a matter of five or six years before the sessions at Minton's, his own musical approach had been revolutionary, and though he failed to condemn many of the experimental methods of the modern jazz soloists on the grounds that music must progress in order to avoid stagnation, he became an absolute reactionary when modern jazz suggested tampering with the rhythmic foundations of jazz. He'd endorse the search for new methods of phrasing, the new use of harmony, and so on, but at the attempts to break up the regular beat of jazz he balked. If jazz does not swing, then do not call it jazz; call it a usage of elements of jazz towards another musical end product, but don't label something as jazz when the core of the musical form has been extracted; these were the Count's musical deductions, and he continued to enforce such a belief within the structure of his own band. The fact that other leaders were giving way did not budge him. Even when modern jazz began to gain ground with musicians and even audiences, he still set his band going with that relaxed, swinging beat, the indomitable child of the Kansas City jam sessions, with its four clear beats to the bar, each one carefully balanced and equally emphasized, confident that with such rhythmic surety the front-line instruments could proceed with their improvised explorations. And with his insistence upon a steady 4/4 time, he retained the guitar to give its lightness and lift to the rhythm section, topping the rich bass notes with its tender yet definite rhythmic chords. The four men of the rhythm team, phrasing together with their four beats to the bar, remained, despite the innovations of modern jazz, a constant with each group of musicians the Count employed, oiling the action of the ensemble at all times.

Basie has waited patiently to prove his point about a sure, unvarying rhythmic pattern being the soundest foundation for any form of jazz improvisation. The structure of the Basie rhythm section, fashioned in the mid-1930's, remained unchanged throughout the rest of the 1930's and the entire 1940's; and, not to be destroyed by the band depression of 1950, it persisted in the style of the septet run by the Count from 1950 to 1951. Today, in the mid-1950's, it is still a decisive factor in the musical policy of the Count's re-established big band. And in the mid-1950's he has really proved his point. The modernists, now consolidating their gains, have realized that while many of their experiments have benefitted jazz, the idea of breaking up the rhythmic foundations of jazz was largely a failure, and, as a result, in the mid-1950's they are anxiously negotiating an alliance of their new use of melody and harmony with a swinging beat in 4/4 time and casting off many of the finicky rhythmic devices which grew up in the 1940's. The tendency of musicians from all schools of thought in jazz today is to praise the Basie band and its decisive rhythmic power. A signpost has been erected by musicians showing that the surest path for the music's progression exists through a co-operation between many of the structural devices of modern jazz and the emotional freedom, the intense superficial excitement and the rhythmic impetus of the swing era. Basie's own band today typifies this ideal, and the modernists working as improvising soloists within its ranks and the arrangers behind it are confirming the soundness of its rhythmic standards. As I have just mentioned, Basie has had to campaign for more than a decade in order finally to by-pass the rhythmic anaemia of certain trends in modern jazz (in particular the Tristano and Russo tangents) and hammer home to musicians his belief that jazz depends so much upon its rhythmic virility if it is to survive. There were times, with his band only just paying its way, when hardly anyone listened to him; in the late 1940's he was regarded by many as unfashionable, his band policy as the dying embers of the swing era. In sustaining his convictions, therefore, he has been fortunate in the fact that his own four-man rhythm section, playing its relaxed and impeccable beat, has contained the finest rhythm guitarist (in Freddie Greene) that the course of orchestral jazz has produced. Greene has completed what has been the most powerful and consistent rhythm section in the past three decades of jazz history, a section whose strength, setting Basie's home in good order as it were, has given him a sound enough case for casting stones at certain of the modernists.

Freddie Greene has been with Basie longer than any other musician in the band; he joined the group early in 1937, and is, in fact, the only member of the present band (the leader apart, of course) who was with the Count in the 1930's. His emphatic guitar playing has been a significant musical feature of each influential combination that the Count has led, from the golden days when Lester and Herschel Evans were in the band to the present group with its renewed success, as well as of practically every small group drawn from the main band over the years for recording purposes; rightly he is regarded as a personification of the leader's ideals over the use of rhythm in jazz.

It was actually as a result of a tip from John Hammond that Basie, soon after bringing his band from Kansas City to New York, went to hear Freddie Greene playing in a little-known Greenwich Village club. The first recording session which the band made for American Decca in New York featured Claude Williams on guitar, but soon after this date Williams left, leaving the all-important rhythm section of the band wide open. Basie was so impressed when he heard Freddie Greene's work that he hired him on the spot, thereby cementing into place the final brick of the most cohesive and consistently-swinging rhythm section in orchestral jazz development. This unit (Basie, Greene, Walter Page and Jo Jones) remained together well into the 1940's, and its playing set a tradition which has persisted in Basie's band through to the present day. In the 1950's musicians still speak with awe of the Basie-Greene-Page-Jones team, and on several occasions recently certain New York recording companies have reunited these four men for specific recording dates, while other companies have attempted an approximation of its sound with other musicians. In Basie's own band of the mid-1950's, the leader and Freddie Greene both employ the same rhythmic patterns which they evolved for use in the late 1930's, while the new bassist and drummer are set to follow pretty closely in the footsteps of Page and Jones.

Though the character of Freddie Greene's guitar playing faithfully adheres to the style of the Kansas City jam sessions, it is a remarkable fact that the man himself had no physical connexions with this legendary musical centre prior to enlisting in the Count's band. He was born at Charleston in South Carolina on 31st March 1911, and, after taking a few lessons in music theory with a local teacher, he began, from the age of twelve onwards, to pick up the rudiments of jazz playing without any real tuition. He worked his way, via a number of musical and non-musical jobs, to New York, and then from meeting Basie his musical career followed a single course. When the Count was forced to disband in 1950 he retained Freddie Greene for the rhythm section of his all-star septet, and later, of course, in 1951 he made him a cornerstone of the reorganized big band.

Greene hasn't changed much over the years. Reliable without being obtrusive, a sound component part of the rhythm section yet with a personal sense of rhythm which is virile and spirited, technically well-versed and a competent reading musician with an interest in jazz composition which suits the band's singular thematic policy, he has been the ideal rhythm guitarist for the Count. He has given both individuality of sound and a rhythmic stamina to the band's propulsive beat. His inherent sense of tempo and his durability when performing a regular beat have set standards well above those of the average band guitarists. One of the Buck Clayton jam sessions, recorded in the 1950's for Columbia, contains instances of Freddie sustaining a set tempo behind a wide selection of improvising soloists for as long as twenty minutes at a time, never faltering over a single chord, and evidencing throughout that essential relaxation which is a part of the familiar Kansas City beat. His fingering and general technique reveal a similar consistency. Unlike so many of his fellow guitarists, who have transferred their attentions to electric instruments, Freddie has continued to use a non-amplified model, showing a preference for the latter's clean, steely sound for the expression of his rhythmic accents. With the non-amplified instrument his touch has been definitive though still delicate, resulting in his supplying each rhythm section that he has worked in with a beat that is emphatic without ever becoming ponderous.

Quite apart from his work with the various Basie bands, and with smaller groups drawn from these bands, Freddie Greene's guitar playing has been constantly in demand for many years now as a rhythmic support at recording sessions featuring many of the outstanding improvising soloists of jazz. In the late 1930's he helped provide the accompaniments to perhaps the finest creative efforts singer Billie Holiday ever recorded (*Sailboat In The Moonlight*, etc.), together with Buck Clayton, Lester Young *et al.* Also while with the old Basie band he found time to make recordings with Benny Carter, Lionel Hampton, Benny Goodman, Joe Sullivan, Illinois Jacquet and many others.

In the 1950's, with so many musicians rediscovering Basie's style of jazz playing, he has been recording more accompaniments than ever; in the past two years alone he has cut literally scores of titles with Joe Newman, Al Cohn, Buck Clayton, Sonny Stitt, Jo Jones and Sir Charles Thompson, as well as extended jam session features with Count Basie and Harry Edison for Clef and one album under his own name for Victor with a group mainly featuring the trumpet work of Joe Newman. On all these sessions his personal musicianship has been impeccable, and his rhythmic certainty has proved invaluable to the musical structure of each group.

So busy, in fact, has Freddie Greene been kept during his career in fulfilling his commitments as a rhythm guitarist, carefully underlining the ensemble of the Basie band and an additional assortment of improvising soloists, that he has never been known as a solo voice. On account of the rhythmic policy set by Basie he has been fully occupied as a section man when working with the band, while on his numerous small-group recordings, though he might be heard playing the occasional introduction or coda (e.g. for *Leonice* on Joe Newman's "All I Wanna Do Is

Eo

Swing" LP. on Victor), he hasn't been known to launch out with his own improvised choruses.

I always do ascribe this absence of recorded solos by Freddie Greene to his continual industry as a rhythm man rather than to any lack of invention. Against those who would argue to the contrary I can bring to bear two pieces of important musical evidence.

The first concerns the compositions which the guitarist has contributed to the Basie band's repertoire—*Down For Double, Right On, Corner Pocket,* and so on. These have all been strong, muscular themes lending themselves to both ensemble variations in the hands of the band's arrangers and to the extended improvisation of the soloists. *Corner Pocket,* for example, a theme which in the 1950's has been recorded by Joe Newman with a small unit for Victor as well as orchestrated by Ernie Wilkins for the full band to record for Clef, comprises a thirty-two bar theme with an interesting chord sequence, a strong, melodic main phrase and a middle-eight phrase which contrasts melodically yet still dovetails neatly into the overall pattern of the theme. Clearly these creations by Greene are not the products of a musician who has failed to gain an understanding of jazz improvisation. Rather, they appear to stem from a line of improvised thought which the guitarist has been unable to project personally on account of his particular role as a kind of back-room boy of the Basie band and instead has stabilized and passed on to the main body of the band.

The other piece of evidence takes the form of a solitary recording which Freddie Greene made in the 1950's (part of a Vanguard LP. featuring the blues and folk-songs and spirituals of Brother John Sellers) on which he can be heard ably improvising the background accompaniments to a documentary-type folk-song by Sellers.

Apart from its rarity in having the guitarist performing an improvised part, this record is something of a collector's item due to the very fact that it links together such superficially-diverse talents as a travelling evangelist and a band guitarist. The historical background attached to the record was in itself quite unusual.

It happened, one learns, that on the day of this recording Freddie Greene had gone into the Vanguard Studios to participate in a revival of three-quarters of the best-known Basie rhythm section. John Hammond, supervising the session, was set to make an album of piano solos with one of Basie's closest disciples, Sir Charles Thompson, and had assembled the formidable Greene-Page-Jones team to back him. Just as the Thompson session drew to a conclusion, however, Brother John Sellers, newly-arrived in New York from Chicago, wandered into the studios in search of an audition. Thompson and the other musicians were just preparing to leave as he entered, yet when they chanced to hear Sellers sing a few bars of one of his own themes, *Doretha Boogie*, they unanimously voted to stay. Without any warning, even without discussing the question of a contract, another recording session was born, Sellers producing one song after another from his repertoire and the musicians in turn fashioning suitable accompaniments. It was when the singer introduced *Boll Weevil* to the session, a song associated many years before with the late Huddie Ledbetter, that Freddie Greene's guitar suddenly sprang into prominence. This sad little theme—about the pest which for so long has been the chief enemy of the cotton crop in the Deep South—has an unusual metre, and at the session it proved a difficult vehicle for the full accompanying quartet to exploit. A solution to the problem was found, however, when the guitarist was persuaded to disengage himself from the rhythm section and fashion an accompaniment after the manner of the guitarists who supported the legendary blues singers of an earlier decade. Thus it was that Freddie Greene's extemporised thoughts as a guitarist were at last shown the light of day—and to good effect.

A feeling for the blues, so vital a part of Greene's musical make-up after years spent in supporting the Count Basie ensemble, was given a logical expression as he delicately moulded the background to Sellers' voice. Using the instrument with a remarkable sensitivity, he intersperses between the series of spread chords and sustained blue notes of the traditional blues accompanists subtle passages of single-string improvisation, weaving first with and then around the vocal line, emphasizing, embroidering, appearing here and there to be about to relax lightly into swing time yet effectively sustaining the melancholy mood of the song.

After hearing the feature I felt an acute sense of regret that Freddie's obvious talent in this direction had not been given an outlet previously; it assured me that he was in no way deficient as an improvising musician, and also that the keen intellect which has for so long supplied the veneer to the Basie rhythm section possesses, behind its immaculate musicianship and outward poise, an intense feeling for the basic roots of jazz music.

With Basie, Freddie Greene has established himself as the outstanding rhythm guitarist of big band jazz; with a solitary and humble accompaniment to Brother John Sellers, and through the thematic strength of his compositions, he has gilded this already imposing status by revealing his awareness of the creative substance behind two widely different facets of jazz music—on the one hand the utter simplicity and moving sentiment of the blues singer, on the other the massive designs involved in the construction of a strong, yet flexible jazz ensemble.

WALTER PAGE

"Walter Page . . . played a mighty wicked string bass, and still does."

COUNT BASIE

I've Got My Captain Working For Me Now ran the title line of the popular song, one of the many maudlin ditties to briefly monopolise the music publishers' attention during the period of suspicious heaven immediately following World War II. Bing Crosby performed one of his casual song-and-dance routines to the tune in a post-war musical film, "Blue Skies", accompanied by various choreographic illustrations of his one-time military superior—with the roles of authority reversed—eating humble pie, and, in order to make a living, operating in a servile capacity.

In 1935 Count Basie, forming his first band to play at the Reno Club in Kansas City, was faced with the position of having a previous employer, bass player Walter Page, seeking an entry into the band. In this instance, however, Page's participation in the Reno Club project presented few of the complications which the trite saying informs us will arise whenever the once-employer becomes the employee. Page and Basie considered their relationship in musical terms before the question of official positions was discussed. Certainly Basie had worked for Page several years before in the Blue Devils group, but they had always operated together on friendly, informal terms rather than on a strictly

132

leader-and-sideman basis. They had admired each other's playing and had proved ideal partners within the musical structure of the Devils' rhythm section. Later they had worked together in the Moten Orchestra. When Page joined Basie at the Reno there were no embarrassments, and the bassist was to lend his powerful underlay to the Count's rhythm section for close on a decade, thereby completing (together with Basie, Freddie Greene and Jo Jones) not only the most musicianly and finely-poised section that the course of jazz music has produced, but also a section which held together for longer than the majority of its contemporaries.

Walter Page, or the "Big One" as he was known to many of the Kansas City musicians in the 1930's, has in turn been one of the most consistent bass players in the course of mainstream jazz, a musician who has mellowed rather than deteriorated over the years. He is still very active today, a greying, bespectacled veteran in his mid-fifties, still massive of frame without having become flabby. In the 1950's, after relinquishing the worries of touring and settling in New York, he has been busier than ever before as a recording musician, and his services are much in demand in the New York City jazz clubs.

Apart from his own activities as a bandsman, Page has also been an important teacher of bass players: during his long career his pupils have included such prominent men as Gene Ramey and Truck Parham, and almost every bass player to work in Kansas City in the 1930's was a beneficiary in one way or another of his firm sense of direction with the instrument. He was the last important technician to use the cumbersome bass purely as a rhythmic vehicle to underline the ensemble of a big band, prior to the late Jimmy Blanton's development of the instrument as a solo voice at the end of the 1930's.

Walter Sylvester Page was born at Gallatin, Missouri, on 9th February 1900, and was the elder half-brother of trumpeter "Hot Lips" Page (though this relationship has been disputed by certain critical sources, despite "Lips" Page's own authority). As a boy Walter became interested in music as a result of hearing folk-songs and spirituals sung by the elder members of his family. His first active participation in music came when a local brass band employed him to beat the bass drum on their parades. Later, at high school, he studied music theory, as well as a practical use of several instruments, including the bass-saxophone,

French horn, tuba and double-bass. (Mary Lou Williams has attested that Walter was one of the first jazz musicians to alternate between the tuba and the string-bass as vehicles for providing the jazz ensemble with its rhythmic support.) In his early teens he played tuba with a large municipal orchestra, performing only classical works but expanding his knowledge of reading and theory; when he later encountered the high musical standards of the Kansas City jazz scene, the thoroughness of this musical background and his experience with several diverse forms of music was to prove its worth. Musicians who were in Kaycee when he first appeared there have since confirmed that at their extended jam sessions he performed with a confidence far in advance of his years.

The bassist was only eighteen when he first braved the stiff competition of the Kaycee school of musicians, but with his already mature rhythmic sense he found little difficulty in obtaining work. Within a few months of his arrival there he graduated to the most important of the Kansas City bands, the one led by Bennie Moten. Even as early as 1918, when Page joined the band, Moten was an intimate of the powerful political and booze racketeers who ran Kaycee, a liaison which brought him in the cream of the musical engagements, the best socials and dances, and so on, and he could afford to hire all the better musicians for his group. Walter's first association with the Moten band lasted until 1923, when he left to join a band in support of a road show. The show later closed in Oklahoma City, but the band stayed intact and quite suddenly Walter found himself a bandleader. Renaming the group Walter Page's Original Blue Devils, the young bassist decided to make Oklahoma City a centre of operations, and gradually he built up a strong musical reputation with it.

The late "Hot Lips" Page has indicated that when he joined the Blue Devils in 1928, the chief musical influences upon the group, at least in its ensemble playing, came from King Oliver, Jelly Roll Morton and Duke Ellington, in that order. The soloists, however, were all firm disciples of the Kansas City school. After "Lips" Page had taken over as lead trumpet, the Devils were further strengthened by the addition of Count Basie at the piano, and, in the late 1920's, the musicians came across blues singer Jimmy Rushing in Oklahoma City and persuaded him to join them. Lester Young also entered the group shortly after this.

134

Jo Jones has stated that the Blue Devils formed the finest band he ever remembers hearing. He maintains that it was chiefly Page's encouragement which stimulated the musical talents of Basie, Rushing, Buster Smith (the altoist said to be a forerunner of Charlie Parker) and himself, even implying that, but for Walter's teaching, his own drumming would not be the musical force it is known as today. It was unfortunate that this band never did make the grade financially, and that it failed to secure a recording contract.

In 1929 Walter Page and The Blue Devils, without money and without instruments, were stranded in Kansas City. The band broke up almost immediately and all the sidemen started chasing after jobs. It was at this point that Bennie Moten stepped in. Knowing the musical qualities of the Devils, Bennie at once reorganized his own band to make room for the redundant men. Walter Page, Lester Young, "Lips" Page, Jimmy Rushing and Basie all joined forces with Bennie, thereby forming the nucleus of the finest band that Kansas City had known. Thus reunited, Page remained with the Moten band until the leader's death, and he recorded with it for Victor, playing both tuba and double-bass.

Upon Bennie Moten's death in 1935, ignoring an offer which Bus Moten, brother of the deceased, made to him to stay on with the band, Page joined the small unit Count Basie had formed to play at the Reno Club; the job meant a lot of rough riding at the outset but later proved to be the better proposition. Walter was teamed with drummer Jo Jones and the Count in a rhythm section which gradually built up and developed a singular style (typical of every Basie band since) with four clear beats to the bar, all equally accented, swinging yet relaxed. Under Walter's expert guidance the young Jo Jones progressed considerably, learning how to phrase and accent and create break passages with his kit. Mary Lou Williams recalls that she "loved to see Jo teaming with Walter Page. Page showed Jo what to do and when to do it, and it was really something to dig those two great musicians". Mary Lou has also said—and this is an exceptional compliment to be payed to any bass player—that several times she caught the Basie band when the only people on the stage were Page and the ensemble, and that the "Big One" still swung the band without any undue effort.

When Freddie Greene joined the band in New York in 1937 the great Basie rhythm section was made complete. With this vital unit, the throb of Page's rich-toned bass can be heard urging on the attack of the ensemble throughout all Basie's Decca recordings of the late 1930's and the Vocalions, Okehs and Columbias made in the early 1940's. On these recordings, with sure-fingered accuracy, and a perfect sense of timing and tempo, and while selecting the sure sequences of notes to underline the melody instruments, he generates a beat which few bass players have since been able to equal for strength and sound intonation. So muscular are his accompaniments on these band recordings that they form a strict contrast with the accompaniments he fashioned with delicacy and gentle charm behind Basie's piano solo recordings on Decca and behind the slight ensemble sound of the 1938 Kansas City Six records on Commodore. After witnessing the impetus he gives to the Basie ensemble as it builds up the final choruses of *Sent For You Yesterday* (recorded 1938), it is revealing to play the Kansas City Six record of *Pagin' The Devil*, and to note the way his deep-toned bass nurtures the featherweight thematic phrases produced by Clayton's trumpet and Lester Young's clarinet with such exceptional sympathy.

Walter Page remained a part of the Basie rhythm section until 1943, in which year, after a slight disagreement with the leader, he left and tried to obtain a job with the Lionel Hampton band, Rodney Richardson replacing him with Basie. The position with Hampton never materialized, however, and in 1946, after freelancing around New York City for the latter part of the wartime period, the bassist returned to Basie for two years more, concluding his regular musical association finally with the Count at the end of 1948.

Since 1948 he has held various band jobs, though he has shown a reluctance to leave New York for long periods on account of his increasing contacts for studio work. In 1949 he played in a small unit with "Lips" Page, and from 1951 to 1952 he toured in the accompanying group to singer Jimmy Rushing. In the autumn of 1952 he appeared for a few weeks with the Chicagoan trumpeter Jimmy McPartland at Lou Terrasi's Club, and then in the November of that year he worked with Eddie Condon's band. He has worked frequently with Condon's group since that date at the guitarist's own club in Greenwich Village, supplementing his earnings with studio jobs.

A further reason to keep Walter Page in New York City in the 1950's, of course, has been the increasing demand for him at recording sessions featuring rejuvenated mainstream jazz. The advent of critic John Hammond's expansion of the Vanguard label, originally only a classical concern, to take in jazz LP. albums alone has furnished him with a series of important sessions. Due to Hammond's careful selection of sidemen, his bass has enlivened no less than four albums with the Vic Dickenson Septet, one with the Mel Powell Septet (featuring Buck Clayton, Henderson Chambers and Edmond Hall), one with Ruby Braff, one with Nat Pierce and two with Jimmy Rushing. The sessions he made with Rushing have produced perhaps the finest recordings ever completed of this outstanding blues singer's voice. In addition to these LP.s he had figured in several revivals of the old Basie rhythm section for the Vanguard label. On 22nd January 1954 he was reunited with Freddie Greene and Jo Jones to accompany an album of piano solos by Basie's disciple, Sir Charles Thompson; and, when the Thompson session was completed, it was these four men who stayed on in the Vanguard studios to accompany Brother John Sellers for a selection of blues and folk songs. On 11th August 1955 the Basie rhythm section was again revived by Hammond, this time for a session, the first of its kind, under Jo Jones' name, and on this occasion Norman Granz released Basie from his Clef contract especially to sit in on a remake of the *Shoe Shine Swing* title, a theme the Count had used on his band's very first recording session back in Chicago in 1936. In the liner notes to the English issue of this album, so aptly entitled "Jo Jones Special", Stanley Dance has written of the reuniting of the original Basie rhythm section in glowing terms, saying: "When the collaboration of Freddie Greene on guitar and Walter Page on bass is added to the talents of Jo Jones and Basie, the jazz soloist's ideal is realised. Such inspiring lift and such heartening, dependable support were for so long merely a cherished dream. Today, so many years after its formation, this unit is still the pattern of perfection." I do not think there is a word of undue flattery in this statement; I can think of no other rhythm section in the history of jazz which has displayed such an intelligent and sympathetic appreciation of the problems confronting the improvising soloist.

In addition to these Vanguard recordings, Walter Page has recently completed albums for Bethlehem with trumpeter Ruby Braff's eleven-piece band, for Period with the veteran trombonist Jack Teagarden, and for Columbia with an all-star, Kansas

City-type jam session unit under the nominal leadership of trumpeter Buck Clayton. These latter sessions with Clayton contain instances of his bass work teaming with Freddie Greene, Jo Jones and Sir Charles Thompson to rhythmically underline, with never a falter, sequences of improvised solos for as long as twenty minutes at a time, an exceptional achievement and a tribute to the musician's feeling for this particular method of jazz expression. These Columbia extended jam sessions, perhaps more so than any other recordings that Walter Page has made, confirm the statements of Mary Lou Williams, Jo Jones, Basie and many other musicians concerning the durability of his work as a bass player. In fact, as a concluding thought, I would say that if Page's reputation had to stand or fall solely on the merits of his playing on these recordings with Clayton, then I would still have no hesitation over describing him as the finest bassist ever to emerge from the Kansas City jazz school of the 1930's.

JO JONES

"Jo Jones reminds me of the wind. He has more class than any other drummer I've ever heard and has been an influence on me ever since I first heard him with Basie. Man, he could drive that band! With Jo there's none of that damn raucous tom-tom beating and riveting-machine stuff. Jo makes sense."

DON LAMOND

Jo Jones, the perfectionist. As such is this articulate and everlastingly virile drummer known, not only to his musical contemporaries, but also to the younger generation of musicians, the disciples of modern jazz.

One night in 1954 Jo was leading a combo. at George Wein's Storyville Club in Boston. Wein, a sincere but certainly not outstanding jazz pianist, was sitting in with the group (as he was accustomed to doing with the majority of the bands visiting his club), thereby making the broadly-smiling, balding Jo Jones at once his employer and employee. After Wein had made one or two errors of judgement at the piano, however, ones which rather offended Jo's unusually sensitive feelings as a musician, the smile began to fade from the drummer's face. At length, after several more slips on the part of the pianist, Jo could stand it no longer —the perfectionist side of him rebelled. Risking his job, but

138

impelled to voice his mind, he draped a paternal arm about Wein's shoulders, and implied very briefly with his voice that it was difficult to perform two tasks, running a night-club and working as a jazz pianist, *well*; his advice was to concentrate on one or the other, but not both, if any success was to be achieved! Fortunately, Wein was under no illusions about his own abilities as a pianist. He tactfully withdrew his services from the group. (I have since met him, and found him to be an exceptionally modest person, despite his extensive services to jazz as an organizer of the Newport Festival, and so on.) Jo, his musical ethics appeased, resumed his position at the drum kit. He is still George Wein's good friend!

Such an action as this is typical of the singular jazz percussionist, a musician who has survived with success two decades of changes and prolific evolution in jazz without having his reputation suffer from any landslide due to the emergence of new faces and styles. Jo today is valued as highly as any of the important drummers to appear with the development of modern jazz (Kenny Clarke, Max Roach, Art Blakey and Roy Haynes to name the leading four), perhaps the only surviving drummer from the swing era to be so revered; yet although he has listened to modern jazz and subtly absorbed certain slight mannerisms from it, the main ingredients of his style have not altered from the time when, with the Basie band, he first burst upon the New York jazz scene and the record-buying world in the late 1930's.

Jo in his lifetime has heard and seen and played with just about every important soloist in jazz. Little wonder, therefore, that he is a musical perfectionist, and now requires his companions to be likewise, for over the years he has had to be 100 per cent perfect himself in order to stimulate and satisfy bands and soloists possessed of widely different temperaments. One must not be misled into believing that Jo is a megalomaniac as a musician, that his head has been turned by critical acclaim. It could have been so quite easily, but it hasn't. The principal victim of Jo's musical perfectionism has been unquestionably Jo himself. No musician in jazz has been more self-critical than this man; no drummer can have worked harder than the gifted Jo in order to maintain his standards and position. He has learnt the real meaning of perfectionism by continual hard work and self-castigation and the searching to broaden his experience. All his life the drummer has had this profound respect for the jazz musicians who have outstandingly combined their creative and emotional energies with good musicianship, and he has gauged his own contribution by his ability to keep pace with such men. Twenty-five years before giving those few words of friendly advice to George Wein, Jo in his late teens, though he had amassed a great deal of experience with bands and had been complimented on his work by a number of jazz soloists, refused to go near Kansas City because he felt himself unworthy of performing with the musicians there; though frequently the recipient of advice to make haste and join up with the Kaycee scene, Jo had first to satisfy himself that he could compete with the high standards of musicianship there.

A Chicagoan, born on 10th July 1911, Jo Jones picked up the rudiments of percussion work instinctively, while he also became, by more contrived study, a competent reading musician and pianist, and he gained a little further experience by playing with a trumpet and saxophone. As a boy he was always giving performances of one kind or another, singing and dancing at youth clubs and church gatherings. When he left school to start playing professionally with a carnival band, he'd been studying music almost continually for about twelve years.

Once working on tour with various carnivals, Jo admits that he had to do a certain amount of improvising as regards equipment. Sometimes, when he was unable to transport an orthodox drum kit with him, he'd arrive in a town, walk into a grocery store and get a wooden box which he'd then break up and whittle away at some of the pieces to make some sticks; he usually carried cymbals with him, using coat-hangers for holders, but he rarely managed a side drum, and if there wasn't a bass drum at the theatre where the act appeared then he had to do without that too. Such limitations naturally taxed Jo's intelligence quite considerably at the outset, but he soon learnt to overcome the absence of a conventional kit, making the most of what he had. His ability to improvise generally, but most of all the accuracy and skilful gradation in volume and force of his cymbal work, so vital a feature of the drumming style he later co-ordinated with Basie, developed greatly with the experience of these years.

Carnival bands provided Jo with his living for some time. He travelled up and down the country with them, and in the course of his various trips had opportunities to familiarize himself with the music of the majority of the well-known bands of the day, including Duke Ellington's, Fletcher Henderson's and McKinney's

Cotton Pickers, while he had jammed with most of the sidemen from these bands. During these years, though, he always gave Kansas City a wide berth. By talking with other musicians he was made aware of Kansas City and its colourful jam sessions in the late 1920's, but, while itching to go there, he exercised self-restraint until he felt his musicianship was sufficiently developed to meet the exalted standards reputed to exist in this musicians' metropolis.

Jo did not enter Kansas City until 1933, and then only very tentatively to take up an offer to join a small band led by saxist Tommy Douglas. Once there, however, he was astonished beyond all previous expectations at the way the musicians' quarter was so permanently alive with jazz. To stay and play in the place became a necessity.

He listened to Pete Johnson playing at the Sunset Café with an alto-saxophone player called Walter Knight, esteemed by Jo to be a vital musical ancestor of Charlie Parker. Invariably these two were augmented in the early hours of the morning for an impromptu jam session by the Kansas City school of tenor players, consisting of Lester Young, Herschel Evans, Dick Wilson and Ben Webster, as well as the trumpeters "Lips" Page and Mouse Randolph (the "Irving Randolph" who later worked with Cab Calloway) and the "Big One", bassist Walter Page. Pha Terrell, the singer from Andy Kirk's band, frequently joined the men there. Most of these men were working either with the Kirk or Moten bands at the time. Joe Turner was singing the blues and working as a barman in one club, while one could also hear in the course of a single evening (for all the clubs and dancing establishments and saloons were tightly compressed within the same small area) Sammy Price, Mary Lou Williams, Buster Smith, Jimmy Rushing, Clyde Hart, Basie, of course, and even the late Art Tatum (who frequently took time off from touring to stay for weeks on end in the place). Jo was both fascinated and inspired by what he heard; the musical standards of the men and their enthusiasm for expressing themselves were unequalled by anything or anyone he'd previously heard. One important thing he realized through listening to them was that only by playing with these men, and facing up to the competition, would he broaden his experience and ultimately attain the same proficiency.

After his initial encounter with the Kansas City jazz scene, Jo found himself unable to leave the place. He started sitting in at one or two of the "after hours" sessions, as a pianist as well as a

141

drummer, and he started sharing a room with the tenor player Herschel Evans, who introduced him to quite a number of the regular Kaycee musicians. Within a matter of months his playing was absorbed into the musical life of the community, and as his rhythmic properties came to be accepted and even admitted, so Jo found himself incessantly being called out to underline different gatherings of musicians. Whenever a travelling band came into Kansas City, no matter what hour of the night or morning it might be, the musicians would want to jam with the residents for a couple of hours, and Jo would be woken up and told to bring his tubs down to where the men were collecting. The drummer nowadays insists that it was working for hours on end in this way in Kansas City, stopping for a shot of crude bootleg whisky occasionally, but otherwise never leaving his kit, which gave his playing such durability, strengthening his muscular actions so that in subsequent years even the most strenuous of sessions failed to tire or unbalance him.

Continually on call for jam sessions, Jo contrived to play with virtually every musician who either lived in or visited Kansas City within the space of the next three years. He also led a unit of his own for several months at one of the smaller drinking clubs, with Lester Young on tenor, George Hunt (the trombonist who later took a solo on Count Basie's renowned recording of *One O'clock Jump*) and Eddie Durham on guitar, and at times in 1934 and 1935 he played drums with Bennie Moten's Orchestra. Whenever it was possible he tried to work with the bass player Walter Page, the man who, more than anyone else in Kansas City, became his musical father. Jo has said that it was Walter who assisted him in the formation of an individual style at the drums by first advising him how to phrase and fashion the rhythmic supports to offset different soloists, also how to make explosive accents which would generate impetus behind the ensemble of a band. The teaming of Jo's drums and Walter's deep-toned bass became an easily identifiable feature of the Kaycee jam sessions. According to the men who played at the important gatherings in this unique musicians' town there was an atmosphere of unselfishness about the jamming which never really appeared anywhere else; when the men began playing together they never got in each other's way, and everyone knew more or less by instinct when to take their three or four solo choruses. Such musical agreement is indeed a rarity in jazz.

Upon Moten's death in 1935, Jo joined several other members of the band, including Walter Page, Eddie Durham, Ed Lewis and Jack Washington, in a small unit which Count Basie was rehearsing to play at the Reno Club. Jo played with Basie at the Reno and at several other Kansas City haunts, including the Tower and Main Street Theatres and the Fairland Park and Pla-mor Ballrooms. Money was extremely scarce then, of course. Early in 1936, in fact, when Jo wanted to purchase some new percussion equipment, he had to go and take a job in St. Louis for several months to make up the price. With the exception of this unavoidable absence though, the drummer stuck with Basie during the all-important period when the unit's musical approach was fashioned, and with Walter Page helped to determine a new style of playing for the jazz rhythm section.

Earlier in the book I explained that certain elements descended from Walter Page's Blue Devils and Bennie Moten's Orchestra came together in the Basie band to produce a supple and evenly flowing rhythm pattern, with four clear, equally-accented beats to the bar—a pattern designed to temper the intense, hard-driving nature of the riff passages unleashed by the ensemble and the fiery, explosive bursts from soloists with the qualities of relaxation and flexibility, while maintaining a generous swing. Of the various large bands functioning in the United States in the 1930's, Basie's alone evidenced this unique blend of force and relaxation.

Jo Jones played a vital part in providing the rhythm section of the Basie band with such ease and elasticity of movement, while propelling and firing the immense attacking impact of the ensemble with a sure swing.

Unlike other important big band drummers of the late 1930's and early 1940's (such men as Jimmy Crawford with the Lunceford band, Gene Krupa with Benny Goodman and Cozy Cole with Cab Calloway) who tended to bear out the theories of the great bandleader and drummer, the late Chick Webb, by driving their ensembles with an unrelenting, all-powerful beat, Jo exercised a less ferocious, more ingenious method of attack. Transferring his main attentions to the high-hat cymbal, he delivered upon it a regulated but unceasing series of stick shots, thereby creating a shimmering rhythmic effect which was unusually fluid and supple, and ideal for swinging—relaxedly but surely—the massed instruments in the ensemble. Generating his principal support to the orchestra in this fashion, Jo was then free to create, with his remaining stick on the snare drum and with his right foot on the pedal of the bass drum, accents upon the main rhythmic pattern. This process, known to Jo as "dropping bombs", meant that with an intelligent and often discreet deployment of snare and bass drum accents he could emphasize certain points of the ensemble's statements, heaping dramatic effect upon the course of a performance by sudden outbursts of force. There are numerous examples among Basie's recordings of Jo, while swinging effortlessly, quite startlingly increasing the emotional tension of a performance by a skilful loosing of accents.

Sensibly acknowledging the fact that a drummer with a big band should be so busily engaged in feeding the ensemble and the soloists that no time is left for vainglorious personal displays, Jo made use of his improvising powers at the drums to distribute further impetus behind and between the voicings of the ensemble. With Basie he never at any time embarked upon one of the prolonged, exhibitionist, *and extremely monotonous* drum displays which have become an integral part of the "Jazz At The Philharmonic" shows and of the programmes of several other big bands. Numerous recordings by the Basie band, however, contain instances of Jo plugging slight gaps which occasionally appear between two ensemble passages with a sudden barrage of stick shots, or, *and proving even more dramatically effective to a performance*, improvising a quick round of his kit during the middle-eight of the last chorus of an orchestral arrangement, ushering in, as it were, the climax of mighty brass unisons. Whenever these drum breaks appear it is noticeable that Jo extracts a wide variety of timbres from his kit, phrasing logically as though relating a personal story.

Jo's approach to the drum kit, innovated in the early days of the Basie band's existence, and delivered with all the musical precision and lightness and sensitivity of touch in his power, combined outstandingly with the unwavering 4/4 time of Walter Page's bass and, later, Freddie Greene's guitar to generate a fluid, immaculate, yet compelling swing—a swing which has distinguished every Basie band since, despite Jo's absence from some of them.

After earning the money for his new drum equipment, and rejoining Count Basie at the Reno Club, Jo Jones remained with the band throughout the period of its gradual revision and enlargement, and he was a part of the force with which the Count carried out his invasion of the jazz scene in New York and the east. On 9th October 1936, in Chicago, he recorded for the first time as part of the Smith-Jones Incorporated unit with Basie, Carl Smith, Lester Young and Walter Page, swinging spiritedly throughout the four Vocalion features: *Shoe Shine Swing*, *Evenin'*, *Boogie Woogie* and *Lady Be Good*. Then on 21st January 1937, in New York City, he was present in the Decca studios for the first recording date by the Basie band proper—the now-legendary session which produced *Honeysuckle Rose*, *Pennies From Heaven*, *Swinging At The Daisy Chain* and *Roseland Shuffle*. Collectors of jazz music recordings all over the world will doubtless recall their incredulity upon receiving these items; incredulity not only at the musical formation of the ensemble as it played short, rhythmic riff phrases with violent intensity, and the fiery, extrovert nature of the chief solo voices, but also at the ease and precision with which Jo Jones and Walter Page swept the whole band along, swinging all the way. Jo made an even greater impression though, upon those people, many of them musicians, who actually witnessed his first performances at the Roseland and The Famous Door in New York, rocking the Basie band and urging on its soloists with a free, uninhibited, yet polished and accurate beat. They watched and heard him generate this powerful, compelling swing, without once resorting to any pile-driver methods.

Jo remained with the Basie band (apart from an absence enforced by military service in 1944 and 1945, when Shadow Wilson deputised for him) until 1948. Within that period he backed the band on several score recordings, as well as accompanying Basie's piano solo recordings and a number of units, quintets, sextets and septets, drawn from the band's personnel. It is interesting to compare such big band items as *Topsy* and *Jumpin' At The Woodside*, which reveal Jo blowing up a storm with his kit in support of a mighty ensemble attack, with Basie's piano solos, *Red Wagon*, *How Long Blues*, *When The Sun Goes Down*, and so on, which find the drummer fashioning such gentle and sensitive accompaniments. Whenever the Basie band was working in New York during these years, Jo would also receive frequent offers to perform freelance jobs, and he sat in at recording sessions organized by a variety of record companies with small units led by Eddie Durham, Billie Holiday, Benny Goodman, Dicky Wells, Harry James, Mildred Bailey, Lester Young, Teddy Wilson, Lionel Hampton and others. Together with Lester Young and

Harry Edison from the Basie band he was prominently featured in the Gjon Mili film, "Jammin' The Blues".

After leaving Basie, Jo worked with Illinois Jacquet from 1948 to 1949, with Lester Young from 1950 to 1951, and then for two full years, 1952 and 1953, with the Joe Bushkin Quartet, mainly at The Embers club in New York City. Featuring Bushkin at the piano, Buck Clayton on trumpet, Milt Hinton on bass, and Jo, of course, at the drums, the latter unit was never accorded the artistic appreciation it rightly deserved. I have heard a number of transcriptions recorded by the Voice of America service of this Bushkin Quartet in action, and I have no hesitation in saying that its musical output, so warm and original in conception, and so sensitive in expression, established it as one of the outstanding east coast jazz units to perform in the 1950's.

Jo has concentrated upon freelance work in New York since the break-up of the Bushkin Quartet, and today is one of the busiest sessioners in the city whose work alternates between radio broadcasts, recording sessions and jazz-club dates. Admired by musicians from all schools of thought, he has been one of the comparatively few jazz percussionists (the late Sid Catlett was another) able to face up to the revolutionary changes wrought by modern jazz in the 1940's without effecting drastic modifications in style. While discreetly employing a number of accents innovated by the modern jazz drummers, Jo has successfully retained all the essentials of the drumming style he originally introduced with Count Basie's first band, and, in the 1950's, performing with his customary polished and articulate methods, has proved ideally suitable for accompanying all manner of soloists. Since settling in New York in the 1950's he has recorded albums with Lester Young (Clef), Roy Eldridge (Clef), Billy Taylor (Roost), Sonny Stitt (Roost), Jack Teagarden (Period), plus the outstanding Buck Clayton LP.s on Columbia, perhaps the nearest point yet reached by any studio recordings to a re-creation of the atmosphere at an extended Kansas City jam session. For John Hammond's Vanguard label he has completed albums with Sir Charles Thompson, Brother John Sellars, Vic Dickenson, Jimmy Rushing (two LP.s), Nat Pierce and Ruby Braff.

On 11th August 1955 Hammond also organized the first recording session ever to be held under Jo Jones' own leadership. For this auspicious, and long-overdue event, Jo used in his group Emmett Berry (trumpet), Benny Green (trombone), Lucky

146

Thompson (tenor-saxophone), Nat Pierce (piano), Freddie Greene (guitar), Walter Page (bass), and for one title only (a new version of *Shoe Shine Swing*) Count Basie at the piano, kindly released for the occasion by Norman Granz, the head of Clef. (This title, therefore, provides a rare reunification of the original Basie rhythm section.)

Jo performed superbly behind the front line for *Shoe Shine Swing*, *Lincoln Heights* and several other features, but steadfastly refused to take any drum solos, asserting that his primary function was to stimulate the other musicians in the group. It was not until several days later, at the end of a Jimmy Rushing session for Vanguard, that Hammond persuaded the reluctant Jo to record a rare display of his improvising abilities with the Duke Ellington theme, *Caravan*. Under pressure from the critic, Jo finally brought his impressive technical abilities into play and created a percussion solo which was imaginative in its use of timbres and accents, wry and humorous in its ideas, yet still possessed of a valid swing. Hammond, in his excitement, insisted that the resulting piece of tape be pieced on to the music from Jo's own session.

This story of Jo Jones' first record album as a leader in his own right explains so clearly why he has given priority to the job of accompanying other soloists and bands over the years, a job at which he has excelled. And it is precisely for this reason, for the sympathy and the stimulating swing of his accompaniments, that Jo is valued so highly by other musicians. Trumpeter Jonah Jones summarised the opinions of a multitude of jazz soloists when he once said to me: "After you've played with Jo behind you, man, it's so hard to find the right kind of support from anyone else."

JIMMY RUSHING

"I remember the lovable Jimmy Rushing, 'Mr. Five-by-Five'. Unlike the run of blues shouters, Jimmy could read music, and he could be heard ten blocks away without a microphone."

MARY LOU WILLIAMS

Count Basie's recording of *Sent For You Yesterday And Here You Come Today* (vintage 1938) contains a vocal chorus by the exuberant Jimmy Rushing which summarizes the effects wrought by the revolutionary Kansas City jam sessions of the early 1930's upon the course of authentic blues singing, as well as serving to define Rushing's position as the most influential exponent of blues singing to appear since Bessie Smith. (It was a cruel stroke of fate that at the very time of Rushing's explosive initial impact upon New York audiences in 1936 as a singer with Count Basie's Orchestra, Bessie Smith was in the throes of a physical and artistic decline and within months of a brutal and neglectful death.) Interpreted by the outstanding member of the Kaycee school of blues shouting, the lyric of *Sent For You Yesterday And Here You Come Today* becomes a symbol of the musical schism which took Rushing and Joe Turner and their companion singers away from the "classic" renditions of the traditional singing form of their race.

Rushing unfolds the story of this blues in a manner that is aggressive as well as heartfelt, urged on by the pulse of the Basie rhythm section and the stabbing phrases from Buck Clayton's trumpet:

> *Don't the moon look lonesome shinin' through the trees,*
> *Don't the moon look lonesome shinin' through the trees,*
> *Don't your arms look lonesome when your baby packs up to leave.*

> *Sent for you yesterday and here you come today,*
> *Sent for you yesterday and here you come today,*
> *You can't love me baby, and treat me that-a-way.*

The reader will notice that the *Sent For You Yesterday* lyric conforms to the metre of a traditional blues song, also that its words express a dissatisfaction with a facet of existence and are an obvious attempt on the part of the singer to relieve the strain of a particular trouble by sharing it with an audience. Any analysis penetrating beyond these points, however, will bring to light deviations from the concept of the traditional blues performance.

Sent For You Yesterday reveals Count Basie and his musicians subjecting the musical structure of the blues to a swiftly-moving rhythm pattern, and building upon it a theme consisting of short, melodic phrases which are exploited by unison riffs from the sections and the ensemble and swinging choruses of improvisation by the soloists. And Rushing, though the words of his song imply

148

a state of melancholy caused by a human problem, aligns his voice with the band's instrumental approach, picking up the beat set by the rhythm section, swinging lustily, spiritedly, continually thrusting forward his words, and often remoulding the melodic shapes of the song's phrases in the manner of a soloist improvising variations upon a theme with his instrument. As he sings, his delivery belies the mood described in the song. Evoking an emotional intensity typical of the Kaycee musical gatherings, Rushing sounds heated, even animated, and not at all dismayed that the gist of what he has to say is a complaint. Only a strong musical sense maintains the balance of his swing and prevents his emotions from boiling over, and it is the white heat of anger rather than a despondent sadness which dominates the emotional content in his voice. The impetus of the musical supports supplied by the Basie rhythm section alienates any tendency to droop or sound downcast.

The immensity of Jimmy Rushing's voice and the direct, aggressive phrases and simple but effective dynamics he projects take his songs a stage beyond the mere outcry of a traditional blues. He becomes increasingly extrovert. He hammers home his words with unusual vehemence, shouting or rhythmically chanting rather than singing them, exposing in all their nakedness his innermost convictions. It is noticeable too that whereas Bessie Smith's voice would only magnify its sound under emotional strain while lamenting an injustice, heightening the tension of her dirge, the ebullient Rushing maintains a considerable volume of voice whenever he sings, and is easily excited so that with the impact of the Basie rhythm section behind him he is prone to using force and repeatedly "hollering" his words to achieve the dynamic effect he desires.

One final point I would draw the reader's attention to with the recording of *Sent For You Yesterday* after stressing the actual musical evolution engendered by Rushing's performance, and that concerns the air of sophistication about the words of the lyric he sings.

It is true that the tune's lyric takes the form of a complaint, but it becomes noticeable that this is not the complaint of the down-trodden Negro plantation worker against social injustice. Here is no outcry against brutal racial discrimination and slavery; or against taxation and poverty. Here is no lament against the elements of nature for spoiling the cotton crop or for causing famine and disease. This lyric has no connection with the life of the Negro agricultural worker. It is a song of the urban dweller, of the city slicker, not of the impoverished country blues singer. It hints of better living; it could easily be taken as the statement of the well-dressed, well-fed man of the world, a dandified figure outlining the story of one of his many love affairs.

The country blues singer, explaining a problem of love, would rarely dissociate himself from the general sadness of his social background. *Sent For You Yesterday* is the statement of an emanicipated Negro, of a rather elegant city type, of a man already ascending the social scale; the message it carries is predominantly romantic, free, or comparatively free, from social worries, while its language has moved closer to that of the popular songwriter of the 1930's. The intensity and feeling in Jimmy Rushing's voice as he renders the song fashions a link between him and the traditional blues singers who preceded him in spite of various musical differences which exist between the two styles of approach, but the urban-type lyric he sings has only slender connexions with the past.

Over the years, Rushing has embodied all the exceptional qualities of Kansas City blues singing in his output, and *Sent For You Yesterday* is just one of the many alliances between his voice and the instrumental patterns of the Count Basie band. In the early 1930's, more so even than the intrepid Joe Turner, he was the prime mover behind this particular style of singing and he has remained its outstanding exponent through to the present day.

An impressive figure, the very antithesis of the pale, aesthetic, professorial jazz interpreter who of late has proved to be the darling of the cultural hounds, Rushing's immensity of voice and intensity of feeling are well complemented by the vastness of his physique. His rotundity, and the appetite for food and drink which is continually maintaining it, out-distance even Count Basie, his long-time friend and musical associate, who by normal standards is no slim man. (Gary Wagner's photographic study in Leonard Feather's "Encyclopedia Of Jazz" of a pensive, heavy-eyed Rushing, a white napkin tucked beneath his ample jowls, about to consume a large portion of chicken, accompanied by the admiring glance of Count Basie, who is sitting close by him, is most apt.) If Basie is stout, then Rushing is enormous. His waistline must be double that of the normal man. And he has all the rumbustious spirit, the human warmth and the abundant

150

humour which invariably accompany such corpulence. Just as Lester Young's features and lethargy of manner appear to match the superficial softness of his tenor-saxophone tone and the retarded melodic phrases of his improvisation, so Rushing's bulk and energetic, often volatile nature well match his methods as a blues singer.

He was born in Oklahoma City on 26th August 1903, the son of a trumpet player. Encouraged by his father, and by his mother and brother, who were both singers in a professional capacity, to make a thorough study of music, Jimmy (who had picked up the rudiments of violin and piano playing by ear as a child) concentrated on music theory while he was a student at the Douglas High School in Oklahoma City. He passed out from school as a competent reading musician, and when he first began to sing professionally with bands his musical sense was already well developed.

In 1925 Jimmy travelled to California and made his public début as a singer, working in various "after-hours" clubs along the western coastal strip. Then in 1927, back in Oklahoma City, Jimmy ran into bassist Walter Page, leader of the Blue Devils, who made him an offer to sing with the group. The two men were not entirely unknown to each other prior to this juncture. Some time before he had decided to concentrate on vocal work, Jimmy had played piano—on a semi-professional basis—in a trio with the bassist and an affinity of musical ideas had sprung up between them. With the Blue Devils group Jimmy did quite a lot of travelling between Oklahoma City and Kansas City, and his singing soon came to be known in most of the Kaycee "after-hours" clubs.

When Walter Page's Blue Devils finally went bankrupt in Kansas City in 1929, Rushing was one of the men engaged by Bennie Moten to work with his reorganized big band, and he remained with this important Kaycee unit until the leader's death in 1935. About the time of the break-up of the Blue Devils group Jimmy collaborated with Walter Page for what appears to have been his début on record. In an earlier essay on Walter Page I lamented the fact that the highly esteemed Blue Devils never obtained a recording contract, thereby causing a source of important musical talent to be lost to later generations of jazz lovers. In actual fact, though, in 1929 Page did manage to get the more important members of his group, including Basie, "Hot Lips" Page, Dan Minor, Buster Smith and Jimmy Rushing, into a Kansas City recording studio to make just two sides for the Vocalion label. The titles of these items, issued under the name of Page and The Original Blue Devils, were *Squabblin'* and *Blue Devil Blues*, and Rushing was featured on the latter item. Needless to say, copies of this Vocalion record are now priceless.

Rushing joined Count Basie's little band at the Reno Club in 1935 and his singing quickly became an integral part of the musical policy which the pianist-leader was fashioning at this period. Basie, who believes that Jimmy Rushing has no equal among blues singers, has since attested that there were times in the early days of this band when but for the encouragement of the buoyant Jimmy he would have given up the ambition of ever making the grade as a leader in his own right. According to Basie, in those days the singer acted as his "right arm", sticking with him in spite of all the troubles which beset the band. As a performer he appeared to be tireless; often he would work all evening serenading the customers at the club where the band was performing, and then go and join groups of musicians in different late-night clubs to sing for kicks. Mary Lou Williams has said that even after all the musicians had tired themselves out at an informal jam session, Jimmy would still be in high spirits and anxious to continue the entertainment, and that frequently he would take over the piano from the exhausted pianist and accompany himself as he sang ballads, or else keep everyone laughing with an endless supply of spicy anecdotes.

Rushing remained with Count Basie until the old band's dissolution in 1950, and from 1936 onwards identified himself with the Count by means of a fine series of blues interpretations, many of them bearing lyrics of his own creation. On 9th October 1936, in Chicago, the singer recorded for Vocalion together with Count Basie and the Jones-Smith Inc. unit, taking choruses on *Evenin'* and *Boogie Woogie*. The latter title, while revealing the musicians combining the simple harmonic structure of the blues with a spirited swing in a musical style typical of Kansas City jazz, shows off Rushing in the rendition of a romantic urban blues lyric; his intensity of feeling is comparable with that of a great "classic" blues performer. The interpretation also set a precedent for many further Rushing recordings by having a trumpet obbligato to cushion his words—a device which Buck Clayton was to so ably exploit when the singer was recording with the enlarged Basie band in New York.

Between January 1937, when the Basie band proper commenced recording for American Decca, and the enforced break-up of the band in 1950, Rushing's strong, boiling, high-pitched voice became almost as well-known a feature of the band's musical policy on record as Lester Young's tenor-saxophone and the leader's own piano playing, so much so that it becomes difficult after continually replaying Basie's recordings not to regard Jimmy's rhythmic, musicianly phrases and melodic ingenuity as the output of one of the band's instrumental soloists. *Good Morning Blues*, a second *Boogie Woogie* and *Don't You Miss Your Baby?* (1937), the mean and sinister *Blues In The Dark* and *Sent For You Yesterday* (1938), *Evil Blues* and *How Long Blues* (1939), *Evenin'* (1940), *Goin' To Chicago* and *Take Me Back, Baby* (1941), *Jimmy's Blues* (1944) and *Goodbye Baby* (1946); these are perhaps the outstanding blues performances resulting from his associations as a recording artist with the band, and serve to define the revolutionary measures as well as the inherent musical qualities vested in his work. These blues themes became intensely personal expressions with Rushing; his recorded versions reveal that he really felt the implications of their words, and it is a significant fact that the majority of them have remained in his repertoire until the present day.

While working with the Count Basie band, Rushing was also called upon to interpret the show tunes and certain of the better popular songs of the day which periodically would be used to augment the band's catalogue of blues arrangements. This task he performed with marked success, singing with a softer, less intense voice but with a considerable amount of warmth and charm. He appeared able to inject a certain feeling and expressiveness into the most maudlin of Tin Pan Alley lyrics, and he learnt to reshape the melodic lines of the songs into new and interesting shapes just as he had done with his blues themes. The band's recordings of *Pennies From Heaven, Boo Hoo, Listen My Children And You Shall Hear, You Can Depend On Me, Do You Wanna Jump, Children?, Stop Beatin' Around The Mulberry Bush, London Bridge Is Falling Down* and the outstanding *I Want A Little Girl* contain vocal choruses by Jimmy which suitably illustrate his talent in this direction.

During *Listen My Children* his singing (which is still extremely rhythmic even though his voice sounds tender and intimate) appears startlingly similar in style to that of the late Fats Waller, and but for the differences in accompaniment the two singers might even be confused in the analysis of this vocal chorus. The record, though, is rather exceptional for Rushing, and the only one I know on which he approximates Fats' style. When comparing a number of Waller and Rushing vocal recordings of standard melodies it becomes fairly obvious that while Fats is a consistent, natural comic, who cannot be serious with any lyric, "Mr. Five-by-Five" is witty only on occasions, and even has a tendency to sound sentimental about these tunes.

Though the long association with Count Basie meant that Jimmy spent so much of his time touring, in the years that he was with the band he found time to appear on a number of recording sessions which were not motivated by the Count. In 1936 Benny Goodman, one of Basie's most enthusiastic supporters in the days when the Kansas City bandleader was struggling to achieve recognition, used the singer for a Victor session with his own widely acclaimed band. And in 1939, in Chicago, bandleader Bob Crosby persuaded Rushing to record the song *What Goes Up Must Come Down* with his band for American Decca—a title which only a month previously the vocalist had performed with Count Basie's band for the same label. One of his own songs, *Jimmy's Round The Clock Blues*, Jimmy recorded in the 1940's with the band of drummer Johnny Otis for the independent Excelsior label, while he broke new ground in 1944 by taking a part in the Olsen and Johnson film "Funzapoppin'".

After the break-up of Count Basie's band the singer formed his own septet, with which he toured for several months and later took up a residency at the Savoy Ballroom in New York City for almost two years (from the end of 1950 until 1952). With sympathetic support from this unit—and he was fortunate in having bassist Walter Page in it most of the time—Jimmy made it plain that despite the end of an era in jazz caused by the dissolution of the Basie band, he would continue as a performer to manifest the ideals of Kansas City jazz. And in June 1952, when the job at the Savoy came to an end and he gave up bandleading to concentrate on solo appearances, his style of singing remained unchanged.

Since 1952 Rushing has been widely acclaimed as a singing attraction, and has performed to capacity audiences in theatres, concert halls and ballrooms throughout the country, as well as making frequent radio broadcasts and appearing in a television series over a leading New York network. Facing up to the various scene shiftings in jazz, and without making any concessions to commercialism, he has managed to widen his public considerably and at the same time enhance his reputation even further with his musical contemporaries. In the mid-1950's, though separated from the Basie band, his performances have made it very obvious where his sympathies lie, and have confirmed that as an interpreter of the Kansas City style of blues singing he is a greater creative force than ever before. His more recent work is a logical extension of the singing style he shaped and so ably expressed with Basie.

Rushing's sustained greatness as an artist has been adequately defined in the mid-1950's by two long-playing albums issued by John Hammond's Vanguard label. The crowning achievement of the singer's lengthy and impressive career, these vital albums possess a profundity of feeling and a powerful expression the equal of his most inspired work in years gone by with the Basie band. Featuring enlargements of several blues and other songs long associated with Jimmy, plus several of his more recent creations, they have documented the qualities of the Kansas City blues singer with an accuracy comparable to that of Huddie Ledbetter's when in 1948 he recorded his last sessions for Fred Ramsey and the Folkways label and documented the art of early Negro folk singing.

The first of the Vanguard albums—the one which Count Basie personally selected as containing the greatest recordings of Rushing's career—is made up of items recorded at a session held in New York City on 1st December 1954. Entitled simply "Jimmy Rushing Sings The Blues" (not a strictly accurate description, for it contains one standard ballad), it features the singer with a small Basie-influenced unit consisting of pianist Sammy Price (an outstanding blues interpreter), Pat Jenkins (trumpet), Henderson Chambers (trombone), Ben Richardson (alto-saxophone and clarinet), Buddy Tate (tenor-saxophone), Walter Page (bass) and Jo Jones (drums). At the time of recording, Jenkins and Richardson were sidemen with Buddy Tate's small band, then playing at the Savoy Ballroom in New York City. Jenkins, a greatly underrated trumpet player, had previously been a prominent member of Al Cooper's Savoy Sultans and had recorded with this group as early as 1938.

Jimmy commences his first Vanguard set with a long and very

moving performance of Leroy Carr's *How Long Blues*, which he dedicates to the memory of his friend, the late "Hot Lips" Page. The dedication is most apt, for although superficially the lyric tells of a romantic interest the actual words carry the pain of loss, and hint at an irremediable departure: the singer enquires how long it is since the last evening train left, the train which would have taken him around the mountain to the home of the girl whose love for him he suspects is waning; he'd heard the train whistle blow, but when he'd reached the station the train itself was already out of sight. He laments that if only he could "holler like a mountain jack" he'd "walk round the mountain and call his baby back", but he despairs of ever seeing her again.

Sammy Price sets the prevailing mood for the occasion with a piano introduction that is sad and downcast, and thereafter remains an important component of the performance, creating a variation upon the blues theme between each stanza that Rushing sings. Rushing himself is considerably stirred emotionally by the song. Without divesting his voice of any of the strength it normally employs when functioning with the propulsive beat of a jazz group, he demonstrates that he can still render a slow, completely sad blues with all the feeling of a traditional singer of the musical form. He indicates his intense grief with a voice that at first expresses enquiry, then concern, then anger and accusation, and finally resignation, so that as he sings the closing line the ferocity leaves his voice and he is reduced almost to tears. Seldom has a blues singer been quite so overwhelming on record.

Boogie Woogie, the performance which has the unenviable task of following *How Long Blues* on the record, is a new version of the title Rushing recorded in 1936 with the Basie Quintet (Jones-Smith Inc.) for Vocalion, and resolves itself into an interpretation that is fast-moving and heated, with audible foot-tapping at the outset (possibly by Jimmy or Jo Jones) to urge the musicians on their way. After adopting the Buck Clayton role behind Rushing's tempestuous first chorus, jabbing short, tight riff phrases in between the bursts of vibrant song, Pat Jenkins sparks the proceedings even more with an aggressive, full-throttle trumpet solo and the men race towards a frantic climax. For *How You Want Your Lovin' Done*, however, a close-fitting mute is in Jenkins' horn as he sets the stage for another of the singer's more melancholy blues, his tone becoming slight and glassy as he blows the introductory phrases over Sammy Price's sombre piano chords. Price actually conceived the melody for this sorrowful little piece, accompanying an original lyric by Rushing, and as a musician he has a prominent say in the interpretation. Besides carving the sensitive supports to the singer's lines, inserting clusters of treble notes whenever a gap appears in this nostalgic tale of a hesitant, inexperienced lover, he effects a superb transitional chorus between the exposition and the reprise of the vocal, punctuating with fragile block chords a series of walking-bass figures stated by Walter Page.

The second half of the album contains three performances which are remakes of well-known items from Rushing's repertoire (*Goin' To Chicago, I Want A Little Girl* and *Sent For You Yesterday*), plus a theme which the singer composed specially for the session in collaboration with Sammy Price entitled *Leave Me*.

Goin' To Chicago reveals the rhythm section ingeniously varying their tempo, dramatically offsetting Rushing's interpretation by dragging the rhythm pattern in relaxed manner behind his voice and then producing short, explosive bursts of a more aggressive rhythm in collaboration with riff figures from the ensemble as punctuations between stanzas of the song. Urged on by these occasional leaping figures the singer shouts out his complaints in stentorian manner against the "so mean and evil" woman who has got her clutches on his "brand new money". As always he makes the lyric entirely personal, even concluding with the lines:

> *If anybody asks you, who was it sang this song,*
> *Anybody asks you, who was it sang this song,*
> *Tell them little Jimmy Rushing, he's been here and gone.*

I Want A Little Girl finds the singer in a wistful mood as he makes a further plea for a woman who will give him just the simple things in life. Perhaps more so than any other popular ballad he has ever rendered since first starting out as a recording artist with Basie, he has made this delicate little theme his own. Here, as on his earlier version with Basie, he injects considerable warmth and charm into his words, while his singing is this time complemented by an exceedingly moving trombone chorus by Henderson Chambers. The new *Sent For You Yesterday* is as much the supporting group's meat as Rushing's. More foot-tapping ushers in a freely-improvised ensemble statement, with Ben Richardson's clarinet weaving about the other instruments after the pattern of a New Orleans front line; and then when the theme is passed over to the soloists, Buddy Tate and Henderson Chambers are given equal prominence with Rushing. The singer gives his rendition of the lyric an unusual twist by augmenting the original words with a section from the *Evil Blues* lyric which he had recorded with Basie many years before.

During *Leave Me* he castigates both his woman and himself for their joint mistakes, and one can imagine him with his fists clenched and the muscles of his face taut with agony as he cries out that he is "mean and evil and full of misery" and that his woman had better leave his house and get right away from him. Jenkins accompanies the greater part of the vocal with a trumpet obbligato and Buddy Tate plays a spirited transitional improvisation. Taken at an ultra-slow tempo, the performance once more allows the ensemble and the rhythm section to periodically unlease explosive accents between the lines of the lyric.

At the later Vanguard session, held in New York City on 16th August 1955, the personnel of the supporting group to Rushing underwent a reshuffle. Buddy Tate, Walter Page and Jo Jones remained from the previous group. Emmett Berry and Lawrence Brown replaced Jenkins and Chambers, Rudy Powell played the alto and clarinet parts and Freddie Greene was added to the rhythm section. Sammy Price vacated the piano stool to make way for his Kansas City contemporary, the ubiquitous Pete Johnson, who gave everyone at the session a fillip as he interspersed the Basie-like chordal struts of his ardent blues accompaniments with occasional spurts of boogie phrasing. At this session Jimmy Rushing produced new editions of *Good Morning Blues*, *Evenin'* and *Take Me Back, Baby*, all songs he had recorded earlier with Basie, plus a spirited adaptation of *Roll 'Em Pete*, the theme conceived in Kansas City by Pete Johnson and named after a jam session call of tenorman Ben Webster. Widening the scope of his material somewhat, he also included at the session versions of *Every Day* (having a tilt at Basie's contemporary band singer, Joe Williams) and a wonderfully feeling interpretation of Ma Rainey's blues song, *See See Rider*.

It is to be hoped that Rushing's association with Vanguard will yield further albums of a musical calibre similar to these two. Having obtained an option on the outstanding blues singer's services at a time when his creative powers are at their most significant, John Hammond has done well to preserve for posterity collections of Rushing's work, giving him the benefits of high-fidelity recording equipment and of spacious long-playing issues, and it behoves him to continue with the project.

Hammond has set a high standard with his Vanguard recordings and has been one of the men largely responsible for awakening the public to a new interest in Kansas City jazz, but his harnessing of Jimmy Rushing's singular inspiration has been the most artistically stimulating event of his recording programme on Vanguard. Jimmy's vital expression and creativeness cause these albums to be rated amongst the best made by any blues singers at any period for any recording company.

CHAPTER V

ADDITIONAL BIOGRAPHIES OF MUSICIANS OF THE OLD BASIE BAND

ORAN "HOT LIPS" PAGE
(*Trumpet and Singer*)

ONE OF THE greatest trumpet players of the Kansas City jazz scene, "Lips" Page was strongly connected with the Basie band in its embryo stages. When Basie first took a group into the Reno Club in Kansas City, Page would frequently sit in with the trumpet section or occasionally sing a blues in his gravel-throated style. Also he acted as an unofficial Master of Ceremonies for the band at the club. He ceased to work regularly with the band after it left Kaycee to go on tour and to New York.

Born in Dallas, Texas, on 27th January 1908, "Lips" began playing trumpet in a brass band at the age of eleven. (Budd Johnson was in the same band.) He was attracted to Kansas City in the late 1920's and speedily adapted his musical approach to the colourful jam sessions there. Describing the Kaycee scene in a story for the "Melody Maker", Mary Lou Williams has said: "Hot Lips was the life of many a Kaycee jam session. After a soloist had blown nine or ten choruses 'Lips' would start a riff in the background which the other horns picked up. Not many arrangers could improve on 'Lips' when it came to backing up a soloist." "Lips" played with Walter Page's Blue Devils from 1927 to 1929. When Basie, Page and the rest of the Blue Devils joined Bennie Moten's Orchestra in 1930 "Lips" teamed up with them and remained with the band until Moten's death in 1935. (He played on the majority of Bennie's Victor recordings.) After that he played briefly with Basie at the Reno as well as freelancing with the band over the local radio network. By the time Basie took his band east, "Lips" was already a soloist of considerable standing in jazz. He travelled east at the same time to seek his fortunes as a freelance, and his solo work deeply impressed the school of musicians in New York. From 1936 to 1941 he had his

Benny Goodman with Count Basie in the late 1930's

Count Basie, Artie Shaw and Duke Ellington at The Bandbox in New York

Harry Edison

Freddie Greene

[photo Parent

Joe Sullivan, Dicky Wells, George Wettling and Walter Page

Count Basie and Jimmy Rushing at Basie's twentieth anniversary dinner

[photo Parent

Lester
Young

Joe
Williams

[photo
Malmqvist

Thad Jones and Joe Newman

[photo Malmqvist

Frank Wess and Frank Foster

[photo Henniger

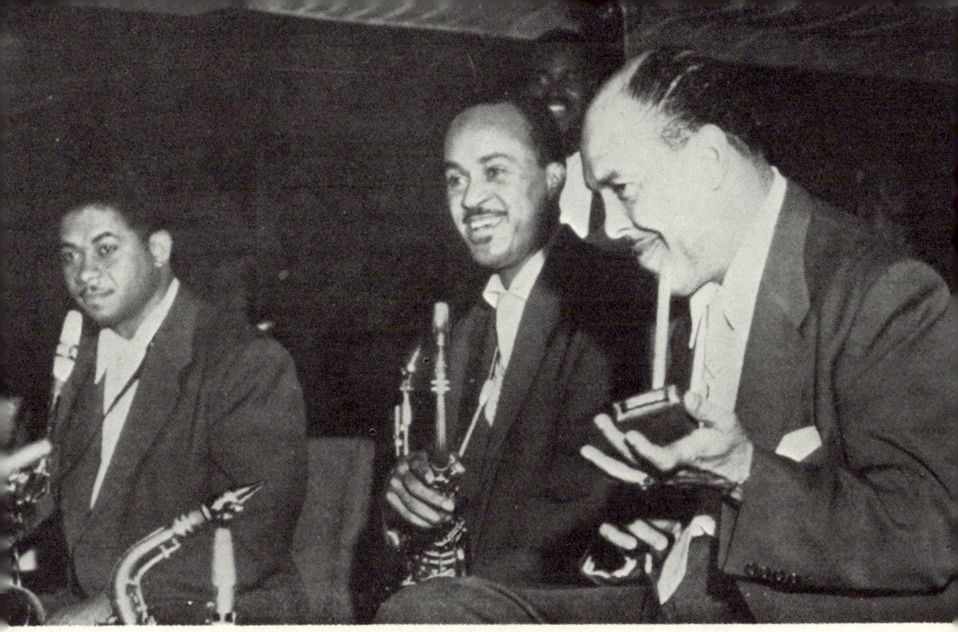

[*photo Henniger*

Frank Wess, Ernie Wilkins and Marshall Royal

Charlie Fowlkes and Henry Coker

[*photo Popsie*

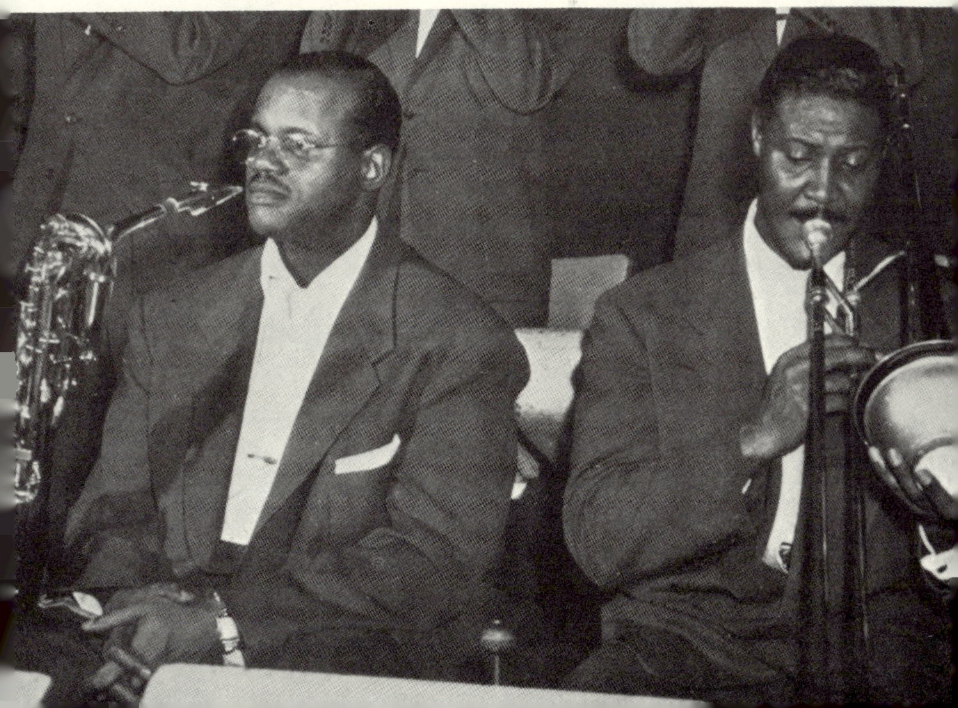

The saxophone section: (l. to r.) Frank Wess, Ernie Wilkins, Marshall Royal, Frank Foster and Charlie Foulkes. Behind: Gus Johnson (drums) and Freddie Greene (guitar)

[photo Popsie

own band in the east, and afterwards he played for a few months as featured soloist and singer with the then great Artie Shaw band. From then, until his tragic death in 1954, "Lips" remained a freelance around New York. In the last years of his life he paid several trips to Europe to play summer seasons at the French and Belgian resorts.

The chief overall influence upon Page's trumpet playing (and also upon his singing) was without doubt Louis Armstrong. His full, powerful tone and economic, yet beautifully-constructed melodic phrases showed that quite clearly. Contact with the Kansas City jam sessions introduced riffs, and so on, into his improvisation. It is unfortunate that he did not record with the real Basie band; the outcome of such sessions would have indeed been interesting. Some of his best recordings were made with Choo Berry for Commodore, and with Moten for Victor. Under the alias of "Pappa Snow White" he played with Mezzrow and Sammy Price on King Jazz, being featured to good effect on *House Party* and *Blood On The Moon*. Two titles—*South* and *Lafayette* —were issued under his name in the Decca "Kansas City Jazz" album. The last records he ever made (for Brunswick on a "Jazz-time U.S.A." session with the Marian McPartland Trio) were sadly below the standard of his other work.

JOE KEYES

(*Trumpet*)

Joe Keyes, who in the early 1930's was a well-known member of the Kansas City jazz scene, and who later came to New York with the first Count Basie band, died penniless in 1950, thought to be the victim of a brutal assault.

It seemed that he was reported missing from his New York lodgings on 2nd November 1950. Four days later his body was found in the Harlem River. At the enquiry the police stated that the body showed signs of having been violently assaulted, possibly the result of an armed robbery. It was estimated that he was aged 43 at the time of death.

As a younger man, connected with the Kaycee scene, Keyes was highly regarded as a trumpet player. Jo Jones has said that he was one of the real thinkers among the musicians there. He was one of the regular members of the Bennie Moten brass section, and played on the majority of Moten's Victor recordings made between 1929 and 1932. He also worked with "Lips" Page for a time, and he was a member of the original Basie band that arrived in New York in 1936 and sat in at the band's first recording date for American Decca.

Leaving Basie in 1937, Keyes freelanced around New York City, and, according to his friends, started to go downhill as a person. In 1940 he was the only trumpeter present at a recording session organized by guitarist Eddie Durham for Decca. (Buster Smith, the altoist so much admired by Charlie Parker, also played on those sides.)

In 1941 Keyes worked with Fats Waller's group for some months, but shortly afterwards went into decline, and had not played his trumpet for several years when he died.

Shad Collins

(*Trumpet*)

Shad was not a product of the Kansas City jam sessions; most of his early playing experience was built up in or around New York. He joined the Basie band in January 1939 and stayed until early in 1940, when he was replaced by the technically-gifted and brilliant high-lead man, Al Killian. Not perhaps given sufficient credit today for his abilities, Shad was one of the more distinctive stylists to pass through the band's ranks. His sharp, fiery tone and short, stabbing, staccato phrases make his solo sound highly personal. When he uses a mute to play ballads he achieves a most delicate result.

Born on 27th June 1910 in Elizabeth, New Jersey, Shad actually is the son of a clergyman. He grew up in Lockport, New York, and, after studying trumpet, got his first important job with a band led by Charlie Dixon. In the 1930's, upon reaching maturity as a jazz stylist, he played with the bands of Chick Webb, Benny Carter and Teddy Hill. With the latter he toured Europe in 1937, and in Paris recorded some of his best solos for the French Swing label with trombonist Dicky Wells; he can be heard to advantage on numbers like *I Got Rhythm*, *Between The Devil And The Deep Blue Sea* and *Bugle Call Rag*. After returning

162

to the United States, in 1939 he joined Basie; this was some time after Dicky Wells went into the Basie band. Perhaps the best recorded example of his solo playing with Basie is to be heard with the small-group feature, *You Can Depend On Me*, in the company of just Lester Young, Basie and the rhythm section. After leaving the Count he worked briefly with Lester Young at Kelly's Stable in New York, and then intermittently in the 1940's with Cab Calloway's Orchestra. He recorded with King Cole in 1942.

Unfortunately, in the 1950's his talents have been buried in various rhythm-and-blues units, though John Hammond has used him for his Vanguard recordings and it is to be hoped that this latter work will revive the interest of collectors in his previous recordings. On Vanguard he is particularly well featured on two Vic Dickenson LP.s in the company of Vic, Ruby Braff, Sir Charles Thompson and Edmond Hall. One number from these sessions, *Everybody Loves My Baby*, finds Shad playing a long trumpet duet with Ruby Braff.

AL KILLIAN

(*Trumpet*)

Killian, one of the finest lead trumpeters and high-note men in jazz, and a gifted soloist when translating the ideals and theories of modern jazz, played with Basie from 1940 until 1944. During this period he developed enormously through contact with Ed Lewis, Basie's lead trumpet, and with the solo style of Harry Edison.

Born on 15th October 1916 at Birmingham, Alabama, Killian first came to the attention of jazz musicians when working with Slim Gaillard's combo. during 1939. Before joining up with Basie in 1940 he also spent a few months with the bands of Don Redman and Claude Hopkins. By the time he was through with the Count's band he was sufficiently experienced and gifted technically to hold down a job with any important jazz group. He could lead a brass section with confidence, spurt up into the highest octave of his instrument and reach all the high notes, and play dynamic, driving improvised choruses in the newly-developing modern jazz idiom. From Basie he moved into the Lionel Hampton Orchestra, then over to Charlie Barnet for almost two years (1945–1946). Then, after touring for a time with Norman Granz' "Jazz At The Philharmonic" unit, he joined Duke Ellington's Orchestra in December 1947. He remained with the Duke until shortly before his death in 1950. When the Ellington band toured Europe in 1950, Al expressed his dislike of being "typed" as a high-note man. However, before the tour commenced, he had recorded an important solo with the band during the *Third Dance* of Duke's *Liberian Suite*, and on the tour Ellington featured one of the trumpeter's own compositions with the band, *Y'Oughta*. He also recorded in Europe: in Sweden he cut four sides for the Baronet label with tenorman Alva McCain and the Ellington rhythm section; in Paris he recorded *Chumpa Leezy* and *Big Al*, features for the five Ellington trumpeters, supported only by piano, bass and drums.

On 5th September 1950 Al met a tragic end, shot to death in his Los Angeles home by his landlord, a paroled murderer, who suddenly ran berserk. His death came as a severe loss to jazz. When Marty Paich came to England in 1956, he mentioned Killian to me, saying: "The American lead trumpeters still speak of Al with awe in their voices."

EMMETT BERRY

(*Trumpet*)

Emmett Berry, one of the finest trumpet players of the school logically descended from the style of Harry Edison, spent five years in the Basie band, joining in 1945 and remaining through to the 1950 dissolution. During these years he shared most of the solo trumpet parts with Edison.

Berry was born in Macon, Georgia, on 23rd July 1916, but actually grew up and started playing in Cleveland. His name first came to the attention of musicians and critics when he played for three years with the various bands led in the late 1930's by Fletcher Henderson and his brother Horace. Later he played with Teddy Wilson (from 1941 to 1942), for nine months with Raymond Scott's pseudo-jazz unit at CBS, with Lionel Hampton and Benny Carter (both in 1943), with John Kirby (1944), and then briefly in 1945 with Eddie Heywood before going into the Count Basie brass section. Already an adherent to the extrovert adventurous style of Harry Edison, Emmett quickly attained maturity with Basie. Playing with a broad, yet fiery tone, a gushing, forceful type of phrase construction and a continual swing, he became at once one of the most powerful, confident and emotional trumpeters of middle-period jazz. He has kept this style through to the present day. Capable as a technician, Emmett is well equipped to play not only extended solos but also the most demanding lead and section parts. Whether playing open or using a mute he is always a gifted improviser, with a flow of ideas never ridden with repetition.

He was present on practically all the orchestral sides Basie made during the late 1940's, as well as the small group sides, *My Buddy*, *Sugar*, *Basie's Basement*, etc., which were recorded under the leader's name for Victor in 1947.

After the 1950 break-up, Emmett worked for about a year with the small unit which Jimmy Rushing took around for his concert and club dates. He then played with Johnny Hodges' fine little band from 1951 to 1954, recording some of his finest work for Clef with solos like *In A Mellow Tone*, *Good Queen Bess*, *Don't Get Around Much Anymore* and—his own favourite—*Jappa*. During this period he also recorded several pieces with the Hodges band under Al Sears' name for King; among these is one superb solo, *Berry Well*, which reveals his glassy-edged tone and immense power of attack to good effect. Since leaving Hodges he has freelanced around New York with Earl Hines, Cootie Williams and others, and recorded albums for Vanguard with Coleman Hawkins, Jo Jones and others. (Some of his best muted work is to be found in the "Jo Jones Special" album on Vanguard.)

He came to Europe in 1956 with a small group led by pianist Sammy Price, and in Paris recorded LP.s for Vogue and Ducretet-Thomson with tenor-saxophone player Lucky Thompson. At the Ducretet-Thomson session he recorded his own theme, *Blues For Frank*.

JIMMY NOTTINGHAM

(*Trumpet*)

Information is scarce on the subject of Jimmy Nottingham's predecessor Ed Lewis, despite the fact that he worked as Basie's lead trumpet for close on twenty years. We know that he worked for Moten for a number of years, and that after the death of Bennie he moved into the early Basie band, but little is known about the groups he worked with prior to his appearance with the Moten band. He played a fierce, aggressive lead trumpet with the Count right through until 1948, rarely taking solos (one exception to this being his support to Jimmy Rushing on *Evil Blues*) and seldom taking time off to play sessions with smaller jazz groups, though he did record some sides for Savoy in 1945 with altoist Pete Brown. During these years with Basie he led the band's brass with strength and precision, but since then has dropped out of the music scene. Recently he has been working as a taxi-driver in New York City.

In 1948, when Ed Lewis left Basie, he was replaced as lead trumpet by a young trumpeter from the Lucky Millinder band, Jimmy Nottingham, a musician who proved his worth with the Count and who has more recently been making a name for himself as an important modern jazz soloist.

Nottingham was born in Brooklyn on 15th December 1925 and picked up his knowledge of music theory from various local teachers. In 1939, in the company of the fine jazz pianist Duke Jordan, he worked with Steve Pulliam's Manhattan Sextet, a group which won the prize for the best amateur combo. in the New York based World Fair of 1939. Later he gigged around Brooklyn with Max Roach and Cecil Payne before serving with the U.S. Navy from 1944 to 1945 and working in a services band led by Willie Smith. Upon release he played lead trumpet with Lionel Hampton (1945–1947), then with Charlie Barnet, Lucky Millinder and, in 1948, Count Basie. Remaining with the Count until the old band was dissolved in 1950, Jimmy proved himself an adept section lead, capable of hitting the very high notes strongly and of drawing the section with him through the more difficult scores.

Since leaving Basie he has held a variety of jobs: with Lucky Millinder again for several months, with Herbie Fields for a year, with Perez Prado and a series of Latin bands, in the pit band for the Hazel Flagg show, on the staff of CBS in 1954, and since then freelancing with TV and radio shows in New York City. He has also been appearing regularly in the New York jazz clubs and recording for the east coast jazz labels. As an improvising soloist he combines a fine all-round technique and a thorough understanding of modern jazz phrasing with an extrovert, dynamic style of attack and a sharp, brassy tone which reminds one somewhat of Charlie Shavers' playing. He can be heard as a soloist on Lionel Hampton's Decca LP. "Hamp's Boogie-Woogie", on two Clef LP. albums with Charlie Barnet and on Sonny Stitt's first Roost 12-inch LP. On the latter LP. he plays a very fine solo during Quincy Jones' arrangement of *Sonny's Bunny*.

CLARK TERRY

(*Trumpet*)

Clark's trumpet playing was featured in the later stages of the old Basie band's existence, his style being used as a foil to the solo work of Harry Edison. After the 1950 break-up he stayed on with Basie to work in the septet (1950–1951).

A native of St. Louis, where he was born on 14th December 1920, Clark had his first musical experience when playing in a local drum and bugle band at the age of fifteen. At high school he studied valve-trombone. From 1942 to 1945, while with the U.S. Navy at the Great Lakes base in Chicago, he really began to use the trumpet to good effect, playing jam sessions in an all-star local unit which also included Willie Smith and Ernie Wilkins. Upon release he decided to work full time as a musician, and he played briefly with Lionel Hampton, and then for a year and a half with George Hudson in St. Louis. (Ernie Wilkins was also to play with this same unit.) After this, Terry's career took him through a variety of bands: ten months with Charlie Barnet on the west coast, briefer periods with Eddie Vinson, Charlie Ventura and again with George Hudson. He joined Basie in 1948.

Originally Clark's trumpet style was influenced by Charlie Shavers, with a sharp, aggressive, brassy tone, a volatile attack and the tendency towards blowing flowery cascades of notes. Later influences upon him were the half-valve effects of Rex Stewart and the intricate phrase constructions and unusual tempo variations of Dizzy Gillespie. Upon joining Basie, however, his solo work came up against stiff opposition in a trumpet section which already included Harry Edison, Emmett Berry and Jimmy Nottingham; he began to reach maturity, moulding into his style

167

the elements already mentioned but displaying also his own flow of ideas, gaining a definite personality with his work. He was featured more with Basie towards the end—the band's arrangement of *Katy* contains an example of his trumpet work. While with the Basie Septet from 1950 to 1951 he played on all the unit's Columbia recordings, and he was in the trumpet section of the big band which the Count formed in the spring of 1951 but which failed to achieve success. Since November 1951 Clark has been with the band of Basie's friend and rival Duke Ellington, and he has recorded some of his best solos with the group. Certainly Terry is one of the finest all-round trumpeters now playing jazz, a phenomenal technician and an inventive improviser.

EDDIE DURHAM
(*Trombone, guitar and arranger*)

One of the important musicians connected with the formative years of the Basie band, Eddie Durham was also one of the best-known figures of the Kansas City jazz scene in the early 1930's, and later in the same decade was to assist several important large jazz groups.

He was born on 19th August 1906 in San Marcos, Texas. When Basie first arrived in Kansas City he found that Durham was already respected there by the other musicians. Apparently he was one of the few men who actually visualized arranging the style of music played at the Kaycee jam sessions to the proportions of a large group with scored section parts and unison voicings; he attempted to stabilize many of the ideas he heard at the jam sessions on to manuscript, and was practically the first to achieve success. From 1929 Eddie had played on and off for several years with Bennie Moten's Orchestra, and he arranged for several of the band's Victor recordings. He also played briefly with Willie Bryant, and then from 1935 to 1937 he worked regularly with Jimmy Lunceford's Orchestra.

Durham was far-sighted as an instrumentalist as well as an arranger; he was one of the first musicians ever to use the amplified guitar in jazz, pointing to a style which was later to blossom into maturity under the gifted fingers of Charlie Christian. He played guitar and trombone with Lunceford, and is credited with a long

168

list of arrangements for the band, including: *Bird of Paradise, Rhapsody Junior, Oh Boy, Hittin' The Bottle, Avalon, Harlem Shout, Running A Temperature, Count Me Out, Pidgeon Walk, Lunceford Special* and *Blues In The Groove.*

He played with Count Basie as a regular member of the trombone section from 1937 to 1938, and orchestrated several themes for the band, amongst them *Good Morning Blues, Out Of The Window, Topsy, Time Out* and *Swingin' The Blues.* After leaving Basie, Durham wrote several arrangements for the Glenn Miller Orchestra and led a number of groups under his own name. For a time in the 1940's he was musical director for The Sweethearts In Rhythm.

To my mind the best things to come from Durham's association with Basie, however, even before his scores for the full band, were the eight sides he recorded for the Commodore label in New York in 1938: *Laughing At Life, Good Morning Blues, I Know That You Know, Way Down Yonder In New Orleans, Countless Blues, Them There Eyes, I Want A Little Girl* and *Pagin' The Devil.* Recorded under the titles of the Kansas City Five and the Kansas City Six, these are some of the most artistic and inspired small group jazz ever recorded by sidemen from the Basie band. No piano was used on the sessions. Durham played trombone and took solos on electric guitar, Buck Clayton played delicate and moving trumpet, and Lester Young played some of his best work ever on both tenor-saxophone and clarinet. His clarinet work has certainly never been more beautifully portrayed than with these sides. Green, Page and Jones supplied the main rhythm for the group.

DAN MINOR

(*Trombone*)

One of the musicians who played in Basie's first regular band, trombonist Dan Minor was born in Kansas City in 1907. One of the members of the earliest Kaycee jazz school, he was a vital part of the city's local jam session music during the formative years of the late 1920's and early 1930's. In 1929 he became a regular member of the Bennie Moten Orchestra, along with Basie, Ben Webster, "Lips" Page, Eddie Durham, Jack Washington and Walter Page, and he remained with the band until

169

Moten's death, recording on all its Victor sessions in the early 1930's.

After Moten's death he worked for some months with Andy Kirk's band, but soon moved into the band which Count Basie organized to make its first tour from Kansas City to New York. He remained with the Count until the middle of 1941, playing on all the band's Decca and Okeh recording sessions up to that date, and improvising tough, growling, hard-swinging solos on *Gone With What Wind*, *You Can't Run Around* and other titles.

Minor played for some time in 1942 with Buddy Johnson's band, then gradually dropped from the limelight as a jazz musician. In recent years he has had a factory job in New York, and has been playing for two or three gigs each week with a calypso band.

BENNY MORTON
(*Trombone*)

Morton, while less important to the musical style of the Basie band as a trombone soloist than, say, Dicky Wells, Vic Dickenson or, latterly, Henry Coker, nevertheless brought an extremely individual voice to bear with the band during its early years in New York and created several effective solos on record with it.

Born in New York City on 31st January 1907, Morton became active as a jazz soloist from about 1924 when he was first heard playing with the band of Billy Fowler. In the late 1920's and early 1930's he worked with Fletcher Henderson, and then from 1932 to 1935 with Don Redman's band. He joined Count Basie in September 1937 and remained with the band until December 1939, within that time recording several fine solos with it, of which perhaps the best known is *Out Of The Window*. Employing a full, round tone and an intense, rhythmic method of phrasing, as well as a forceful, direct attack, his trombone work proved well suited to the style of the Basie band.

Upon leaving Basie, Benny Morton joined the sextet of pianist Joe Sullivan at Café Society in New York, and he remained on and off at this jazz club for several years, working with a variety of groups, including Teddy Wilson's, Edmond Hall's, Red Allen's, and, in 1946, his own. In 1940 he recorded with Red Allen for American Decca two features which are now well known to jazz collectors, *Canal Street Blues* and *Down in Jungle Town*. In 1944, given a recording date of his own by Keynote, he caused a sensation by organizing a unit which consisted of a trombone choir and a rhythm section, an instrumental combination which was thought extremely revolutionary in those days. (The three trombonists who worked with him on this project were Bill Harris, Vic Dickenson and Claude Jones.)

Since 1946 Benny has worked mainly with a series of pit bands for New York shows, including *Memphis Bound, St. Louis Woman, Lend An Ear, Regina* and *Guys And Dolls*, and he has played around New York City with a number of small jazz units.

In the 1950's he has recorded with trumpeter Charlie Shavers for Bethlehem, and also for John Hammond's Vanguard label with pick-up units led by Sir Charles Thompson and Buck Clayton.

Vic Dickenson

(*Trombone*)

When discussing the trombonists who worked with the Count Basie band in the 1940's it is perhaps only natural that most of the talk revolves about the great Dicky Wells. Yet there were a number of other trombone players—including Vic Dickenson, who worked with the band from 1940 to 1941—who if they were not liberally featured on records with Basie still possessed very personal and impressive solo styles.

It has only been within the last two or three years that Dickenson's talents as a jazz soloist have been recognized by a wider public, yet he is certainly one of the most singular slide trombonists to pass through Basie's ranks. More recently the Count was heard to describe his playing as "the greatest". I include him in this section of sidemen because his style (at last given a free rein by John Hammond's Vanguard recordings) reveals him to belong very definitely to the same musical atmosphere as Basie. He was not given as many solos as he might have had with Basie if the great Wells had not been in the same section, but his many later recordings as a freelance soloist place his style well in keeping with Basie and middle period jazz. When not typed to play a dull Dixieland trombone style, Vic's ideals have usually taken him into the same company as the Basie sidemen.

Born in Xenio, Ohio, on 6th August 1906, Vic in the early part of his musical career actually played with Bennie Moten. However, it was when he moved into the Claude Hopkins band (to play from 1936 to 1939) that Vic caused a stir amongst musicians with his style. He joined Basie as a replacement for Benny Morton. After well over a year in the band he left to work in turn with "Lips" Page, Sidney Bechet, Frankie Newton, and then in California with Coleman Hawkins. A long illness interrupted his career on the west coast, and afterwards, when returning east, he suffered greatly in the hands of promoters who repeatedly cast him in the role of trombonist with various Dixieland groups, a setting quite out of keeping for his essentially swing-style solos.

Dickenson's style is intensely rhythmic, and the phrases which he creates are always emphatic, giving the impression that he is very definite in what he wishes to say. His mood of attack varies considerably. Perhaps on one record he will be heard playing with a hard, brassy tone, directing a series of slashing broadsides at the audience; he has a strong sense of humour and doesn't hesitate to use it when the occasion demands. His playing contains enormous strength, and there are few other trombonists in jazz able to create the same tension with a hard-swinging approach and an effective use of vibrato as Vic. On the other hand, if the record is a slow-tempo one, he can be warm and composed, playing phrases which are sensitive and very melodic.

Dickenson has made many records over the years, varying from appearances with middle-period jazz musicians like Lester Young and Coleman Hawkins to traditional-style sessions with Art Hodes and Pee Wee Russell. Yet his outstanding work I find is that contained in the series of records he made under his own leadership in the mid-1950's for John Hammond's Vanguard label. On titles such as *Russian Lullaby, Jeepers Creepers, Old Fashioned Love, Everybody Loves My Baby* and *Suspension Blues,* together with Edmond Hall, Sir Charles Thompson, Shad Collins, Ruby Braff, Jo Jones, Walter Page *et al*, Vic Dickenson's artistic greatness as a soloist has been fully captured.

JAY JAY JOHNSON
(*Trombone*)

Jay Jay, the most important trombone stylist of modern jazz, played with the Basie band for almost two years (1945–6), and during this stay many of the ideas which were later to give him an ascendancy over all the younger trombonists reached maturity. His solos with the band at this time reveal that his radical style was already well advanced in its development.

Jay Jay was born in Indianapolis on 22nd January 1924. He studied piano at the age of eleven, then took up the trombone at fourteen. His first professional experience was with Clarence Love (1941–2). He also played in 1942 with Snookum Russell's band, and then, from 1942 to 1945, he was with Benny Carter. It was actually with the Carter band that he first impressed his fellow musicians; he was the first musician to adopt the revolutionary theories of Parker and Gillespie on trombone, and his swift articulation and dazzling array of fresh and inventive ideas so overwhelmed the New York school that many people concluded quite wrongly that he was playing a valve instead of a slide trombone. With Basie he began to co-ordinate his newly-discovered technique and imagination into a definite style—a style now aspired to by almost every younger jazzman who owns a trombone. His solos on *The King* and *Rambo* with Basie fully demonstrate his nimble mind and agile technique.

Johnson's approach to jazz has never really belonged to the style of the Basie band. Rather I mention him here as one of the many interesting leaders of modern jazz who have passed through the band's ranks with a new style still partially in its embryo stages. Since leaving the group he has worked with a variety of groups, most of them pick-up units in New York. He toured with Illinois Jacquet (1947–9), and then briefly with the Herman and Gillespie big bands. In 1951 he toured the Far East with Oscar Pettiford's group. Then, due to the scarcity of freelance work in New York, he was forced to work in a factory for almost two years, playing, writing and studying in his spare time. This situation, however, has been fortunately rectified since August 1954, the date when he formed the successful quintet with fellow trombonist Kai Winding. With this group, due to the success of his recordings and his tours, Jay Jay has at last been awarded the credit which his innovation deserves.

Earl Warren

(*Alto-saxophone*)

Earl Warren occupied a position with the old Basie band roughly comparable to the role fulfilled by Marshall Royal with the new group, being deputy leader, and as a result responsible for much of the organization and rehearsing so necessary to the continued musical unity of a large jazz unit. On his shoulders were also heaped many of the worries of transport, accommodation, band discipline, and so on. In addition to this, Earl was leader of the reed section, a task which he never failed to perform conscientiously; credit must be given to him for the brilliant unison reed voicings which so distinguished the recordings by the old band.

Earl was born in Springfield, Ohio, on 1st July 1914. He had his own unit in Springfield when he first commenced to play professionally, and then for several years in the mid-1930's he worked with Marion Sears in Cleveland. (Buster Harding also worked with Sears in the 1930's.) It was in 1936, however, when leading his own large band in Cincinnati, that he first came to Basie's attention. The pianist made him an offer and he took the post of lead alto with the band in the spring of 1937. After joining, his responsibilities were gradually enlarged from just a section leader to deputy bandleader, and his work as deputy relieved the Count considerably, allowing him to concentrate more upon public relations, and so on. Occasionally Warren also sang with the band, and he may be heard as a vocalist on such records as *Our Love Was Meant To Be, Let Me Dream, You Betcha My Life* and *Fancy Meeting You*. He played with the band until 1945, when he left to lead briefly his own small group in Cincinnati and New York. He returned to the band, however, late in 1948 to play for a few months, and then again from the autumn of 1949 to early 1950. Since 1950 he has worked on several projects: as manager for Johnny Otis, as the director of orchestras at the Apollo Theatre in New York and the Howard Theatre in Washington, and in 1954 and 1955 as director of the musical show supporting pianist Eddie Heywood.

Apart from his obvious head for business and managing matters, Warren is a brilliant musician, a fine reading man and section leader, and also a capable soloist. His alto playing is identified by its smooth, pure tone, simple, melodic ideas and strong rhythmic sense. Some of his best solos with Basie are to be found with the recordings of *Out Of The Window*, *9.20 Special*, *Miss Thing*, *Pound Cake* and *Take Me Back, Baby*. Yet to play over almost any one of the band's recordings made between 1937 and 1945 is to hear an example of the remarkable unity he injected into the reed section which he controlled so confidently. An example of his more recent work is to be heard with one of John Hammond's Vanguard albums; issued under Sir Charles Thompson's name, this session finds Warren in the company of Coleman Hawkins and Benny Morton.

A final point about Warren's connection with the Basie band concerns the many themes which he contributed to the Count's repertoire. Though not an arranger, Warren conceived quite a number of themes, some just typical blues riffs, but several consisting of strong, melodic material based on the thirty-two-bar popular song structure. Some of his better-known compositions for the band have been *9.20 Special*, *Rocking The Blues*, *Wiggle-Woogie* and *Tom Thumb*. The majority of Warren's themes were orchestrated by Buster Harding for use by the band.

TAB SMITH

(*Alto-saxophone*)

Tab played with Basie's band of the early 1940's, and even at this period displayed broad hints of the sweeping, driving phrases and overforceful tone which were later to aid him as a leading exponent of rhythm-and-blues music. His gutty style of attack when improvising at the faster tempos, and his excessive lushness as an interpreter of ballads formed a strict contrast to the more dignified playing of his companion altoist with Basie, the sleek-toned and delicately-phrasing Earl Warren. Warren's playing had much in common at this time with the elegant Benny Carter, while Smith's was nearer to the jump style of Pete Brown.

175

Tab, who was born at Kingston, North Carolina, in 1909, started playing a C-melody saxophone at the age of thirteen; later he added the alto and tenor-saxophones to his collection. His first job was with the Carolina Stompers in 1929 and this led to further work with Fate Marable, Dewey Jackson and Eddie Johnson. Jazz musicians began to hear him much more prominently after 1935, however, when he joined Lucky Millinder's band. It was from this band that he joined Basie in 1940, following in the footsteps of Harry Edison, who had also been with Millinder in the late 1930's before he teamed up with the Count. After his stint with Basie, Tab returned to Lucky Millinder for just over a year, and then branched out with his own group. In the late 1940's and early 1950's he has been very successful playing rhythm-and-blues music, utilizing his ability to force a rasping tone and generate a driving beat to good effect.

Of his various recordings, other than his out-and-out rhythm-and-blues numbers, perhaps the best examples of his jazz solo style will be found with sides like *Rosetta* and *Stardust*, which he made with Charlie Shavers and Earl Hines in 1944 for Mercury. and a number of sides recorded in 1939 for the Vocalion and Commodore labels (*Long Gone Blues*, *Strange Fruit*, *Some Other Spring*, *Them There Eyes* and *Swing, Brother, Swing*) in support of singer Billie Holiday. In more recent times he has recorded sessions for the King and United labels.

BUDDY TATE

(*Tenor-saxophone*)

Buddy Tate was yet another of the musicians playing in Kansas City during the important formative years of its jazz. He worked occasionally with Basie's first small group in Kaycee, but didn't join up with the band as a regular member until 1939 when he took over from the already ailing Herschel Evans. Basie's opinion of him always remained high. "We were a little rough when we made a change after Herschel, but Buddy Tate caught on in a hurry and fit right in," the leader once remarked.

Buddy was born on 22nd February 1915 and was launched professionally as a musician with Troy Floyd in San Antonio in 1931. He worked with Torrence Holder (1930–3) and with

Andy Kirk (1933-4) before joining Basie's first experimental unit in Kansas City. Afterwards he went to work with Nat Towles. In 1939, however, when Basie was searching for a replacement for Herschel Evans he remembered Buddy from the earlier days and sent for him. Buddy stayed with the band for ten years, practically through to the 1950 break-up. After that he worked with Lucky Millinder and "Hot Lips" Page, but latterly he has been leading his own band, playing at the Celebrity Club and the Savoy Ballroom in New.York City, a group which still adheres to the ideals of middle-period jazz.

In style Buddy is a logical descendant from the Coleman Hawkins school of tenor playing, possessed of a full, rich tone, a weaving, rhapsodic style of phrasing and a strong, attacking sense of rhythm. He was an ideal deputy for Herschel and for several years acted as a perfect foil for Lester Young's lighter tone and radical phrasing. Right through until he left the band he upheld Herschel's style, though he is by no means a reactionary in his views and his favourite tenormen include Lester and Stan Getz. Of his own numerous features with Basie his favourite solos are *Rock-a-bye Basie* and *Super Chief*. He has recorded with other mainstream stylists such as Roy Eldridge and Mel Powell. Of late, however, he has been recording once more with sidemen from the Basie Band. His best LP.s so far to my mind are both on Vanguard, the first with Buck Clayton and Ruby Braff, containing fine solos by him on *Kandee* and *I Can't Get Started*, the other a Jimmy Rushing album for which the great blues singer used not only Buddy but also two members from the tenorman's own jumping little band, trumpeter Pat Jenkins and altoist Ben Richardson. He is also featured on the Buck Clayton "Jumpin' At The Woodside" LP. on Columbia; he plays one chorus during *Rock-a-bye Basie*, and two choruses, plus a chase series of four and eight-bar alternations with Coleman Hawkins during *Broadway*.

DON BYAS

(*Tenor-saxophone*)

Though Basie at all times appears to possess a sixth sense when estimating whether or not a man will fit in with the band's musical style, he has registered over the years a particular success with tenor-saxophone players. The band was never without a brace of outstanding tenor-soloists in the 1940's despite inevitable personnel changes; as one left, so the leader picked up another as if by magic, and usually succeeded in improving the new man's reputation by featuring him with the band. Don Byas played with Basie in 1941, joining shortly after Lester Young had left the band to lead his own small group, and though of a different style he successfully breached the gap in the band's ranks for a year before he too passed on. He recorded several outstanding solos with Basie.

Born in Muskogee, Oklahoma, on 21st October 1912, Don was the son of a clarinettist, and while at college led his own small jazz group. Prior to joining the Basie group in 1941 he had played in turn with Eddie Barefield, Don Redman, Lucky Millinder, Eddie Mallory and Andy Kirk. His style has always been deeply influenced by the playing of Coleman Hawkins, and all his solo work reveals him to have a big, rich tone, a dramatic, direct way of phrasing and an openly emotional expression of ideas. His early work is all typified by an exciting attack. Perhaps the outstanding example of his solo work with the Basie band is the recording of *Harvard Blues*, while one cannot afford to ignore the small-group sides, *Royal Garden Blues*, *St. Louis Blues*, etc., which he recorded with just Buck Clayton and the Basie rhythm section.

After leaving Basie he took a notable interest in modern jazz, working with various small groups along 52nd Street in New York City. He was a member of the first modern jazz group, a quintet which Dizzy Gillespie formed, and he actually recorded with the trumpeter for Victor. Yet although he worked with these men, Byas changed his playing style but little. He never went to a harmonic source for his improvisation and he never modified his tone to the smaller, more pure sound demanded by Lester Young. In 1946 he came to Europe with the Don Redman band, and, according to a number of European critics, when he arrived he was at the very peak of his artistic power. He has remained in Europe ever since, one of the most-admired figures of the Paris jazz scene. In 1950, when Duke Ellington toured Europe, Don played with the band, having one important solo feature, *Danny Boy*. Unfortunately, due to the lack of competition and the absence of strong rhythm sections in Europe, Byas of late has been beset by a lethargy and has resorted to blowing mainly slow, out-of-tempo ballads. Certainly his greatest period of playing, judging by his records, appears to have been from 1940 to 1946.

ILLINOIS JACQUET
(*Tenor-saxophone*)

Though frequently the subject of adverse criticism on account of his tendency to blow freak notes and other exhibitionist devices, Jacquet, when away from the excitement of the concert hall and the recording executives who want only gallery-rousing tactics, can indeed play with imagination and taste. The fact has been noticeable that most of his better recorded work has been either with the Basie band or in the company of Basie sidemen on small-group sessions. He was with the band from 1945 to 1946 as a regular sideman, while many of his more recent Clef recordings have found him using Basie soloists.

Jacquet was born on 30th October 1921 in Houston, Texas, and played soprano and alto-saxophones before switching to the tenor. After work with a number of lesser-known bands, he joined Lionel Hampton on the American west coast in 1941, a band with which he was to achieve considerable public acclaim *and* critical notoriety on account of his exhibitionist tenor-saxophone playing on Hampton's recording of *Flying Home*. His high-note screams were in the worst possible taste, but sufficiently exciting to the less-discerning, sensation-seeking public to earn him nation-wide recognition. He continued with his policy of erotic, tasteless improvisation while with Cab Calloway's Orchestra (1943–4), but for his period with Basie he sobered down somewhat and recorded a number of less-extrovert solos with the band, including *The King* and *Mutton Leg*. Also in 1944 he took part with Lester Young and Harry Edison in the Gjon Mili film "Jammin' the Blues". After leaving Basie, the exhibitionism returned to his playing and with it commercial success. Occasionally he would record a tasteful solo like *Black Velvet*, but normally he turned on his series of freak notes when entering the recording studio. During the last few years he has alternated between leading his own small group and appearing with the "Jazz At The Philharmonic" touring unit. He brought a group to Europe in 1954 which included trombonist Matthew Gee, altoist Sahib Shihab, Osie Johnson and his brother, trumpeter Russell Jacquet.

When Jacquet chooses to play well he will reveal a fresh flow of ideas and an exciting, well-constructed style, partially descended from the Coleman Hawkins-Herschel Evans conception. Usually his concert appearances are all spoilt for the lover of more sincere jazz by his pandering to the rabble sections of his audiences, but a number of his more recent Clef recordings show that he has not lost his ability to play jazz that is in keeping musically with the Basie tradition. He has recorded a number of items such as *Learning The Blues* with a group including trumpeter Harry Edison, while some of his best solos have been *Port Of Rico* and *Cool Rage*, accompanied by Basie at the organ.

LUCKY THOMPSON
(*Tenor-saxophone*)

Lucky, in many ways the most distinctive tenor-saxophone player to appear in jazz since Coleman Hawkins and Lester Young, played with Basie in the mid-'forties (1944–5), and then again briefly in the late spring of 1951 with the Count's unsuccessful attempt to break up his septet and reform his big band. His early inclusion in the band again reveals Basie's ability at ferreting out great, yet little-known talents and featuring them prominently with his band.

Lucky was born Eli Thompson in Detroit on 16th June 1924. He studied under the father of trombonist Bobby Byrne and with Francis Hellstein of the Detroit Symphony Orchestra. (In later years, when unable to find work in the jazz field, Lucky was to play clarinet for a time in a symphony orchestra.) He also studied theory and harmony under John Phelps.

His first work was with the Alabama State Collegians. Then, in 1943, he moved to New York, working out his Local 802 union card before playing in turn with Lionel Hampton, Ray Parker, drummer Sid Catlett, Don Redman and the first modern jazz orchestra of Billy Eckstine. After a brief period spent working with small groups he joined Basie, earning the praise of both critics and musicians with his playing. In the mid-1940's, after leaving the Count, he settled in Los Angeles, and actually became the most heavily-recorded jazz soloist in the city. To my mind his greatest up-tempo solo was recorded during this period: *How High The Moon*, with pianist Dodo Marmarosa, for the now non-existent Atomic label. After this Lucky suffered from an unfortunate neglect. Always outspoken about the many injustices and rackets which go on behind the glittering façade of the musical profession, Lucky was almost squeezed out of the jazz scene by both booking agents and recording executives who deliberately passed over his talents. He made several attempts to lead his own group, only to find that he was purposely starved of work. His own publishing company, *Great Music*, met the same fate: recording companies time and time again refused to use his compositions despite their musical merits. He travelled to Europe in 1956 in an attempt to break what has amounted to an unofficial ban upon his work. In Paris, working with French groups and recording frequently, he gained some of the artistic recognition which his playing rightly deserved.

Fortunately, despite this harsh treatment, Lucky's creative standards have never been lowered. As a tenor-player he combines the best of both the swing and the modern jazz schools into his work. From Coleman Hawkins he has taken the melodic richness of phrasing and dramatic style of delivery, from Lester Young the smooth, pure tone. These qualities are added to an elegant turn of phrase and an effortless invention which are entirely his own. His work is technically perfect, tasteful and distinguished by a facile swing.

With Basie he recorded a number of fine solos, including *Taps Miller*, *Avenue C* and *I Didn't Know About You*. After several years of neglect on the part of recording companies, John Hammond of the Vanguard label used Lucky for his "Jo Jones Special" album, together with Basie, Benny Green, Emmett Berry and the Greene-Page-Jones rhythm section. Lucky proved to be the outstanding soloist on the session, and his improvisation on *Loverman*, *Lincoln Heights* and *Shoe Shine Swing* equals the standard of his best recorded work. In Paris he once more teamed up with Emmett Berry to record albums for Vogue and Ducretet-Thomson.

Wardell Gray

(*Tenor-saxophone*)

Wardell Gray, one of the outstanding tenor-saxophone players of modern jazz, was destined to make contact with Basie on several occasions prior to his untimely death in 1955. In fact, it is significant that whenever questioned about his tastes in music, Wardell always asserted that the Basie band was the finest in jazz, both for playing with and for listening. As a tenor stylist Wardell was a natural swinger, and the easy, flowing rhythm which distinguished everything he played in jazz found a sensible musical companion in Basie's style of music.

Born in Oklahoma City in 1921, Wardell had his first music lessons on clarinet, only switching to tenor-saxophone when he entered high-school. As a jazz musician he rose to fame with the Earl Hines band in 1943. Already by this date his style had attained comparative maturity. Though in many ways a descendant of Lester Young, Wardell possessed certain additional qualities which made his style at once singular and easily identifiable. He phrased in the same subtle, searching way as Lester, but though he had the modern pioneer's purity of tone his sound was considerably greater in volume. Wardell's technique, his automatic swing and his ability to go on building up chorus after improvised chorus without ever running out of ideas have placed him alongside Lucky Thompson as one of the two finest tenormen of the younger generation in jazz.

After two years with Hines he worked in turn with Vernon Alley, Benny Carter, Billy Eckstine and Gene Norman's various concert groups. He came to New York with Benny Goodman in 1948, and in that same year played for the first time with Basie, sitting in with the band at the Royal Roost as deputy for Buddy Tate. He did not record with the band at this time. At the end of 1948 he worked with Benny Goodman's big band, though he later admitted that he was not happy with the group. He returned to Basie to play with the septet (1950–1) and took solos on the unit's Columbia recordings of *Little White Lies* and *I'll Remember April*. When the Count tried unsuccessfully with a large group in April 1951, Wardell and Lucky Thompson were the band's

182

tenors. This group recorded four sides for Columbia, and one of these, *Little Pony*, was an arrangement by Neal Hefti designed to feature Wardell's playing. (This same feature is still in the band book, with Frank Foster playing the Wardell role.) After leaving Basie, the tenorman continued to hold an admiration for the band and its leader; he played on the Clef jam session with Basie, the date which produced *Blues For The Count* and others. The last years of his life were spent largely as a freelance musician on the west coast of America. When he met his somewhat mysterious death he was working with Benny Carter.

JACK WASHINGTON
(*Baritone and Alto-saxophones*)

Jack Washington was one of the permanent fixtures with the old Basie band. One of the founder members of the group in Kansas City, apart from one or two very brief absences, he remained loyal to his leader right through until the dissolution of 1950. During this period he missed only a few of the band's scores of recordings.

A fine reading musician and section man, Washington was actually a native of Kansas City, being born there in 1912. He was familiar with the informal jam-session type of music which grew up in the city, and he played with the Bennie Moten Orchestra for several years, joining Basie's new group at the Reno Club shortly after Moten's death. With Basie he played both alto and baritone-saxophones with equal facility when he first joined. After the band was enlarged in preparation to make the first trip to New York, Basie settled him mainly on baritone, in which position he acted as the anchor for the remainder of the reed section. He played prominently on a number of the early Basie recordings on Decca, including *Doggin' Around*, *Topsy* and *Jive At Five*. In the mid-1940's, however, when forced to leave the band to serve with the army, Jack returned after his service in 1946 to find the baritone book being played by Rudy Rutherford. Basie reinstalled him in the second alto position. After that he became once more a utility man, frequently swopping over when required from alto to baritone positions. He played baritone on the two Victor small groups sessions which Basie made in May 1947.

After the 1950 break-up he retired to Oklahoma City, there to work at an airport and play occasionally with local groups.

BUSTER HARDING
(*Arranger*)

Harding's arranging talents have played an important part in the musical life of both the old Basie band and the new one. Though in the early days Basie relied mainly upon head arrangements, by the 1940's he began to have many of the familiar head themes turned into written arrangements. Harding was the band's chief arranger during the 1940's, a man who skilfully reconciled the characteristics of Kansas City type jazz with the sheet of music manuscript. He has continued to write for Basie's new band; his quantity output for the latter group has only been outdistanced by Neal Hefti and Ernie Wilkins.

Born Lavere Harding in Cleveland, Ohio, on 19th March 1917, most of Buster's early arranging knowledge was acquired from books and from listening to records; he had no set tutor at the outset. When he later settled in New York he studied the Schillinger system. He is also a competent pianist, again largely self-taught.

After playing with various small groups around Cleveland, he lived and worked for a year in Canada, not moving to New York until 1938. He was deputy pianist and arranger with the big band which Teddy Wilson led from 1939 to 1940, and since then has been busily occupied writing for many leading jazz groups, including Artie Shaw, Cab Calloway, Dizzy Gillespie and, of course, Count Basie. More recently he has been writing background accompaniments for Billie Holiday.

Harding's writing for Basie had always succeeded in retaining the essential virility of Kansas City jazz; simple and direct in its melodic lines, powerful and unrelenting in ensemble voicings, invariably distinguished by a swinging 4/4 time, his work is a logical extension of the typical Kansas City approach to the blues construction. There is a lack of complication in everything he creates, and often he will use a repetitive riff figure in his writing as effectively as the musicians themselves might pick up a phrase and mould it into a riff head arrangement.

184

For the Basie band in the 1940's Harding wrote many of the outstanding items in the repertoire, and arranged many others from ideas which some of the sidemen had created in the course of their solos, like Earl Warren's *Rocking The Blues*. Scores such as *Mad Boogie, Hobnail Boogie, 9.20 Special* (featuring Coleman Hawkins) and *Wild Bill's Boogie* helped the band to make some of its best recordings.

His work for the contemporary Basie band is easily recognized, for, unlike his fellow arrangers Neal Hefti, Johnny Mandel and Ernie Wilkins, he has not used the devices of modern jazz very frequently in his work. Some of his best things for the new band include *Nails, Howzit, Blee Bop Blues, Rails, Tippin' On The Q.T.* and the feature for Eddie Davis on tenor and the Count on organ, *Paradise Squat*.

HELEN HUMES

(Singer)

It has been noticeable that Basie has never, during all his years as a bandleader, given a great deal of prominence to female singers. He has shown a definite predilection for the male voice, not only by featuring blues shouters like Jimmy Rushing and Joe Williams, but even allowing sidemen like Earl Warren and Harry Edison to occasionally take a vocal. The female voice is rarely identified with the band's musical style. Billie Holiday did not have a happy period of work with the band, and never recorded with it even though she made a memorable series of records with small groups from the band, including Lester Young and Buck Clayton. Helen Humes appears to have been the only female voice to have contributed successfully to the band on record—and also probably the only one to please the leader with her work.

Born in Louisville, Kentucky, in 1913, Helen was singing professionally while still only a young girl. At the age of fifteen she recorded with James P. Johnson. Singing with the Basie band from 1938 to 1942, however, she earned more of a nation-wide reputation. The Count—normally very sceptical about girl singers in jazz—was moved once to comment that Helen Humes "handled the vocals the way we all felt they could best be handled". An even better sign that the leader was satisfied with

Helen is the way he used her frequently for recording sessions; among her many records with the band may be numbered such items as *Dark Rapture, My Heart Belongs to Daddy, Thursday, Blame It On My Last Affair, Don't Worry About Me, If I Could Be With You, And The Angels Sing* and *Someday Sweetheart.*

All these recordings reveal that Helen had a strong jazz sense, which she succeeded in injecting into all the popular ballads she sang with the band. Her pliable phrases moulded well into the band's very rhythmic pattern. Since leaving Basie her claims as a jazz singer have unfortunately lessened. Her phrasing has tended to become exaggerated, developing into a rhythm-and-blues approach. Her concert recording of *If I Could Be With You* (Modern) is a suitable illustration of her change of style as a singer in recent years.

CHAPTER VI

THE PRINCIPAL SIDEMEN OF THE NEW BASIE BAND (1950–   )

REUNALD JONES

"Reunald Jones, lead trumpet, is the real work-horse of the band."

ERNIE WILKINS

THE PROGRAMME OF work which the Basie band undertakes each year is a strenuous one. For the individual musicians in the organization life must often appear similar to a fast-moving game of baseball; everyone spending the greater part of their time rushing from point to point, only in this particular case with the points becoming the concert hall, the ballroom, the recording studio and the door of the band-bus. Sleep is something of a rarity in this programme, an item which a man must fit in where and when he can.

With the consequent strain which such a hectic pace of life imposes upon the bodies and the minds of the men in the band it follows that, in order to ensure a sustained maximum of musical efficiency at all the orchestra's public appearances, there has to be a co-operative effort by everyone concerned in the band. The leader cannot afford to carry any passengers, for if one man slacks then the whole balance of the ensemble can easily be disturbed, perhaps even crippled. Everyone has his allotted task to perform within the musical pattern, but, even further, it is essential that the men must help each other at all times, so co-ordinating the various tasks into producing the band's singular musical style.

In a band like Basie's, which carries so many gifted jazz soloists, it is to be expected that individual temperaments vary considerably. The Count makes no attempt to throttle these temperaments with regard to their improvised solos, knowing

187

full well that a temperament is usually something which adds colour and individuality to a musician's creation. Solos are things to be freely created. In return, however, he expects musicians to fulfil their roles conscientiously when the ensemble is playing, contributing unselfishly to the section voicings or to a background support behind another improvising soloist. It's a give-and-take policy, relying upon the sincerity of both leader and sideman. Within the Count's band it has proved its worth. The sidemen know that the leader appreciates their abilities, that he respects their individual talents, even more that he is using those talents in the band's overall musical expression. With this knowledge in mind the men go about their various tasks in an enthusiastic manner. This is important, for over a period of time it is enthusiasm which binds the musicians together and keeps the band's high musical efficiency secure.

Reunald Jones, Basie's lead trumpet, has probably the most difficult section job in the entire orchestra to hold down. The band's trumpet team is its crowning glory, a section without rival in the contemporary jazz field, and much of the credit for its generally superior musicianship and cohesion must be laid at the feet of the veteran Jonesy, its more-than-able commander.

The lead trumpeter's role in a group of this type means a lot of hard, gruelling work—and not much popular acclaim in return. At one of the band's concerts, when Joe Newman or Thad Jones come to the end of their exacting solo features they stand full in the beam of the spotlight to receive the congratulations of the audience. In return for their labours they are talked about long after the concert has ended. In many cases their names will be on the lips of numerous fans in a town or a city even when other memories of the concert have faded dimly into the past. Should the band visit a certain town again, then the local jazz enthusiasts will be listening out for them. They frequently record albums under their own leadership with small, all-star jazz units, so that their names are constantly on display in the records shops and their solo work comes under discussion by the critics in the various music periodicals. There is none of this glamour attached to the lead trumpeter's job.

Reunald Jones has the worries of controlling and leading the brass section throughout almost every number of every concert, without ever receiving much popular acclaim. The critics may understand his problems, and the other musicians in the band may appreciate the tireless energy he displays in coping with these problems, yet he is probably one of the Basie sidemen least known to the general public. Despite this lack of glamour, however, Reunald carries out his responsibilities in a brilliant manner. In the four years that he has been lead trumpet with Basie, the band's brass section has successfully vanquished all its rivals in the field of orchestral jazz.

The qualities which constitute a good lead trumpet in jazz are not forged overnight; all the things which a lead man requires in order to manage his section through a long concert programme, the calm authority, the confidence and surety of attack, the stamina to keep abreast, and at times ahead of the band's pace, the continual awareness of what is going on around him, the nimble mind necessary for making split-second adjustments to a section's playing in a crisis, ₁ nd so on, are only built up as a result of long periods of practical experience with big bands in jazz where the standards of musicianship are high. Reunald Jones has had a considerable amount of experience with such bands, and the knowledge which he has amassed and the power which he has developed over the years have been vital contributions to the mastery which he now displays with Basie.

Born in the city of Indianapolis on 22nd December 1910, Reunald comes from a very musical family; both his parents were musicians, and his two brothers, Reginald and Leopold, play double-bass and trombone respectively. At first he studied trumpet and music theory with his father, then later he took up formal studies at the Michigan Conservatory.

The first work which Reunald had as a professional musician was with various local groups in the Minneapolis and Milwaukee areas, but in 1930 he broke through in to the circuit of the better-known bands when he obtained a job with Speed Webb. Playing in the same section with Webb at this time was another rapidly-developing trumpeter, the young Roy Eldridge, from whom Reunald learnt quite a lot of ideas. After this, during the 1930's and early 1940's, Reunald played with a series of leading swing bands, including Fess Williams, Chick Webb, Willie Bryant, Teddy Hill, Charlie Johnson, Don Redman (for two years, 1936–1938), Jimmy Lunceford, Duke Ellington and Erskine Hawkins. His periods of work with the last three bands mentioned all took place in 1946. Also in the 1930's he played at a number of recording sessions with small jazz groups. One of these was the well-known Mezz Mezzrow session with Benny Carter, Floyd O'Brien, Willie "The Lion" Smith and Chick Webb; the session which produced *Apologies* and other interesting items. In 1938 he played trumpet on some Decca recordings with an all-star group composed of Lil Armstrong, Buster Bailey, J. C. Higginbotham, Wellman Braud and O'Neil Spencer.

Reunald Jones has described himself as being "a protégé of Sy Oliver". There are actually strong grounds for making this statement, because in the late 1940's and early 1950's, when he was living mainly by freelance work in New York, it was Oliver who provided him with his best studio jobs. Sy at this time was a musical director for American Decca, and, realizing the enormous powers of stamina and control in Reunald's playing, he used him on as many sessions as possible. If one were to examine the files relevant to Decca's many commercial recordings over these years, then the chances are that Reunald's name would be found in the personnels of quite a number of accompanying groups, and to some rather surprising artists as well. Reunald lived mainly by studio work until February 1952, when he went in to the Basie band as lead trumpet. He has been with the band continuously since that date.

In 1955, when collaborating with Alun Morgan in preparing the book *Modern Jazz*, one of my tasks in the book was to discuss the Basie band. Commenting upon the trumpet section of the band, I wrote:

"Behind these personal fancies for the saxophones [meaning, of course, Basie's love for two tenor-saxophone soloists playing in contrasting styles] there looms the brass in all its immense splendour. A splendour which will unbend to suit the mood of an arrangement, yet which remains a tremendous item of power in the band. The rugged voicing of the trombones, topped by the clean, decisive bite of the trumpets make up a section which has not seen an equal in recent years from any other band. The trumpets are not tied to any one sound; not characterized by an impression of heavy armour like Kenton's brass. They sway and swing, playing in complete concord, yet appearing alive to the emotions of jazz. They've revived the style of playing deep and low down behind the other sections, then of welling out, to finally rise loud and clear above everything else with a sudden passionate surge. When they soar above the remainder of the orchestra the impact of their attack gives the impression that Clayton and

Edison are still furiously blowing there. Once the trumpets are given their full head by the arrangements the natural fire is only matched by the superb quality of the musicianship. Tonally their display is faultless, achieving a unique vibrato in the more direct, open work and a crisp, stinging sound in the muted choruses. Whether in unison, or working against each other in certain contrapuntal passages, the trumpets are a tower of strength, able to lift up the entire band in one sweep or just to continue the warm mood of the composition."

It must indeed be very taxing upon the lead trumpet player's reserves of strength to keep the section under his control playing consistently well. While there must be many musicians who envy Reunald Jones his abilities, there cannot be many who envy him the task he has to face night after night when the band takes the stand. Few musicians would be able to keep the Basie trumpets playing so well. Reunald belongs to the school of hard-blowing trumpeters, the school which grew up in the swing era of the 1930's, the great age for large bands in jazz. The members of this school have dwindled in the 1940's and 1950's; somehow jazz doesn't seem to be producing so many confident lead men nowadays. If the cool, unemotional jazz school now situated in Los Angeles ever gains complete control over the jazz scene, then the chances are that such trumpet men will disappear altogether, for I don't know of one of the west coast atonalists who has the necessary power to last one night on the stand with the bands of Ellington, Basie, Erskine Hawkins, Lionel Hampton and the other large Negro jazz units now in existence.

There are so few trumpet players with the durability and assurance of delivery, the power of attack and the commanding authority required to lead a brass team of the Basie calibre; Jonah Jones, Walter Williams, Cat Anderson and one or two others could conceivably take over the position, but the list of "possibles" is lamentably short.

Reunald Jones is a natural section commander. He takes no solos; that field is left entirely to the other members of his team, Joe Newman, Thad Jones, and to a lesser extent, Wendell Culley. This arrangement leaves Reunald completely free to concentrate upon the task of leadership.

The power and durability of Jonesy's work leave nothing to be desired. Bringing up the whiplash of the brass section, or just setting the whole section swinging soft and low down behind the reeds, can be as varied and as difficult a job as shouldering the majority of the solo parts. Reunald has the trumpets completely under his command, setting with them the many moods and contrasts of voicing which give the brass such a distinctive character in the arrangements played by the Basie band. Like Ed Lewis, the lead man in the old Basie trumpet section, Reunald Jones is a vital corner-stone in the musical construction which the Count has aimed for and achieved. He deserves a great deal of credit for what he has accomplished with his section, as much in his way as Joe Newman deserves for his inspired improvisation.

JOE NEWMAN

"Joe Newman's presence would make any trumpet section sound good."

ROY HAYNES

The American west coast jazz scene does not entirely revolve around stave lines, pen and ink and the Kenton band agency, even though many of the white modernists there have marched boldly into the frustrating cul-de-sac deceptively labelled: "The technical experiment and the long, long bridge leading to the classics."

From time to time one or other of the clubs along the Californian coastal region will reverberate with the blasting of a powerful Negro trumpet player, a sound to remind local inhabitants that jazz has not always been the prerogative of the conservatoire and the composition class. Few of the area's white modernists care to engage in battle with this lion-like character, for they know full well that his trumpet playing helped to lay the foundations for modern jazz; that he is just as likely to beat them at their own game where complicated phrasing is concerned. Even more they fear the sheer force of his playing; the massive tone which turns so many knees to jelly, and the emotional, direct swing, certain to outpace those courageous enough to reach the stand. Heads topple when someone tries to carve this man. The music courses in atonality are of little use in trying to combat his punching, energetic trumpet style. Recording engineers cannot tame his jazz, and they realize, even if they secretly begrudge him his strength, that it would be disastrous to team any local horn players with him.

The man himself is little affected by the awe with which he is regarded in California. One of the five or six most powerful trumpet players in jazz, he disregards the opportunity of achieving greater national fame by touring with a large band or an all-star jazz troupe. He is loath to quit his home and car and the hot Californian sun. Whenever Norman Granz' glittering collection of jazz musicians does some recording on the west coast he is usually roped in—one of the rare men who dare play sessions with giants like Tatum and Hampton. Occasionally he records for a local company with just a rhythm section, and he plays most of the jazz clubs in turn. He makes a living.

On account of this somewhat detached existence, however, perhaps Harry Edison is able to view the jazz scene and his own previous effect upon it quite clearly. He may still have a handful of the recorded solos he made during twelve years with Count Basie's Orchestra; solos which exerted an influence second only to that of Roy Eldridge upon brassmen in the development of modern jazz. No doubt he experienced many moments of private humour when he played on the recordings of Shorty Rogers' west coast tribute to Count Basie, without being given even one solo. The only ex-Basie man present at the session, one can guess that his exclusion came through fear!

Perhaps he has records in his home by the important jazz trumpet players he has influenced over the years. Records by the Hampton and Lunceford bands when Snooky Young was in their brass sections. Records of Taft Jordan with Duke Ellington. Records of Emmett Berry, some with Basie, others more recently with Johnny Hodges. Many critics and collectors are only just realizing the full reach of Edison's style in jazz. Perhaps he has some records by the contemporary Basie band, containing trumpet solos by Joe Newman. I'm sure he must be pretty pleased with what he hears of Newman. Certainly, of the many Edison disciples Joe is the one now being praised by both critics and musicians.

The fact that Newman—an adherent to the trumpet style of Harry Edison rather than of Buck Clayton—is the principal soloist in the Basie band's present trumpet section provides interesting food for thought. Does it mean that Basie himself secretly had a higher regard for Edison's style during the days of the old band, even though Buck Clayton was given most of the recorded solos? I do not think so. Such a suggestion is rather taking matters to an extreme. I do feel, however, that Newman's presence today denotes the fact that Basie understood and appreciated Edison's singular talents even in the early days when the public obviously did not, and that his private admiration has persisted right through until today.

We know that the Count loves contrasts between the solo styles of the sidemen in his band. He earlier had Lester Young as a foil for Herschel Evans, and since their departure he has always employed two tenormen of different approaches. In the trumpet section of the old band Harry Edison, with his broad, full tone, adventurous phrasing and boisterous attack, played in direct opposition to the tight, stinging tone, the delicacy and the more conventional phrase ideas of Buck Clayton. The only links between them were a spontaneous swing and an emotional approach to jazz.

When recording with a small unit drawn from the orchestra, Basie usually selected Buck to join it from the trumpet section. Yet there is a story—rumoured to come from Basie himself— that while Buck could be relied upon to play with the precision desired for a timed recording or for the rendition of a written passage, in the course of a freely-improvised jam session, away from all the rules set by promoters and engineers, it was Edison who was most likely to come out with something in his solo work destined to inspire the men around him. Of technique he was hardly conscious—he just wanted to swing. Yet technique—in a natural way—abounded in his work. His phrasing was always straining to go beyond the pale of convention, always saying something new, always keeping up the session's tension with its surprise ideas. Basie loved to play with Edison for kicks. He loved the man's energy, his feeling, his enormous generation of swing, his largely unconscious artistry. In the course of a jam session, where the musicians and not the public called the tune, Edison was the trumpeter to give Basie and the other soloists present that little extra fillip. And seemingly, though Edison cannot now be tempted away from his home on the Pacific coast to tour for any length of time, Basie still wants a reminder of his sound to linger with the existing orchestra.

When dealing with the trumpet playing of Joe Newman, to begin by writing a lengthy discourse upon the work of his principal influence might seem a little uncomplimentary. Yet I think that to discuss Edison's position in this way does enable one to view Newman's presence in the brass section of the existing Basie band more easily. To realize how, as an Edison disciple, he has been able to fit so snugly into the singular style of the band, taking the largest solo book with complete assurance. To dwell upon an influence is not detrimental, unless one means to point out that the disciple is a mere copyist. Newman is certainly no such thing. He gained a vital inspiration from Edison, a rock-like foundation, and from there the natural jazz musician took over. He had his own ideas about where to move to from the anchorage, about what to retain and what to replace.

Joe had a personal store of ideas, a great imagination, allowing him to use a style without repeating the actual improvised thoughts which originally went with it. He took a keen interest in all the modern jazz developments which followed Edison (he still does if his recent records are anything to go by), picking out in his own time and absorbing the music's most choice devices. These two qualities, allied with a most adept handling of the technical side of his instrument, go a long way to explaining Joe's freshness as a soloist and the fact that his playing can be original, stimulating, artistic and yet the means of continuing one of Count Basie's most fruitful trumpet traditions.

Joseph Dwight Newman—small in height, yet a trumpet player with the heart of a lion—was born in New Orleans on 7th September 1922. Though the general exodus of jazz musicians from the Crescent City had been completed several years before, Joe grew up with his roots deeply entrenched in the native music of the place. His father, Dwight Newman, was a Dixieland pianist who led the Creole Serenaders at the Absinthe House in New Orleans during the depression years. He was also one of the first Negro bandleaders to do radio shows in those early days.

The boy's first attraction was for the tenor-saxophone. He had heard some of the things Dick Wilson was doing with Andy Kirk, and, later, he heard Herschel Evans and Lester Young with Count Basie. He took part in a local schoolboys' venture where everyone was more or less forced to make their own instruments. Joe blew into a zinc pipe that had elbows curved like a tenor and holes drilled into it. He blew through it as one would blow into a trumpet mouth-piece and he was able to play some melodies on it. Due to his father's occupation, however, instruments were often left lying around the house and one day Joe took a trumpet to the schoolboys' session instead of his zinc pipe. He was at ease with the instrument from the word "go". The session ended with all the others listening to him.

His father let him take lessons after that. He studied for a month with David Jones, who had played mellophone with Louis Armstrong on the riverboats. Then when Joe joined the band at the Daniel Public School he received some tuition from the leader—one Earl Bostic. (The only other private studying he did was in New York in 1944 with Al Stern.) Later Joe won a music scholarship to the Alabama State Teachers College, joining a class there which also included trombonist Matthew Gee, and his period at the College was fated to be the launching base for his professional career. When Joe was eighteen the members of his class interested in jazz heard that Lionel Hampton's band was scheduled to play at nearby Birmingham. Joe was flat broke at the time, but two of his colleagues, Isaac Livingston and Barney Williams (brother of trumpeter Cootie Williams) scrounged the money from somewhere to make the trip. At the dance they talked to Hampton with such enthusiasm about the trumpet work of Newman that the leader asked them to send him over on the next night. The boys arrived back, pawned some of their clothes, bought a ticket for Newman and packed him onto the train. He blew like fury that night, impressing both Hampton and the audience. Some months later Hampton made the trumpeter an offer to join the band. Joe took it up and stayed with the band until the end of 1943.

In December 1943 Buck Clayton left the Count Basie trumpet section to join the army. The band's drummer, Jo Jones, suggested that Newman should sit in with the band, and the young man sidled tentatively into the chair next to the mighty Edison.

Joe has been associated with the Basie band on and off ever since. His first period in the trumpet section lasted for about a year and a half; he left to work out his Local 802 union card in New York, playing with various pick-up groups around the city, then rejoining the Count again for a brief period. He next left to join Illinois Jacquet when the tenorman decided to form a small band, a unit whose style of ensemble was reminiscent of Basie's even if the leader's tenor wasn't always in the same tradition! Then when Illinois joined Norman Granz' "Jazz At

The Philharmonic" troupe Joe worked for several months with J. C. Heard. The drummer was leading a fine little group at this period, including Benny Green and Wardell Gray. Joe recorded with the band for Apollo.

Illinois Jacquet reformed his band in 1947 and Joe went on the road again with the tenorman's group, ultimately staying with it until the middle of 1950, playing on the band's recording sessions during the period. He left to freelance once more around New York, until the end of 1951 when Count Basie made him an offer. The Count had just broken up his septet; he was reorganizing ready to go back on the road with another big band. Joe took the job of featured trumpet soloist with him. He has been there ever since; one of the group's most widely acclaimed stylists, an automatic choice for all the Count's recordings (small groups and full band) and for many of the east coast jam sessions where record promoters like John Hammond and George Avakian have sought to reconstruct a Basie atmosphere. Perhaps one can gain some estimate of his importance to the Basie band by the fact that when Basie toured Europe in 1954, in a nightly programme when the band played on average twenty-six arrangements Newman was usually playing solos in at least twelve of those arrangements!

In an interview with Nat Hentoff of *Downbeat*, Joe intimated that the first trumpet stylist to impress him was Louis Armstrong, and that when he was young he used to wait up to listen to the radio when Louis revisited New Orleans and made broadcasts from the Club Forest Café. "Louis was my first inspiration—even before I had a trumpet," he explained. "I'd stay up at night and often would fall asleep waiting for him to come on the radio."

By the time Joe had made some records, however, he had been playing with and listening to Harry Edison in the Basie band, and his style had taken on many of the famed swing trumpeter's characteristics.

Proximity with Edison brought the more daring phrase constructions, the more elaborate designs upon the melody as opposed to the sparse notes and obvious lines of the traditional jazz trumpeters. He learned to maintain a continual wave of attack, building forceful runs and cascades of notes from the punching swing riffs, and always keeping them firmly poised upon the beat. He learnt to play with attack and impact, keeping the senses of

197

the listener alert constantly. As his confidence grew he also learned that one can be forceful and yet still portray relaxation. Like Edison he loved to play bold and adventurous phrases—to occasionally break the expected runs of notes with unusual intervals, to stretch the phrases just that little bit extra beyond the accepted sequences, letting his imagination and technical range wander just sufficiently away from the clearly-revealed course, enough to be interesting while still maintaining a grip on the essentials of jazz. To play one after the other all the records by Newman and Edison will show that despite the sheer bulk of their work they have never had recourse to clichés.

The final touch from Edison came with the creation of Joe's matured tone; a tone broad and full, heated by the agitation of an explosive, emotional attack. Even when caressing a ballad it remains full, firm and rounded. Just occasionally its normal purity is ruffled by a spasm of vibrato—a sort of crying sound which Edison has long featured. This adds to the emotional expression, if anything, being rather similar to the buzzing which one hears through the tone of Coleman Hawkins' tenor-saxophone when he is obviously excited by the course of his solo. With his broad and forceful tone Joe was one of the few hot trumpet stylists able to stick a foot in the doorway of jazz appreciation at a time when the door seemed to be closing against all but the cool and intellectual musicians.

However, Edison was not the final port of call before Joe's style reached its completion. The finished product contained one more quality—the presence of modern jazz overtones. Joe went out of his way to listen to Eldridge, Gillespie and Navarro, to listen to the added ornaments of phrasing evidenced in their work. The time with the Jacquet and J. C. Heard groups—spent largely in the company of modernists—brought the opportunity to familiarize himself thoroughly with the execution of such ideas. Thus the last coating of varnish was added to his playing.

When he rejoined Basie he was possessed of a style which not only pleased lovers of mainstream jazz with its heated, volatile attack and broad tone, but also delighted the more progressive minds with its apt modern touches. It has enabled him to fit in with recording sessions of widely diverse approach—one day to take part in an entirely improvised, middle-period jam session, the next to work with facility through a batch of interesting modern scores such as those penned by Al Cohn for a series of

Victor recordings or the writing by Ralph Burns for his "Jazz Studio 5" album.

Joe has been well represented by records, even in Britain, many of them extended jam sessions revealing his durable blowing power and continual unfolding of invention. Unfortunately, the records he made with Jacquet contain few solo passages, and the J. C. Heard coupling issued in Britain by Vogue (*Ollopa* and *This Is It*) boasts only short stabs of his trumpet work. However, since rejoining Basie his recorded solos have made an ever increasing pile.

There are many solos with the full Basie band (on Clef/Columbia). Just a few of the Clef pieces to feature his improvisation are: *Blues Backstage*, *Soft Drink*, *Jumpin' At The Woodside*, *Stereophonic*, *Plymouth Rock*, Manny Albam's *I Feel Like A New Man*, *16 Men Swingin'* and *Bunny*. It is interesting when playing the 12-inch LP. "A Count Basie Dance Session" to compare Joe's muted sixteen bars during the Johnny Mandel arrangement of *Straight Life* with the middle-eight played by Joe Wilder in the Hefti arrangement of *Softly With Feeling*. Wilder, the Count's other featured trumpet soloist at this time, sounds very much softer in tone, and his notes appear to flow lucidly into one another, recalling at times the playing of the late Frankie Newton. Newman's playing boldly articulates every single note, making a very clear construction. He is always definite rather than subtle. His attack comes up like the crack of a whip. Apart from his solos on most of the full band sides, Joe can be heard to advantage on the Clef/Columbia "Count Basie Sextet" LP., playing with tenorman Paul Quinichette and with Basie at the organ.

His various jam sessions on record are of a high standard. The chase choruses he effects with trombonist Benny Green on Decca's "Jazz Studio 1" still appear to me to be the highlights of that very fine album. His Columbia sessions with Buck Clayton provide examples of his more relaxed moods, particularly during the long *Robbins Nest* in Volume 1. His own Vanguard LP., leading musicians drawn from the Basie and Jacquet bands, contains perhaps his most beautiful slow-tempo solo on the twelve-bar *Blues For Slim*. Some of his more exciting work will be found in a Sir Charles Thompson Vanguard album, sharing a front line with altoist Pete Brown and trombonist Benny Powell. Though Joe does not orchestrate he has been the creator of several fine melodic themes. One is recorded in this Thompson album entitled *Oh, Joe!* Another theme by him, a very delicate ballad called *Leonice,* was orchestrated by Manny Albam for one of Joe's Victor sessions.

Joe's interest in the more advanced modern writing can be gauged by his Victor sessions with Al Cohn (though one of these groups, Al Cohn's Natural Seven picks a mood going right back to the days of Count Basie's Kansas City small groups with Lester, Dicky Wells and Clayton). Also by Ralph Burns' "Jazz Studio 5" album.

Of the younger generation of jazz trumpet players, Joe Newman is one of the remarkably few stylists who has been able to please critics of both the mainstream and the modern schools of thought, sharing a distinction with Joe Wilder and Ruby Braff. His work has certainly contributed much to the renewed success of Count Basie's band.

THAD JONES

"Thad Jones' playing with Basie has surprised a lot of people . . . all the guys who said he wouldn't make the grade with the Count have had to eat their words."

JIMMY JONES

Jones complimenting Jones. No blood relationship between the two, just a musical admiration of one for the other. The time was 1954, the place was a U.S.A.F. camp in East Anglia, and the person I was talking to was Jimmy Jones, notable jazz pianist and accompanist to singer Sarah Vaughan.

I had been fortunate enough to run to earth a number of jazz musicians allowed into Britain for the purpose of entertaining the American troops stationed in the country. The meeting yielded hours of interesting conversation with Roy Haynes, Jimmy Jones and others. It was from Jimmy that I received the first verbal plaudits about the playing of a young and talented trumpeter by the name of Thad Jones. Jimmy was the first person to inform me that Thad had just replaced Joe Wilder in the Count Basie trumpet section; he told me also that in his opinion Thad would soon be an important figure in the jazz scene, a soloist of considerable ability. Ultimately his forecast has been proved correct. In the last two years, both as a featured sideman with Basie and as a freelance with the New York modernist sessions, the trumpeter's name has emerged from its comparative obscurity to become a much-talked-of subject.

Strange to say, although Thad's rise to prominence has been quite recent, he has been connected with music for many years— doubtless one of the many good musicians with an experienced background who had to wait patiently for a lucky break in order to reveal their talents to a wider public.

He was born in Pontiac, Michigan on 28th March 1923, a member of a very musical family. His brother Hank plays piano, another brother, Elvin, plays drums and an uncle plays trumpet. The latter was responsible for starting Thad on his career as a musician. The youngster had heard Louis Armstrong play an engagement in Detroit; was so impressed that for weeks he could talk of nothing else. In consequence the uncle handed one of his old, unused trumpets over to the enthusiast. Thad patched up the instrument and immediately joined the junior high-school orchestra. He didn't have a case for the trumpet and on many a cold morning he would sit trying to warm up the frozen horn while the rest of the orchestra waited impatiently for him. The only lessons he received were the ones given at the school, and really these only consisted of being shown how to hold a horn and how to blow it and use the valves. The rest he learned from instruction books, and after that the creative musician took over.

Even to this day he has never had any formal training with his instrument. "As a result," he has said, "there are certain things I do in certain ways that nobody else does. A schooled musician has, I imagine, a more crisp style than mine, but there is a freedom in the way I play . . . I feel whatever I'm doing." Jazz was the first music to attract him as a boy. He had an admiration for a trumpet player called Herbert Clark, a concert musician who wrote numerous solo trumpet books, yet at the same time he was listening to Louis Armstrong, to the trumpet section of the Ellington band which contained then Cootie Williams, Rex Stewart and a fine lead man, Wallace Jones, and to the lead man with the Basie band, Ed Lewis.

When he could read and play music Thad started out as a semi-professional in a small band with his brother Hank. Known as the Arcadia Club Band, the group played for school and club dances and week-end affairs, not playing very well, but allowing

Thad to gradually save a hundred and fifty dollars to pay for his first new trumpet. After two years it grew into a larger band, being joined by musicians from Pontiac, Flint, Saginaw and Lansing to play for an entire summer at the Sunshine Gardens in Saginaw. All the members were between 15 and 18 years old, and they included Sonny Stitt and George Nicholas.

"It was a crazy reading band," says Thad. "I remember, we swung like friends, and used to blow out the other bands that came through. One favourite trick was to team up on a trumpet player from a travelling band. A couple of us would blow with him *and at* him during the sessions, but we'd keep one high-note man in the background. Then when we'd taken this cat over the obstacle course and worn him down a bit, we'd bring on our screech man to finish the job. It was a dirty trick, I guess, but it was a lot of fun."

Thad left this group in 1941 to tour Mississippi, Georgia and Alabama with Connie Connell's band. In all he stayed two years with Connell, ultimately leaving to play a short engagement with Red Calhoun's twelve-piece group until his draft number came up. He was inducted at Camp Walters, Texas, in 1943, where the army passed over his musical talents and gave him a job checking cargo. In the last few months of service, however, he managed to join the band in the G.I. show sponsored by the 8th Air Force Special Service Division. Eventually he was discharged at Des Moines, Iowa, where he stayed for seven months playing at the Sepia Slipper Club, saying: "I was so anxious to get back into the swing, I took the first job I could get!"

More important work followed. First of all with arranger and multi-instrumentalist Charles Young in Oklahoma City. "It was a band of real fine musicians," he recalls. "Charles Young was the most talented cat I've ever met. He played trumpet, clarinet, baritone, piano, could swing on everything, sing like a bird and write like a demon. He had so much soul. He had intense powers of concentration, so keen that his health wouldn't stand up to them. They had to collapse one of his lungs, and after that he could only sing, direct and write for the band. At 26 he was dead."

Thad took over leadership of the group for six months, but his father's illness caused him to return to Pontiac, there to lead a quintet for local engagements. Brother Elvin played drums with the group. Work proved rather difficult to find in the area and it wasn't long before Thad was forced to go on the road again. He toured for a year with Candy Johnson's band and then for two and a half years with Jimmy Taylor's band in support of Larry Steele's "Smart Affairs" show. Then an even better opportunity came for him with tenorman Billy Mitchell's group. This unit, which also employed pianist Terry Pollard, bassist Jimmy Richardson and drummer Elvin Jones, was to retain Thad's services for two more years, taking his career up to 1954. "That group was about the best five-piece combo I've heard," he has since remarked. Certainly it built up his reputation to a greater extent in jazz circles. Musicians who heard the group marked him down as a trumpeter with enormous potentialities. He also made his first few records with the Mitchell Quintet for Dee Gee—just a handful of sides, but including in their number a beautiful ballad improvisation by Thad upon the theme of *Alone Together.*

In 1954 tenorman Frank Wess of the Basie band approached Thad over the possibilities of him joining the Count's trumpet section. Actually, when with Jimmy Taylor in Boston in 1951, Thad had sat in for a week with the Basie Septet as a deputy for the sick Clark Terry. He didn't think that Count Basie would remember him in the years which followed, but the pianist had evidently been impressed and had made a mental note of the young trumpeter's qualities. When the band arrived back from Europe in 1954 and Joe Wilder left the trumpet section, the Count used Frank Wess as his envoy to encourage Thad to fill the vacant chair. He has remained with the band ever since, splitting most of the solo work with Joe Newman, playing some of the deputy lead parts to Reunald Jones, and, despite the fatigue of touring, he still manages to record and play frequently in after-hours jam sessions with the New York modernists. Part of the time with Basie he uses a cornet, expressing a liking for the instrument's big, broad tone. He is certainly an adventurous jazz soloist; in his phrasing and ideas he is the most modern in concept of the Basie trumpeters, bold in his searchings, intricate in construction and progressive in his use of technique. Yet he has combined his love for the experiments of modern jazz perfectly with the overall style of the Basie band. The purists who complained at first that he would be a misfit when he joined the band have all been proved wrong, and his numerous features like

Shiny Stockings at the band's concerts have revealed his value over and over again. One of his best solo choruses with Basie on record is to be heard on *April In Paris* (Clef); others may be heard during the recorded scores of *She's Just My Size, Soft Drink* and *Ska-di-dle-dee-bee-doo.*

Thad's physical features convey an impression of a well-integrated, resolute personality, with strong lines of character in the face which remind one somewhat of Red Allen in appearance. This impression bears out, moreover, the mind behind the features, for Thad is a man of purpose, a deep thinker and an idealist in his music almost to the point of aestheticism. He possesses very firm beliefs about the music he plays, about the standards it needs to maintain, and so on. Musical taste is a matter which concerns him deeply. He abhors flashy, gallery-fetching tactics in music, believing that if a musician doesn't set out to be creative then there is no point in his playing at all. Don't imagine from this that Thad is a fanatical extremist or that his sincerity has turned him into a bigot. He admires all jazz as long as it is tasteful, and as long as the musicians are striving to achieve something. He values the trumpet playing of Joe Newman very highly, for example, even though Joe plays with a vastly different style. It is only that Thad cannot tolerate a shallow musician—a man who debases the musical form he is using by indulging in bouts of showmanship. Nor is he afraid to air his views on this subject. Some remarks of his about that cancer in the side of jazz, rhythm-and-blues, make quite interesting reading. In an interview with Nat Hentoff of *Downbeat*, when discussing the possible future of his baby son, Bruce Thaddeus Jones, he exclaimed: "If he became a musician that would please me, but it depends on what *he* wants to do. I would want him to have a musical background so that he'll know what's happening and so that he doesn't get side-tracked by rhythm-and-blues. If only he stays out of rhythm-and-blues, I'll be satisfied."

Thad wants to remain a musician as long as he can. If he ever has his own group he has remarked that it would need to have five men in the front line doubling as many instruments as possible so that the scope and the musical patterns of the unit could be very elastic. When playing small-group jazz he has firm ideas about the men who give his improvisation its best support. Bassist Charlie Mingus he describes as "the most fabulous"; his brother Hank as "a beautiful and sensitive pianist". Of the Basie men he

204

is attracted by Frank Wess's change of pace from "real gutty to slow ballad style", Frank Foster's "crisp style" and the playing of the trombonists Henry Coker and Benny Powell. On the question of trumpeters Thad is emphatic about the might of Gillespie. "Dizzy is *the* man," he says. "No one, absolutely no one approaches his artistry and mastery. He has fabulous technique and endurance. It always amazes me to hear him in front of a big band, screaming over the whole band then going right back and playing parts with the band."

The recent *Downbeat* critics' poll which voted a "New Star" award to Thad would appear to be well-supported in its verdict by the quality of the trumpeter's playing. He is certainly one of the most individual stylists to appear in the last few years, a man who may be mentioned in the same breath as a Clifford Brown. His tone is as broad and as big as a house; finely rounded, full of power, full of purity. When he sustains a note—and he has the confidence to do this often—the tonal quality is never ruffled by any hints of vibrato. His phrasing is full to the brim with confidence, and he has the assurance of all the great jazz trumpet stylists in his playing when he launches from the complicated melodic line of the written ensemble into an attacking improvised solo. His phrasing is full of cleanly-tongued runs and variations, whether he is extemporising in his rugged, adventurous, always aggressive style over a difficult chord sequence and a swiftly-moving rhythm pattern or weaving with delicacy and tasteful expression through the melody of a slow ballad. And though deeply conscious in the way he phrases of the constructions developed by Gillespie and the modernists, Thad's playing is always completed by a spontaneous swing—it has to be or he wouldn't be playing with the Count Basie band.

While Thad is well known in the United States for his work with Basie, his reputation has been even further enhanced within New York musical circles by the two LP.s he has recorded under his own name for the Debut label. Bassist Charlie Mingus founded this label in order to exhibit the playing talents of some of the underrated members of the modern New York school. Thad's ability to play extended improvised solos with a continually unfolding invention has been ably demonstrated by his two sessions for Mingus. It was the authority of his work in these albums which brought such critical acclaim to his solo creation, and which won him the *Downbeat* poll.

One LP. features Thad with just a rhythm section and well displays his musical ideals regarding taste and a desire to be constantly producing. The second LP. (which features a quintet of musicians) I like even more. The trumpeter was aided for this session by Frank Wess, who brought both his tenor-saxophone and his flute along to the studio, brother Hank on piano, Charlie Mingus on bass and Kenny Clarke on drums.

One can play through this album, listen in detail, analyse Thad's every solo, yet they will all prove to be free from clichés. His contrasts of approach are well in evidence: the imagination, the bold, fresh phrases as he attacks the two up-tempo original compositions, *Illusive* and *Bitty Ditty* with their tricky chord progressions; then the grace of delivery, the charm of the melodic lines, the richness of improvised statement as he plays, at medium-slow tempo, *I'll Remember April*. His playing is never terse, never disjointed or bitty. He develops each idea logically and at length, driving it home to a sound conclusion, never leaving any loose ends trailing. The slow ballads in the album, *You Don't Know What Love Is* and his own tune, *Sombre Intrusion*, are distinguished by a flowing beauty as he explores each theme, leaving behind a decorative display, yet never articulating a single note which is not vital to the intrinsic body of the solo; *Chazzanova*, a moody, introspective theme by Charlie Mingus, reveals Thad's technical excellence, his ability to cope with a difficult written line, then to develop that line into a strong and imaginative solo.

Thad Jones is the youngest trumpeter in the present Count Basie section (born one year later than Joe Newman), yet he plays with the power and experience of a veteran. Clearly he has a lot to say in his solo work. He may be a new addition to the school of Basie trumpeters, but his stature as a jazz soloist is considerable, his voice a strong and important one.

HENRY COKER

"Henry Coker . . . I judged him to be something of a perfectionist. Thus when the section acquitted itself particularly
well, he would shake hands with both of his team-mates. If he
was dissatisfied with one of his solos, a wry grimace let the
audience know it too."

STANLEY DANCE

Stanley Dance has related a further anecdote concerning the
behaviour of the imposing Henry Coker; one which goes a long
way towards defining the singular trombone stylist's search for
personal perfection and his corresponding self-criticism and acute
awareness of musical values, also the sense of purpose vested in
his forceful, and at times, dominating personality.

The incident referred to in Stanley's tale occurred on-stage
during one of the Basie band's Paris concerts of the 1954 tour. At
this particular concert the musicians had settled nicely into their
programme and were in a state of animation and blowing quite
freely when Basie signalled the band into one of the many blues
arrangements which adorn its repertoire. After a stimulating
opening ensemble, the theme as usual was turned over to the
soloists, and then certain things unforeseen by the arranger, and
certainly not catered for by the disciplined format on the manuscript, began to unfold. Frank Foster, the young tenorman who
had been with the band only a few months at this time, was the
first soloist; the arranger had allowed him three improvised
choruses on the theme. By the time his allocation was drawing to a
close, however, the saxist's improvisation had been fully stimulated
and he was unfurling such an inventive flow of ideas that he went
beyond the limit of his three choruses, still creating strongly. He
had stretched himself to six choruses before he finally quit, and
by that time the audience and the supporting musicians had
caught on to the excitement of his mood.

Coker meanwhile, patiently awaiting his turn to solo, had been
standing just behind Foster for the latter's final three choruses.
When eventually he eased into the position before the microphone he doubtless realized that Foster had set an unusually
high standard, even for him, and that everyone had caught on and

appreciated his strong attack and imaginative outpouring. The pace he had to follow was a hot one, to say the least. Coker more than rose to the occasion. He too went beyond his allocation to six choruses and during that time he blew with everything he'd got. He lifted the pitch of emotional excitement even above the level set by Foster, increasing the dramatic tension with each and every phrase he expressed, improvising aggressively and fluently, gradually but surely overriding what the tenorman had accomplished before him. The band responded to his call and in turn gave their best in supporting him, quickly fashioning a head arrangement for the ensemble to build up and urge the trombone on in its efforts.

When Coker was ultimately through with what he had to say, and had returned to his place, and when the last notes by the ensemble had died away, the beam of the spotlight was directed at the stage, groping its way over the band's ranks in an effort to pick out the soloist for the benefit of the audience. As it passed along the saxophones the enthusiastic Frank Foster jumped up, ready to take a bow for his solo. Then it was that Henry Coker exercised his authority. Standing up, the trombonist clamped his hands upon Foster's shoulders and gently but firmly pressed him back into his seat. Clearly the occasion demanded that he take the bow. The easily-excited Gallic audience was applauding because he had resolutely followed and set about countering the effect of a very handsome solo, surpassing it with an even better one of his own manufacture.

Coker's appropriation of this bow should not be casually dismissed as the action of an egotistical frame of mind allowed to run without check. For this behaviour is typical of a musician who is only happy when he has excelled himself by his own high playing standards, who knows what it feels like to play well and in consequence is never satisfied by the average performance. On this particular occasion he was well aware that he had extended himself beyond his normal confines and it had made him feel good; the audience and the other musicians had also sensed his inspiration, and to have feigned an excessive modesty would have been as embarrassing as a Uriah Heep's unctuous hand-rubbing and eye-drooping. To a person who time after time sets out to perform the well-nigh impossible, a sudden realization of his aims can bring a glow of intense satisfaction. Henry Coker, a perfectionist in his solo work, is so rarely satisfied with his normal, well-above-average playing, that when he does excel himself and knows it he does not conceal his exuberance. Had he failed to answer Foster's challenge on this occasion and created a competent but not (in his own opinion) outstanding solo, then he would have clapped the tenorman, and, shrinking away from the spotlight, glumly complained to his colleagues about his own insufficiency. Whenever he does play what he considers to be a poor solo his countenance usually conveys the fact. On the rare occasions, however, when he is pleased with something he has expressed, then his sense of musical values is appeased and he can justly smile over achieving his purpose.

Henry Coker, this massive-framed man with a vigorous personality, an iron will to succeed and a musical prowess to support his aspirations, has been with Count Basie since February 1952; he has been probably the most individual-sounding trombone stylist to work with the band since the final departure of Dicky Wells.

A Texan, born at Dallas on 24th December 1919, Henry was a friend of drummer Gus Johnson in his early schooling days. His first musical studies were with the piano and the harp at highschool in Washington, Texas. Later, when at Wiley College, he switched to trombone and began to develop an interest in jazz; mainly in the type of jazz being featured by the important large coloured bands of the mid-1930's, with its improvised solos set between organized ensemble passages.

Coker's own early career as a musician followed rather a strange pattern. Encouraged by the significant jazz sounds he'd heard from the Duke Ellington Orchestra and from several other important name bands, the trombonist launched himself upon the professional road in 1937 when he joined Nat Towles. Now this job could and should have been a logical stepping-stone for Henry, providing him with the necessary experience and confidence to eventually move on and take his place in the ranks of a leading jazz group. To all intents and purposes he treated the job as such when he first joined. Yet for some reason he postponed the final step towards entering one of the top bands of the day. In the time spent with Towles his playing developed considerably and he was soon the owner of a personable jazz style, but instead of consolidating his position he suddenly retired from the jazz scene and the circuit of touring bands. He left the United States for Honolulu in 1938, there to bury his talent in a Hawaiian band, in fact in a series of Hawaiian bands, for he was to remain at this diminutive American outpost through the war years.

The trombonist did not return to the American mainland until 1945, and then had to set about picking up the threads of his career as a jazz musician all over again—not the easiest of tasks for someone whose solo abilities had been given scarcely any outlet in the previous five or six years. As it happened though, luck was with him on this occasion, and shortly after arriving in California he obtained a job with Benny Carter's band. In this improved environment his sense of invention as a jazz performer, which had lain dormant for so long, reappeared in a welcome and impressive form, and from the date of joining the altoist his stature as a soloist began to grow in the eyes of other jazz musicians.

After a year with Carter, working mainly on the west coast of America, the trombonist left the band and went on tour with the Eddie Heywood Sextet, playing with it his first important jazz dates before New York audiences. The sextet's particular musical style called for the presence of two trombonists. When Coker first joined the group his section-mate was the lean-framed, humorous and immensely spirited Vic Dickenson; later Britt Woodman, the young modern stylist subsequently to achieve fame with Duke Ellington's band, merged his abilities with Heywood. Marshall Royal also played with the unit for a few months. Coker held on to this job until 1947, when he returned to California to freelance in the clubs and play studio engagements. (Shortly after his departure the Heywood Sextet was dissolved, due to its pianist-leader suffering from a partial paralysis of the hands, an unfortunate event which forced him to give up playing for four years.)

Henry recorded a number of solos with the Heywood Sextet for American Decca, the most interesting perhaps being *Pom Pom* and *It's Only A Paper Moon*. After this his appearances on wax became rather more frequent. In 1949 he joined the band led by tenorman Illinois Jacquet, contributing towards a musical style which closely resembled that of a Basie small group. He recorded several improvised solos (*Hot Rod, Flying Home*, etc.) in the couple of years he was to remain with Illinois, and he also played a prominent part on an EP. recorded under trumpeter Russell Jacquet's name for King Records. Rather in contrast, on 31st October 1950 he led the trombone section of the twenty-three-piece orchestra (including strings, horns and woodwinds) organized by Discovery to cushion eight virtuoso solos by Dizzy Gillespie. Manfully he led his section through Johnny Richards' tricky background orchestrations on this date.

Fluctuations of bad and good fortune continued to upset and then reshape the course of the trombonist's career. A long illness forced him to relinquish his job with Jacquet, and for some months in the early 1950's the going was rough for him financially. Soon after his recovery, however, a vacancy appeared in the brass section of the recently re-formed Basie band, and Coker's playing so impressed the Count on first hearing that he landed the post of section lead and principal trombone soloist with the band. He joined up with Basie early in 1952, and since then has contributed mightily to the band's written and improvised attack.

Coker has resolutely combined his duties as chief whip and foremost solo orator of the Basie trombone section. He leads the section with obvious spirit when an aggressive, pile-driver unison is demanded by arrangements like *Jack And Jill* and *Tom Whaley*, while he can also get it off on a smooth, delicate voicing when the band slides into a theme of the *Straight Life* variety. Even in the early 1940's, when Vic Dickenson and Dicky Wells were both with the band, it is doubtful whether the Basie trombones played *as a section* with such an energetic and forceful attack as they have unleashed under Coker's direction. Some of the open salvoes punched out by the present team outshine not only the trombone passages on Basie's earlier recordings, but even the majority of those on Duke Ellington's more swinging band features when Nanton and Lawrence Brown were enlivening the Ducal team.

Switching over to the purely improvised side of the band's musical pattern, Coker has been equally busy colouring the arrangements with inventive and stimulating solos. His highly personal style as an improvising performer has been prominently displayed by the scores of *Jumpin' At The Woodside*, *Peace Pipe*, *Down For The Count*, *16 Men Swinging*, *No Name*, *Red Head*, *Bootsie*, *Straight Life*, *Yesterdays*, *et al* (the majority of which have now been recorded for Clef). *Yesterdays*, by the way, is a slow ballad performance, arranged by Frank Wess, and featuring Coker's improvisation above the ensemble throughout; normally it is played at all the band's concerts. It is a rare occurrence for the Basie band, which relies so much upon twelve-bar blues themes scored at medium-tempo and interpreted with a predominance of ensemble, to use virtuoso performances by individual sidemen; usually not more than two slow ballad solos are employed at each concert, with Coker's *Yesterdays* and a solo by Marshall Royal invariably making up the quota.

The solo style of Henry Coker displays a powerful technical command (one he is acutely aware of, and for which he acts in a responsible way) fluently allied to (a) a head crammed with intelligent and original musical thoughts, and (b) a heart generating an intense jazz feeling with which to penetrate everything he expresses. It bears a strong relationship to the style of his illustrious predecessor in the Basie band, Dicky Wells, not in the construction of phrasing (for Coker has been deeply influenced in this direction by the methods of modern jazz), but because it has this rare combination of an immense musicality and a vital and profound jazz spirit.

Coker's approach to jazz improvisation is very direct. He operates at all times with a lusty, swinging attack, delivering each phrase in a robust, bellicose manner. The phrases themselves are manufactured with expert care, with finely-wrought melodic curves and undulations, and (no doubt due to his typical perfectionist attitude) they are always poised accurately and firmly in relation to their particular chord sequence and rhythm pattern; nevertheless, though so much fine designing and casting goes into their creation, the phrases are punched out with an almost passionate force. Each note is made full and round, and is in turn accentuated by a big, brassy, brilliant, belligerent tone. Rather like another musician in a different school of jazz playing, the gushing, tempestuous, tragic modern pianist Bud Powell, Henry Coker's expression comes only through the medium of strong, forthright statements. He is never subtle, never timid or restrained in what he plays. He speaks his mind broadly and bluntly. The mood behind the improvisation, the vein of feeling controlling his mind and senses, might undergo a swift transition between one solo and the next. It might cause him to spit out phrases in a most vindictive manner at one moment, issuing one slashing broadside after another; then to let him subside into a series of disgruntled growls; perhaps at another time it will lead him into throwing away affable phrases with gay abandon, crackling humour and chuckling in the throat of his trombone; or yet again it might have him project a dark, sombre melancholy, like the sixteen bars of improvisation he set in the Clef recording of Johnny Mandel's

Straight Life. Always, however, his phrasing is distinguished by a noticeable strength.

This strength of application is as vital a component of his improvisation as his musical sense and illuminating and inventive thoughts. It colours his swing, his tone, his articulation, his designing of phrases—everything, in fact, which goes into his solo attack.

It is also the chief thing which distinguishes the character of his solo work from that of his present section-mate amongst the Basie trombones, Benny Powell. Benny is more subtle, more slippery in his phrasing than Coker; his tone is softer, his melodic designs devious. A solo by Powell, sleek, suave and swift of movement, appears to have the lightning flash of a rapier; one by Coker to have the strong, broad-bladed slash of a cutlass. Both the rapier and the cutlass are sharp and effective weapons in the hands of skilled exponents, though it is the cutlass which requires the greater strength of arm to wield. So it is with Powell and Coker. The former is agile, but rarely bold in his attack. Coker, on the other hand, favours a bold definition and a rugged vitality in his approach.

The various essential characteristics of Henry Coker's improvisation (his purposeful attack, his sense of musicianship and resultant perfectionism, his vivid imagination and his vital jazz spirit) may be easily singled out when listening to one of his recorded solos with either the full Basie band or with one of several smaller groups drawn from its ranks. Coker has completed a number of interesting small-group dates. These include two LP. albums for Period with units led by drummer Osie Johnson, and one under Joe Newman's name for George Wein's Storyville label. This latter session was organized by Wein just after the Basie band had given a concert at his club in Boston; the impresario collected all the leading soloists to record for him, and even had Basie adopt an alias and sit in at the piano. On the resulting LP., Coker takes rousing solos on the blues features, *In Case You Didn't Know* and *Ingin' The Ooh*, as well as sixteen bars on *Peter Pan* and thirty-two bars on *Ain't It The Truth* (all themes having been dreamed up by Newman). Perhaps his best small-group work, however, has been accomplished in the company of the Basie tenorman-cum-flautist Frank Wess. He sounds very impressive throughout the two LP. albums made under Wess's name for Commodore, creating one of his most sensitive fragments of improvisation on record during sixteen bars of the moody *Some Other Spring* feature. His other successful session with Wess was the first date held in New York under Kenny Clarke's leadership for the Savoy Record Co. Sharing a front line with Wess and the Basie baritone-saxist Charlie Fowlkes, Coker growled and thrust his way through the various titles—*Telefunken Blues, Baggin' The Blues, Klook's Nook* and *Inhibitions*—with a considerable degree of inspiration and a vigorous swing. These solos reveal, in the same way that his features with the full Basie band do, that Coker has been probably the most gifted trombonist (with fine musicianship allied to a keen jazz feeling) to rise to the fore in jazz in the 1950's. He has reconciled the style of the great swing trombonists of the 1930's with the methods of the modern jazz pioneer Jay Jay Johnson to give the instrument a fresh significance in jazz.

MARSHALL ROYAL

"I think that Marshall Royal is the best deputy leader a band could have. He's a thoroughly-schooled and experienced musician, and knows his job inside out. We think he gets a little hard at times, but sometimes one has to, to get results; you know how playful and erratic a bunch of guys can get at times. He's a great section leader, knows how to rehearse a band and shoulders a lot of the responsibility that would become too demanding of Basie. I learnt so much under his leadership."

ERNIE WILKINS

The deputy leader's problems in a large permanent jazz group of the type led by Ellington, Hampton, Basie and a few others are numerous, unrelenting and exacting. Different problems present themselves pressingly at different times, and though they may be temporarily solved as they arise they usually pay frequent return visits. A deputy may be paid a larger salary than the rest of the sidemen, but he has to fight like a Trojan to keep abreast of his many responsibilities, and, like the lead trumpeter, he gets very little public recognition for his services; the audiences at the band's concerts and ballroom dates applaud the musical output for what they consider it to be worth, and seldom do they give a thought to the enormous amount of preparatory work which has gone into creating the end product.

There are so many behind-the-scene tasks to be performed for a band of Basie's kind, and so much of the bandleader's own time is monopolized by public appearances, press receptions, interviews, and so on, that the band's organization and rehearsing have in the main to be delegated to a competent deputy. Earl Warren shouldered the many and varied commitments of deputy leader for quite lengthy periods with the old Basie band; Marshall Royal has been facing up to them with the new band; moreover, both men have performed the job in addition to their work as leader of the band's saxophone section.

The deputy has to cope with major and minor troubles. His first and foremost task is to take charge of the band at rehearsals, to put individual sections and then the complete ensemble through their paces with the written passages, ensuring that collective voicings are always kept clean and fresh and that the familiarity of the musicians with a well-used score doesn't cause them to lose the bite in their attack when they play yet another rendition. He has to satisfy himself that the band's overall sound is crisp and clear, and that the men perform accurately and precisely, without ever becoming too automatic. When one of the band's staff arrangers brings forth a new score, the deputy has to guide the men through an interpretation of it, breaking down the band and rehearsing each section singly before bringing everyone together for a collective and final version. If a particular voicing or passage just will not fit with the band, then he has to take a snap decision to amend the score until it is suitable. Royal's worries are greater than Earl Warren's were in this respect, for the new band relies more upon written scores than the old one did when "head" arrangements were the order of the day.

In order to weld a variety of temperaments into a well-disciplined unit (the most important step in maintaining musical consistency) and yet ensure that the men are still contented and relaxed and not operating like a set of robots who give only the barest essentials, the deputy needs to possess enormous strength of character. He has to be a fine and experienced musician, so that the men will respect his artistic judgement at all times; just imagine how the important soloists would resent being drilled at rehearsals by an inferior musician! At the same time he must know the capabilities of each and every musician under his command very thoroughly, and be able patiently to persevere with a section struggling with a new and difficult passage. A show of temper can so easily upset a band. He must be able to laugh informally with the members of the band and earn their friendship, yet he must never let the various energetic spirits beneath his control get out of hand, and he must know when to tactfully *and* conclusively exercise his authority. When a difficult situation arises, whether off-stage or even in the middle of an actual performance, he must immediately be prepared to assume command, to restore calm, to decide the next move. To gain this vital authority over a virile, energetic collection of jazz musicians, the deputy must be admired, trusted, respected *and liked as a person* by all the men under his jurisdiction.

Quite apart from maintaining discipline within the band's ranks in order to guarantee with it a correct and consistent musical functioning, the deputy has to ensure that all the musicians fall in with the band's tight schedule of appearances. He is responsible for having all the men in their places on stage, with their books of scores open at the appropriate pages, when the curtains between the band and the audience are raised. On tour his command has to be strict. The band's road manager might book the coach and arrange accommodation at the various hotels en route; the deputy has to make sure that the men catch the coach, that they get their baggage on the coach after each night, that the coach gets them all to the theatre on time, that "after-hours" jam sessions don't delay the coach (and it must seem cruel breaking up a party that one is personally enjoying) and that no one gets too loaded to play their part competently at the next concert. He needs to have the legendary hundred eyes from the peacock's tail to watch the leader, fourteen other musicians, the road manager, the coach-driver, the band-boy, theatre managers, theatre staffs, and last, but not least, the people who pay their money over at the box-office and want good value for it. It's a job conducive to grey hairs and stomach ulcers.

Marshall Royal, the quietly-efficient, pleasantly-spoken, greying deputy leader of the present Basie band, has withstood the strains and responsibilities of his position for some time now, and although a veteran jazz musician, shows no sign of throwing in the towel for some time to come. He joined the Count in April 1951 and actually helped the leader to organize the new big band which was launched that year and which has since gone from strength to strength. A calmly confident, experienced administrator, liked and obeyed by all the sidemen, he has proved a first-rate deputy, and has freed Basie from numerous exhausting tasks. He rehearses the band with meticulous care and a minimum of temper, urging and persuading, cajoling and commanding, until he has achieved the section and ensemble sounds which he requires. The band's precision and timing, its clarity and definition when rendering the written parts, and its forceful, yet relaxed attack— qualities which have made many other bandleaders jealous of Basie in the 1950's—all owe a great deal to Marshall's thorough rehearsing. As deputy and musical director, he has an important say regarding the new material which enters the band's repertoire, and he ensures that the skeleton of stock items is liberally fortified with new and interesting scores from the pens of arrangers like Ernie Wilkins and Neal Hefti. Fully appreciative of Basie's long musical tradition and his solid ideals regarding jazz, he guards the band's musical policy jealously, yet he is no stick-in-the-mud, and any new idea which shows a possibility of acclimatizing itself with the band's style is always enthusiastically received.

There isn't much Marshall Royal doesn't know about the running of big bands. He's served too many years in the ranks himself to be caught off balance in an emergency; like the sergeant major, he knows all the whys and wherefores because he's lived to learn the answers to band problems time and time again. He knows when to check a musician and when to be lenient, when to be stern and when to be sympathetic. He gives a great deal of thought to the welfare of the band, and though he is firm with the musicians he is also just.

As a teacher and musical pointer Marshall's powers of patience and endurance are acknowledged by the remainder of the band. Although he has had many years of hard work to endure as a musician and has doubtless seen many injustices within his profession, he has not been soured in any way by his experiences. The long and often tedious life spent in band-coaches, the hurried meals, the strange hotels, the stranger and tougher audiences, the working for tough bandleaders and crooked agents have turned many a fine musician into a stoic. Not so with Basie's deputy. He has fought his battles and still retained a love for his music. He is enthusiastic about his work with Basie, the zenith of a sound career, and, despite his heavy administrative duties and his work as leader of the saxophones, he manages to be one of the busiest soloists in the band, with both clarinet and alto-saxophone.

Marshall Royal was born at Sapulpa, Oklahoma, in 1912. As a boy he studied the violin as well as the various reed instruments, and by the age of ten he could read a severe score. He can remember playing professionally as early as 1925, when he was aged only thirteen, and he has been fully occupied as a musician ever since.

Most of his early jobs were with lesser-known bands on the west coast of America; in 1929 he can recall playing with a band led by one Curtis Mosby. In 1930, however, he obtained his first important job when he joined Les Hite's Orchestra, and he remained with this group for the best part of ten years. During the 1930's the Hite band was frequently called upon to accompany Louis Armstrong on the recordings which the solo trumpet star was contracted to make for the Okeh label, and Marshall Royal was one of the musicians who contributed the background supports to such acknowledged Armstrong classics as *Confessin'* and *I'm A Ding Dong Daddy*. (It is interesting to note here that Lionel Hampton and trombonist Lawrence Brown were also in the Hite band when it made these records.) Marshall also became a familiar soloist at the after-hours jam sessions which Hite's sidemen would hold with the resident musicians in the towns which the band visited, and he became known to most of the important jazz musicians of the 1930's as a result. In 1937, when pianist Art Tatum was organizing his first small-group session for American Decca, he had Marshall Royal bring his clarinet along for the date, and featured him quite prominently on most of the sides.

In 1940, after leaving Hite and working for several months with Cee Pee Johnson's band, Marshall joined forces with vibist Lionel Hampton, who was struggling to make the grade as a bandleader after achieving fame as a sideman with the Benny Goodman Sextet. Playing alto and clarinet, he was first of all in the Hampton Sextet, a group which included pianist Sir Charles Thompson and saxist-violinist Ray Perry, and he recorded with this unit for Victor, playing notably artistic solos on *Bouncing At The Beacon* and other sides. Then, when Hampton enlarged his group to the proportions of a big band, Marshall stayed on for a time as lead alto. He left the band finally in 1942, to play lengthy engagements with Jack McVea and Eddie Heywood, and then to settle in California, concentrating upon freelance work in the film and recording studios. He remained in California, making his living with a variety of studio and commercial jobs, until 1951 when he joined the Basie band and again set out upon his travels.

Marshall Royal's extensive practical experience has quite clearly been of immense value to him in dealing with the problems of a deputy leader and a musical director, and also, of course, in guiding him through his work as leader of the Basie saxophone team. I have already mentioned that he performs his control of the band's reeds in addition to all his other chores. When the band is in motion, however, one gains the impression that Marshall devotes his whole musical life to the one task of leading the saxophones, so brilliantly does he carry out the duty.

His knowledge of collective saxophone work, forged as a result of many years' labour as an executive member of many and varied reed teams, has obviously been a decisive factor in his faultless leadership of the existing Basie section. There can be hardly a jazz reed voicing or texture yet produced which he has not encountered at some stage or other of his career; he knows how every nuance and subtlety is achieved. As a result, the unity and flexibility of the new Basie band's reed team are quite exceptional; they certainly allow the section to compare quite favourably with the more important reed teams in jazz history: with Lunceford's saxophones, so expertly handled by Willie Smith in the late 1930's, with the various sections formed and drilled by Benny Carter and with the Ellington reeds of the early 1940's. Audiences have been amazed at the versatility evidenced by Basie's reeds—at the lightning alternations between soft, light voicings and incisive, attacking ones, at the complex phrases which the quintet of reeds weave in perfect unison and at the contrapuntal developments against the band's brass section which they carry out with such accurate timing. In some of the arrangements, when the mood calls for delicacy and ultra-relaxed voicings, Marshall will take up his clarinet and top a very melodic reed sound which is light and airy and sensitively-constructed; at other times, when the band is launched upon an up-tempo rendition of the blues, he will lead the other alto, the two tenors and the rock-like baritone of Charlie Fowlkes in a broad, gutty, sweeping surge of attack, with all five reed men swinging zestfully and in perfect concord. He always keeps the section pliable and relaxed, so that even when called upon to play a series of complex melodic phrases at a fast, driving tempo, it still operates with surety and taste. Naturally, he is fortunate in that he has sound musicians in the reed section to support his ideals, but his own organizing, welding and directing of their sounds and his own into the finished voicings, portrays the touch of a master musician.

The air of authority, so distinctive an element of Marshall Royal's work as deputy leader of the Basie band and as leader of the saxophone team, also pervades when he steps out from the section during the band's programme to play his solo features. When he is improvising, whether by preaching a blues with his clarinet or playing a slow ballad performance on alto, he creates with a noticeable depth of feeling and with a fertile line of thought, but these qualities are always expressed through a very assured technique. Marshall is always immaculate in his delivery; fluent in phrasing, pure in tone and facile in rhythmic movement. Every idea he perpetrates is perfectly placed in relation to the supporting scenery supplied by the remainder of the band; every turn and twist of phrase he executes in his improvisation is firmly related to the melody and the set of chords he is using as his source of inspiration. His sense of musical proportion is such that he can balance his phrases surely against the mounting strength of the ensemble, delicately stressing the most telling points of light and shade, steadily elevating himself to an emotional climax via a faultless technical display. This does not mean to say, however, that his musical confidence has caused his jazz improvisation to become glib; rather it has gilded the thoughts which he conceives with a remarkable degree of elegance; his urbanity and poise are vital components of his solo style, in the same way that they are essential parts of Benny Carter's solo style.

Basie's concert and recording programmes have called upon Marshall's services as an improviser frequently. His gaily-swinging, lucid, pure-toned clarinet has been liberally utilized in the scores of *Basie Talks* and *Blues Inside Out* (both of which have been recorded by the band for Clef). His fluent alto style has been effectively worked into the solo sequences of the Ernie Wilkins' arrangements of *Basie English*, *The Moon's Not High* and *Small Hotel*, as well as having several lengthy ballad features to itself, the most notable of which are *Falling In Love All Over Again* (scored by Neal Hefti), *You're Not The Kind* (scored by Ernie Wilkins), and Harold Arlen's lovely theme, *Over The Rainbow*. These latter performances, of which at least one is used at each of the band's concert appearances, demonstrate fully his consummate skill as a soloist with the alto-saxophone. His alto style may be immediately identified with Benny Carter's on account of its suave, polished and always musicianly delivery, and also its sense for beauty or form and design, but there are also hints of Willie Smith's playing in the bold, incisive tone which he uses, and of the opulent Johnny Hodges in the lyrical turn of phrase which he will occasionally slide out for dramatic effect during a ballad interpretation. These characteristics, allied to his confident technical mastery, his flowing ideas and his ability to carve and shape his ideas into exquisite forms and constructions, give Marshall a very strong and personable jazz style, eminently suitable for both virtuoso and shorter solo roles with the Basie band. A style not without its sympathy for modern jazz and for the alto theories of Charlie Parker, but one with its largest and strongest roots firmly embedded in the swing or "middle period" of jazz improvisation.

In conclusion I would again stress the fact that Marshall Royal has performed enormous feats of strength in helping to resurrect the success of the Count Basie band. He threw in his lot with Basie when the new band was still a very dubious proposition, and he played a major part in steering the group through the multitudinous teething problems which beset it in its embryo stage. The music world was very much opposed to big bands when the Count reorganized his in 1951 and the road to success was strewn with pitfalls and booby-traps. In the middle 1950's, after having to fight for practically every inch of the way, the Count and the musicians who have stuck by him through the lean times have *made* the period ripe for a large jazz group to be appreciated by the public. Marshall Royal has been a valuable general in this struggle.

FRANK WESS

"Wess's swinging tenor is in the Hawkins' tradition, a vein he proves is still a significant one, and his flute sound is of impressive jazz quality."

NAT HENTOFF

Frank Wess has effectively donned the "Jekyll and Hyde" cloak through his playing with the Count Basie band. On the one hand, he is the more conservative of the band's two tenor-saxophone soloists, a man whose improvisation has been noticeably influenced by the musical theories of modern jazz yet who has also maintained strong ties in his playing with the earlier tenor school of Hawkins, Webster and Byas; he is less advanced in the thoughts which he projects through the instrument than his younger colleague, Frank Foster, an adherent to the amalgamated Sonny Stitt–Sonny Rollins school. The two Franks are a natural continuation of Basie's policy to have two tenor-saxophone players with contrasting styles of approach. On the other hand, Frank Wess has caused a minor revolution within the musical pattern of the Basie band by using his second instrument, the flute. His style of tenor playing is well in keeping with the tradition of earlier Basie groups, but his use of the flute is something quite new to the band's musical designs, an experiment which startled many of the critics when it first occurred, yet one which Frank has carried out so efficiently that already he has made the hitherto scorned sound of the flute an integral part of the Count's programme. He now takes three or four solos on the instrument at each of the band's concerts, and even the sternest of critics are really beginning to regard Frank's advance in this direction as a permanent addition to the Basie group.

The flute has had rather a curious history in the gradual evolution of jazz; for many years even its claim to be termed a "jazz" instrument lived a chequered existence. Only now, in the 1950's, has the instrument gained a wider acceptance with musicians, critics and audiences, and much of the credit for bringing about this change of attitude must be laid at the feet of Wess, the flute's most gifted exponent in jazz.

Really the flute is far from being the easiest of musical instruments to turn into a vehicle for improvised jazz. A wind instrument less suited to the form from the rhythmic and emotional standpoints would be hard to imagine. For while a musician like Benny Carter might well be able to master most of the reed family of instruments and still express his own individual style of approach through each one of them, even he would find it a tough proposition to sound individual with the flute. The embouchure provides a major snag for jazz musicians. The mouthpiece, which necessitates a very delicate breathing control, makes it terribly difficult for the soloist to create any of the tonal inflections which he might be able to produce with the various saxophones. Hard-blowing saxophone stylists like Coleman Hawkins and Ben Webster would be stripped of their emotional attacks from the first note if they tried to express themselves through the flute. The instrument has an essentially polite sound—sweet, but rarely exciting. It irons out all the dirty tones of the saxophone players, but manages to desecrate most of the rich, lusty tones as well. In fact, to forge any personality through it at all, the soloist has to rely mainly upon a set of esoteric ideas suited only to the flute's technical construction with its special embouchure and fingering system, plus his own determination to inject some sense of swing and impetus into what is really a very dignified, inhibited instrument. Though saxophone players are normally the ones who attempt to utilize the flute for jazz, they are forced to create quite a different set of ideas for it to the ones they would project through their reeds; typical saxophone phrases just will not fit the flute, which demands its own special construction of phrases.

Tone is a difficult thing to make individual on the flute, swing too is difficult, and even the phrasing of notes has very much of a sameness unless the soloist is outstanding. The instrument's awkward approach and expression have caused it to be branded as a poor relation of jazz; its tasteful sound is not usually regarded as sufficient compensation for the discouragement it offers to those who seek to express improvised jazz fluently and with a definite swing. Few musicians have been able to alleviate the problem. The flute yields success grudgingly; so grudgingly that only a handful of jazz musicians have had the patience and determination to master it.

In the 1930's Wayman Carver made a lone attempt to give the flute a definite place as a solo instrument in jazz. When the British arranger Spike Hughes went to America in 1933 and recorded a number of his compositions with Benny Carter's fourteen-piece orchestra, he was greatly impressed by some of the things he heard Carver playing with his gold-plated flute. Spike made use of this singular talent in some of the ensemble voicings of his orchestrations. He also, after the orchestral works had been safely achieved, included Wayman in the informal jam session features he recorded with Henry "Red" Allen, Coleman Hawkins, Choo Berry, Dicky Wells and Sidney Catlett. *Sweet Sue, Just You* and *How Come You Do Me Like You Do* from these sessions, re-issued on Spike Hughes' London LP., contain examples of Wayman's tasteful conception and technical mastery as a flautist. Later in the 1930's Wayman worked with Chick Webb's famous band at the Savoy Ballroom in Harlem, and he recorded several more solos with his flute for American Decca.

Despite Wayman Carver's pioneering efforts, however, the flute attracted few jazz musicians in the 1930's and then lapsed even further, to suffer from a total neglect in the 1940's.

It was not until well into the 1950's that an interest in it commenced to grow, this time mainly due to the creative efforts of its newly-matured and finest exponent Frank Wess.

Some of the credit for the flute's more general acceptance in the mid-1950's must be attributed to the widening outlook of both critics and audiences in these years. The modern jazz developments of the 1940's had by this time changed from being controversial issues to become an established force, and with their acceptance the stringent boundaries placed about jazz by some of the purist critics were broken down, allowing a more liberal set of views to prevail within the music. As a result of these views many musicians desirous of experimenting with instruments hitherto little-exploited in jazz have been shown greater leniency by the critics of a more discerning nature. The flute has been one of several instruments to benefit from these concessions.

On the other hand, this lessening of the purist grip on jazz does not detract from the credit due to Wess and the part he has played in exploiting the flute as a jazz instrument. It has been Wess who, after convincing Count Basie that he could fit the instrument into the band's musical policy, has persevered with flute solos at Basie's concerts in all the leading cities of the United States, and he has recorded with it on several occasions. The renewed success of the Basie band itself in the 1950's and Wess's determination, have therefore given this shrill-voiced woodwind nation-wide publicity. After hearing the flute operate successfully with the most virile large jazz group in the United States, audiences have gradually grown to enjoy its sound, while critics have penned their acceptance of it as part of the Basie pattern. In turn, this new appreciation has encouraged other musicians to come out into the open with their desire to improvise solos on the flute. Frank Wess's courage has set the ball rolling, and though in the mid-1950's he has remained the instrument's outstanding exponent, a thriving school of jazz flautists has sprung into being. On the west coast of America, where of late jazz musicians have become highly-conscious of new sounds and instrumental experiments, the flute now has able exponents in Bud Shank, Bill Perkins and Buddy

Collette. In the east, with the New York modern jazz school, it has found champions in Gigi Gryce, Jerome Richardson and Herbie Mann. Its use in jazz, therefore, would now appear to be a permanent thing.

One of the most-discussed soloists to rise to the fore in jazz during the 1950's, winner of the "New Star" award in the 1954 *Downbeat* critics' poll, Frank Wellington Wess is a native of Kansas City. He was born there on 4th January 1922. His first instrument was the alto-saxophone, and with it he played a number of public engagements, mainly with local groups around Oklahoma, where he was living at the time. Later he moved to Washington, D.C., and switched to tenor-saxophone, a medium which proved better for his particular style of improvised expression. In Washington he began to concentrate upon music as a full-time profession. His first job was with Billy Baldwin's band, and this was followed by a regular post with the pit band at Washington's Howard Theatre. In his free hours he was busy studying and sitting in with small local jazz groups.

Frank's first real experience with a "name" band was gained with Blanche Calloway's Orchestra (a band which at one time had contained another important tenor-saxophone player in the making, the mighty Ben Webster). He toured with this group for a year, and then in 1941 he was drafted into the army for a period of service which was to last for almost four years.

Upon release, the tenorman stepped almost straight away into his first really important job as a jazz soloist when he signed with Billy Eckstine's Orchestra. In the mid-1940's this large band, which toured as a supporting group to the popular singer, was virtually the sole breeding ground and experimental centre for the rapidly-maturing modern jazz school; it was the first large jazz group (thanks mainly to the enthusiasm of its leader) to perform in public modern jazz arrangements, and its ranks in the mid-1940's were full to overflowing with developing soloists of the new musical generation in jazz playing: Dizzy Gillespie, Charlie Parker, Lucky Thompson, Benny Green, Jerry Valentine, Tommy Potter, Art Blakey, Fats Navarro, Miles Davis and Doug Mettome were just a few of the important modern jazz figures to pass through the band's ranks. Frank Wess played tenor with the band through most of 1944 and 1945 and was able to mix with and learn from musicians who represented the cream of a new and expanding era in jazz history. The providing of stiff competition is usually the best means of drawing out into the open a man's potential abilities. Frank Wess had to pit his strength against some important soloists in the Eckstine band, an effort which gradually changed him from a potentially-good jazz tenor-saxophone player into a confident and freshly-inventive one. The job was the turning point in his career. He became known to many jazz musicians—and respected by them.

After leaving the Eckstine band Frank toured for quite lengthy periods with first Eddie Heywood and then Lucky Millinder. Then when the financial depression hit jazz in the late 1940's, and work was scarce for the sincere and artistic soloists, he took a bread-and-butter job for a year with Bull Moose Jackson's rhythm-and-blues band. In 1949, somewhat dispirited by the music scene, he retired to Washington, there to renew his musical studies and to play jazz chiefly for pleasure. Also in Washington at this time were pianist John Malachi (who had played in the Eckstine band), and bassist Eddie Jones, another man destined to link up with Basie in the 1950's, and frequently the tenorman worked with these two on local engagements.

More important, however, Frank began to apply himself to a serious study of the flute, and after long perseverance, with constant practical and experimental work, he evolved a singular and satisfactory style of jazz improvisation with the instrument. It was a lengthy process but one which has since proved artistically rewarding. Frank remained in Washington, studying hard and playing spasmodically, almost up to the time he joined Basie. The Count made him an offer in June 1953, and he entered the band immediately, just ahead of his fellow tenorman, Frank Foster. In the mid-1950's these tenormen have become two of the Basie unit's most attractive solo features.

The two Franks are now the solo spearheads of the Basie saxophone team. Apart from their duet feature, *Two Franks*, a composition and arrangement by Neal Hefti, they each have a heavy quota of solo parts to get through at every concert. Frank Wess has taken over the Eddie Davis part in the arrangement of *Paradise Squat*, as well as solo tenor features during *Bubbles, Blee-Bop Blues, Stereophonic, Straight Life, Two For The Blues, Peace Pipe, Bunny, Plymouth Rock, Wess's Mess, Fawncy Meeting You* and other scores. His talents as a flautist are in evidence when the band works through *Why Not, She's Just My*

Size, *The Midgets*, *Flute Juice* and *Perdido*. Most of these scores have now been recorded by the Basie band on Clef, featuring Wess to good advantage as an instrumentalist. Particularly recommended for his tenor playing are the recorded renditions of *Straight Life* (containing sixteen bars of Frank improvising sensitively at a slow-medium tempo) and two up-tempo features —*Peace Pipe* and *Bubbles*—which reveal his playing in its more exciting vein.

In addition to the prominence Frank has achieved with Basie as an instrumentalist, he is also quite a capable arranger, and several items from his pen are now part and parcel of the band's repertoire. These include the original compositions, *Wess's Mess* and *Basie Goes Wess*, and the background score for Henry Coker's solo feature, *Yesterdays*. *Basie Goes Wess* is one of the scores contained in the first "Count Basie Dance Session" album on Clef, and proves to be a remarkable exercise for the band's brass section, dramatically contrasting immense, high-register voicings for the open trumpets with soft and lightly-swinging figures in which the trumpets play muted.

I have already mentioned that as a tenor-saxophone soloist Frank Wess is rather more conservative in his style of expression than his colleague, Frank Foster; also that he has definite connections with the school of tenor-players founded upon the original conceptions of Coleman Hawkins, a school which enjoyed its greatest period of popularity with jazz musicians in the 1930's. Let me now, therefore, in order to define Frank Wess's style more closely, examine his ties with the methods of Coleman Hawkins and the pre-modern tenor school.

I must first explain that these ties join Wess tonally, emotionally, and, to a limited extent, rhythmically with the Hawkins-Webster-Byas school. They do not, on the other hand, join the entire form and construction of his playing with the Hawkins approach, nor the source of his improvising material.

Tonally Wess has much in common with Coleman Hawkins; he produces a big, fat, full-sounding tone, richly and maturely moulded and devoid of harshness. It reminds me very much of Hawkins as he was playing in the 1930's. In recent years the Hawk has tended to rasp, and, when excited, to produce a buzzy sound through his instrument, allowing a strong vibrato to disturb the purity which once so distinguished his tone. Wess doesn't employ a strong vibrato; his tone retains a smoothness and purity, despite its bulging proportions. He may bark the odd note when excited or sound breathy when handling a slow, sensitive ballad performance, but he maintains a consistently pure tone usually.

Emotionally he resembles Hawkins because he prefers to express his feeling directly rather than subtly. Like Hawkins (and unlike Lester Young, who has influenced the majority of the young jazz tenor-saxophone players to appear in the 1940's and 1950's with his soft, cool approach), Frank will not disguise his excitement through a series of devious, searching phrases; everything he feels he expresses strongly and directly. Whereas Lester Young will approach a phrase with the stealth of a burglar creeping through the back window of a house, Wess (following in the footsteps of Hawkins) will approach the phrase with the boldness of the landlord walking through the front door. Frank's expression has the surface intensity of pre-modern jazz, and each phrase he delivers in a gushing, forceful manner. Even when improvising over the theme of a ballad at slow tempo he uncovers his emotions at the outset.

Rhythmically Wess's playing is again in keeping with the jazz ideals of the 1930's, but more, one feels, through his contact with Basie than as a result of his admiration for Hawkins. When he plays he poises each one of his phrases upon a strong, unwavering beat—upon the same firm, regular, swinging type of beat that the Basie rhythm section produces. The forthright delivery he favours in his phrasing is best served by this straight beat. Hawkins, of course, can play very well on the beat in the same way, but his playing is frequently distinguished by the use of double-time, a modern jazz mannerism which is found but rarely in Wess's playing. Even on his small group dates Frank has not revealed any marked predilection for the broken beats and the unusual cross-rhythms of modern jazz, thereby differing from the Hawk who has embraced these rhythmic devices.

It is in the designing and fashioning of his phrases, however, that Frank Wess has really deviated from the approach of Coleman Hawkins. He is content for his tone and his style of attack to be identified with the Hawk's school of playing, but the phrases he creates are of a very personal nature and their construction bears little resemblance to Coleman's rhapsodic outpourings.

There are reminders of previous jazz forms in his phrasing: of the Kansas City jam sessions and their use of the blues structure;

of the particular type of tenor figure which Ben Webster played so well in the early 1940's with Duke Ellington and which Herschel Evans played with the old Basie band—the sweeping, full-sounding, yet lucidly swinging figure which would leap up and weave its melodic line above the unison riffs of a large ensemble with dramatic effect; of early modern jazz, evidenced by the occasional unusual interval or run of notes, and the ability (when required) to improvise upon an angular chord-sequence instead of upon a simple melody. These reminders, however, do not constitute the whole of Frank Wess's creation. He has a most individual turn of phrase, and is able to project ideas which remind me, with their melodic strength and harmonic symmetry, of a beautiful pattern executed in wrought-iron. He employs an economical number of notes (far fewer than Frank Foster uses) with telling effect and he seems to prefer fairly simple, direct melodic phrases to the meaningless scale exercises which too often result from a purely harmonic source of improvisation. The ideas which he builds into strong, pliable improvised phrases invariably display simple melodic designs, yet they are always very original and inventive, and he always succeeds in arranging them so as to build an exciting climactic development.

One final difference between Wess and Hawkins as tenor-saxophone players concerns the former's liberal use of the well-tried blues structure as a source of improvising material. Hawkins —essentially a very sophisticated jazz musician—has displayed over the years a preference for the standard ballad as a source of improvisation. He has utilized the blues form but rarely, and then only to build his own elaborate figure upon it. In contrast, Wess, though confident with a ballad and even with a complex modern jazz chord-sequence, is never happier than when working with the blues. He is a true child of the Kansas City jazz scene in this respect. He evidences a great deal of feeling when he interprets a blues solo, projecting statements like the typical Kaycee blues shouters which are forceful and rhythmically stimulating, yet still very sincere.

With the flute, though he has not fallen into the trap of trying to push typical saxophone phrases through the instrument (a mistake which Bud Shank made with his early flute improvisations), Frank does express the main component qualities of the musical approach he has adopted for his tenor-saxophone work with Basie. He has evolved a separate system of phrase building for the flute; a style of construction better suited to the instrument's limited range and special fingering system, mixing the legitimate trills and runs with a singular conception of jazz melody and harmony. Otherwise the personality he expresses runs on a parallel with the personality behind his tenor work with Basie.

He does not treat the flute as a fragile instrumental voice. Though the phrases he designs and plays flow tastefully and sensitively, they are never over-restrained. He blows in an energetic manner, fashioning a full, bold and piercing tone (larger in volume of sound than the legitimate flute tone), and he swings unreservedly. His technical control is immaculate, his embouchure confident, his articulation facile and clean, but even more he injects a feeling warmth and a strong, rugged attack into his work. He isn't afraid of making the flute sound loud and bold when he plays jazz solos on it, and he has used strength where other jazz flautists have been hesitant. The virility (in tone, in creative ideas and in swing) imparted by Frank Wess through his improvised solos with Basie has placed him far in advance of any other jazz flautists. He has become the real pace-setter with the instrument in jazz, and it will require an exceptionally inventive and fiery spirit to steal this lead away from him.

Much of Frank Wess's solo playing on record, both with the tenor-saxophone and the flute, has been accomplished in the environment of the small jazz unit (usually with groups partially or totally composed of sidemen from the Basie band). To conclude this essay, therefore, I would like to briefly mention some of the better sessions he has completed in the small group idiom. The small jazz recording unit, a kind of band within a band, has frequently acted as a supplement to the Count Basie Orchestra, allowing various sidemen to display their gifts as improvisers in extended solos, frequently using instrumental combinations and forms of musical material less suitable for exploitation with the full band. Wess has completed a prolific number of recording sessions with small groups, and some of his outstanding work has been issued in LP. albums from these sessions.

There are two albums on Vanguard which feature Frank quite prominently as a sideman: one, under the leadership of trombonist Urbie Green, teams the tenorman alongside Urbie, Ruby Braff and Med Flory in the front line; the other finds him in a band composed of Basie and Jacquet sidemen, placed under the nominal leadership of Joe Newman. (In the Newman album Frank plays one flute solo during the Frank Foster arrangement of *Close Quarters*.) Another session under Joe Newman's name which Frank played on has been made available by Storyville Records; this collection, entitled: "Joe Newman And The Boys In The Band", was taped after a concert by Basie's band in Boston, and the Count actually sat in at the piano and at the organ under the alias of "Bill Bailey". Two LP.s under drummer Osie Johnson's name on Period also feature Frank extensively, while for an example of his ability to improvise upon difficult modern jazz chord sequences one should hear his solos on the Thad Jones Quintet LP. on Debut.

Commodore has issued two very fine albums under Frank Wess's own name. The first finds him the leader of a group which includes the Basie trombonists, Henry Coker and Benny Powell, pianist Jimmy Jones, bassist Oscar Pettiford and drummer Osie Johnson. The solo highlights of this album are reached with Frank's lovely rendition on tenor of the ballad (first popularized by Teddy Wilson and Billie Holiday in the late 1930's) *Some Other Spring*, a breathy-toned and sensitively-phrased piece of improvisation, and also his slow-tempo flute solo, *You're My Thrill* (accompanied only by Jimmy Jones at the piano), a gem of delicacy and feeling. The second Commodore LP. adds trumpeter Joe Wilder and trombonist Urbie Green to the group.

Finally, there are the various albums which Frank has taken part in for the Savoy Record Co. under the expert supervision of A. and R. man Ozzie Cadena.

"Flutes And Reeds", a Savoy LP. featuring Frank, Ernie Wilkins, Jerome Richardson and the Hank Jones Trio, contains several outstanding tenor and flute improvisations, the most noteworthy perhaps being the flute duet between Frank and Jerome Richardson on the old Basie tune, *Shorty George*. "Opus De Jazz", another Savoy LP., teams Frank with the Modern Jazz Quartet leader, Milt Jackson, and contains further illustrations of his flute work.

However, the finest of all Frank Wess's small-group session work, to my mind at least, is contained in the first album issued by Savoy under drummer Kenny Clarke's name. Superbly recorded by engineer Rudy Van Gelder, the actual group on this date consisted of Clarke, Wess, Henry Coker, baritone player Charlie Fowlkes, Milt Jackson at the piano, and the

Basie bassist, Eddie Jones. Ernie Wilkins provided the four original compositions used at the session: *Telefunken Blues, Klook's Nook, Baggin' The Blues* and *Inhibitions.* These items were recorded on one of those rare occasions when every member present in the recording studio was inspired by the prevailing musical mood; certainly everyone functions admirably on the resulting LP., but most of all Frank Wess who really attains a peak of artistic and emotional perfection. *Telefunken Blues,* a relaxed, medium-tempo twelve-bar theme, contains not only what I feel to be his best recorded flute solo, but also an extended tenor-saxophone improvisation by him which deserves to be ranked alongside the most feeling and inventive work of Hawkins, Webster, Young and Lucky Thompson. Wess's feeling for the blues form, his musicianship, his rich invention and his rhythmic sense all combine to provide this solo with true creative and expressive greatness by any jazz standards.

FRANK FOSTER

"Frank Foster is something of a Wardell Gray without the final coating of varnish. Once that coating is added then he should achieve an artistic status similar to that of Wardell. I think that he'll go very far in jazz."

ALUN MORGAN

Count Basie is not a reactionary; he believes in progress and in worthwhile musical changes. He believes that in music nothing is static, and that only by a sensible forward development from the known substance will jazz remain fresh and free from stagnation.

The Count has lived through a lot of developments in jazz since he made his early records in the 1920's with the St. Louis-blues singer Edith Johnson. He has listened to them all, picked out and used everything which he has found of value, and has still succeeded in keeping his individuality intact by skilfully absorbing them into the style which he has turned into something of a legend with his band—the Kansas City jazz style. The Basie band today, although it is still playing essentially a swing style in an age which has experienced modern jazz, does not sound in the least bit outmoded. The swing period in jazz is commonly

232

supposed to have been out of favour since the mid-1940's, yet Basie is now in greater favour than ever. Just how, one might well ask, does he manage it? The answer is simply that Basie has behaved very sensibly with regard to modern jazz. He has not chased a series of new sounds, but instead has made the new sounds dance to his own tune. He has retained the chief qualities of the Kansas City style which the band adopted in the 1930's, and has subtly used modern jazz in with this style. At the moment there are distinct modern jazz overtones to be heard when the band plays, yet so carefully and subtly have they been introduced that they in no way smother the elements of the swing style. When the band moves into action it still projects the most compelling, propulsive beat of any jazz orchestra, a beat that is simultaneously forceful and relaxed. As Basie says: "We keep a beat in the back line, solid and relaxed, behind the horns. So it doesn't matter so much what they do up front with the solos and the ensembles, the audience always gets that beat."

Given this strong rhythmic foundation, the modern devices which have been injected into the band's arrangements and into the improvisation of certain soloists have acted as a stimulus, not only providing the Basie band with a further fountain-head of creative ideas, but also helping the band to satisfy two lines of thought in jazz, the swing school and the modern jazz school. In the 1950's Basie's style has done much to reconcile these two schools, and the alliance of their ideologies may well be the key to jazz development in the future.

The musical policy of the existing Basie band has made its concessions to modern jazz in four definite ways. Firstly, in allowing Neal Hefti, Ernie Wilkins and the remainder of its panel of staff arrangers to carefully blend certain of the phrase constructions of modern jazz into their scores. Then by allowing Frank Wess to use his flute, both for solos and for scored parts. Thirdly, by employing a number of soloists—Joe Newman and Henry Coker are two of them—whose improvisation contains certain melodic and harmonic mannerisms from modern jazz. Finally, by employing three soloists (Thad Jones, Benny Powell and Frank Foster) whose improvisation clearly belongs to the school of modernists now based in New York, young stylists who have grown up as disciples of modern jazz and who now have merged their knowledge of it with the rhythmic theories of the Basie band. Of these three, Foster, the younger of the band's two tenor-saxophone players, is the most heavily-featured in the normal Basie programme.

Foster has filled one of the more difficult positions within the Basie organization. Since the real return of Basie as a leader in 1951 the band has been fired by a tremendous enthusiasm, and there have been comparatively few changes of personnel. The notable exception to this, however, came in 1953 when Basie found himself without both of his tenor-saxophone stars, Paul Quinichette and Eddie Davis. He filled these two positions with young and, at that time, little-known stylists. Frank Wess was one, Foster the other. Time has proved his judgement on both to be sound. For his part, Frank Foster has taken over a large solo book and played it with confidence. He quickly overcame his lack of experience to become one of the band's biggest assets. Basie regards him as a natural jazz musician, quite obviously a modernist in his conception of improvisation but nevertheless a musician to whom swing is an automatic action. A thinker, a fluent technician and a feeling improviser, he is capable of imparting a deeply emotional outflow of jazz to the listener.

One instance of his power came with the Count's first Stockholm programme during the band's European tour in the early months of 1954. The band had visited Europe with very little advance publicity, and in consequence there were doubts in many minds over the abilities of the new names contained within its ranks. As the musicians undertook the various concerts, however, these fears were soon dispelled. Basie let every soloist have his say. Unlike his fellow bandleader Duke Ellington, who has frequently "typed" musicians in order to express a certain composition, Basie stands by the individual at all times. There were young soloists in the band certainly, but they had all been hand-picked for their invention and for their ability to suit the style of a very swing-conscious group. Their names might not be well-known, but he wasn't going to gag them. However, two concerts a day and a lot of strenuous travel has its effect on a band. There may be an occasion when one musician's power is undermined by the pace of a tour. The first Stockholm concert was unfortunate in that the musicians had barely arrived in the country before they were on the concert platform. Naturally, quite a number of the men were feeling jaded at the prospect of playing without any rest. The curtains parted to find a band heavy with fatigue, struggling to get into its normal musical stride. It was Frank Foster who saved the day. When the band played its fifth number, the blues *Jumpin' At The Woodside*, Foster stood up and swept through ten improvised choruses, blowing with great emotional intensity all the time. As he went on, building up chorus after chorus, the rest of the band pricked up their ears. Bit by bit his playing injected its enthusiasm into the other musicians. They commenced to build up a unison riff behind him, and by the time he finally gave up they were giving him tremendous support. At first the audience was dazed by his power. Then the applause broke out. It was so deafening that the leader was unable for some time to continue with the programme. After Foster's solo the band got into its stride and turned the concert into an important artistic success.

Frank Benjamin Foster was born on 23rd September 1928, in Cincinnati, Ohio. At school, and later at Wilberforce University, he studied clarinet and alto-saxophone, trying to follow on the latter instrument the style of the late Charlie Parker. Then at the age of nineteen he took up the tenor-saxophone. For two years he played professionally in Detroit (part of the time with Wardell Gray) before being conscripted into the army in 1951. Working with a military band fortunately caused little interference with the logical development of his style. He toured Japan and Korea, gaining his discharge in May 1953. It was at this time that Count Basie was in the dilemma over his reed section. Ernie Wilkins was chiefly responsible for getting Foster the job.

Ernie remembers his first meeting with the young tenorman. "I met him at the university," he recalls. "My brother, Jimmy Wilkins, was also there at that time and was leading the college dance band. We were playing in Dayton, Ohio, close by. We got in town early so I went over to the school to visit my brother. We had a jam session that afternoon and that's when I heard Frank for the first time. He was playing alto then. Later he changed to tenor and I heard him again. When Eddie Davis was leaving the Basie band some time afterwards I heard that Frank was due to be discharged from the army, so I told the Count about him. Billy Eckstine had also heard him and backed up my story. One night soon after, the band was playing in Detroit, and we got Frank to sit in. That was it!" The Count didn't need any more convincing. The tall, slim saxist (who also plays piano with considerable skill) joined the band in July 1953.

As a soloist Foster has one of the most nimble minds in contemporary jazz. With a strong command of his instrument and a remarkable sense of timing, he co-ordinates ideas into a logical flow, swinging all the way, never letting his solo become just a string of empty phrases. His favourite tenormen are Don Byas and Sonny Stitt. The explanation is obvious. In Byas he sees the fluent, assured musician, gifted with a beauty of melodic expression. (When Foster came to Europe with Basie in 1954 he just couldn't resist going into the jazz club where Byas was playing in Paris and pitting his strength against his idol!) In Sonny Stitt he admires the rhythmic stamina and the strong attack. Tonally he is very close to the Sonny Stitt-Sonny Rollins school of hard-blowing modern tenor players, and his playing is always distinguished by a tone which applies a mature, ripe edge to a fairly full sound. As a practical soloist he is never over-controlled. His phrasing is gushing, and he obviously appreciates the meaning of strength and emotional force in a jazz solo. Without being erratic he creates purely from his moods; consequently, it is comparatively simple to trace the feeling which runs through his work. He has never sold his emotions in the search for musical progression. He approves only of the jazz sounds which use a definite rhythmic foundation. To him swing *is* feeling and feeling is jazz. In this sense, at least, he's a typical Basie sideman.

Foster is heavily featured in the Basie band's normal programme, usually taking nine or ten solos at each concert. The arrangements of *Blues Backstage*, *Rails*, *Basie English*, *Soft Drink*, *The Moon's Not High*, *Two For The Blues*, *Jumpin' At The Woodside*, *Ain't Misbehavin'*, and *Plymouth Rock* all contain passages designed for his improvisation. Neal Hefti's *Two Franks* is a score which features Foster in a duet with his partner, Frank Wess. *You For Me* is a score designed entirely for Foster's work, while *Little Pony* is a solo job which he took over as a reminder of the days when Wardell Gray was with the band.

In addition to his tenor playing, however, Frank is also a competent arranger, to a certain extent self-taught. He has penned a number of originals for the Basie repertoire, including *Blues Backstage* and *Down For The Count*. Also he has been responsible for many of the background scores supporting singer Joe Williams. He has offset Williams' voice with striking success by writing scores like *The Comeback* (which also contains an exciting solo by Frank himself), *Alright, O.K., You Win*, *Send Me Someone*

To Love, My Baby Upsets Me, Ev'ry Day I Fall In Love and *In The Evening*, and he most certainly deserves a little of the credit for the blues singer's rise to fame.

Since achieving a wider recognition for his solo talents as a result of working with Basie, Frank Foster has made a great number of recordings with small modern jazz groups in New York. Until 1953 he had not made a record with any known jazz label. Now, however, he is highly in demand as a soloist and he has been recording with many of the leading New York modernists. For Blue Note he has participated in several albums: one with pianist Elmo Hope; one with George Wallington, playing arrangements by Quincy Jones; one under his own name, a quintet group including trombonist Benny Powell. For the Prestige label he has completed an album with Thelonious Monk and trumpeter Ray Copeland. Then there is the superb album on Decca, the famed "Jazz Studio 1" session featuring Foster in the company of Joe Newman, Benny Green, Paul Quinichette, Hank Jones and others. His improvised choruses on the *Tenderly* theme in this album are for me some of the most stimulating emotionally that he has ever created. Dramatic in attack, melodically so fine and direct, and rhythmically so fluid, they allow Frank to outblow the more experienced Paul Quinichette at every stage.

Perhaps the most revealing recording session that Foster has completed, though, at least for his invention and stamina as a modern jazz soloist, is the isolated album which he made for French Vogue in 1954. Frank was the only soloist from the Basie band to record in Europe during the band's tour. A few months before, eight members of the Lionel Hampton band had lost their jobs and had been involved in grave difficulties with the American Musicians Union as a result of making records in Paris. French Vogue had arranged to record a number of the Basie soloists, but at the eleventh hour all save Foster decided not to make the session through fear of union reprisals. The tenorman arrived at the studio on his own and cut an entire LP. with just the support of a European rhythm section. Let me emphasize the fact; Foster has recorded with better rhythm sections in his time, and he has recorded moments which I find possess greater emotion, greater intensity of feeling; he has played against stiff opposition at times and proved amply his confidence and his ability. Yet I think that his invention, his expression of improvised thought, is at its finest on these recordings for French Vogue. His moods and his material in the album vary considerably, and I think that they provide the best illustration of his literally teeming ideas, also his remarkable technical accomplishment. Supported by Henri Renaud (piano), Jean-Marie Ingrand (bass) and Jean-Louis Viale (drums), he was able to play considerably extended solos, and the resulting album explains just why he is considered one of the outstanding new thinkers in modern jazz.

Discussing the six solos which make up the album in a liner note for English Vogue, I wrote:

"The beautiful Richard Rodgers' composition *My Heart Stood Still* is taken by the tenorman at medium tempo. He states the melodic theme very gently at the outset, then plays an out-of-tempo break heralding four improvised choruses. The grace of delivery is most apparent here. The ideas flow easily and are offset by the clarity of tone. Thirty-two bars in the familiar neat style of Henri Renaud serve as a quiet transition before Foster returns for two more choruses. In the second and final chorus he restates the theme but leaves the middle-eight to Renaud.

"*Fat Shoes* has a thirty-two bar theme based upon the harmonies of *I Got Rhythm*. This is actually a seven-chorus solo, although the tenor uses choruses five and six for a series of four-bar alternations with Viale's drums.

"Seven choruses also constitute the succeeding *I'll Take Romance* feature. This waltz—converted to 4/4 time—is a perfect vehicle for the tenorman's melodic sense of expression. With the exception of a middle-eight from Renaud in the final chorus Frank shoulders all the solo work on this track. He culminates with a most restrained theme reiteration and a beautiful coda.

"While still a comparatively young jazz soloist, Frank Foster is possessed of a wide imagination and he has the courage to utilize material often thought unsuitable for jazz improvisation. He ascribes to the theory that a jazzman's limitations should be governed by his own abilities and not by current fashions. This is most evident in his selection of the charming French melody *Escale à Victoria*. He plays the theme statements in very formal manner, with long, simple lines to preserve the typically Gallic melody. Between these statements, however, he gains the maximum swing and invention from the tune and its clearly-defined chord sequence.

"A piano quotation from *Mean To Me* constitutes Renaud's

238

introduction to the sixty-four bar *The Things We Did Last Summer*. Using a slow-medium tempo, Foster begins with just one, very relaxed chorus, holding closely to the composer's original lines for the first thirty-two bars, then gradually projecting the melody more freely. This is followed by a half chorus from Renaud in which the ideas are presented in an orderly, rather polite manner. The tenorman then uses half a chorus of the theme to form a suitable conclusion.

"Finally, at up-tempo, he weaves impressively through *Just 40 Bars*, an original composition by Henri Renaud. Roughly its title describes two measures of the twelve-bar blues, a bridge of eight bars and then one further measure of the blues. Foster improvises from the opening bars, then gradually works towards the written theme for his conclusion. The accuracy of his phrasing may be realized from the final chorus as he executes the closely-knit, repetitive main phrase of the theme with perfect finesse. Not one note is delivered in a slovenly manner and the tonal beauty is maintained throughout."

I still find this album thoroughly absorbing whenever I play it through. With its fresh and interesting ideas it has acted as my answer to those who blandly inform me that everything has already been said by the tenor-saxophone in jazz, and that there are no younger minds capable of creating anything new with the instrument. All Foster's work sets a high artistic and emotional standard in jazz, but I think that these six solos together provide the most varied and interesting introduction to his playing for the newcomer to the modern jazz scene. Having heard this album, one should have a pretty good idea of his capabilities. The faith of Count Basie in the fertility of Foster's mind and the sureness of his swing can well be understood after experiencing the full range of these six improvisations.

NEAL HEFTI

"The master of simplicity . . . his writing has been a big factor in the resurgence of the Basie band."

ERNIE WILKINS

Neal Hefti can rightly lay claim to the distinction of having his arranging and composing talent act as a lever behind the ascent to success of two of the most influential and acclaimed large bands in jazz history. In the mid-1940's he was one of the principal scoring minds for the Woody Herman Orchestra. This was for the particular Herman Herd which overthrew so many critical barriers in jazz with its animation and musical prowess when performing scores like *Wild Root, Caldonia, The Good Earth* and *Apple Honey*; undoubtedly the finest of the various bands which Herman has led, it earned the unanimous praise of jazz critics as being the most important large white jazz group of its decade. Coming more up to date, in the 1950's Neal has added to his laurels by becoming one of the two leading staff arrangers for Count Basie's new band —without question the most discussed and influential large jazz group of *its* decade.

To have helped in steering two jazz groups from their experimental stages to established success is no mean feat, and something which I personally have no wish to belittle. On the other hand, Neal has accomplished a further successful task with his arranging, and it is one which I feel enhances his reputation as a jazz scoring mind to an even greater extent, namely that as a white arranger he has assisted in the ultimate establishment before the public of a coloured jazz orchestra. His writing for Basie does not actually set a precedent in this direction, but it is a rarity for a white musician to compose and arrange outstandingly for a coloured group; usually in jazz these roles have been reversed and it has been the Negro, the music's first cause, the spearhead in every major jazz development and the teacher for the majority of the white musicians, who has penned the music's more important arrangements. Hefti's writing for Basie deserves to be ranged alongside the better jazz arranging of the Negro school, admittedly falling short of the most inspired creative efforts of Duke Ellington, Benny Carter, Don Redman and John Lewis, but worthy of comparison with the greater proportion of the Negro orchestral designs in jazz.

Hefti has the advantage, of course, that he is writing for an exceptional jazz group, a group which will fight many of his battles for him in its significant rendering of his scores. The Basie band has its own ideals, its own sense of direction and a knowledge of its own capabilities, and Hefti's task has been to offset and draw out the musical qualities inherent in its powerful jazz style. He has never had to score for a finer jazz group (not even during his days with the Herman band). And though his writing has enabled the Basie band to realize much of its musical potential, it is safe to suggest that no other jazz group would have interpreted his scores with such spirit and defined his talents so accurately. Nat Hentoff explained this situation so aptly in a *Record Whirl* article on the new Basie band when he wrote: "Neal has written several of the Count's most powerfully popular arrangements and originals. On a recent LP. under Neal's own name, the arranger-conductor conducted a crack crew of sidemen in several of the same numbers. The results was quite pleasurable but still rather pallid compared to the way the scores sound when played by the Basie band." The liaison between the arranger and the band has been on a very definite give-and-take basis.

Hefti has worked well for the Count, penning scores which have broken into fresh and interesting territory in their material and their technical structure, and which always maintain the virility, the emotional front and the other characteristics of the band's style. He has revealed in his writing an extensive knowledge of the qualities of the various sidemen and a sympathy for their creative gifts, and he has fused their wares in with his ensemble writing as neatly as any arranger who has worked with Basie in the past. His rhythmic insight in composing for this most swing-conscious of jazz groups has likewise left nothing to be desired. Taking such matters as these into consideration it may be truthfully said that he has exploited the band quite fully. In return, however, the Basie musicians have projected the ideas Hefti has employed in his writing with more musical verve, more emotional impact, more rhythmic facility and certainly with a far greater collective jazz sense than any other large band of today could have produced. As Hentoff's statement about Hefti will surely bear out, the best arranger in the world can be easily crippled if he has not the right group at his fingertips to fully illustrate his ideas. Hefti has the attributes of an intelligent, imaginative *and sensitive* jazz arranger, but without the strength of the Basie band to enhance his thoughts with their spirited interpretation then his writing would be forced to go without its gilt finish.

Though he has been playing and arranging for important American bands since the early 1940's, and was actually one of the first musicians to consider moulding the theories of modern jazz into orchestral scores, Neal Hefti is still a comparatively young man. He was born at Hastings, Nebraska, on 29th October 1922, and from his earliest college days music has dominated his life, creating within him an appetite which has varied in its tastes from the jazz forms to Stravinsky and other modern composers. The first jazz records which attracted his attention were by the Casa Loma Orchestra and Duke Ellington's Orchestra. For a man still in his thirties his own output of orchestral writing has already been considerable, and it is still sharply on the ascent, with the demands upon his arranging becoming so heavy that he now has little opportunity to appear in public as an instrumentalist (though he is an excellent modern jazz soloist on trumpet, as well as being a capable pianist).

After playing in the brass sections of several lesser-known groups, Neal broke into the circuit of "name" bands when he joined Bob Astor's Orchestra for about six months in 1941, working mainly around New Jersey. Then in 1942 he went to Cuba with Les Lieber on a job which gave him the opportunity which he needed to study West Indian rhythms at close quarters, thereby gaining a knowledge which was to prove more than useful in his writing in later years. Towards the end of his season with Lieber he began to seriously apply himself to arranging— with encouraging results. By the end of 1942 he was back in New York, there to embark upon a series of engagements with the bands of Bobby Byrne, Charlie Barnet, Charlie Spivak and several others, and wherever he went he usually managed to work several of his own arrangements into the band's repertoire.

By the time he joined the Woody Herman Orchestra in the closing months of 1944, Neal had fallen under the musical spell, both as a trumpet player and as an arranger, of the musicians who had been experimenting with new and revolutionary jazz theories at Minton's Playhouse in New York City. At this club, a meeting place for the radical jazz musicians to exchange and build upon their ideas, he had listened to Lester Young and Clyde Hart and Jimmy Blanton and Charlie Christian, the men who were to give modern jazz its musical beginnings; also to the younger men who were gradually advancing from the ideas of these pioneers, and who had a fresh approach to jazz improvisation within their grasp—to people like Dizzy Gillespie, Charlie Parker and the enigmatic Thelonious Monk.

Neal was fired with the desire to express some of these theories in his writing and the job with Herman brought him just the opportunity. By 1944, Woody Herman was ready to break away from the rather pallid blues arrangements which had been the identity tags upon his early bands. He had just built up a strong and virile orchestra, capable not only of enormous technical feats in its section and ensemble playing, but also of generating a forceful, propulsive swing as a result of its superior rhythm section, the renowned Ralph Burns–Billy Bauer–Chubby Jackson–Dave Tough rhythm team. Hefti joined the band and played in its trumpet section for more than a year, and in that time he was allowed a considerable amount of freedom by Woody in the type of material he wished to use in his orchestrations for the group. Harnessing the might of the ensemble and the rhythm section to good effect, Neal's arranging declared his fluent understanding of modern jazz in a series of notable scores, the best of which were perhaps *Wild Root*, *The Good Earth* and a new version of *Woodchopper's Ball*. The brass writing in particular which he effected in these scores subsequently paved the way for many other arrangers who were struggling to utilize the devices of modern jazz in their work.

While with Woody Herman, Neal married the band's vocalist, Frances Wayne, and at the end of 1945 he decided to leave the group and settle with his wife in the Los Angeles area, there to concentrate more and more upon arranging. He continued to write for the Herman band for some time after actually relinquishing his post with it as an executive musician, and he began to extend his activities until he was writing regularly for several other "name" bands.

In the five years which followed his departure from the Herman band, Neal wrote prolifically, not only for a variety of jazz groups, but also for several commercial concerns. In 1946 he played with the short-lived Charlie Ventura big band and wrote several scores for it including *Misirlou* and *How High The Moon*. Other arrangements which he placed with important leaders in these years were *Mo Mo* (with Georgie Auld), *Some Of These Days* (with Benny Carter), another *How High The Moon* (this time for Stan Kenton), *Frustration* and *Everything Happens To Me* (with Bill Harris and a small modern jazz recording group for Keynote) and several more commercial items with Harry James. He also recorded two more modern jazz originals—*Sloppy Joe* and *I Woke Up Dizzy*—with his own small group on Keynote. All these illustrations of his writing are linked together by one vital musical thread, namely his employment of a strong, clearly-defined rhythmic basis. The groups are set to play with an unreserved swing no

243

matter what he might have written melodically and harmonically for the various instrumental combinations. Unfortunate exceptions to this rule are the two scores which Norman Granz commissioned him to write in 1949 for an unwieldy twenty-five piece recording group, *Rhumbacito* and *Repetition*. His handling of a combination consisting of a full-size jazz orchestra, plus string, woodwind and Afro-Cuban percussion sections, sounds fidgety, taut and very contrived; quite clearly it was more Granz' idea of a practical orchestral jazz sound than his own.

Neal's association with Count Basie commenced in 1950 when he settled in New York and, amongst numerous arranging commitments, undertook to write for the all-star septet which the Count was leading at this time; he contributed *Neal's Deal* and other items to the unit's library. The arranger was working upon several important projects at this period, including background material for Nat Cole, Frank Sinatra and other singers, and commercial scores for radio and television broadcasts, but so pleased was Basie with the contributions he had made to the septet's programme that in 1951, when he was drawing up the plans for his new big band, the pianist commissioned Neal to write the greater part of the band book.

The arranger set about completing this batch of scores for Basie with all the skill and industry and determination he could muster, giving them top priority over all his other writings, and, after repeatedly burning the midnight oil in order to finish the job on schedule, he was able to present the Count with a pile of manuscript destined to get the new band off to a rousing start. It is perhaps significant that several of the scores which Neal created for the band's début are still, in the mid-1950's, among the most frequently interpreted items in its programme.

Since his initial success in helping to make up the band's preliminary book of arrangements, Neal has continued to contribute fairly regularly to the Basie repertoire. He now shares the position of chief staff arranger with Ernie Wilkins, and each new composition which he conceives and orchestrates for the band reveals (at least, on recorded evidence) that he has retained all his initial enthusiasm for the job.

Writing for Basie has been, I feel, the most interesting, stimulating and artistically rewarding work of Neal's lengthy career as a jazz musician. Admittedly, there are other musical projects completed by him which are worthy of praise. I have already mentioned his many activities in the 1940's. In the 1950's he has been busy as a bandleader in his own right in addition to his writing for the Count. He led a large band from 1951 to 1953; a band which closely resembled Basie's group in its musical style and ideals, though it lacked the immense ensemble impact and the solo strength of the Count's band. With this band Neal rearranged and recorded for Coral a number of the themes he'd originally written for Basie. Then in the mid-1950's he formed another big band, which included many important east-coast jazz soloists, to record for Epic and to play a number of New York club dates. (Neal played piano in this latter band.) These orchestral jobs he has undertaken in addition to his heavy schedule of commercial writing (for the Arthur Godfrey television show on CBS, etc.). Nevertheless, it has been the writing for Basie which has afforded Neal his most significant expression as a jazz arranger in recent years. No other group of musicians in the 1950's has proved itself capable of propagating Neal's mature line of thought with the same jazz spirit allied to musical efficiency as the Basie band has done; the jazz critic cannot escape from this fact.

The compositions conceived and orchestrated by Neal for the Basie band have been very imaginative, with themes of strong and original melodic substance expressed through a wide selection of masterly orchestral devices. Ranging from the notable orchestral pieces such as *Fawncy Meeting You, Sure Thing, Two For The Blues, Bubbles, Why Not?, Softly With Feeling, Ska-Di-Dle-Dee-Bee-Doo, Cherry Point* and *Plymouth Rock* (some of them built up from ideas appearing with head arrangements which the musicians in the band have created) to the features for the various sidemen (*Two Franks, Little Pony, You For Me, Falling In Love All Over Again*, etc.), his scores have sensibly deployed the soloists, the sections and ensemble of the band to embellish the pliable thematic lines with a host of interesting instrumental voicings, textures, tone colours, structural designs, and so on. Neal has been quite successful in reconciling the band's enormous emotional impact with a steady and necessary flow of technical ideas. Without damaging the band's essential jazz style, he has successfully taken the musicians over the arranger's obstacle course with his many and varied devices, exploiting the whole gamut of ensemble and section voicings, gilding the main swing style with numerous modern jazz overtones in his writings. And he has pulled more than his share of plums out of the pie in his search for fresh instrumental shapes and designs within the band's musical pattern.

In the main his writing is simple, direct, melodic and invariably founded (whether his mood of attack is aggressive or gentle) upon a firm, emphatic rhythmic pattern—a swinging rhythm pattern on 4/4 time which "puts wheels on all four beats in the bar", to borrow a phrase from the critic Whitney Balliett.

Neal has not time for over-elaborate, fussy writing, with broken rhythms and complex ensemble phrases; instead he prefers to project his rich melodic lines in simple terms, with the orchestra performing cleanly and precisely, holding to the maxim that if the thematic material has substance then it is disastrous to clutter it up with a too-busy orchestration. This same rule also applies to the various technical designs and the section and ensemble voicings he has unearthed for use with Basie. One can pick out at random a selection of the structural ideas, the tone colours and the section voicings Neal has hallmarked for his Basie arrangements: the clarinet-led reed section subtly fusing with the Count's organ sound, for instance, which is used during the score of *Softly With Feeling*; the juicy question-and-answer technique for unison brass and unison saxophones during *Sure Thing*; the tightly-muted trumpet section delicately picking up and repeating Basie's piano phrases from the introduction to *Bubbles* for the theme's main phrase; not least, the frequently used voicing which has the baritone-saxophone against the trombones accompanying muted trumpets (often with three trumpets using harmon mutes and one using a cup mute). Rarely, if ever, does one hear these arranging devices jerked through a series of angular or abstract harmonic variations. They are all employed to enhance—simply and directly—the main melodic statement of their respective twelve or thirty-two-bar theme, and to assist Neal in gradually urging the might of the orchestra towards an emotional climax. In the course of an arrangement, in order to engineer a climactic development, Neal may push his melody through a number of interesting sectional and collective voicings and at times bend it into varied shapes and designs, yet he never allows the melody to lose its substance, and he will certainly not juggle with it through garish tone colourings and knotty phrase designs in order to impress his fellow musicians; he keeps everything he writes, melodically and technically, very simple and forthright.

At all times Neal's writing has encouraged and nurtured the

natural technical attributes and the collective spirit of the Basie band; with plump and solid, but never fussy, ensemble figures, strong, melodic riffs and phrase designs, and a perfect sense of timing and tempo, he has accentuated the group's broad range of sounds, its surging attack, its intense jazz feeling, its ability to produce a fluid, easy swing at a second's notice and the stylistic characters of the various improvising soloists to good effect.

As Basie's other staff arranger, Ernie Wilkins, has explained, Neal's scoring has been an important factor in the success story of Basie's band in the 1950's. He has been one of the most tenacious fighters in helping to establish the band's style and ideals in the public's mind. I always like to think of Neal Hefti's position with Basie as an addition to a short description of the band which Nat Hentoff once expressed. The well-known American jazz critic wrote in one of his articles: "The Basie band roars as if all its members had been blown into one jazz John Henry, a steel-driving band that can create jazz that always wails no matter how long the night." Well certainly, if the band gives this impression of being an efficient work-gang, with Basie wielding the biggest hammer and setting the pace of industry, then Hefti has surely been one of the truck-drivers, regularly transporting the men to their appointed place of work.

ERNEST WILKINS

"Wilkins' composition for the Basie band has a definite strong rhythmic pulsation and is more or less in the swing idiom, with the importance lying on groove rather than linear interest. I've never heard a Wilkins' score yet that didn't swing and I'll buy that any day."

QUINCY JONES

In his book "The Music Of Ralph Vaughan Williams", the English critic Frank Howes wrote:

"Composers do not live in ivory towers, nor are they spiders spinning silken threads out of their own guts. They live in the world and their minds are nourished by events in the world, and their emotions are stirred as other men's are."

Such a remark, intended by its author to reveal how a particular age in history and the international events relevant to it

247

had a profound effect upon Vaughan Williams in his symphonic creation, might well be taken out of its original context, framed, and liberally quoted by critics in essays analysing sincere composition and thought displayed over several centuries of evolution in music. Indeed, if any creative person, be he artist, sculptor, writer or musician, is at all sensitive to life, then his work can hardly escape being influenced in some way by his environment. He may be emotionally moved by the violence of man, like Goya depicting on canvas the horrors of Napoleon's occupation of Spain. Perhaps by the normalities of everyday life like the Impressionist painters with their cry "Get to grips with real life instead of painting the monotonous pink nudes so popular with the Official Salon. Take your canvas into the cafés and the boulevards, and paint people as they really are". Or again by the natural properties of a place as with Sibelius whose music was so influenced by the mountains, the forests and the lakes of his native Finland.

Of course, it stands to reason that the influence of an age and of environment will not always be so dramatic in its effect upon an artistic mind as it has been in the case of Goya. A man's creation may only reflect one aspect of the life which surrounds him, say happiness if the people who surround him are happy, or melancholy if his background has been difficult. It frequently happens that a man's creative expression is largely the expression of the immediate circle in which he moves. Yet in one way or another age and environment do have their influence. Only by transplanting one's mind deliberately into a mystical world of dreams or else by creating purely for technical effect can one entirely shake off the effects of the men, the age and the trends in thought and life which surround one's existence.

The truth of Frank Howes' remark goes beyond its intended application to the music of a master like Vaughan Williams. It reaches out to the other main branches of art; it even finds itself suited to the various minor artistic forms, including jazz. The creative men to be influenced by environment and the way of life immediately surrounding them are legion.

The composing and arranging talents of Ernie Wilkins form a perfect example in jazz of the creative orchestral mind being stimulated by its immediate environment, and as a result producing music which reflects the qualities of that environment.

248

In this particular instance the environment has been the musical life of the Count Basie band.

"When I joined Basie," Ernie recalls, "I'd done a certain amount of arranging, but with the Count the most important thing to me at first was blowing my horn and being a good section man. After a few months, however, the Count became disappointed with me because I wasn't writing often. Clark Terry had told him that I knew a lot about arranging, so I guess he expected big things of me. Anyway I started to concentrate more and more upon arranging, and then I came to realize that I could help myself more by writing more, artistically as well as financially."

As this statement explains, Wilkins wasn't an established arranger when he joined Basie. His writing attained its maturity while he was with the band. He was impressed by the musicians and the musical policy which surrounded him in the band, and on the style of writing which he created for himself the musical ideals of the band became the foremost influence. Being on the "inside" he had the opportunity to study every man in the band thoroughly, to get to know all the qualities and all the weaknesses of the various people, and as a result when he developed his style of arranging he brought out with great success the full power of the ensemble and the soloists. Even more, his writing, developed within this unique organization, contained something of the musical atmosphere that accompanied the Basie musicians; something of the gaiety, the high spirits, the "I'm having a ball with this music" attitude. It still does for that matter. Basie's musicians have long been distinguished by their spirit and enthusiasm, by the forceful attack, confident relaxation and constantly-flowing invention which are evident in their creation; all the qualities, in fact, which have grown as a result of the remarkable freedom of speech which their leader allows them in their solos. And Wilkins—reaching maturity with his arranging in the company of such men—has been influenced by these self-same qualities and has projected them through his own work.

Wilkins' writing contains all the elements we have come to associate with the new Basie band and its concept of jazz: the relaxed swing, the simplicity of approach, the forceful impact of the ensemble, the melodic riffs developed from the Kansas City jam sessions fortified by a sprinkling of modern jazz overtones, and so on. Using Basie's normal musical style as a means of delivery, Ernie has been able to unfold a considerable flow of musical ideas. He has been one of the most inventive minds connected with the new Basie band, a fine example of the creative jazz arranger who has been given a true sense of direction through contact with the Count's ideals and musical aims.

Ernest Brooks Wilkins was born in St. Louis on 20th July 1922. He had his first music lessons at the piano from his mother, but later, while at Wilberforce University, he took up the alto and tenor-saxophones. He became more deeply involved with jazz in the early 1940's when he spent three years in the U.S. Navy. Stationed at the Great Lakes base in Chicago he regularly took part in jam sessions with Clark Terry, Willie Smith and Gerald Wilson. After taking his release he decided to turn professional musician. His first regular job was back in St. Louis with George Hudson, but late in 1948 he had a taste of touring with a first-rate jazz group when he worked for a spell with Earl Hines' last big band. When the job with Hines came to an end he went back to St. Louis to play with George Hudson and other local groups and to continue his studies.

It was in 1951 that Ernie linked himself with the New York jazz scene when he took part in a rehearsal with Count Basie's new big band. "I was recommended to the bandleader by trumpeter Clark Terry," he remembers, "though up to that time I'd never actually met Basie. I'd been seeing the band for years, and wishing that I could play with it."

At the rehearsal Ernie's playing passed the Count's penetrating examination with flying colours. He joined the band immediately, officially to take over the second alto-saxophone book, but in actual fact, at the band's concerts to do that and also play improvised choruses on tenor-saxophone. After several months of thoroughly orientating himself with Basie's musical style he began to arrange for the band, and as his stay lengthened so the number of scores to come from his pen increased from a mere trickle to a veritable flood. It has been as an arranger that he has made his most important contribution to the Basie story.

The list of arrangements by Ernie Wilkins in the repertoire of the present Basie band is quite imposing. Though quite a number of his scores have not yet been recorded the ones actually in use with the band at its concerts and so on include: *Paul Meets Prez* (originally scored to feature Quinichette), *Bread, Bootsie* (named after Ernie's wife), *Smooth Sailing, The Moon's Not High* (a variation on *How High The Moon*), *One O'clock Jump*, *Peace Pipe*, *Blues Go Away*, *The Blues Done Come Back*, *16 Men Swinging*, *She's Just My Size*, *You're Not The Kind*, *Stereophonic*, *Basie's Back In Town*, *Flute Juice* (featuring Frank Wess), *Sweetie Cakes*, *The Midgets* (featuring Newman's trumpet and Frank Wess's flute), *Serious Business*, *Big Red*, *Blues Inside Out*, *Basie Jones*, *Jack The Riffer*, *Basieville*, *No Money Blues*, *Basie's Loaded*, *Small Hotel*, *Perdido*, *The Sleeper*, *Long Sam*, *Fo-De-Fee*, *Basie Talks*, *Corner Pocket* (an original by Freddie Greene) and an original by Reunald Jones. In addition he has arranged a number of the background scores for singer Joe Williams, including the best-selling *Every Day* and the popular ballad *Teach Me Tonight*. Then there is one rather more ambitious score, a jazz score in extended form entitled *Concerto From Coast To Coast*. The work got its name because Ernie wrote it specially for use on a package tour which the Basie band made across America in the company of George Shearing and Billy Eckstine. This would certainly be an interesting score for the band to record. As Ernie says: "The Count asked me to work on this piece and I think it's my best effort even though the band doesn't have much chance to play it any longer. As you know, things like this are often pretentious, but I tried my best to avoid it with this score. We got a favourable response from the audience wherever we played it."

Ernie's chief aims in writing for Basie have been to exploit fully the band's musical style and yet portray "freshness and originality". "I like to write good, simple melodic lines," he says, "eliminating anything that sounds banal or trite, so that the arrangement sounds cohesive and uncluttered. I also like the arrangement to be easy to play, so that the men can relax and blow. I try to write lines that suggest what Basie himself might play at the piano, and in that way I'm usually able to maintain the identifiable Basie style for the band. I like to hear a clean, hard-hitting brass section, a flexible reed section, and plenty of solo space, but, of course, with a loose, relaxed precise rhythm section carrying the whole thing."

Talking about his practical methods for achieving these aims Ernie explains: "I use simple voicings for the ensemble, mostly with closed voicings for the brass but at times letting them play open for colour. In hard-hitting ensembles I usually keep the brass closed and the saxes open, with the baritone-saxophone acting as the anchor for the whole thing. Like Neal Hefti, however, there are times when I want a voicing in which the whole ensemble plays close. I let the lead alto double the lead trumpet an octave lower, and the baritone doubles the lead alto another octave lower. That gets a full, brilliant ensemble sound and doesn't sound too heavy or bogged down through one section being stronger than the other. While all this is going on I let the rhythm section ride along like mad, with the drummer accenting here and there with the ensemble to help give more impact."

Ernie admits quite frankly that he has learnt a lot from his fellow arrangers Neal Hefti, Buster Harding and Johnny Mandel. "In music you can't ever afford to stop learning," he emphasizes. He has also been impressed by Andy Gibson's arrangements. "He hasn't done anything for the band in the past few years, but Basie still uses some of his older things and I always got a kick out of playing them." Outside the Basie style he most admires Manny Albam, Al Cohn and Quincy Jones. Quite recently he has collaborated with Quincy in the formation of a music publishing house for jazz compositions.

The success of Ernie Wilkins' writing for Basie has quite naturally brought numerous further commissions from other bandleaders for arrangements. After his first year with Basie he discovered that the amount of freelance work which he handled was steadily mounting. At times the volume of work almost defeated him, and while he was continually touring with the band he didn't have a lot of free time to settle down with a pile of clean manuscript. Yet he remained an active sideman with Basie until the beginning of 1955, when he reluctantly handed in his resignation and settled permanently in New York. "I hated to leave the band," he admits, "and it took me a year to make up my mind. Although I was being swamped by arranging jobs I enjoyed the atmosphere at a concert with the band and I'd made so many friends within it. However, I'm kept pretty busy in New York now. I'm happy in what I'm doing and I can still get my thrills listening to the band." And even though he has left the band he still sends more arrangements in to Basie than to anyone else, while he has also recorded prolifically with the various Basie sidemen on small-group sessions in New York over the past two years.

So many additional commissions have come Ernie's way since leaving the Basie band that, apart from a period in 1956 (when he joined a large orchestra organized by Dizzy Gillespie and

Quincy Jones to undertake a tour of the Far East), he has hardly been able to budge out of New York. He has contributed jazz scores to the books of the Dan Terry and Tommy Dorsey Orchestras, and late in 1955 he made up an entire repertoire of arrangements for a new Harry James band.

He has written for so many small-group recording sessions in New York that I can only find space within this essay to briefly summarize the better-known ones.

There are first of all the items he has contributed to various Joe Newman albums; one LP. under Newman's name on Vanguard contains an orchestration of his theme *The Sleeper*, while for the trumpeter's Victor sessions he has scored a number of things, including Freddie Greene's *Corner Pocket*, the standard *Dream A Little Dream of Me*, and his own originals, *Pretty Skinny Bunny* and *The Daughter of Miss Thing*. The latter theme, incidentally, is a melodic riff based upon a phrase improvised by trumpeter Harry Edison on the old Basie band's recording of *Miss Thing*.

For Savoy he has completed some of his finest small-group work. He wrote and arranged four pieces for the first Kenny Clarke Savoy album with Henry Coker and Frank Wess: *Telefunken Blues* (which has the best improvised flute solo by Frank Wess that I have ever heard), *Baggin' The Blues, Klook's Nook* and *Inhibitions*. Later he organized a septet session with Kenny Clarke for Savoy, on which he played alto and tenor-saxophones (his alto work reveals a satisfying blend of elements from the styles of Benny Carter and Charlie Parker) and penned a number of arrangements, including ones of his own compositions *Cute Tomato, I Dig You The Most* and *Oz—The Wizard*. For the same label he orchestrated a session entitled "Flutes And Reeds" featuring Frank Wess and Jerome Richardson. The originals he produced on this date were *Blues In A Cold Water Flat, Stereophonic* and *Bouncin' With Boots*. Also at this session he recorded a spectacular alto solo, entitled *That's A Woman*.

Ernie's most adventurous writing for Savoy, however, is in the "Top Brass" album which contains scores for five jazz trumpeters (Joe Wilder, Ernie Royal, Ray Copeland, Donald Byrd and Idrees Sulieman) with just a rhythm section. The themes which he composed and orchestrated to exploit this unusual instrumental combination (*58 Market Street, Trick Or Treat, Speedway* and *Top Brass*) successfully display some of the

253

finest brass scoring to be conceived by any jazz arranger in recent years. The group presents some of the choicest devices in modern jazz allied to a Basie-type rhythmic foundation. Whether scoring the trumpets in unison or setting off each trumpet with a different line to create a contrapuntal design for the section, Wilkins' writing comes through in a freshly-inventive and interesting manner, containing all the fire and forceful impact which have typified his ensemble writing for the Basie band.

The arrangements by Ernie Wilkins have been a decisive factor in the renewed success of the Count Basie Orchestra. It has been a case where Basie's faith in a young and gifted, but comparatively-unknown musician ultimately has reaped its own reward. Both arranger and bandleader have gained considerably by their musical association. Wilkins, as a result of the musical environment of the Basie band, being placed amongst a unique bunch of jazz musicians and learning to write for them, has developed into one of the finest arrangers of the contemporary jazz scene. Basie, on the other hand, having nurtured the arranger's talents in their infancy, has been able to draw upon a large supply of fine arrangements since Wilkins has found his feet and reached maturity as a jazz composer. It has certainly been a most satisfactory musical union.

JOE WILLIAMS

"Joe is a spellbinding artist to watch. Much of the time he stands very still, hands in front of him with fingers touching— as if in prayer. Sometimes he throws a syllable away as casually as an old-time blues singer who can't hold a note; at other times, he grasps a tone and bends the syllable into half a dozen different notes for a wild, dramatic effect. And on one or two numbers he just takes a note, sung falsetto, and holds on to it for an entire 12-bar blues chorus, while the band builds up the tremendous intensity behind him. Again, he will take a simple phrase like 'Oh, well; oh, well' and repeat it like some magic incantation throughout the 12 bars."

LEONARD FEATHER

David Stone Martin, commissioned by impresario and record magnate Norman Granz to design a sleeve for Joe Williams' first album of recordings with the Basie band on Clef, effectively depicted with his brush not only something of the singer's extrovert nature but also a thought about his artistic relationship with his employer, the discerning Count.

The finished piece of art-work reveals (covering about a third of its area) the figure of a singer in black evening clothes, hands clasped together, chest swollen, head held tensely back—obviously an impression of one of the passionate stances adopted by Williams for his public appearances—surrounded by a bank of vivid crimson paint. To one already conversant with Williams' intrepid, exciting, and, at times, startling attack, the brightly-coloured backdrop serves to confirm an existing impression. Stone Martin has achieved this emphasis well. Over the figure of the singer looms a huge facial sketch of Count Basie, the unmistakable features captured with shadings of brown and dull purple. Viewing the painting at a distance the face appears to be even more imposing. It gives Basie such proportions that he would seem to be director, mentor and guardian-angel for the singer all at the same time. Stone Martin has hit the nail on the head with this impression; Williams and Basie both require representation, having helped each other considerably of late over a remarkable musical project, but Basie is still the more important figure musically, the senior partner, as it were, in the project.

Joe Williams' regular connection as a singer with the Count Basie Orchestra dates from Christmas Day 1954. Since then he has figured prominently in several of the band's achievements, not the least of these being to provide Basie with his first really big commercial success on record (*Every Day*) in a long time. (I mention this record specifically because it was also Williams' first with the band, a thing which gives the event even further significance.)

When Williams joined Basie the band was badly in need of a blues singer. The old band had fortunately possessed (in Jimmy Rushing) the leading singing product of the Kansas City jazz scene, and the finest all-round singer of blues with a band that jazz music has known. When the present Basie band was formed, however, Rushing was managing so well as a solo artist that he refused the offer of reinstatement—a refusal that ripped a jagged hole in the new band's façade, for despite many inherent musical qualities and a galaxy of freshly-interesting sidemen, the band did need a blues singer. Basie tried several. Then he tried Joe Williams. Public reaction was immediately favourable and the relationship hardened into permanence. Williams' success with the group has been an upward spiral ever since. By this, of course, I mean commercial success; commercially Joe has filled the gap left by Rushing. Artistically he has *partially* filled it.

Joe has covered a lot of ground commercially with Basie. He has impressed the general public on a gigantic scale through both his recordings and his appearances with the band, taking the musicians with him into new venues, gaining favour with countless thousands of people who had previously been unable to appreciate the band's instrumental talents and the degree of inspiration in the jazz it creates. This much has been accomplished *because he sings in a particular way*; he is a blues singer with a difference, and the difference takes the form of a sensational front. Williams sings the blues capably, but he also has something else to offer: showmanship. We know how the public loves showmanship. After one concert the band played in Philadelphia, Basie turned to his musicians and reflected: "I might just as well not be here—all they want to hear is Joe." A modest statement, but containing a germ of truth. For while part of the audience appreciated the band's singular style of jazz, the sensation seekers in the audience, and there were many there, went wild over Williams! How the public loves a showman!

Williams has become a distinct asset to the band in that he is able to act as a kind of "public relations" man, helping with his singing-plus-stagecraft to take the band's artistry before new and larger audiences. Call it, if you like, the sugar coating on the vitamin pill. It serves its purpose, and while Williams' singing takes in showmanship he remains a capable blues singer and causes no deterioration to the band's musical policy. Joe doesn't use gimmicks; he wouldn't be with Basie if he did. He is simply a more extrovert performer than anyone else in the Basie organization, well able to sing the blues but in a flamboyant manner which is liable to catch the attention of an audience before the solid qualities of the band catch it.

Unfortunately, however, Joe's showmanship has been picked up by the poorer section of the press (the "yellow guttersnipe" press as Richard Aldington aptly refers to it), mistaken for musical ability and touted out of all proportion to its actual value. Frequently nowadays one reads statements describing Joe as "the greatest", "another Jimmy Rushing", and so on. The air grows hot as the press showers him with superlatives. It is not uncommon to find him being described as the only reason for Count

Basie's renewed musical success. It is a bubble which I feel requires pricking.

Let me, before I proceed any further, précis my own observations concerning Joe Williams' talents.

He has impressed me first of all as a good blues singer, possessed of an exciting and individual style, and being well able to function and fit his talents in with the style of the Basie band; he is not, on his showings so far, a *great* blues singer, and he is certainly not the equal of a Jimmy Rushing as regards emotional intensity. (He may well be the best *since Rushing* in emotional projection, impetus of phrasing and rhythmic sense, but this is quite a different definition to the one being touted by so many of the popular magazines.) He is of distinct value to the Basie band commercially; but one must not confuse this value to such an extent that one begins to describe him as the *cause of the band's renewed musical success*; he has helped it, yes, but not caused it. If Williams has been the one person responsible for Basie's current acclaim as a musical unit by the critics, then why did he not elevate the bands he worked with previously (Hampton's, Kirk's, and so on) to a similar position?

Let us forget some of the wilder statements of the sensationalist press. Williams needed the Basie band's support to draw out his capabilities, to give him the necessary rhythmic urge, to give him an opportunity to sing the blues in a manner both powerful and relaxed. No other band in the United States could have allowed Joe to realize his potential as a singer in the way that Basie's has, because no other band plays the blues so consistently well. Though his presence is desirable in the new Basie band, the fact remains that the band could, if necessary, function reasonably well on its own (it managed to survive without him from 1952 to 1954), whereas Joe's singing would be far less effective if placed with any other band. Williams' debt to the Count outweighs what he has achieved in popularity for his leader and he is the first to recognize the fact; he is full of praise for the band and he regards his job as the finest musical experience in his life. As he says: "I'm having a ball working with the band."

If the cheap press would only stop confusing Williams' sensational front and showmanship with his artistic merits, then perhaps people would begin to think more about him as a real blues singer, and to praise him for the qualities of style which he genuinely possesses.

Io   257

Well, now, after having placed Joe Williams in what I consider a true perspective with regard to his stature as a singer and his relationship with the Basie band, perhaps I can move into calmer waters and say something of his previous career, and also discuss the characteristics of his highly-personal style.

Joe was born Joseph Goreed on 12th December 1918 in Cordele, Georgia. When he was aged only three, however, his family moved to Chicago and it was there that he first became interested in the blues. The Windy City's South Side, a vast Negro district, contained innumerable well-known and lesser-known singers in the years when Joe grew up there; it is an interesting fact that he first heard the song *Every Day* in Chicago when he was quite young, then being sung by Memphis Slim. As a boy Joe picked up some knowledge of the piano, and often he would try to pick out unidentified blues melodies he'd heard being performed by unknown singers. Before long he was singing the musical form himself.

In 1938 Joe obtained his first job when he joined Jimmy Noone's little band, a job which required him not only to sing but also to act as a personal servant to the great clarinettist. Jimmy treated the young singer well; he was always ready with a word of advice or encouragement when it was most needed. "He was a wonderful, warm human being. It was a pleasure even to carry his bags," the singer remembers.

Joe might have stayed with Noone much longer, but the clarinettist moved eventually to the west coast of America, and the aspiring blues singer didn't want to leave Chicago. He free-lanced for a while, and then, in 1941, joined a new big band which tenorman Coleman Hawkins had organized for a long engagement at Café Society in Chicago.

When the job with Hawkins came to an end, Joe did consent to tour for a while when he joined the new big band which Lionel Hampton had formed. He joined the unit as a ballad singer, a role which he gradually found insufferable because it prevented him indulging his first passion, the inspiration to sing the blues. At least, however, the work furthered his confidence with a large jazz group.

Joe was never away from Chicago for really very long in the 1940's and early 1950's. He held the post with Hampton for a while; he also worked for periods of a few months with a rhythm-and-blues unit led by Red Saunders, with Andy Kirk's band, and

258

with the piano team of Pete Johnson and Albert Ammons; after a few months of one-night stands, though, he always returned to Chicago to work as a freelance.

His first contact with Count Basie came in 1950 when the pianist-leader was fronting his septet at the Brass Rail in the Windy City. Joe had the job of singing with the unit during its two-month engagement at the club, sparking off a mutual admiration between singer and leader which was to have enormous musical repercussions in later years. Basie never forgot about him; as with so many other musicians in whom he recognized a natural talent, the pianist made his personal assessment and stored it away in a mental corner, allowing it to lie dormant but never to fade. Whenever the Count played in Chicago after that he always got in contact with Joe, either to just talk about jazz and the blues, or if time allowed to draw him into a jam session which the musicians were holding. In December 1954 he asked the singer if he'd join the band; it was an offer which Joe felt unable to refuse, even though it meant forsaking Chicago to go on the road with the band.

In the time he has been working with Basie as a band singer, Joe has learnt a great deal concerning the handling of an audience; about how to use the impact of the band to build up a dramatic tension behind the voice; how to generate excitement amongst those listening in order to engineer a free emotional response; how to use varying moods of melancholy and gaiety in his attack; how to keep the attention of an audience riveted upon his every word and move.

He is certainly a brilliant actor. When singing he always displays an intense figure. No cavorting about the stage, no hysterical waving of hands. Instead Joe will usually set a single passionate stance and hold to it; a stance which is simple, forthright and emotionally obvious, and which to the listener appears to be pregnant with power and feeling. People who would normally jump and scream when confronted by the antics of Calloway and Hampton tend to be hushed and overawed at first by this emotional expression. Joe is always to the point. He uses gestures with economy so that each one comes to mean something. He has his listeners following each of these gestures. Unlike Lionel Hampton, who exhausts his audience with a non-stop barrage of head, hand and leg shaking, Joe takes his along with him. At every concert he changes the moods skilfully and effectively; from the outset the audience's emotions will only move with Joe's. If he swings the blues, lightly tapping his feet and gently swaying his shoulders in rhythm with his words, then thousands of feet will tap with him; if he stands very still and sings a sad blues then all will be hushed and grave about him.

As an interpreter of the blues Joe Williams' style can be traced back directly to Jimmy Rushing, Joe Turner and the other Kansas City shouters. He too uses the blues form for its rhythmic impact and melodic strength as well as for its emotional effect. He moulds words and melodic lines after the style of a jazz instrument's improvisation, functioning like an additional horn with the band. He can swing and force and bend and rebuild the twelve-bar structure in the accepted Kaycee manner, using it for a happy lyric as well as an outcry. On the other hand, quite apart from his improved platform technique, there are certain schisms in his work which serve to place him somewhat apart from the style of Jimmy Rushing. He is a child of the Kansas City movement, but not a streamlined copy of it.

His voice (at least on record) appears to be rounder and smoother, with a less incisive edge than Rushing's. Each word he delivers is big and full and very articulate, and when he sustains a high note he is clear and confident. His range is extremely good, and he will often use a startling interval with dramatic effect. He can hold the high notes well, and can reach down for the rich, low ones with the same facility. At slow tempo he has a way of preaching rather than singing his phrases, and even, at times, of talking them over the ensemble, yet retaining also a tremendous power to thrust each and every syllable out at the audience. Frequently he uses his musician's sense to catch and chant a single word or phrase *ad lib* just like a soloist repeating a riff figure. All these devices he uses to advantage.

While I admire his musical sense, however, I feel that at times his delivery is just too slick. He is smooth and sophisticated, much more than Rushing. He uses his voice intelligently to shape phrases in an individual manner, yet despite his obvious power he lacks the tremendous intensity of voice that is Rushing's, the raw edge and uncontrolled emotional statement which connect the ebullient Mr. Five-By-Five with the earthy singing of the early blues performers. He has elegance, craftsmanship, musicality, an individual turn of phrase and an enormous reserve of energy, yet he noticeably lacks the profundity of feeling vested in Rushing.

Perhaps it is the added degree of sophistication, the result of his stage-craft, which tempers his emotions with restraint. I find that on all his recordings, though he expresses a feeling for the blues its roots do not go down so deeply as do the great Rushing's; his singing is altogether more superficial than Jimmy's heartfelt utterances.

A further aspect of Joe's singing which I feel leaves him Rushing's inferior concerns his renditions of standards, particularly when he takes the tunes at slow tempo. While the popular ballad composition obviously plays second fiddle as a source of material for the blues singer, Rushing, given a strong, pliable melody (like *I Want A Little Girl*), can sing with tenderness, and usually inject his innate feeling through a maudlin lyric. Joe Williams achieves less success artistically with this type of material. Unlike Rushing, who tends to take the melodic line of a standard ballad and convert it to the mood of a blues singer, Joe tends to keep the ballad within its own field, treating it in the same style as would an experienced singer of show tunes, and in this field he consequently suffers by comparison with its wily masters like Frank Sinatra and Mel Tormé. I find his slow ballads uneventful, at times even downright amateurish. Joe's real assets to my mind are his strength of voice, his extrovert, gushing attack and his spirit and verve—qualities which he wields to good effect when swinging a blues over the rhythmic impetus of the Basie band. He can interpret a faster-moving show tune in a blues style with equal facility, punching out each word with obvious enthusiasm, chanting zestfully in unison with the might of the Basie ensemble. Yet when he tries to sing it straight and at a slow tempo these qualities are unfortunately lost to him; he sounds quite ordinary, just one of many light-weight singers in the field of light music.

Joe has a large repertoire of songs. The various blues themes which he uses with the band provide almost an historical survey of the musical form, ranging as they do from early items like Leroy Carr's *In The Evening*, through the Kansas City period with Pete Johnson's *Roll 'Em Pete*, to more modern developments with his own composition *My Baby Upsets Me*. It is noticeable that when he picks up and renders an early blues lyric he will often substitute modern terms and descriptive phrases for some of the original ones. To his blues collection he has added a number of obvious band vocals, such as *Right Smack Dab In The Middle*, and a proportion of the tunes which register his exploits into the field of standard ballad singing. Though I find his interpretations of popular ballads quite unexciting compared with his treatment of the blues, I must say that he shows a remarkable sense of taste in the standard tunes he selects to sing. Few other band singers nowadays feature such superior melodies as Vernon Duke's *April In Paris* and Harold Arlen's *The Girl That Got Away*.

Joe's first LP. album with the Basie band on Clef is a varied and interesting introduction to his singular brand of blues singing. It reveals him in moods warmly composed as well as ones where he really bawls his lyrics.

Both his long features, *Every Day* and *The Comeback*, are contained on the LP. *Every Day*, his big-seller, goes on for close on six minutes and spotlights the singer in fine form. Ernie Wilkins has scored a series of immense brass voicings in his background arrangement for this record, and they spur Williams' singing very successfully. The vocalist pulls several highly personal tricks out of the hat during his choruses, one of them (typical of his extrovert style) being to yodel one or two phrases in the upper register of his voice. *The Comeback*, a feature of similar length, proves to be a medium-tempo swinger scored by tenorman Frank Foster. Frank has built up interesting section voicings around Joe's vocal here, mainly with clipped trombone phrases and lines for the open reeds. He inserts between the two vocal sections of the score a spurting, furious passage of tenor improvisation by himself, a solo which is ably backed by Sonny Payne's belting drums.

Ernie Wilkins' second arrangement in the album is the slow-tempo ballad *Teach Me Tonight*, a varied and imaginative score which is spoilt by a very ordinary performance by Williams. His voice is rich and full, but he injects no obvious feeling into the lyric and makes no effort to remould any of the phrases into the personal shapes so typical of his blues features. *Teach Me Tonight* and *Ev'ry Day I Fall In Love* (scored by Foster) are the two least-inspired efforts by Joe in the album.

In The Evening When The Sun Goes Down (another Frank Foster score) also requires Joe to sing at slow tempo, but back with the blues formula the singer sounds much more himself. Leroy Carr was perhaps the greatest of blues lyric writers and his poetry has been treated with respect and sensitivity by this performance. Joe imbues a feeling into the words of true sadness, almost as though he is announcing the facts about his own life; this ring of sincerity, a way of making the song sound quite personal, is one of the hall-marks of the true blues singer. In the delicate orchestral accompaniment Frank Foster has made effective use of Frank Wess's flute and of muted trumpet (I think played by Wendell Culley).

Three further numbers scored by Frank Foster are *My Baby Upsets Me, Please Send Me Someone To Love* and *Alright, Okay, You Win*. The first, Williams' own theme, is a blues rendered at slow-medium tempo and provides a fine example of the way Joe will often pick on a phrase and chant it *ad lib*, just like a preacher determined to impress his point upon the congregation. "My baby upsets me, upsets me, upsets me," he sings, and several other lines of the lyric are treated in the same manner. *Someone To Love* is another slow ballad, but one which he handles rather more sensibly. After a spectacular introduction by trumpeter Thad Jones, Joe takes up the song, kneads the words into a personal expression of feeling and evokes a genuine spirit. Unlike the dead-pan *Teach Me Tonight*, his voice here does sound concerned with the words it is singing. *Alright, Okay, You Win* is a medium-tempo rendition of a boogie-woogie type theme, a track outstanding for the enthusiastic attack by both the singer and the band.

The final item on the LP., *Roll 'Em Pete*, finds Williams really shouting the lyric in the true Kansas City manner, with the band building up a tremendous head arrangement behind him. Like Joe Turner, who sang the words on Pete Johnson's earlier recording of the number, Joe unleashes a fine rhythmic attack. He re-phrases a number of lines and in others he places his emphasis upon different words, while his timing of the melody tends to be more polished than Turner's, yet the spirit of the Kansas City jam session is very much in evidence. The band plays magnificently. Basie leads off with a piano introduction, then after Joe's first rendition of the lyric there are rousing solos by Benny Powell (how the American polls can place the banal Bill Harris at the top of the trombone division when soloists like Coker and Powell are around really puzzles me) and tenorman Frank Wess. High-register brass riffing provides a fine climax.

It is true that there are weak items in the album, but there are also these others which feature Williams at his best; which exploit his vitality, his stamina, his exciting sense of swing and his full, powerful voice. Williams has his weaknesses, and, as I have said, I feel that he is a good blues singer without being a great one.

However, he has a number of fine qualities which should impress any blues lover save the perfectionist; qualities which I have attempted to describe in a rational way in this article.

One additional point I will make in his defence, and one which must form my conclusion: he may be an inferior blues singer to Jimmy Rushing, but he is one of the very few blues singers to emerge in the 1950's with a strongly-individual character.

CHAPTER VII

ADDITIONAL BIOGRAPHIES OF MUSICIANS OF THE NEW BASIE BAND

WENDELL CULLEY
(*Trumpet*)

KNOWN AS "The Professor" to most of the men in the band, Wendell has been in the brass section ever since Basie reorganized his big band at the end of 1951. Born on 8th January 1908 in Worcester, Massachusetts, he first played trumpet with a small local band at the age of seventeen. In 1930, encouraged by the praises of his fellow musicians in Worcester, he travelled to New York, full of determination to break into the upper strata of the band business. His strong, rounded tone and facile phrasing quickly impressed musicians and he was given a year's engagement with Horace Henderson's band. Later, he played for a year with Cab Calloway, and then for eleven years as featured soloist in the trumpet section of the Noble Sissle Orchestra.

From 1944 to 1949 he was importantly featured with the Lionel Hampton big band, playing in one of the most swinging brass sections of the decade. Hampton fully appreciated Wendell's inventive and musicianly playing; he used him on practically all his recording sessions with small groups drawn from the band at this period. A particularly fine example of the trumpeter's solo work may be heard on the Hampton recording of *Midnight Sun* on Decca. Also he proved a sensitive accompanist for the band's singer, Dinah Washington. He played the obbligato on her Decca recording of *Blowtop Blues*, and when the band played at Carnegie Hall in 1945 he delicately embroidered her rendering of *Evil Gal Blues*. Wendell returned to Noble Sissle for fourteen months prior to joining Basie.

Though playing a less glamorous role than Joe Newman and Thad Jones, Wendell has been very busy with the Basie band, playing accompaniments, deputy lead parts, and, on occasions, lead parts. He plays the lead during the arrangement of *Small*

Hotel, a feature designed to show off the brass section, and when on occasions the band slows down its tempo to play an orchestral ballad, he invariably plays any solo parts which appear with the arrangement. As a soloist he is at his best with slow, sensitive ballads.

JOE WILDER

(*Trumpet*)

Joe Wilder is one of the very few completely fresh and original trumpet stylists to emerge with modern jazz in the 1950's. Certain facets of his style have much in common with Basie's musical policy, and he actually toured Europe with the band in the spring of 1954 as well as making records with sidemen from the Basie school; such facts warrant his inclusion in this section.

Born Joseph Benjamin Wilder at Colwyn, Pennsylvania, on 22nd February 1922, Joe is the son of a bandleader. He was raised in Philadelphia, where his father today still leads a dance band. After learning a certain amount of theory, the boy made his début at a local amateur contest, organized by a Philadelphia radio station. His playing was praised after the show, and thus encouraged he entered the Mastbaum School of Music, joining a class which also included Red Rodney and Buddy De Franco and which stimulated his desire to play jazz after hours.

He was launched as a full-time musician when he joined Les Hite's Orchestra in 1941; with this band he stayed for a year, working in a trumpet section which included the radical Dizzy Gillespie. From 1942 to 1943 he worked with the Hampton band, a job which was terminated with the arrival of his service papers. For the next two years he played in a U.S. Marine band, ultimately achieving the position of assistant bandmaster. Then in 1945 he obtained his discharge and commenced a series of lengthy jobs with name bands; first with Hampton for a year, then in turn with Lunceford (until the leader's death), Lucky Millinder, Sam Donahue, Herbie Fields and Noble Sissle. (With the Millinder band he recorded one of his first solos: *I Ain't Got Nothing To Lose* on Victor.) The job with Sissle was the last touring work Joe wanted to undertake for some time. He settled in New York, playing in the pit bands with a series of Broadway shows, including "Alive And Kicking" and three years with "Guys And Dolls", as well as studying in his spare time at the Manhattan School of Music where he obtained his B.A. in 1954. He undertook the European tour with Basie and made a number of recordings with the band for Clef, but left soon after his return to New York in order to concentrate upon freelance work around the city. Since then he has appeared frequently on TV with Camarata and various other commercial orchestras, as well as playing in the city's jazz clubs and making records for Ozzie Cadena's Savoy label.

Wilder's trumpet style is very distinctive, and is certainly one of the most original to be heard in contemporary jazz. Rhythmically he is in agreement with the style of the Basie band, while his phrasing shows that he has wedded some of the melodic devices of the swing era with the harmonic devices of modern jazz. His tone, however, though it conveys warmth, is pure and clean, almost a legitimate tone. These qualities of tone are emphasized because of the way he improvises his phrases—so softly, so delicately, so sensitively, making them seem elegant and beautifully-poised, weaving them with the same symmetry and formal balance as in a piece of hand-made lace. At times he seems to make his notes deliberately soft, so that they merge into each other, rather in the same style as the late Frankie Newton. This makes his improvisations appear on the surface very pliable and smooth, even when he is playing at a fast tempo or when he is blowing in the upper register of his instrument. I don't think that I have ever heard a solo by Wilder in which he sounded in the least bit ruffled. He plays with great technical assurance and an elegance which may be compared with that of Benny Carter. Moreover, his imagination matches his musicianship; he never repeats himself.

The middle-eight which Joe plays on the Basie band's recording of *Straight Life* illustrates perfectly the qualities in his style: the smooth, lovely tone, the carefully-constructed, economical phrases, the thought which he gives to melody, the wonderful control and timing which he exercises. I feel that Wilder has been one of the most important younger trumpeters to pass through the Basie band, and that his influence will be greatly felt in jazz in future years. Since leaving Basie he has recorded a number of fine albums in New York; one on Commodore with Frank Wess, one on Bethlehem with Pete Brown (containing superb improvisations by Joe on *Tea For Two* and *Used Blues*), a third with Ralph Burns on M.G.M. ("Winter Sequence"). Three Savoy albums feature him to even better advantage. The first is "The Trio With Guests", containing Joe's long improvisation at slow-tempo upon the well-tried harmonies of *How High The Moon*, backed by the Hank Jones Trio. The second is Ernie Wilkins' "Top Brass", which features Joe in several solo parts, the most memorable being a ballad chorus on *Willow Weep For Me*. Finally, there is his own album—just trumpet backed again by the Hank Jones Trio—in which he improvises upon a superior selection of standard melodies at a variety of tempos.

BENNY POWELL
(Trombone)

Benjamin Gordon Powell—one of the finest trombone products of the younger modern jazz school—joined Basie in 1951, and may be justifiably described as a founder member of the new band. He shares most of the trombone solos with Henry Coker (who did not actually join the band until some three months later) as well as playing deputy lead to him in the section work. Though still comparatively young, his solo style has displayed a maturity in ideas and technique well in advance of his years.

Though New Orleans is no longer looked upon as an important base for jazz musicians, having yielded up its one-time monopoly upon the music to other cities such as Chicago, Kansas City, New York and, latterly, Los Angeles, it still seems capable of producing important jazz musicians, even though evolution has required new standards of playing and a new technical approach to visit the jazz scene. In the present Basie band both Joe Newman and Benny Powell sport college ties which have their origins in the Crescent City. "It must be something in the air in New Orleans," one critic once ribbed me, "which causes it to produce jazz musicians as fast as a doe rabbit produces young." Perhaps there is something in this! Anyone born in New Orleans certainly inherits a strong jazz tradition.

Benny was born on 1st March 1930 and remembers taking his first lessons on drums at the age of eight. By the time he was twelve he was playing regularly in his grammar-school band, and

268

in that same year he acquired his first trombone. So well did he master the rudiments of this latter instrument that on New Year's Day 1944 he made his début as a professional musician. At fifteen he was playing gigs with a local band led by one Dooky Chase, but he quit this job in order to study for a while at the Alabama State College. By 1946 he was playing professionally once more, this time with King Kolax's band in Texas. "I starved for a year with them," he ruefully recalls, "and then I joined Ernie Fields' band in Tulsa and starved for another year." Things improved for the young musician in 1948, however, when he obtained a job in the trombone section of the Lionel Hampton band. This job lasted until 1951 and it gave Benny plenty of experience, the kind of experience which only a nameband can bring, and his confidence and musicianship improved considerably. In 1951 he lived for a short while in Ottawa in Canada, singing, studying, playing trombone and bongo drums. In October of that year he travelled to New York, sat in at one of the early rehearsals of the new Basie band and secured a job. Since then he has been entrusted with a large solo book by Basie.

In style Benny obviously owes a great deal to the remarkable modern trombone theories of Jay Jay Johnson, even though he is only too ready to admit an admiration for the earlier school of Vic Dickenson and Trummy Young. Possessed of a most facile technique, he phrases very like Jay Jay, with fast, clean runs of notes interspersed with intricate, though often quite melodic figures. He appears to delight in introducing variations to the rhythm pattern, one moment launching upon a series of short staccato phrases, the next slipping out his ideas in a more flowing, legato style. Unlike Henry Coker, who phrases in a very extrovert style, despite its modern overtones, Benny will often project his ideas in a subtle, devious manner, weaving about his theme instead of stating it directly. In tone too he is different from his sectionmate; his tone is clean and rounded, but its edges are softer and more pliable, thereby fashioning an interesting contrast with Coker's brilliant, brassy tone.

The Basie repertoire features Benny fairly well with arrangements like Ernie Wilkins' *The Moon's Not High, Jumpin' At The Woodside, Basie's Loaded* and *Blues Backstage*. A typical solo by him is to be heard on the band's Clef recording of *Tippin' On The Q.T.* For solos of greater length by him one can easily refer to a fine series of small group recordings he has made for various labels, mostly with Basie sidemen. He recorded one LP. for Blue Note with Frank Foster (a Quintet date), a second for Period with drummer Osie Johnson, and yet another for Vanguard in the company of Joe Newman, Sir Charles Thompson and Pete Brown. On the latter date he played fine improvisations on three tunes: *Bop This*, *Oh! Joe* and *For The Ears*. He was a prominent sideman on the first LP. which tenorman Frank Wess led on Commodore, creating some of his best recorded work on the twelve-bar blues *Basie Ain't Here* and Osie Johnson's original, *Frankosis*. Finally, he took part on one of the superior Buck Clayton jam sessions, recorded for Columbia. One of the 12-inch LP.s issued subsequently from these sessions, "How High The Fi", contains full solo choruses by Benny on *Sentimental Journey* and *Moten Swing*.

Johnny Mandel

(*Trombone and Arranger*)

When Basie auditioned for the new band at the end of 1951, he settled on a trombone section comprising: Henry Coker, Benny Powell and Jimmy Wilkins. The latter, a brother of altoist Ernie Wilkins, stayed with the band until June 1953, when he left to go to Detroit as manager of his uncle's restaurant there. It's actually Jimmy who takes the trombone solo on the Clef recording of Ernie Wilkins' *Basie Talks* arrangement. "Now he's sorry he ever left the band," comments Ernie.

As a replacement for him, the Count engaged the white musician, Johnny Mandel, who took over the third trombone book, and, after studying the musical style of the band thoroughly, contributed a number of arrangements to the band's repertoire. (Marty Paich thinks about ten arrangements in all.) Johnny toured with the band for about five months, and then left to settle on the American Pacific coast, working as a freelance arranger. His place was ultimately filled by Bill Hughes.

Born in New York City, on 23rd November 1925, Mandel is one of the most brilliant orchestral minds yet produced by the modern jazz school. A thoroughly schooled musician, who has studied under a number of the best minds in American music, he is one of the very few arrangers to succeed in combining classical writing techniques sensitively with the elements of jazz. To play through a Mandel score is to hear interesting ensemble writing, yet also a strong sense of jazz rhythms and melody. He has arranged for almost every important big band in the United States as well as for films, radio and television, yet when handling jazz material he never lowers his artistic standards and all his writing maintains a consistently inventive level.

It is difficult to pick out highlights from the prolific store of arrangements which Mandel has contributed to jazz, so meticulous is his orchestration. His own compositions all contain a strong melodic substance. I can only select the ones which have personally pleased me so much. These include: *The Song Is You* (recorded on Coral), which he wrote for the Willis Conover Orchestra; the "Pacific Jazz Album", which he arranged for Cy Touff, where all the writing is similar to that for a Basie small group; the compositions *Hershey Bar* and *Pot Luck*, recorded by Stan Getz; and, of course, *Straight Life*, which he composed for Basie. This latter theme has been recorded on Clef.

Straight Life is quite one of the outstanding arrangements in the repertoire of the contemporary Basie band. Consisting of a thirty-two-bar theme, scored at slow-medium tempo, Mandel uses it to make the band sound emphatic and yet restrained, its rhythmic power definite but with the swing lightly imposed. The supple, flowing melody of the main phrase is enhanced by the delicacy of the reed voicing which he uses, while the middle-eight phrase, surprisingly, has been lifted from his previous composition, *Pot Luck*. Only after sixteen bars of improvisation each by Frank Wess, Joe Newman (tightly muted for the occasion), Basie and Henry Coker, does Mandel unleash the might of the band's brass —and then only for sixteen bars. The final chorus and coda are as quiet as the introduction. The score is a thing at once warmly beautiful and technically articulate, imaginative and perfectly poised.

BILL HUGHES
(*Trombone*)

Born in Dallas, Texas, on 28th March 1930, Bill Hughes cropped up from a position of comparative obscurity to take the place in the trombone section vacated by Johnny Mandel at the end of 1953. Though a competent reading musician and section man, for a long time he was featured very little as a soloist with the band. During the European tour of 1954 his trombone was rarely heard as a solo voice, although Ernie Wilkins had scored one part for him in the arrangement of *Basie English*. More recently, however, his stature as an improviser has been given greater recognition. He has recorded one fine solo with the band: *Magic* on Clef. He is also featured on an Osie Johnson LP. on Period.

BILL GRAHAM
(*Alto-saxophone*)

A capable performer on both baritone and alto-saxophones, Bill was born in Kansas City on 8th September 1918, though he was actually brought up and made to study music in Denver. At the University in Denver he first met tenorman Paul Quinichette and the two musicians led a small semi-professional group to play for local dances. Later Bill studied at the Tuskegee Institute in Alabama and at Lincoln University in Missouri. On turning professional musician he worked briefly with Basie, and then in turn with the bands of Lucky Millinder, Erskine Hawkins and Eddy Wilcox. In the early 1950's he worked mainly with Dizzy Gillespie, usually playing baritone in the various small units which the trumpeter led during these years. He toured Europe with Gillespie. Then for two years he led his own small group at Snookie's Club in New York.

When Ernie Wilkins left the Basie band early in 1955 the leader first tried to get Earl Warren to rejoin. The former deputy-leader, however, was too tied up with work to go on tour. Graham's name was then suggested to Basie. The leader sought him out and persuaded him to revert to alto-saxophone, taking over the book normally played by Wilkins.

PAUL QUINICHETTE
(*Tenor-saxophone*)

"The man more like Lester than Lester himself" was the phrase frequently chanted by the critics in the early 1950's when

Paul Quinichette was gracing the saxophone section of the new Basie band. Paul, who worked with the Count's new band from 1951 to early in 1953, certainly did resemble Lester tonally, in his designing of phrases and in his subtly-shifting swing at this period, though he lacked the imagination and the greater inspiration of the master.

Born on 7th May 1921 at Denver, Colorado, Paul Quinichette has had a thorough musical training as well as a lengthy professional career as a jazz musician. While at Denver University he practised clarinet and alto-saxophone before finally deciding that the tenor was his true medium; later, he majored in music at Tennessee State College. The first jobs he had as a musician were with Nat Towles, Lloyd Hunter and then one in Chicago with a quintet led by Shorty Sherock. After this he rose to the fore via a long series of jobs with touring bands. He was with Jay McShann from 1942 to 1944 (taking a solo on the band's American Decca recording of the Gene Ramey composition, *Say Forward, I'll March*), then he worked in turn with Johnny Otis, Louis Jordan, Lucky Millinder and Eddy Wilcox. Then he settled in New York, playing for a time with J. C. Heard's small group at Café Society, later freelancing with musicians like trumpeter "Hot Lips" Page until 1951, when he went into the Basie band. Once with the Count his reputation grew enormously. He recorded a great many solos with the band for Clef, including *Paul Meets Prez, Cash Box, No Name, Jack And Jill, Basie Talks* and *Bootsie,* as well as a number of fine small-group features like *Preview, Shad Roe, Crew Cut, Samie* and *The Hook* with Buck Clayton, Dicky Wells and the Count at the organ. Wardell Gray, who had advised Basie to hire the tenorman, seems to have been a sound judge, for Paul functioned extremely well with the band. His improvisation was always tasteful, carefully constructed and well suited to the singular Kansas City rhythm pattern. Since leaving the band he has successfully led his own small group around New York, though he did take time off in 1955 to go on tour with the Benny Goodman Octet (a group which also included Ruby Braff and Urbie Green).

Paul's various recordings prior to joining the Basie band were almost all styled after the playing of Lester Young. His Decca sides with McShann, his Excelsior sessions with Johnny Otis (including one feature shared with blues shouter Jimmy Rushing, *My Baby's Business*), his sides with "Lips" Page for Victor and for Rudi

273

Blesh's Circle label and his solos like *Blow Top Blues* with Dinah Washington for Mercury, all register Lester's influence with their cool tone, easy phrasing and lagging swing. Since leaving Basie, however, Paul's style has changed somewhat, at least if one is to judge from his recorded performances. He still designs many of his phrases along the same lines as Lester, but his tone has gradually become more forceful, his swing more firmly poised upon the beat. Nowadays his playing reminds one somewhat of the late Dick Wilson, prominent tenorman with Andy Kirk's band in the 1930's and claimed by Paul to have been one of his early influences. His more important records since leaving the Basie band—and which reflect the new character in his playing—are the "Jazz Studio One" LP. on Decca, a Roost LP. with Johnny Smith (using the alias of "Element X"), a trio date for Vanguard with Mel Powell and Bobby Donaldson, a small-group date for Emarcy and a variety of sides with his own group on American Decca (some of them with Marlowe Morris on organ).

EDDIE DAVIS

(*Tenor-saxophone*)

The predilection for two contrasting tenor-saxophone stylists, first encouraged by Basie with Lester Young and Herschel Evans, and later with Lester Young and Buddy Tate, has continued with the contemporary band. From May 1952 until July 1953 Eddie Davis, a gutty, hard-blowing tenorman, with improvisations which obviously spring from the Hawkins' concept, worked with the band. Naturally his playing proved a marked contrast from the softer, more relaxed tenor playing of the Lester Young-influenced Paul Quinichette. (Now that both have left the band the contrast of tenor styles is still continued with Franks Wess and Foster.)

Born in New York City in 1921, Davis was largely self-taught as a musician. He first came to the notice of musicians when appearing at Monroe's Uptown House in Harlem, a club similar to Minton's Playhouse, where in the early 1940's musicians gathered to play largely for their own enjoyment. It became a minor experimental centre and many new musicians possessed of new ideas had their first opportunity to broadcast their theories in the club. From 1942 to 1943 Eddie toured with Cootie Williams, and then worked in turn with Lucky Millinder, Andy Kirk and Louis Armstrong, before settling in New York to lead his own small group. Apart from the recent year with Basie he has worked with small groups ever since. He has recorded with Benny Green (Prestige), Dinah Washington (Emarcy), Gene Krupa (Clef) and for various labels with groups under his own leadership, perhaps the most noteworthy of these being the Savoy sides which feature some of the best recorded work by the late Fats Navarro on trumpet.

Always a forceful tenorman, at times coming close to the rhythm-and-blues style, with strong, attacking phrases and a ripe tone which on occasions slips into a coarse vibrato, Eddie was prominently featured with Basie both on record and at the band's concerts. Perhaps his most spectacular solo is on *Paradise Squat* (Clef), accompanied by Basie on organ, but he can also be heard to advantage on the recorded arrangements of *Bread* and *Tom Whaley*.

CHARLIE FOWLKES

(Baritone-saxophone)

"Charlie Fowlkes has the baritone chair well covered—and in more ways than one, for he's six feet four high and weighs two hundred and ninety pounds." This physical assessment of the reed section's rock-like anchor by Ernie Wilkins ties up well with the musical contribution that Fowlkes makes to the band's playing. For while his adept handling of the baritone parts acts as the foundation stone for most of the reed voicings, he is also responsible for creating much of the attacking impact which the section evidences when playing a fast, swinging figure in unison. His importance to Basie may well be compared favourably with the importance of Harry Carney's baritone to Duke Ellington, though in the band arrangements, of course, both men are used in entirely different ways.

Brooklyn-born on 16th February 1916, Charlie when at college practised with all the saxophones, and clarinet and violin as well. The musical experience which he holds is impressive: six years with Tiny Bradshaw, then, after a year spent at war defence work, four years with Lionel Hampton, followed by shorter periods with Arnett Cobb and acting as an agent for his wife, singer Wini Brown. He played in the big band which Basie tried to keep together unsuccessfully in the spring of 1951, and has been with the new band since its inception.

Until the period commencing when he joined Basie, Charlie Fowlkes wasn't known as a soloist in jazz. He'd even been known to exclaim: "I'm not a soloist. I'm a utility man." Basie drew him out, however, and bit by bit discovered that the baritone-saxist had been hiding his light beneath a bushel, being in actual fact no mean soloist on his instrument. Since then his ripe-edged tone, deep, sonorous phrasing and extrovert sense of humour have been used to good effect by the band. At almost every concert now the band plays an arrangement of *Rock-a-bye Basie* featuring his big, full, shuddering baritone phrases extensively; usually it proves to be one of the most rousing items in the band's repertoire. In contrast, he occasionally plays a rich, rhapsodic solo on *Eventide*.

Small-group sessions by the Basie men have been calling upon his services as a soloist too. One discovers him featured quite prominently on the Buck Clayton Columbia jam sessions, playing solos in his normal booting, uninhibited way on *The Hucklebuck*, *Robbins Nest* and *Sentimental Journey*. Osie Johnson used him on his Period LP. Kenny Clarke used him for his first Savoy LP. together with Henry Coker and Frank Wess.

GENE RAMEY

(*Bass*)

When Basie re-formed his big band in 1951 he kept as his bassist Jimmy Lewis, the same man that he had used with his septet in 1950. In November 1952, however, Lewis left and was replaced by Gene Ramey, one of the most gifted younger jazz-men to emerge from the Kansas City scene.

Born on 4th April 1913 at Austin, Texas, Gene's first musical instrument was a sousaphone which he played in a band also including the great tenorman Herschel Evans; that job was in 1930. Two years later he moved to Kansas City, where Walter Page taught him to play the string bass. (The fact that today Walter is still Gene Ramey's favourite bass player speaks well for his tuition.) By the time 1938 arrived he had mastered the new instrument sufficiently to work in Kansas City with Countess Johnson. This was followed by a period of six years spent with Jay McShann's Orchestra, taking his career up to 1944. Settling in New York towards the end of 1944, he worked for a year with Luis Russell, and then, finding increasing interests in the rapidly-developing modern jazz, he played along 52nd Street with groups led by "Lips" Page and the already legendary Charlie Parker. He remained with various small modern jazz groups until 1952, when he joined Basie.

A versatile musician, able to fit in with groups of different size and style in jazz, Gene is respected by both the traditional and modern schools. His big, clean tone, sure-fingered accuracy and steady drive underlined the Basie band's ensemble to good effect during his period with it.

Apart from the Basie band's recordings which he made for Clef (including a small group date with Newman, Coker, Royal and Quinichette) Gene has recorded scores of sessions over the years, including many sides with Jay McShann (Decca), Horace Silver, Lou Donaldson and Thelonious Monk (Blue Note), Lester Young (Clef), Pete Brown and Joe Wilder (Bethlehem), Stan Getz (Prestige) and Fats Navarro (Savoy). In March 1954 pianist Duke Jordan used him for a Vogue LP. Usually on records Gene has concentrated on producing a fine rhythm behind the group. The Sir Charles Thompson Sextet LP. on Vanguard (the one with Joe Newman and Benny Powell) contains some of his rare solo work.

EDDIE JONES

(Bass)

It was in August 1953 that Basie, badly in need of a good bass player, engaged Eddie Jones, a young man previously little known in the New York school of jazz musicians. The Count's ability to estimate very quickly a man's potential power, however, had not gone amiss. Jones has been with the band ever since and is now being recognized by musicians as one of the finest rhythm men of the younger generation of jazz musicians. "He was an eager, but inexperienced kid when he joined us,"

Ernie Wilkins remembers, "but he's improved so much that he's now one of the best bass players in the business." An impressive figure (Basie has a number of plump men in the band, though Charlie Fowlkes is way ahead of everyone where size is concerned), Eddie controls his instrument like a man cuddling a docile toy doll. Yet this appearance can be deceptive. Although he makes playing seem easy, he is one of the hardest-worked men in the band, for Basie relies so much upon his rhythm section. With a facile touch Eddie evinces a tremendous drive from his bass, and when he's working in partnership with Freddie Greene the two men swing together as though they have worked in each other's company for many years.

Eddie was born in New York City on 1st March 1929. He was actually raised in Red Bank, New Jersey, living only two doors away from the Basie family there. It wasn't until he joined the band after an audition that Basie realized that this fine musician was in fact the kid who'd originally been a friend of the family! Starting on bass while at Howard University in 1946, Eddie's experience in the front ranks of the jazz world was comparatively slight up to joining Basie. In 1951 he'd been away from jazz for a whole year when he went to teach in Beauford, South Carolina. He returned to jazz, however, in 1952, when he lived for a year in Washington, working in a post office by day and playing and singing in a trio every evening. Frank Wess and pianist John Malachi were studying in Washington at the same time. From Washington he joined Basie.

His influences as a bassist come from Walter Page, and from modern jazz stylists such as Ray Brown, Nelson Boyd and Milt Hinton, though he is no copyist. All the more recent recordings by the Basie Orchestra on Clef feature his propulsive work, while he has made a number of small-group sessions, notably for Vanguard with Joe Newman, for Period with Osie Johnson, for Decca in the "Jazz Studio One" album and for the Kenny Clarke first Savoy LP. (playing in a group which also included Henry Coker, Frank Wess and Charlie Fowlkes). In a more recent Savoy album, the Hank Jones Quintet (with Donald Byrd), his solo work during one long jam session type feature entitled *An Evening At Pappa Joe's* reveals him to be a confident improviser, capable of playing melodic ideas on his instrument in the best Jimmy Blanton tradition.

GUS JOHNSON
(*Drums*)

"Even when a photographer and an electrician were battling off-stage, and Gus was delightedly digging every blow, the beat kept coming sure and steady." These words, written by the English critic Stanley Dance in a review of a concert played by the Basie band in Paris in 1954, aptly summarize the way in which Gus Johnson competently took over the difficult Jo Jones' role in the Count's group. Gus followed Jo Jones in the Basie band in 1948. Apart from brief periods when Shadow Wilson and Butch Ballard deputized for him, he held this position outstandingly through until December 1954.

Born at Tyler, Texas, on 15th November 1913, Gus studied piano, bass and drums at school; he was a class-mate of Henry Coker. At the age of nine he had his first professional work in Houston, appearing as a child prodigy. As he grew up he played with various small bands in Texas and later in Kansas City. Once he became a member of the Kaycee school he developed considerably as a jazz musician. He was a prominent sideman with the Jay McShann band at the same time as Charlie Parker, and he played drums on Parker's first recordings, such as *Hootie Blues* and *Dexter Blues* with McShann. In 1941 Gus travelled to New York with this band, but soon after was forced to leave it when his army papers arrived, his place being taken by Harold "Doc" West. It is interesting to note that, after Gus left, McShann recorded one of the drummer's compositions, *Get Me On Your Mind*.

Upon release Gus rejoined the McShann band for a short spell. This job was followed by engagements with Eddie Vinson and with the last Earl Hines big band (a group which included Ernie Wilkins). In 1948 he took over the drum stool with Basie, and between that date and the end of 1954 managed to make most of the band's recording sessions, including the ones with the 1950–1951 septet. He has worked since December 1954 as a free-lance in New York City, and with the Larry Sonn band.

In style Gus is obviously a disciple and admirer of the great Jo Jones. In fact, when the Basie band was in Paris in 1954 and one evening Gus was being showered with praise by a number of critics after one of the concerts, he stated his view very firmly. "Thanks," he said in acknowledgment, "but don't knock my predecessor with Basie. Nobody has ever swung the band like Jo did."

Though a fine technician, Gus is not a pretentious drummer in any way. He rarely, if ever, took solos with Basie; instead he just concentrated upon sending the band with a strong, propulsive beat—and he coped surprisingly well. He was able to blow up a storm behind the ensemble whenever the occasion demanded, accenting figures in the arrangement forcefully, generating a prodigious swing on items like *Basie Talks*, *Tom Whaley*, *Peace Pipe* and *Basie Goes Wess*. He also proved his ability with brushes on *Straight Life* and other slow-tempo features in the repertoire, performing in a sensitive, relaxed and articulate way. I feel that the best all-round study of his work is to be found on the first "Count Basie Dance Session" LP. on Clef, though he can also be heard to advantage on the small-group sides which the Count made in 1952 for Mercury with Buck Clayton, Paul Quinichette and Dicky Wells. An example of his playing since leaving Basie may be discovered on "The Modern Art Of Zoot Sims" LP. on the Dawn label.

Sonny Payne

(*Drums*)

One of the most recent additions to the Basie Orchestra, Sonny was brought in to replace Gus Johnson in December 1954. Born in New York City in 1926, he is the offspring of another notable jazz percussionist, Chris Columbus. Prior to joining Basie he had worked with a number of bands, the most important being the Erskine Hawkins Orchestra. He recorded with Hawkins for Coral.

An articulate, stylish musician, Sonny is well able to generate a powerful and exciting rhythm behind the ensemble. His ability to push the full orchestra strongly can be easily gauged by the band's recordings of *The Comeback*, *Every Day* and *Roll 'Em Pete* with blues shouter Joe Williams. On the other hand, *In The Evening*, also featuring Williams, reveals that Sonny can also furnish a soft, sensitive rhythm for an ultra-slow blues. Like his predecessor, Gus Johnson, Sonny prefers the job of driving the band with a strong, steady beat to playing overlong, elaborate percussion features. Only when playing to an audience where the demand is more for spectacle than for music does he bring out a long and exciting demonstration of jazz drumming with the Basie arrangement of *With Friends*.

BIXIE CRAWFORD
(*Singer*)

A trained musician as well as a singer, Bixie Crawford was born on 2nd August 1923 in Oklahoma City. At first singing came more as a sideline for her; she majored in music at Lincoln University, and, apart from a knowledge of composition, she has played piano and 'cello. Benny Carter heard her singing at a picnic one day and offered her a job.

After singing for a year with the Carter band, she was with the Lunceford band immediately prior to the famous leader's death. Her first work with Basie was for three months in 1949. From 1949 to 1950 she sang with Louis Jordan, but then left the musical profession to become a school-teacher in Los Angeles. She rejoined Basie for a time when he went on the road with his new big band in 1951.

For recorded examples of her work there is a session on United under her own name, aided by a septet drawn from the Basie band. She has also recorded *Like A Ship At Sea* with the full band for Clef. On account of Basie's rightful featuring of the band to such an extent at concerts, of course, it has meant that a girl singer with the band usually performs on only one or two numbers in the programme; in Europe in 1954 Bixie was often excluded from concerts altogether. When she does sing she is an average performer in a style reminiscent of Ella Fitzgerald. Once Joe Williams joined the band there was little call for her services.

A COUNT BASIE DISCOGRAPHY

by ALUN MORGAN

IN COMPILING THIS discography I was confronted with the problem of setting out the various details in the most suitable manner. Most discographical listings of jazz artists are based on the strict chronology of the recording dates. In the case of this Count Basie listing I have tried to simplify the task of the reader who wishes to refer to any recordings made under the names of Basie sidemen. Consequently the discography is divided into two sections. Part I is devoted to those sessions on which Basie himself was present as a participating musician; this part contains all the recordings made under the title *Count Basie and his Orchestra* plus those other records on which Basie played but not as the actual leader. Part II gives details of representative records made by musicians and singers from within the band and is listed in alphabetical order under the leaders' names. In this second section I have had to use my own powers of discretion, omitting records which contain Basie musicians in settings which fall outside the scope of this book. Similarly I have included some records, notably *Shorty Courts The Count* by Shorty Rogers and his Orchestra, made by bands attempting a literal transcription of the Basie formulae although not actually featuring any of the Count's men.

Readers unfamiliar with discographical layout may care to note that the band title appears on the first line, followed by the personnel. The date and place of recording is given beneath the personnel and is followed by the list of titles made at that session. The numbers on the left of each title are the individual matrix numbers (where known) allocated by the record company in question while the catalogue or issue numbers appear on the right-hand side. A key to the abbreviations used in the discography will be found at the end of Part II.

Due to the tremendous increase in gramophone-record production it has been impossible to include the catalogue numbers of every reissue; for example, the fact that some of the tunes first recorded for the American Victor company have ultimately appeared on Indian HMV is considered to be of very limited interest. Consequently I have included only British and American catalogue numbers.

I must apologise for a certain lack of information appertaining to those Count Basie records made for the Clef, Norgran and Verve labels.

PART I

A LISTING OF RECORDS ON WHICH COUNT BASIE PLAYS

BENNIE MOTEN'S KANSAS CITY ORCHESTRA
Joe Keyes, Dink Stewart, Hot Lips Page (tpt); Dan Minor (tbn); Eddie Durham (tbn, g); Eddie Barefield, Jack Washington, Ben Webster (reeds); Count Basie (p); Leroy Berry (g); Walter Page (bs); Willie McWashington (d); Buster Moten (p, acc); Jimmy Rushing (vo).

Chicago—October 23, 1929

57301	*Rumba Negro*	Vi 23037, HMV B4845
57302	*Jones Law Blues*	Vi 23357
57303	*Band Box Shuffle*	Vi 23007
57304	*Small Black*	Vi 23342
57305	*Every Day Blues*	Vi V38144

Chicago—October 24, 1929

57312	*Boot It*	Vi V38144
57313	*Mary Lee*	Vi V38114
57314	*Rit-Tit Day*	Vi 23342
57315	*New Vine Street Blues*	Vi 23007
57316	*Sweethearts Of Yesterday*	Vi V38114

WALTER PAGE AND THE ORIGINAL BLUE DEVILS
Hot Lips Page, James Le Grand, James Simpson (tpt); Dan Minor (tbn); Buster Smith, Ted Manning, Reuben Reddy (reeds); Count Basie (p); Reuben Lynch (g); Walter Page (bs); Alvin Burroughs (d); Jimmy Rushing (vo).

Kansas City—November 10, 1929

KC612	*Blue Devil Blues*	Vo 1463
KC613	*Squabblin'*	Vo 1463

EDITH JOHNSON
(Count Basie has stated that he recorded with singer Edith Johnson. The following titles have "unknown piano accompaniment" which may be the records on which Basie played.)

Chicago—November 16, 1929

W403308		
W403309	*Ain't No More To Be Said*	OK 8748, HJCA 118
W403310		
W403311	*Heart Achin' Blues*	OK 8748, HJCA 118

BENNIE MOTEN'S KANSAS CITY ORCHESTRA
Personnel as before.

Kansas City—October 28, 29, 30, 31, 1930

62909	*Won't You Be My Baby*	Vi 23028
62910	*I Wish I Could Be Blue*	Vi 22734

62911	*Oh Eddie!*	Vi 22793, HMV B4986
62912	*That To Do*	Vi 22793, HMV B4912
62915	*Here Comes Marjorie*	Vi 23391
62916	*The Count*	Vi 23391
62921	*Liza Lee*	Vi 23023
62922	*Get Going*	Vi 23023
62923	*Professor Hot Stuff*	Vi 23429
62924	*When I'm Alone*	Vi 22734
62925	*New Moten Stomp*	Vi 23030
62926	*As Long As I Love You*	Vi 22660, HMV B4912
62927	*Somebody Stole My Gal*	Vi 23028, HMV B4844
62928	*Now That I Need You*	BB B6711
62929	*Bouncin' Around*	Vi 23030

New York City—April 15, 1931

54012	*Ya Got Love*	Vi 22680, HMV B4889
68900	*I Wanna Be Around My Baby*	Vi 22680

Harlan Leonard (sax); Buster Smith (sax) replace Washington.

Camden, New Jersey—December 13, 1932

74846	*Toby*	Vi 23384, HMV B6425, B4986
74847	*Moten's Swing*	Vi 23384, HMV B6377
74848	*Blue Room*	Vi 24381, HMV B4990
74849	*Imagination**	Vi 23378
74850	*New Orleans*	Vi 24216
74853	*The Only Girl I Ever Loved**	Vi 23378
74852	*Milenberg Joys*	Vi 24831, HMV B4953
74851	*Lafayette*	Vi 24216
74854	*Prince Of Wails*	Vi 23393
74855	*Two Times*	Vi 23393

* Add Sterling Russell Trio (vo).

COUNT BASIE AND HIS QUINTET (PaE)
JONES-SMITH INCORPORATED (Vo)
Carl Smith (tpt); Lester Young (ten); Count Basie (p); Walter Page (bs);
Jo Jones (d); Jimmy Rushing (vo).

Chicago—October 9, 1936

c1657	*Shoe Shine Swing*	Vo 3441, PaE R2636, Epic LN3107
c1658	*Evenin' v*JR	Vo 3441, DeE J13
c1659	*Boogie Woogie v*JR	Vo 3459, PaE R2874, Epic LN3107, CoE SEG7576
c1660	*Lady Be Good*	Vo 3549, PaE R2636, Epic LN3107

COUNT BASIE AND HIS ORCHESTRA
Joe Keyes, Carl Smith, Buck Clayton (tpt); George Hunt, Dan Minor (tbn);
Caughey Roberts (alt); Hershal Evans, Lester Young (ten); Jack Washington
(bar); Count Basie (p); Claude Williams (g); Walter Page (bs); Jo Jones (d);
Jimmy Rushing (vo).

New York City—January 22, 1937

61542	*Honeysuckle Rose*	De 1141, BrE O2496, LAT 8028
61543	*Pennies From Heaven* vJR	De 1121, BrE O2379, LA 8589
61544	*Swinging At The Daisy Chain*	De 1121, BrE O2379, LAT 8028
61545	*Roseland Shuffle*	De 1141, BrE O2515, LAT 8589

Ed Lewis, Bobby Moore (tpt); Freddie Greene (g) replace Keyes, Smith and Williams. Eddie Durham (tbn, arr) added.

New York City—March 26, 1937

62078	*Exactly Like You* vJR	De 1252, BrE O2521
62079	*Boo Hoo* vJR	De 1228, BrE O2427
62080	*Glory Of Love*	De 1228, BrE O2427
62081	*Boogie Woogie* vJR	De 1252, BrE O2521

Earl Warren (alt, vo) replaces Roberts.

New York City—July 7, 1937

62331	*Smarty* vJR	De 1379, BrE O2490
62332	*One O'Clock Jump*	De 1363, BrE G2466, LAT 8028
62333	*Listen My Children* vJR	De 1379, BrE O2490
62334	*John's Idea*	De 1363, BrE O2466, LAT 8028

New York City—August 9, 1937

62511	*Good Morning Blues* vJR	De 1446, BrE O2496
62512	*Our Love Was Meant To Be* vEW	De 1446, BrE O2543
62513	*Time Out*	De 1538, BrE O2543
62514	*Topsy*	De 1770, BrE O2684

(N.B.—Two different masters of 62511 have been issued.)

Bobby Hicks (tpt) replaces Moore. Benny Morton (tbn) added on 62683 only.

New York City—October 13, 1937

62682	*I Keep Remembering*	De 1581
62683	*Out Of The Window*	De 1581, BrE O2595, LA 8589
62684	*Don't You Miss Your Baby* vJR	De 1770, BrE O2797
62685	*Let Me Dream* vEW	De 1538, BrE O2870

New York City—January 3, 1938

| 63122 | *Georgianna* vJR | De 1682, BrE O2581 |
| 63123 | *Blues In The Dark* vJR | De 1682, BrE O2581, LAT 8028 |

New York City—February 16, 1938

63286	*Sent For You Yesterday* vJR	De 1880, BrE O2619, LA 8589
63287	*Every Tub*	De 1728, BrE O2595, LA 8589
63288	*Now Will You Be Good* vJR	De 1728, BrE O2940
63289	*Swinging The Blues*	De 1880, BrE O2619, LAT 8028

286

Benny Morton (tbn); Harry Edison (tpt) replace Hunt and Hicks.

New York City—June 6, 1938

63918	*Mama Don't Want No Peas* vJR	De 2030, BrE O2668
63919	*Blue And Sentimental*	De 1965, BrE O2644, LAT 8028
63920	*Doggin' Around*	De 1965, BrE G2644

New York City—August 22, 1938

64471	*Stop Beatin' Around The Mulberry Bush* vJR	De 2004, BrE O2658
64472	*London Bridge is Falling Down* vJR	De 2004, BrE O2668
64473	*Texas Shuffle*	De 2030, BrE O2668, LAT 8028
64474	*Jumping At The Woodside*	De 2212, BrE O2684

COUNT BASIE (p solos with usual rhythm)

New York City—November 9, 1938

64731	*How Long Blues*	De 2355, BrE O2762
64732	*The Dirty Dozens*	De 2498, BrE O2825
64733	*Hey Lawdy Mama*	De 2722, BrE O2929
64734	*The Fives*	De 2722, BrE O2929
64735	*Boogie Woogie*	De 2355, BrE O2762

COUNT BASIE AND HIS ORCHESTRA

Personnel as for August 22, 1938, plus Helen Humes (vo).

New York City—November 16, 1938

64746	*Dark Rapture* vHH	De 2212, BrE O2797
64747	*Shorty George*	De 2325, BrE O2745, LA 8589
64748	*The Blues I Like To Hear* vJR	De 2284, BrE O2728
64749	*Do You Wanna Jump, Children* vJR	De 2224, BrE O2711, LAT 8028
64750	*Panassié Stomp*	De 2224, BrE O2711, LAT 8028

Add Shad Collins (tpt).

New York City—January 5, 1939

| 64851 | *My Heart Belongs To Daddy* vHH | De 2249, BrE O2870 |
| 64852 | *Sing For Your Supper* vJR | De 2249, BrE O2940 |

COUNT BASIE (p solos with usual rhythm)

New York City—January 26, 1939

64954	*Oh! Red*	De 2780, BrE O3028
64955A	*Fare Thee Honey, Fare Thee Well*	De 2780, BrE O3028, LA 8589
64955B	*Fare Thee Honey, Fare Thee Well*	De 2780
64956	*Dupree Blues*	De 3071, BrE O2955
64957A	*When The Sun Goes Down*	De 2498, BrE O2825
64958	*Red Wagon*	De 3071, BrE O2955, LA 8589

COUNT BASIE AND HIS ORCHESTRA

Personnel as for January 5, 1939, except that the first side was made by Collins (tpt), Young (ten) and the rhythm section, also, although H. Evans (ten) is officially present on the session, he is not evident and Choo Berry (ten) definitely deputises for him on 64984-5.

NOTE: It is probable that henceforward B. Morton (tbn) is not present on all sessions up to the time he leaves the band (March 1940).

New York City—February 2, 1939

64978	*You Can Depend On ME* vJR	De 2631, BrE O2838
64979	*Cherokee Pt. 1*	De 2406, BrE O2780
64980	*Cherokee Pt. 2*	De 2406, BrE O2780
64981	*Blame It On My Last Affair* vHH	De 2284, BrE O2728
64982	*Jive At Five*	De 2922, BrE O2894, LAT 8028
64983	*Thursday* vHH	De 2325, BrE O2745
64984	*Evil Blues* vJR	De 2922, BrE O2894, LAT 8028
64985	*Lady Be Good*	De 2631, BrE O2838

Buddy Tate (ten) for Berry.

New York City—March 19, 1939

W24238	*What Goes Up Must Come Down*	Vo 4734, CoE DB5062
W24239	*Rock-A-Bye Basie*	Vo 4747, CoE DB5066, PaE R2912
W24240	*Baby Don't Tell On Me* vJR	Vo 4747, CoE DB5066
W24241	*If I Could Be With You* vHH	Vo 4748
W24242	*Taxi War Dance*	Vo 4748, PaE R2862, Epic LN3107
W24243	*Don't Worry About Me* vHH	Vo 4734, CoE DB6052
W24244	*Jump For Me*	Vo 4886, PaE R2874, Epic LN3107, CoE SEG 7576

Same but Basie (organ) on first title.

Chicago—May 19, 1939

| WC2596 | *Nobody Knows* | Vo 5169, PaE R2755 |
| WC2597 | *Pound Cake* | Vo 5085, CoE DB5076, PaE R2918, Epic LN3168 |

New York City—June 15, 1939

W24337	*And The Angels Sing* vHH	Vo 4784, CoE DB5064
W24338	*If I Didn't Care* vHH	Vo 4784, CoE DB5064
W24339	*Twelfth Street Rag*	Vo 4886, PaE R2862, Epic LN3107
W24340	*Miss Thing Pt. 1*	Vo 4860, PaE R2855, Phi BBR8036
W24341	*Miss Thing Pt. 2*	Vo 4860, PaE R2855, Phi BBR8036

Chicago—June 24, 1939

WC2632	*You Can Count On Me* vHH	Vo 4967, CoE DB5069
WC2633	*You And Your Love* vHH	Vo 4967, CoE DB5069
WC2634	*How Long Blues* vJR	Vo 5010
WC2635	*Sub-Deb Blues* vHH	Vo 5010

New York City—August 4, 1939

| W24978 | *Moonlight Serenade* vHH | Vo 5036 |
| W24979 | *Song Of The Islands* | Vo 5169, PaE R2755, Epic LN3107 |

288

W24980 *I Can't Believe That You're In*
     Love vJR   Vo 5036
W24981 *Clap Hands, Here Comes Charlie* Vo 5085, CoE DB5076, Epic LN3107

COUNT BASIE'S KANSAS CITY SEVEN

Clayton (tpt); Wells (tbn); Young (ten, clt) plus usual rhythm.

                     New York City—September 5, 1939
W25296 *Dickie's Dream*   Vo 5118, CoE DB5073, Epic LN3107
W25297 *Lester Leaps In*   Vo 5118, CoE DB5073, Epic LN3107

COUNT BASIE AND HIS ORCHESTRA

Personnel as for August 4, 1939.
                     New York City—November 6, 1939
WCO26276 *The Apple Jump*   OK 5862
WCO26277 *I Left My Baby* vJR   Co 35321, PaE R2822, Epic LN3168
WCO26278 *Riff Interlude*   Co 35321, PaE R2822, Epic LN3168
WCO26279 *Volcano*   OK 6010
WCO26280 *Between The Devil And The*
         Deep Blue Sea   Co 35357, PaE R2748
WCO26281 *Ham 'n Eggs*   Co 35357, PaE R2822, Epic LN3168
WCO26282 *Hollywood Jump*   Co 35338, Epic LN3168
WCO26283 *Someday Sweetheart* vHH Co 35338

BENNY GOODMAN SEXTET

Benny Goodman (clt); Lionel Hampton (vib); Count Basie (p); Charlie
Christian (g); Artie Bernstein (bs); Nick Fatool (d).

                     New York City—February 7, 1940
WCO26494 *Till Tom Special*   Co 35404, PaE 2752, CoE DC603
WCO26495 *Gone With What Wind* Co 35404, PaE 2752, CoE DC603

COUNT BASIE AND HIS ORCHESTRA

As for November 6, 1939, but Al Killian (tpt) and Vic Dickenson (tbn) replace
Collins and Morton.
                     New York City—March 19, 1940
WCO26655 *I Never Knew*   Co 35521, PaE R2759, Epic LN3168
WCO26656 *Tickle Toe*   Co 35521, PaE R2759, Epic LN3168
Next title only. Arranged by Buck Clayton for four tpt and rhythm.
WCO26657 *Let's Make Hay While The*
         Moon Shines   Co 35500
WCO26658 *Louisiana*   Co 35448, PaE R2768, Epic LN3168
WCO26659 *Easy Does It*   Co 35448, Epic LN3168
WCO26660 *Let Me See*   OK 6330, Epic LN3168
WCO26661 *Blues* vJR   OK 5862
WCO26662 *Somebody Stole My Gal* vJR Co 35500

As before, but Tab Smith (alt) added for first title only.

New York City—May 31, 1940

WCO26870	*Blow Top*	OK 5629, PaE R2782, Epic LN3168
WCO26871	*Gone With What Wind*	OK 5629, PaE R2782

On the last title Dan Minor plays his first recorded tbn solo with the band.

WCO26872	*Super Chief*	OK 5673
WCO26873	*You Can't Run Around*	OK 5673

Chicago—August 8, 1939

WC3254	*Evenin'* vJR	OK 5732
WC3255	*The World Is Mad Pt. 1*	OK 5816, PaE R2748, Phi BBR8036
WC3256	*The World Is Mad Pt. 2*	OK 5816, PaE R2748, Phi BBR8036
WC3257	*Moten Swing*	OK 5732, PaE R2768, Epic LN3107
WC3258	*It's Torture* vHH	OK 5773
WC3259	*I Want A Little Girl* vJR	OK 5773

Add Tab Smith (alt, sop)

New York City—October 30, 1940

29006	*All Or Nothing At All* vHH	OK 5884
29007	*The Moon Fell In The River* vHH	OK 5884
29008	*What's Your Number*	OK 5897, PaE R2795
29009	*Draftin' Blues* vJR	OK 5897, PaE R2795

BENNY GOODMAN SEPTET

Cootie Williams (tpt); Benny Goodman (clt); Georgie Auld (ten); Count Basie (p); Charlie Christian (g); Artie Bernstein (bs); Harry Jaeger (d).

New York City—November 7, 1940

CO29027	*Wholly Cats*	Co 35810, PaE R2787
CO29028	*Royal Garden Blues*	Co 35810, PaE R2787
CO29029	*As Long As I Live*	Co 35901, PaE R2961, CoE 33 SX1035
CO29030	*Benny's Bugle*	Co 35901, CoE 33 SX1035

COUNT BASIE AND HIS ORCHESTRA
As for October 30, 1940.

New York City—November 19, 1940

29087	*Five O'Clock Whistle*	OK 5922
29088	*Love Jumped Out*	OK 5963
29089	*My Wanderin' Man* vHH	OK 5922
29090	*Broadway*	OK 6095, Epic LN3168

Paul Bascombe (ten) replaces Young.

New York City—December 13, 1940

29246	*It's The Same Old South* vJR	OK 5963
29247	*Stampede In G Minor*	OK 5987
29248	*Who Am I?*	OK 5987
29249	*Rockin' The Blues*	OK 6010, PaE R2796

SAM DONAHUE AND HIS ORCHESTRA

Harry Gozzard, Mitch Paul, Bud Davis (tpt); Ken Meisel, Ken Houghey

(^tbn); Sam Donahue, Bill Nichol, John Forys, Max Kriseman, Paul Petrilla (reeds); Count Basie (p); John Jordan (g); Walter Sherman (bs); Hal Kahn (d).

New York City—December 26, 1904

29297   *It Counts A Lot*   OK 6334

NOTE: Wayne Herdell plays piano on the other three titles from this session.

BENNY GOODMAN SEPTET
As for November 7, 1940.

New York City—January 15, 1941

CO29512	Breakfast Feud	Co 36039, CoE 33 SX1035
CO29513	On The Alamo	Co 35938, PaE R2798, CoE 33 SX1035
CO29514	I Found A New Baby	Co 36039, PaE R2961
CO29519	Gone With What Draft	Co 35938, PaE R2798

NOTE: Gap between last matrices are not Benny Goodman items.

THE METRONOME ALL STAR BAND

Harry James, Ziggy Elman, Cootie Williams (tpt); Tommy Dorsey, J. C. Higginbotham (tbn); Benny Goodman (clt); Toots Mondello, Benny Carter, Coleman Hawkins, Tex Beneke (saxes); Count Basie (p); Charlie Christian (g); Artie Bernstein (bs); Buddy Rich (d).

New York City—January 16, 1941

060331	Bugle Call Rag	Vi 27314, HMV B9195
060332	One O'clock Jump	Vi 27314, HMV B9195

COUNT BASIE AND HIS ORCHESTRA
As for December 13, 1940

New York City—January 20, 1941

29521	It's Square But It Rocks vHH	OK 6047, PaE R2796
29522	I'll Forget vHH	OK 6122

BENNY GOODMAN AND HIS ORCHESTRA

Alec Fila, Jimmy Maxwell, Irving Goodman, Cootie Williams (tpt); Lou McGarity, Cutty Cutshall (tbn); Benny Goodman (clt); Gus Bivona, Hymie Schertzer, Bob Snyder (alt); Georgie Auld, Jack Henderson (ten); Count Basie (p); Mike Bryan (g); Artie Bernstein (bs); Dave Tough (d).

New York City—January 21, 1941

Co29529   *I'm Not Complaining*   Co 36022

NOTE: Teddy Wilson plays piano on the remaining three titles from this date.

COUNT BASIE AND HIS ORCHESTRA
As for December 13, 1940.

New York City—January 22, 1941

29533	You Lied To Me vHH	OK 6267
29534	Wiggle Woogie	OK 6157, PaE R2951
29535	Beau Brummel	OK 6122

C3677	*I Do Mean You*	OK 6180, PaE R2814
C3678	*9.20 Special**	OK 6244, PaE R2836
C3679	*H & J*	OK 6365
C3680	*Feedin' The Bean**	OK 6180, PaE R2814
C3681	*Goin' To Chicago Blues* vJR	OK 6244

* Add Coleman Hawkins (ten).

Don Byas (ten); Ed Cuffee (tbn) replace Bascombe and Dickenson.

New York City—January 28, 1941

29580	*Music Makers*	OK 6047
29581	*Jump The Blues Away*	OK 6157, Epic LN3169
29582	Unknown title	Unissued
29583	*The Jitters*	OK 6095, PaE R2982, Epic LN3169
29584	*Tuesday At Ten*	OK 6071, Epic LN3169
29585	*Undecided Blues* vJR	OK 6071

Kenny Clarke (d) for Jones on first two titles only.

New York City—June 2, 1941

30520	*You Betcha My Life* vEW	OK 6221
30521	*Down, Down, Down*	OK 6021, Epic LN3169
30522	*Tune Town Shuffle*	OK 6267, Epic LN3169
30523	*Tired Of Waiting For You*	rejected

Robert Scott, Eli Robinson (tbn) replace Wells and Minor.

New York City—July 2, 1941

30831	*One Two, Three O'Leary* vJR	OK 6319
30832	*Basie Boogie*	OK 6330, PaE R2836, Epic LN3169
30833	*Fancy Meeting You* vEW	OK 6319
30834	*Diggin' For Dex*	OK 6365, Epic LN3169
?	*Let Me See*	OK 6330

Dickie Wells (tbn) replaces Cuffee. Lynne Sherman (vo) replaces Helen Humes.

New York City—September 24, 1941

31353	*My Old Flame* vLS	OK 6527
31354	*Fiesta In Blue*	OK 6440, PaE R2831, Epic LN3169
31355	*Tom Thumb* vLS	OK 6527
31356	*Take Me Back Baby* vJR	OK 6440, PaE R2831

Paul Robeson (vo) added on 31373-4.

New York City—October 1, 1941

31373	*King Joe Pt. 1*	OK 6475, PaE R2966
31374	*King Joe Pt. 2*	OK 6475, PaE R2966
31375	*Moon Nocturne* vEW	OK 6449
31376	*Something New*	OK 6449, Epic LN3169

New York City—November 3, 1941

31642	*I Struck A Match In The Dark* vLS	OK 6508

| 31643 | *Platterbrains* | OK 6508, Epic LN3169 |
| 31644 | *All Of Me* vLS | Co 36675 |

New York City—November 17, 1941

31765	*Feather Merchant*	Co 36845, CoE DB2288, Epic LN3169
31766	*Down For Double*	OK 6584
31767	*More Than You Know* vLS	OK 6584
31768	*Harvard Blues* vJR	OK 6564, PaE R2847
31769	*Coming Out Party*	OK 6564, PaE R2847

THE METRONOME ALL STAR BAND

Harry James, Roy Eldridge, Cootie Williams (tpt); J. C. Higginbotham, Lou McGarity (tbn); Benny Goodman (clt); Toots Mondello, Benny Carter (alt); Vido Musso, Tex Beneke (ten); Count Basie (p); Freddie Greene (g); Doc Goldberg (bs); Gene Krupa (d).

New York City—December 31, 1941

| 32079 | *Royal Flush* | Co 36499, PaE R2967 |

METRONOME ALL STAR LEADERS

Cootie Williams (tpt); J. C. Higginbotham (tbn); Benny Goodman (clt); Benny Carter (alt); Charlie Barnet (ten); Count Basie (p); Alvino Rey (g); John Kirby (bs); Gene Krupa (d).

New York City—January 16, 1942

| 32261 | *I Got Rhythm* | Co 36499, PaE R2967 |

COUNT BASIE AND HIS ORCHESTRA

Personnel as for November 3, 1941.

New York City—January 21, 1942

32274	*One O'Clock Jump*	OK 6634, PaE R2951
32275	*Blue Shadows And White Gardenias* vEW	OK 6626
32276	*'Ay Now*	OK 6626

Jerry Blake (alt, clt) replaces Tab Smith.

Chicago—April 3, 1942

| C4225 | *Basie Blues* | Co 36601, PaE R3003 |
| C4226 | *I'm Gonna Move To The Outskirts Of Town* vJR | Co 36601 |

COUNT BASIE AND HIS ALL AMERICAN RHYTHM SECTION

Piano solos with usual rhythm.

Hollywood—July 24, 1942

HCO873	*How Long Blues*	Co 36710, CoE SEG7578
HCO874	*Royal Garden Blues**	Co 36710, PaE R2982, CoE SEG7578
HCO875	*Bugle Blues**	Co 36709, PaE R2964
HCO876	*Sugar Blues**	Co 36709, PaE R2964
HCO877	*Farewell Blues*	Co 36712
HCO878	*Café Society Blues*	Co 36711, PaE R2970, CoE SEG7578
HCO879	*Way Back Blues*	Co 36712
HCO880	*St. Louis Blues**	Co 36711, PaE R2970, CoE SEG7578

*Add Buck Clayton (tpt); Don Byas (ten).

COUNT BASIE AND HIS ORCHESTRA

Ed Lewis, Al Killian, Buck Clayton, Harry Edison (tpt); Dicky Wells, Robert Scott, Eli Robinson (tbn); Earl Warren, Jack Washington, Buddy Tate, Don Byas, Caughey Roberts (reeds); Count Basie (p); Freddie Greene (g); Walter Page (bs); Jo Jones (d).

Hollywood—July 27, 1942

HCO888	Rusty Dusty Blues vJR	Co 36675, PaE R2994
HCO889	Ride On vEW	Co 36647
HCO890	Unknown title	Unissued
HCO891	Time On My Hands vEW	Co 36685
HCO892	It's Sand, Man!	Co 33647
HCO893	Ain't It The Truth?	Co 36845, PaE R3003
HCO894	For The Good Of Your Country	Co 36685

Probably similar personnel to last session.

Los Angeles—November 23, 1943

87	Dance Of The Gremlins	"V" D 34
118	G.I. Stomp	"V" D 34
495	Yeah Man/Rhythm Man	"V" D 175

KANSAS CITY SEVEN

Buck Clayton (tpt); Dicky Wells (tbn); Lester Young (ten); Count Basie (p); Freddy Greene (g); Rodney Richardson (bs); Jo Jones (d).

New York City—March 22, 1944

HLK21	After Theatre Jump	Key 1302, Mer 599, MG25015, MerE MG25015
HLK22	Six Cats And A Prince	Key 1303, Mer 600
HLK23	Lester Leaps Again*	Key 1302, Mer 599, MG25015, MerE MG25015
HLK24	Destination K.C.	Key 1303, Mer 600, MG25015, MerE MG25015

*Clayton and Wells out.

LESTER YOUNG

Lester Young (ten); Count Basie (p); Freddie Greene (g); Rodney Richardson (bs); Shadow Wilson (d).

New York City—May 1, 1944

S5454	Blue Lester	Svy 581, MG9002, SvyE 581
S5455	Ghost Of A Chance	Svy 552, MG9002, SvyE 552
S5456	Indiana	Svy 581, MG9002, SvyE 581
S5457	Lester's Savoy Jump	Svy 552, MG9002, SvyE 552

COUNT BASIE AND HIS ORCHESTRA

Personnel probably similar to July 27, 1942 session.

New York City—May 27, 1944

| 711 | Kansas City Stride | "V" D 258 |
| 712 | Beaver Junction | "V" D 258 |

| 731 | *Circus In Rhythm* | " V " D 289 |
| 733 | *Gee Baby Ain't I Good To You* vJR | " V " D 552 |

New York City—October 30, 1944

| 1002 | *Harvard Blues* vJR | " V " D 369 |

Harry Edison, Al Killian, Ed Lewis, Joe Newman (tpt); Dicky Wells, Ted Donnelly, Eli Robinson, Louis Taylor (tbn); James Powell, Rudy Rutherford, Buddy Tate, Earl Warren, Lucky Thompson (reeds); Count Basie (p); Freddie Greene (g); Rodney Richardson (bs); Shadow Wilson (d); Jimmy Rushing, Thelma Carmenter (vo).

New York City—December 6, 1944

CO33953	*Taps Miller*	Co 36831, PaE R2994
CO33954	*Jimmy's Blues* vJR	Co 36831, PaE R2992
CO33955	*I Didn't Know About You* vTC	Co 36766
CO33956	*Red Bank Boogie* vJR	Co 36766, PaE R2992

Same or similar personnel.

New York City—January 11, 1945

1115	*Taps Miller*	" V " D 419
1120	*Playhouse No. 2 Stomp*	" V " D 439
1176	*Old Manuscript*	" V " D 575
1280	*Jimmy Blues* vJR/*Take Me Back Baby* vJR	" V " D 460

String section added for following session only.

New York City—February 26, 1945

| CO24353 | *This Heart Of Mine* vLS | Co 36795 |
| CO24354 | *That Old Feeling* vLS | Co 36795 |

Similar personnel to previous " V " D session but with Buck Clayton, Karl George, Snooky Young (tpt) in place of Al Killian and Joe Newman.

New York City—May 14, 1945

1356	*High Tide*	" V " D 483
1357	*Jimmy's Boogie Woogie* vJR/*Sent For You Yesterday* vJR	" V " D 534
1686	*Tippin' On The QT*	" V " D 627
	Down For The Double	" V " D ?

Ed Lewis, Eugene Young, Harry Edison, Emmett Berry (tpt); Dicky Wells, Ted Donnelly, Jay Jay Johnson, Eli Robinson (tbn); Preston Love, George Dorsey (alt); Buddy Tate, Illinois Jacquet (ten); Rudy Rutherford (bar); Count Basie (p); Freddie Greene (g); Rodney Richardson (bs); Shadow Wilson (d); Jimmy Rushing, Ann Moore (vo).

Hollywood—October 9, 1945

HCO1563	*Blue Skies* vJR	Co 37070
HCO1564	*Jivin' Joe Jackson* vAM	Co 36889
HCO1565	*High Tide*	Co 36990, CoE DB2288
HCO1566	*Queer Street*	Co 36889

Joe Newman (tpt); George Matthews (tbn); James Powell (alt) for Young, Wells and Dorsey.

New York City—January 9, 1946

CO35602	*Patience And Fortitude* vJR	Co 36946
CO35603	*The Mad Boogie*	Co 36946, PaE R3014
	Goodbye Baby	Co CL6079, CoE 33S1054
	Wild Bill's Blues	Co CL6079, CoE 33S1054

Earl Warren (alt); Jo Jones (d) replace Love and Wilson.

New York City—February 4, 1946

CO35730	*Lazy Lady Blues* vJR	Co 36990, PaE R3009
CO35731	*Bambo*	Co CL6079, PaE R3014, CoE 33S1054
CO35732	*Stay Cool*	Co CL6079, PaE R3009, CoE 33S1054
CO35733	*The King*	Co 37093

Preston Love, Jack Washington (alt); Walter Page (bs) for Warren, Powell and Richardson. Add Eugene Young (tpt).

New York City—July 31, 1946

CO36702	*Hob Nail Boogie*	Co CL6079, CoE 33S1054
CO36703	*Danny Boy*	Co 39075, CL6079, CoE 33S1054
CO36704	*Mutton Leg*	Co 37093

Bill Johnson (tbn); Paul Gonsalves (ten) replace Jay Jay Johnson and Illinois Jacquet. Omit Joe Newman.

New York City—August 9, 1946

CO36747	*Fla-Ga-La-Pa* vAM	Co 37093
	Lonesome Miss Pretty	Co CL6079, CoE 33S1054

Ed Lewis, Emmett Berry, Eugene Young, Harry Edison (tpt); Bill Johnson, Ted Donnelly, George Matthews, Eli Robinson (tbn); Preston Love, Jack Washington (alt); Paul Gonsalves, Buddy Tate (ten); Rudy Rutherford (bar); Count Basie (p); Freddie Greene (g); Walter Page (bs); Jo Jones (d); Ann Moore, Jimmy Rushing, Harry Edison (vo).

New York City—January 3, 1947

D7VB402	*Bill's Mill*	Vi 20–2148, HMV B9557
D7VB403	*Me And The Blues* vAM	Vi 20–2127, HMV JO51
D7VB404	*Free Eats*	Vi 20–2148, HMV B9557
D7VB405	*Brand New Wagon* vJR	Vi 20–2529
D7VB406	*Open The Door Richard* vHE	Vi 20–2127, HMV JO51

Same but Ann Moore and Jimmy Rushing replaced by Ann Baker and Bob Bailey (vo).

New York City—March 13, 1947

D7VB652	*One O'clock Boogie*	Vi 20–2262, HMV B9593
D7VB653	*Meet Me At No Special Place* vAB	Vi 20–2262, HMV B9593
D7VB654	*I'm Drowning In Your Deep Blue Eyes* vBB	Vi 20–2346, HMV B9604
D7VB655	*Futile Frustration*	Vi 20–2529

Emmett Berry (tpt); George Matthews (tbn); Paul Gonsalves (ten); C. Q. Price (alt); Jack Washington (bar); Count Basie (p, organ); Freddie Greene (g); Walter Page (bs); Jo Jones (d).

New York City—May 20, 1947

D7VB886	*Swingin' The Blues*	Vi 20–2696, LPT4, HMV B9691
D7VB887	*St. Louis Boogie*	Vi 20–2694, HMV B9703
D7VB888	*Basie's Basement**	Vi 20–2695, HMV B9703
D7VB889	*Backstage At Stuff's*	Vi 20–2693, HMV B9761

*Basie plays organ on this title.

New York City—May 21, 1947

D7VB890	*My Buddy*	Vi 20–2693, HMV 7EG8147
D7VB891	*Shine On Harvest Moon*	Vi 20–2694, HMV JO93
D7VB892	Unknown title	Unissued
D7VB893	*I Never Knew*	Vi 20–2695, HMV B9761
D7VB894	*Sugar**	Vi 20–2696, HMV B9691

*Gonsalves; Basie; Greene; Jones only.

Count Basie and his Orchestra

Personnel as for last full orchestra session except C. Q. Price (alt) replaces Rutherford. Add Taps Miller (vo).

New York City—May 22, 1947

D7VB895	*You Call Yourself Jungle King* vJR	Vi 20–2314
D7VB896	*Take A Little Off The Top* vHE	Vi 20–2435
D7VB897	*I Ain't Mad At You* vTM	Vi 20–2314
D7VB907	*House Rent Boogie*	Vi 20–2435
D7VB908	*South*	Vi 20–2346, HMV B9604, 7EG8221

Dickie Wells, George Simon (tbn) replace Matthews and Robinson. Bob Bailey, Jimmy Rushing, Jean Taylor (vo).

New York City—October 19, 1947

D7VB1090	*Don't You Want A Man Like Me ?* vJR	Vi 20–2602
D7VB1091	*Blue And Sentimental* vBB	Vi 20–2602
D7VB1092	*Seventh Avenue Express*	Vi 20–3003, HMV B9718, 7EG8147
D7VB1093	*Mister Robert's Roost*	Vi 20–3003, HMV 7EG8147

George Matthews (tbn) for Simon.

New York City—December 8, 1947

D7VB2167	*Sophisticated Swing*	Vi 20–3255
D7VB2168	*Guest In A Nest*	Vi 20–2168
D7VB2169	*Your Red Wagon* vJR	Vi 20–2677
D7VB2170	*Money Is Honey* vJR	Vi 20–2771

New York City—December 9, 1947

| D7VB2171 | *Just A Minute* | Vi 20–3051 |

| D7VB2172 | *Baby Don't Be Mad At Me* vJT | Vi 20–2948 |
| D7VB2173 | *I've Only Myself To Blame* vJT | Vi 20–2850 |

George Washington (tbn) replaces Wells.

New York City—December 12, 1947

D7VB2186	*Robbins Nest*	Vi 20–2677
D7VB2187	*Hey Pretty Baby* vJR	Vi 20–2948
D7VB2188	*It's Monday Every Day* vJT	Vi 20–2850
D7VB2189	*Bye Bye Baby* vJR	Vi 20–3051
D7VB2190	*Ready Set Go* vJT	Vi 20–3003, HMV B9718

Harry Edison, Emmett Berry, Clark Terry, Jimmy Nottingham, Gerald Wilson (tpt); Dicky Wells, Ted Donnelly, George Matthews, Melba Liston (tbn); Paul Gonsalves, Jack Washington, C. Q. Price, William Parker (reeds); Count Basie (p); Freddie Greene (g); Singleton Palmer (bs); Butch Ballard (d); Bobby Troup, Taps Miller, Jimmy Rushing (vo).

Hollywood—April 11, 1949

D9VB600	*Brand New Doll* vBT	Vi 20–3449
D9VB601	*Cheek To Cheek*	Vi 20–3449
D9VB602	*Old Manuscript*	Vi LPM 1112
D9VB603	*Katy*	Vi LPM 1112, HMV 7EG8221

Melba Liston out.

June 29, 1949

D9VB1766	*She's A Wine-O* vJR	Vi 20–3542, HMV B9891
D9VB1767	*After You've Gone* vJR	Vi 20–3528
D9VB1768	*Shoutin' Blues*	Vi 20–3514

July 13, 1949

| D9VB1767 | *Did You See Jackie Robinson* vTM | Vi 20–3514 |
| D9VB1821 | *St. Louis Baby* vJR | Vi 20–3601 |

July 22, 1949

D9VB1897	*Wonderful Thing*	Vi LPM 1112, HMV 7EG8147
D9VB1899	*Mine Too*	Vi 20–3699
D9VB2100	*Walking Slowly Behind You* vJR	Vi 20–3572

Add Jimmy Taylor (ten); Billy Valentine (vo).

August 5, 1949

D9VB2138	*Normania*	Vi 20–3601
D9VB2139	*Rocky Mountain Blues* vBV	Vi 20–3572
D9VB1898	*The Slider*	Vi 20–3542, HMV B9891

Harry Edison (tpt); Dicky Wells (tbn); Georgie Auld, Gene Ammons (ten); Count Basie (p); Freddie Greene (g); Al McKibbon (bs); Gus Johnson (d); Deep River Boys (vo).

February 2, 1950

| EOVB3187 | *If You See My Baby* | Vi LPM 1112, HMV 7EG8221 |

EOVB3188   *Solid As A Rock* vDRB   Vi 20–3699
EOVB3189   *Rat Race*   Vi LPM 1112
EOVB3190   *Sweets*   Vi LPM 1112, HMV 7EG8221

COUNT BASIE SEXTET

Clark Terry (tpt); Buddy De Franco (clt); Charlie Rouse (ten); Serge Chaloff (bar); Count Basie (p); Freddie Greene (g); Jimmy Lewis (bs); Buddy Rich (d).

New York City—May 16, 1950

CO43261	*Neal's Deal*	Co 39075, CoE SEG7576
CO43262	*Bluebeard Blues*	Co 38888
CO43263	*The Golden Bullet*	Co 38888

Wardell Gray (ten); Rudy Rutherford (bar); Gus Johnson (d) for Rouse, Chaloff and Rich.

Hollywood—November 3, 1950

Little White Lies	Epic LG1021, Phi BBR8036
I'll Remember April	Epic LG1021, Phi BBR8036

COUNT BASIE AND HIS ORCHESTRA

Clark Terry, Al Porcino, Lamar Wright, Bob Mitchell (tpt); Matthew Gee, Leon Comegys, Mike Woods (tbn); Marshall Royal, Bernie Peacock (alt); Wardell Gray, Lucky Thompson (ten); Charles Fowlkes (bar); Count Basie (p); Freddie Greene (g); Jimmy Lewis (bs); Gus Johnson (d).

New York City—April 10, 1951

CO45658	*Little Pony*	Co 39406
CO45659	*Beaver Junction*	Co 39406, CoE SEG7576
	Nails	Epic LG1021, Phi BBR8036
	Howzit	Epic LG1021, Phi BBR8036

Joe Newman, Wendell Culley, Paul Campbell, Charlie Shavers (tpt); Jimmy Wilkins, Henry Coker, Bennie Powell (tbn); Marshall Royal, Ernie Wilkins (alt); Floyd Johnson, Paul Quinichette (ten); Charlie Fowlkes (bar); Count Basie (p); Freddie Greene (g); Jimmy Lewis (bs); Jo Jones (d).

New York City—January 19, 1952

665–4	*New Basie Blues*	Clef 8964, LP120, CoE LB10003
666–3	*Sure Thing*	Clef 8964, LP120, CoE LB10003
667–2	*Why Not?*	Clef 8988, LP120
668–4	*Fawncy Meeting You*	Clef 8988, LP120

Gus Johnson (d) replaces Jones.

New York City—January 25, 1952

688–6	*Jive At Five*	Clef 8987, LP120
	Jumpin' At The Woodside	Clef 8987
691–5	*Every Tub*	Clef 8987, LP120

PAUL QUINICHETTE AND HIS ORCHESTRA

Paul Quinichette (ten); probably Count Basie, organ; Bobby Tucker (p); Freddie Greene (g); Jimmy Lewis (bs); Gus Johnson (d).

New York City—circa January, 1952

YB4574	*Sandstone*	EmA MG26021
YB4580–1	*Preview*	EmA MG26021
YB4581	*No Time*	EmA MG26021

Buck Clayton (tpt); Dicky Wells (tbn); Paul Quinichette (ten); Count Basie (p); Freddie Greene (g); Walter Page (bs); Gus Johnson (d).

New York City—February, 1952

YB4815–1	*Shad Roe*	Mer 8287, EmA MG26022, EmAE ERE1502
YB4816–1	*Paul's Bunion*	Mer 70020, EmA MG26022
YB4817–	*Crew Cut*	EmA MG26022, EmAE ERE1502
YB4818–1	*The Hook*	EmA MG26022, Mer 8287, EmAE ERE1502

Omit Buck Clayton and Dicky Wells

YB4819–1	*Samie*	Mer 70020, EmA MG26022, EmAE ERE1502
YB4820–2	*I'll Always Be In Love With You*	Mer 8272, EmA MG26022
YB4821–2	*Sequel*	Mer 8272, EmA MG26022

COUNT BASIE AND HIS ORCHESTRA

As for January 25, 1952, but Reunald Jones (tpt) and Eddie Davis (ten) replace Shavers and Johnson.

New York City—July 22–23, 1952

823–2	*Bread*	Clef 89085, LP633, CoE SEB1000
824–7	*Small Hotel*	Clef 89070, LP633, CoE SEB1000
825–7	*Hob Nail Boogie*	Clef 89014, LP120, CoE LB10013
827–3	*Paradise Squat*	Clef 89014, LP120, LP639, CoE LB10013
830–5	*Tippin' On The QT*	Clef 89085, LP633
831–3	*Blee Bop Blues*	Clef 89070, LP633, CoE SEB1000
	You're Not The Kind	Clef LP647, CoE 33CX10044
	Bunny	Clef LP148, CoE SEB10033
	Jack And Jill	Clef LP148, CoE SEB10023
	Basie Talks	Clef LP148, CoE SEB10023
	Nylon	Clef

ILLINOIS JACQUET AND HIS ORCHESTRA

Illinois Jacquet (ten); Count Basie (organ); Hank Jones (p); Freddie Greene (g); Ray Brown (bs); Jimmy Crawford (d).

New York City—July 24, 1952

818–3	*Lean Baby*	Clef 89021, LP129, CoE SEB10016
819–6	*Somewhere Along The Way*	Clef 89001, LP129, CoE SEB10016
820–8	*Cool Rage*	Clef 89021, LP129, CoE SEB10016
821–3	*Port Of Rico*	Clef 89001, LP129, CoE SEB10016

COUNT BASIE AND HIS ORCHESTRA

Previous full band personnel except Ray Brown (bs) replaces Lewis.

300

Bootsie	Clef LP148, CoE SEB10033	
Cashbox	Clef LP148, CoE SEB10023	

Eddie Davis, Paul Quinichette (ten); Count Basie (organ); Oscar Peterson (p); Freddie Greene (g); Ray Brown (bs); Gus Johnson (d).

Same date

Extended Blues	Clef LP633, CoE SEB10060
Be My Guest*	Clef LP633, CoE SEB10060
Blues For The Count And Oscar	Clef LP633, CoE SEB10060

* Full band personnel on this title.

As for previous full band except Gene Ramey (bs); Buddy Rich (d) replace Brown and Johnson. Add Al Hibbler (vo).

December 13, 1952

965-4	*Sent For You Yesterday* vAH	Clef 89028, LP633
966-1	*Goin' To Chicago* vAH	Clef 89028, LP633
	Redhead	Clef LP148, CoE 10033
	No Name	Clef LP148, CoE 10033
	Tom Whaley	Clef LP148, CoE SEB10023

COUNT BASIE NONET
Joe Newman (tpt); Henry Coker (tbn); Marshal Royal (alt); Paul Quinichette (ten); Charlie Fowlkes (bar); Count Basie (p, organ); Freddie Greene (g); Gene Ramey (bs); Buddy Rich (d).

Same date

967-1	*I Want A Little Girl*	Clef 89033, LP633, CoE LB10057

COUNT BASIE SEXTET
Omit Coker, Royal and Fowlkes.

Same date

968-6	*Lady Be Good*	Clef 89033, LP633, CoE LB10057
969-4	*Song Of The Islands*	Clef 89061, LP633

December, 1952

977-3	*Basie Beat*	Clef 89101, LP146, CoE 33C9010
979-1	*Count's Organ Blues*	Clef 89101, LP146, CoE 33C9010
980-1	*K.C. Organ Blues*	Clef 89102, LP146, CoE 33C9010
982-1	*Stan Shorthair*	Clef 89102, LP146, CoE 33C9010
984-4	*Royal Garden Blues*	Clef 89061, LP146, CoE 33C9010
	She's Funny That Way	Clef LP146, CoE 33C9010
	Blue And Sentimental	Clef LP146, CoE 33C9010
	As Long As I Live	Clef LP146, CoE 33C9010

JAM SESSION
Harry Edison (tpt); Buddy De Franco (clt); Benny Carter, Willie Smith (alt); Stan Getz, Wardell Gray (ten); Count Basie (p); Freddie Greene (g); John Simmons (bs); Buddy Rich (d).

Hollywood—Summer, 1953

Apple Jam	Clef LP4003, CoE 33CX10030
Lady Be Good	Clef LP4004, CoE 33CX10021
Blues For The Count	Clef LP4004, CoF 33CX10021

COUNT BASIE AND HIS ORCHESTRA

Wendell Culley, Reunald Jones, Joe Newman, Joe Wilder (tpt); Henry Coker,
Bennie Powell, Henderson Chambers (tbn); Marshall Royal, Ernie Wilkins
(alt); Frank Wess, Frank Foster (ten); Charlie Fowlkes (bar); Count Basie (p);
Freddie Greene (g); Eddie Jones (bs); Gus Johnson (d).

December, 1953

1403-3	*Peace Pipe*	Clef 89115
1405-2	*Softly With Feeling*	Clef 89112
1407-6	*Cherry Point*	Clef 89120
1408-1	*Basie Goes Wess*	Clef 89112
1409-2	*Right On*	Clef 89120
1410-1	*The Blues Done Come Back*	Clef 89115
	Plymouth Rock	
	Straight Life	
	Blues Go Away	
	Bubbles	

NOTE: Above ten titles on Clef LP626 and CoE 33CX10007.

JOE NEWMAN AND THE BOYS IN THE BAND

Joe Newman (tpt); Henry Coker (tbn); Frank Wess (ten, fl); Frank Foster
(ten); Charlie Fowlkes (bar); Count Basie (p, organ); Freddie Greene (g);
Eddie Jones (bs); Gus Johnson (d).

Boston—July, 1954

	Ingin' The Ooh	Storyville LP318
	Confessin'	Storyville LP318
	Peter Pan	Storyville LP318
	In Case You Didn't Know	Storyville LP318
	These Foolish Things	Storyville LP318
	Ain't It The Truth	Storyville LP318

NOTE: Above six titles issued on Vogue LDE126.

COUNT BASIE AND HIS ORCHESTRA

Previous full band personnel but Thad Jones (tpt); Bill Hughes (tbn) replace
Wilder and Chambers.

New York City—August, 1954

1887-6	*Slow But Sure*	Clef 89126
1888-3	*Soft Drinks*	Clef 89126
1890-4	*You For Me*	Clef 89131
1891-2	*Two For The Blues*	Clef 89131
1893-4	*Sixteen Men Swinging*	
1895-7	*Stereophonic*	Clef 89137
	Mambo Mist	
	I Feel Like A New Man	Clef 89137
	She's Just My Size	

NOTE: Above nine titles on Clef LP647 and CoE 33CX10044.

Blues Inside Out	ARS 402
Lady In Lace	ARS 402
Sweety Cakes	ARS 402

New York City—Late 1954

Blues Backstage	Clef LP666, CoE 33CX10065
Down For The Count	Clef LP666, CoE 33CX10065
Eventide	Clef LP666, CoE 33CX10065
Ain't Misbehavin'	Clef LP666, CoE 33CX10065
Perdido	Clef LP666, CoE 33CX10065
Ska-di-dle-dee-bee-doo	Clef LP666, CoE 33CX10065
Two Franks	Clef LP666, CoE 33CX10065
Rails	Clef LP666, CoE 33CX10065

Bill Graham (alt); Sonny Payne (d) for Wilkins and Johnson. Joe Williams (vo).

New York City—May, 1955

2347-2	*Every Day I Have The Blues* vJW	Clef 89149, LP678
2348-5	*The Comeback* vJW	Clef 89151, LP678, CoE LB10017
2349-2	*Alright, Okay, You Win* vJW	Clef 89152, LP678
2350-3	*In The Evening* vJW	Clef 89152, LP678
2358-2	*Roll 'Em Pete* vJW	Clef 89162, LP678, CoE LB10022
	April In Paris	Clef 89162, CoE LB10022

New York City—June, 1955

Teach Me Tonight vJW	Clef LP678
My Baby Upsets Me vJW	Clef LP678
Please Send Me Someone To Love vJW	Clef LP678
Ev'ry Day vJW	Clef LP678, CoE LB10012
Smack Dab In The Middle vJW	Clef 89169, CoE LB10028
Amazing Love vJW	ARS 402, Clef 89171, CoE LB10040
Magic	ARS 402, Clef 89171, CoE LB10040

NOTE: Clef LP678 issued in Britain as CoE 33CX10026.

JO JONES SPECIAL

Emmett Berry (tpt); Benny Green (tbn); Lucky Thompson (ten); Count Basie (p); Freddie Greene (g); Walter Page (bs); Jo Jones (d).

New York City—August 11, 1955

Shoe Shine Boy (Take 1)	Vng VRS8503, VngE PPL1102
Shoe Shine Boy (Take 2)	Vng VRS8503, VngE PPL1102

NOTE: Basie does not play on any other titles from this session. See under Jo Jones in Part II of this appendix for details of the remaining sides.

A Night at the Apollo

This record was made at the Apollo Hall in New York during an evening concert. The Basie Band provides accompaniment to a number of stage acts including dancers Coles and Atkins; comic-impersonator George Kirby; the Keynoters; comedienne Jackie (Moms) Mabley; singer Doreen Vaughan, etc.

New York City—January 16, 1956

A Night At The Apollo   Vng VRS9006

Count Basie and his Orchestra

Personnel as before. Joe Williams (vo) on all tracks.

Hollywood—Spring, 1956

Thou Swell	Verve MGV–2016, HMV CLP1109
There Will Never Be Another You	Verve MGV–2016, HMV CLP1109
'S Wonderful	Verve MGV–2016, HMV CLP1109
Our Love Is Here To Stay	Verve MGV–2016, HMV CLP1109
My Baby Just Cares For Me	Verve MGV–2016, HMV CLP1109
Nevertheless	Verve MGV–2016, HMV CLP1109
Singin' In The Rain	Verve MGV–2016, HMV CLP1109
A Fine Romance	Verve MGV–2016, HMV CLP1109
I Can't Believe That You're In Love With Me	Verve MGV–2016, HMV CLP1109
This Can't Be Love	Verve MGV–2016, HMV CLP1109
I'm Beginning To See The Light	Verve MGV–2016, HMV CLP1109
Come Rain Or Come Shine	Verve MGV–2016, HMV CLP1109

PART II

A listing of records considered to be representative of the Count Basie band, its musicians and arrangers.

KENNY CLARKE

Kenny Clarke Volume 1

Henry Coker (tbn); Frank Wess (ten, fl); Charlie Fowlkes (bar); Milt Jackson (p); Eddie Jones (bs); Kenny Clarke (d); Ernie Wilkins (arr).

New York City—Autumn, 1954

Telefunken Blues	Svy MG12006, LonE LTZ–C15004
Klook's Nook	Svy MG12006, LonE LTZ–C15004
Baggin' The Blues	Svy MG12006, LonE LTZ–C15004
Inhibitions	Svy MG12006, LonE LTZ–C15004

The Kenny Clarke-Ernie Wilkins Septet

Eddie Bert (tbn); Ernie Wilkins (alt, arr); George Barrow (ten, bar); Cecil Payne (bar); Hank Jones (p); Wendell Marshall (bs); Kenny Clarke (d).

Pru's Blooze	Svy MG12007, LonE LTZ–C15008
I Dig You The Most	Svy MG12007, LonE LTZ–C15008
Cute Tomato	Svy MG12007, LonE LTZ–C15008
Summer Evening	Svy MG12007, LonE LTZ–C15008
Oz The Wizard	Svy MG12007, LonE LTZ–C15008
Plenty For Kenny	Svy MG12007, LonE LTZ–C15008

Kenny Clarke (d solo).

Same date

Now's The Time	Svy MG12007, LonE LTZ–C15008

BUCK CLAYTON

BUCK CLAYTON WITH THE ALIX COMBELLE BAND

Buck Clayton (tpt, arr); Alex Rénard, Pierre Selin, Aime Hanuche, Andre Simon (tpt); Réné Godard, Jean-Jacques Leger (alt); Alix Combelle, Henri Bernard (ten); Henri Jouot (bar); Jean-Claude Pelletier (p); Roger Chaput (g); Yvon Le Guen (bs); Christian Garros (d); Chonanard (bongo).

Paris—October 20, 21, 1953

54–V–4758	*Who*	Vg LD182, VgE LDE140
54–V–4759	*Relax Alix*	Vg LD182, VgE LDE140
	Sahiva Boogie	Vg LD182, VgE LDE140
	Strolling Blues	Vg LD182, VgE LDE140
	Jumping On The Rebound	Vg LD182, VgE LDE140
	Blues In Brass	Vg LD182, VgE LDE140
	Beatin' The Count	Vg LD182, VgE LDE140
	Basie Days	Vg LD182, VgE LDE140

BUCK CLAYTON JAM SESSION

Buck Clayton, Joe Newman (tpt); Urbie Green, Benny Powell (tbn); Lem Davis (alt); Julian Dash (ten); Charlie Fowlkes (bar); Sir Charles Thompson (p); Freddie Greene (g); Walter Page (bs); Jo Jones (d).

New York City—December 14, 1953

Sentimental Journey	Co CL567, PhiE BBL7040
Moten Swing	Co CL567, PhiE BBL7040
Lean Baby	Co CL882

Henderson Chambers (tbn) replaces Powell.

New York City—December 16, 1953

The Hucklebuck	Co CL548, PhiE BBL7032
Robbins Nest	Co CL548, PhiE BBL7032
Christopher Columbus	Co CL614, PhiE BBL7068

Buck Clayton, Joe Thomas (tpt); Urbie Green, Trummie Young (tbn); Woody Herman (clt); Lem Davis (alt); Julian Dash, Al Cohn (ten); Jimmy Jones (p); Steve Jordan (g); Walter Page (bs); Jo Jones (d).

New York City—March 31, 1954

How Hi The Fi	Co CL657, PhiE BBL7040
Blue Moon	Co CL657, PhiE BBL7040
*Jumpin' At The Woodside**	Co CL701, PhiE BBL7087

*Parts of this tape were joined with sections of a tape made August 13, 1954.

BUCK CLAYTON BAND

Buck Clayton, Ruby Braff (tpt); Benny Morton (tbn); Buddy Tate (ten); Jimmy Jones (p); Steve Jordan (g); Aaron Bell (bs); Bobby Donaldson (d).

New York City—July 1, 1954

*Just A Groove**	Vng VRS8009, VngE PPT1206
Kandee	Vng VRS8009, VngE PPT1206
I Can't Get Started	Vng VRS8009, VngE PPT1206
Love Is Just Around The Corner	Vng VRS8009, VngE PPT1206

*Omit Morton and Tate.

BUCK CLAYTON JAM SESSION

Buck Clayton, Joe Newman (tpt); Urbie Green, Trummie Young (tbn); Lem Davis (alt); Coleman Hawkins (ten); Charlie Fowlkes (bar); Billy Kyle (p); Freddie Greene (g); Milt Hinton (bs); Jo Jones (d).

New York City—August 13, 1954

Don't Be That Way	Co CL614, PhiE BBL7068
Undecided	Co CL614, PhiE BBL7068
Blue And Sentimental	Co CL701, PhiE BBL7087
*Jumpin' At The Woodside**	Co CL701, PhiE BBL7087

*Parts of this tape were joined with sections of a tape made March 31, 1954.

Buck Clayton, Ruby Braff (tpt); Benny Green, Dick Harris (tbn); Coleman Hawkins, Buddy Tate (ten); Al Waslohn (p); Freddie Greene (g); Milt Hinton (bs); Jo Jones (d).

New York City—March 15, 1955

*Rock-A-Bye Basie**	Co CL701, PhiE BBL7087
Broadway	Co CL701, PhiE BBL7087
Blue Lou	Co CL882

*Add Jack Ackerman (tap dancer) on this track only.

FRANKIE LAINE WITH BUCK CLAYTON AND HIS ORCHESTRA

Frankie Laine (vo) acc. Buck Clayton, Ray Copeland (tpt); Urbie Green (tbn); Hilton Jefferson (alt); Bud Johnson, Nick Nicholas (ten); Dave McRae (bar); Sir Charles Thompson (p); Clifton Best (g); Milt Hinton (bs); Jo Jones (d).

New York City—October 24, 1955

ZEP37276	*Baby, Baby All The Time*	Co CL778, PhiE BBL7080
ZEP37328	*S'posin'*	Co CL778, PhiE BBL7080
ZEP37329	*That Old Feeling*	Co CL778, PhiE BBL7080
ZEP37330	*You Can Depend On Me*	Co CL778, PhiE BBL7080
ZEP37331	*Stars Fell On Alabama*	Co CL778, PhiE BBL7080

Lawrence Brown (tbn) replaces Green. Add Jay Jay Johnson, Kai Winding (tbn).

New York City—October 25, 1955

| ZEP37278 | *Roses Of Picardy* | Co CL778, PhiE BBL7080 |

Omit Brown. Bobby Donaldson (d) replaces Jones.

New York City—October 26, 1955

| ZEP37277 | *Taking A Chance On Love* | Co CL778, PhiE BBL7080 |

Buck Clayton (tpt); Urbie Green, Dickie Wells (tbn); Hilton Jefferson (alt); Bud Johnson, Al Sears (ten); Dave McRae (bar); Sir Charles Thompson (p); Clifton Best (g); Milt Hinton (bs); Bobby Donaldson (d).

New York City—October 26, 1955

ZEP37342	*Until The Real Thing Comes Along*	Co CL778, PhiE BBL7080
ZEP37343	*If You Were Mine*	Co CL778, PhiE BBL7080
ZEP37344	*My Old Flame*	Co CL778, PhiE BBL7080

BUCK CLAYTON JAM SESSION
Buck Clayton, Ruby Braff, Billy Butterfield (tpt); Tyree Glenn, J. C. Higginbotham (tbn); Julian Dash, Coleman Hawkins (ten); Kenny Kersey (p); Steve Jordan (g); Walter Page (bs); Bobby Donaldson (d); Jimmy Rushing (vo).

New York City—March, 1956

Don't You Miss Your Baby vJR	Co CL882
All The Cats Join In	Co CL882
Out Of Nowhere	Co CL882
After Hours	Co CL882

AL COHN

AL COHN'S NATURAL SEVEN
Joe Newman (tpt); Frank Rehak (tbn); Al Cohn (ten); Nat Pierce (p); Freddie Greene (g); Milt Hinton (bs); Osie Johnson (d, vo).

New York City—Spring 1955

A Kiss To Build A Dream On	Vi LPM1116
Doggin' Around	Vi LPM1116
Jump The Blues Away	Vi LPM1116
Jack's Kinda Swing	Vi LPM1116
The Natural Thing To Do	Vi LPM1116
AC Meets Osie	Vi LPM1116
Baby Please	Vi LPM1116
9.20 Special	Vi LPM1116
Pick-A-Dilly	Vi LPM1116
Count Me In	Vi LPM1116
Freddie's Tune	Vi LPM1116
Osie's Blues vOJ	Vi LPM1116

VIC DICKENSON

Vic Dickenson Septet

Ruby Braff (tpt); Vic Dickenson (tbn); Ed Hall (clt); Sir Charles Thompson (p); Steve Jordan (g); Walter Page (bs); Les Erskine (d).

New York City—December 29, 1953

Russian Lullaby	Vng VRS8001, VngE PPT12000
Jeepers Creepers	Vng VRS8001, VngE PPT12000
I Cover The Waterfront	Vng VRS8002, VngE PPT12005
Sir Charles At Home	Vng VRS8002, VngE PPT12005
Keeping Out Of Mischief Now	Vng VRS8002, VngE PPT12005

Shad Collins, Ruby Braff (tpt); Vic Dickenson (tbn); Ed Hall (clt); Sir Charles Thompson (p); Steve Jordan (g); Walter Page (bs); Jo Jones (d).

New York City—November 29, 1954

When You And I Were Young Maggie	Vng VRS8012, VngE PPT12015
You Brought A New Kind of Love To Me	Vng VRS8012, VngE PPT12015
Everybody Loves My Baby	Vng VRS8012, VngE PPT12015
Nice Work If You Can Get It	Vng VRS8012, VngE PPT12015
Old Fashioned Love	Vng VRS8013
Suspension Blues	Vng VRS8013
Running Wild	Vng VRS8013

HARRY EDISON

Harry Edison Quartet

Harry Edison (tpt); Arnold Ross (p); Joe Comfort (bs); Alvin Stoller (d).

"Haig" Club, Los Angeles—July 1, 1952

282	*September In The Rain*	PJLP-4, PJ 612, VgE LDE-118
283	*Pennies From Heaven*	PJLP-4, PJ 612, VgE LDE-118
284	*These Foolish Things*	PJLP-4, PJ 613, VgE LDE-118
285	*Indiana*	PJLP-4, PJ 613, VgE LDE-118

FRANK FOSTER

Frank Foster Quartet

Frank Foster (ten); Henri Renaud (p); Jean-Marie Ingrande (bs); Jean-Louis Viale (d).

Paris—April 4, 1954

My Heart Stood Still	Vg LD209, VgE LDE112
Fat Shoes	Vg LD209, VgE LDE112
I'll Take Romance	Vg LD209, VgE LDE112
Escale A Victoria	Vg LD209, VgE LDE112
The Things We Did Last Summer	Vg LD209, VgE LDE112
Just Forty Bars	Vg LD209, VgE LDE112

FRANK FOSTER QUINTET

Benny Powell (tbn); Frank Foster (ten); Gildo Mahones (p); Percy Heath (bs); Kenny Clarke (d).

New York City—May 5, 1954

Little Red	BN LP5043
How I Spent The Night	BN LP5043
Blue For Benny	BN LP5043
Out Of Nowhere	BN LP5043
Gracias	BN LP5043
The Heat's On	BN LP5043

FREDDIE GREENE

MR. RHYTHM

Joe Newman (tpt); Henry Coker (tbn); Al Cohn (clt, ten); Nat Pierce (p); Freddie Greene (g); Milt Hinton (bs); Osie Johnson alternating with Jo Jones (d).

New York City—Early 1956

Up In The Blues	Vi LPM1210
Down For Double	Vi LPM1210
Back And Forth	Vi LPM1210
Free And Easy	Vi LPM1210
Learnin' The Blues	Vi LPM1210
Feed Bag	Vi LPM1210
Something's Gotta Give	Vi LPM1210
Easy Does It	Vi LPM1210
Little Red	Vi LPM1210
Swinging Back	Vi LPM1210
A Date With Ray	Vi LPM1210
When You Wish Upon A Star	Vi LPM1210

BILLIE HOLIDAY

BILLIE HOLIDAY (vo) acc. Joe Newman (tpt); Paul Quinichette (ten); Oscar Peterson (p); Freddie Greene (g); Ray Brown (bs); Gus Johnson (d).

New York City—July, 1952

839–6	*My Man*	Clef 89089, LP144, CoE SEB10035
840–4	*Lover Come Back To Me*	Clef 89037, LP144, CoE SEB10009
841–3	*Stormy Weather*	Clef 89064, LP144, CoE SEB10009
842–2	*Yesterdays*	Clef 89037, LP144, CoE SEB10009
843–6	*He's Funny That Way*	Clef 89089, LP144, CoE SEB10035
844–3	*I Can't Face The Music*	Clef 89096, LP144, CoE SEB10035

ILLINOIS JACQUET

ILLINOIS JACQUET AND HIS ORCHESTRA

Joe Newman, Russell Jacquet, Fats Navarro (tpt); Jimmy Powell (alt); Illinois Jacquet (ten); Leo Parker (bar); Sir Charles Thompson (p); Freddie Greene (g); Al Lucas (bs); Shadow Wilson (d).

137AL	*Blow Illinois, Blow*	Ald 3001, LP701, Esq 10–063
138AL	*Illinois Blows The Blues**	Ald 3001, LP701, Esq 10–063
	Goofin' Off	Ald 3011, LP701
	It's Wild	Ald 3011

NOTE: Ald LP701 issued in Britain on Felsted EDL87014.

*Jacquet and rhythm section only on this title.

JAZZ STUDIO ONE

JAZZ STUDIO ONE

Joe Newman (tpt); Benny Green (tpt); Frank Foster, Paul Quinichette (ten); Hank Jones (p); Johnny Smith (g); Eddie Jones (bs); Kenny Clarke (d).

New York City—October 10, 1953

| MG3539 | *Tenderly* | De DL8058, BrE LAT8036 |
| MG3540 | *Let's Split* | De DL8058, BrE LAT8036 |

JO JONES

JO JONES SPECIAL

Emmett Berry (tpt); Benny Green (tbn); Lucky Thompson (ten); Nat Pierce (p); Freddie Greene (g); Walter Page (bs); Jo Jones (d).

New York City—August 11, 1955

	Lover Man	Vng VRS8503, VngE PPL11002
	Georgia Mae	Vng VRS8503, VngE PPL11002
	Lincoln Heights	Vng VRS8503, VngE PPL11002
	Embraceable You	Vng VRS8503, VngE PPL11002

See under Jimmy Rushing and Part I of this appendix for other titles from this session.

THAD JONES

THAD JONES QUINTET

Thad Jones (tpt); Frank Wess (ten, fl); Hank Jones (p); Charlie Mingus (bs); Kenny Clarke (d).

New York City—August 11, 1954

	Bitty Ditty	Debut DLP12, VgE LDE172
	Chazzanova	Debut DLP12, VgE LDE172
	Illusive	Debut DLP12, VgE LDE172
	Sombre Intrusion	Debut DLP12, VgE LDE172

Omit Wess.

Same date

| | *I'll Remember April* | Debut DLP12, VgE LDE172 |
| | *You Don't Know What Love Is* | Debut DLP12, VgE LDE172 |

THAD JONES-CHARLIE MINGUS

Thad Jones (tpt); John Dennis (p); Charlie Mingus (bs); Max Roach (d).

New York City—March 10, 1955

One More	Debut DLP17
I Can't Get Started	Debut DLP17
More Of The Same	Debut DLP17
Get Out Of Town	Debut DLP17

KANSAS CITY GROUPS

KANSAS CITY FIVE

Buck Clayton (tpt); Eddie Durham (tbn, g); Freddie Greene (g); Walter Page (bs); Jo Jones (d).

New York City—March 18, 1938

P22580-1	*Laughing At Life*	Cmd 510
P22581-1	*Good Mornin' Blues*	Cmd 511
P22582-1	*I Know That You Know*	Cmd 510

KANSAS CITY SIX

Add Lester Young (clt, ten).

New York City—September 8, 1938

P23421-2	*Way Down Yonder In New Orleans*	Cmd 512, FL20021
P23422-1	*Countless Blues*	Cmd 509, FL20021
P23423-2	*Them There Eyes*	Cmd 511
P23424-1	*I Want A Little Girl*	Cmd 509, FL20021
P23425-1	*Pagin' The Devil*	Cmd 512, FL20021

*vo by Freddie Greene.

Bill Coleman (tpt); Dicky Wells (tbn); Lester Young (ten); Joe Bushkin (p); John Simmons (bs); Jo Jones (d).

New York City—March, 1944

4746	*Three Little Words*	Cmd 573, FL20021
4747-1	*Jo-Jo*	Cmd 555, FL20021
4748-1	*I Got Rhythm*	Cmd 555, FL20021
4749	*Four O'clock Drag*	Cmd 573, FL20021

JOE NEWMAN

JOE NEWMAN AND HIS BAND

Joe Newman (tpt); Matthew Gee (tbn); Frank Wess (ten, fl); Frank Foster (ten); Johnny Acea (p); Eddie Jones (bs); Osie Johnson (d).

New York City—March 9, 1954

Close Quarters	Vng VRS8007, VngE PPT12001
Jose Beguines	Vng VRS8007, VngE PPT12001
Blues For Slim	Vng VRS8007, VngE PPT12001
The Sleeper	Vng VRS8007, VngE PPT12001

Joe Newman Octet

Joe Newman (tpt); Frank Rehak (tbn); Ernie Wilkins (alt); Al Cohn (ten);
Nat Pierce (p); Freddie Greene (g); Milt Hinton (bs); Shadow Wilson (d).

New York City—February 8, 1955

F2JB1285	*It's A Thing Of The Past*	Vi LPM1118
F2JB1286	*I Could Have Told You*	Vi LPM1118
F2JB1276	*Corner Pocket*	Vi LPM1118, HMV DLP1114
F2JB1277	*Dream A Little Dream Of Me*	Vi LPM1118, HMV DLP1114
F2JB1278	*Topsy*	Vi LPM1118, HMV DLP1114
F2JB1279	*Leonice*	Vi LPM1118, HMV DLP1114
F2JB1280	*Jack's Wax*	Vi LPM1118, HMV DLP1114
F2JB1281	*Limehouse Blues*	Vi LPM1118, HMV DLP1114
F2JB1282	*Captain Spaulding*	Vi LPM1118, HMV DLP1114
F2JB1283	*Soon*	Vi LPM1118, HMV DLP1114
F2JB1284	*If I Could Be With You*	Vi LPM1118, HMV DLP1114
F2JB1287	*Pretty Skinny Bunny*	Vi LPM1118, HMV DLP1114

Joe Newman (tpt); Urbie Green (tbn); Gene Quill (alt); Al Cohn (ten);
Dick Katz (p); Freddie Greene (g); Eddie Jones (bs); Shadow Wilson (d).

New York City—January, 1956

Top Hat, White Tie And Tails	Vi LPM1198
You Can Depend On Me	Vi LPM1198
We'll Be Together Again	Vi LPM1198
It's Bad For Me	Vi LPM1198
Exactly Like You	Vi LPM1198
Shameful Roger	Vi LPM1198
The Daughter Of Miss Thing	Vi LPM1198
Sometimes I'm Happy	Vi LPM1198
Sweethearts On Parade	Vi LPM1198
Slats	Vi LPM1198
Lament For A Lost Love	Vi LPM1198
Perfidia	Vi LPM1198

The Count's Men

Joe Newman (tpt); Benny Powell (tbn); Frank Foster, Frank Wess (ten);
Sir Charles Thompson (p); Eddie Jones (bs); Shadow Wilson (d).

New York City—March, 1956

Sidewalks Of New York	Jazztone J-1220
Careless Love	Jazztone J-1220
Jumping At The Woodside	Jazztone J-1220
Casey Jones	Jazztone J-1220
The Midgets	Jazztone J-1220
Alone In The Night	Jazztone J-1220
Annie Laurie	Jazztone J-1220

I Feel Like A Newman

Joe Newman (tpt); Billy Byers (tbn); Gene Quill (alt); Frank Foster (ten); John Lewis (p); Freddie Greene (g); Milt Hinton (bs); Osie Johnson (d).

New York City—April, 1956

This Time The Dream's On Me	Storyville STLP905
Imagination	Storyville STLP905
Midgets	Storyville STLP905
Diffugality	Storyville STLP905
I Feel Like A Newman	Storyville STLP905
King Size	Storyville STLP905

Joe Newman (tpt); Frank Wess (ten, fl); Sir Charles Thompson (p); Eddie Jones (bs); Shadow Wilson (d).

New York City—April, 1956

Sweetie Cake	Storyville STLP905
East Of The Sun	Storyville STLP905
Gee Baby, Ain't I Good To You	Storyville STLP905
My Blue Heaven	Storyville STLP905

PAUL QUINICHETTE

PAUL QUINICHETTE AND HIS ORCHESTRA

Joe Newman (tpt); Henry Coker (tbn); Marshall Royal (alt); Paul Quinichette (ten); Charlie Fowlkes (bar); Bobby Tucker (p); Freddie Greene (g); Jimmy Lewis (bs); Gus Johnson (d).

New York City—Late 1952

YB9346	*Bustin' Suds*	EmA MG26035
YB9347	*Let's Make It*	EmA MG26035
YB9348	*P.Q. Blues*	EmA MG26022
YB9349	*Bot Bot*	EmA MG26022

SHORTY ROGERS

SHORTY ROGERS AND HIS ORCHESTRA

Shorty Rogers, Harry Edison, Maynard Ferguson, Conrad Gozzo, Clyde Reasinger (tpt); Harry Betts, Milt Bernhart, Bob Enevoldsen (tbn); Bob Cooper, Herb Geller, Jimmy Guiffre, Bud Shank, Zoot Sims (reeds); John Graas (fr-h); Paul Sarmento (tu); Marty Paich (p); Curtis Counce (bs); Shelly Manne (d).

Hollywood—February 2, 1954

E4VP3021	*Topsy*	Vic LJM1004, HMV CLP1041
E4VP3022	Unknown title	Unissued
E4VP3023	*Basie Eyes*	Vic LJM1004, HMV CLP1041
E4VP3024	*It's Sand Man*	Vic LJM1004, HMV CLP1041
E4VP3025	*Doggin' Around*	Vic LJM1004, HMV CLP1041

313

Pete Candoli (tpt); Bob Gordon, Bill Holman (reeds) replace Reasinger, Cooper, Sims.

Hollywood—February 9, 1954

E4VP3026	*Jump For Me*	Vic LJM1004, HMV CLP1041
E4VP3027	*Over And Out*	Vic LJM1004, HMV CLP1041
E4VP3028	*Down For Double*	Vic LJM1004, HMV CLP1041
E4VP3029	*Swingin' The Blues*	Vic LJM1004, HMV CLP1041

Bob Cooper, Zoot Sims (reeds) replace Holman and Gordon.

Hollywood—March 3, 1954

E4VP3052	*H And J*	Vic LJM1004, HMV CLP1041
E4VP3053	*Tickle Toe*	Vic LJM1004, HMV CLP1041
E4VP3054	*Taps Miller*	Vic LJM1004, HMV CLP1041
E4VP3055	*Walk, Don't Run*	Vic LJM1004, HMV CLP1041

JIMMY RUSHING

JIMMY RUSHING SINGS THE BLUES

Jimmy Rushing (vo) acc. Pat Jenkins (tpt); Henderson Chambers (tbn); Buddy Tate (ten); Ben Richardson (clt, alt); Sam Price (p); Walter Page (bs); Jo Jones (d).

New York City—December 1, 1954

Goin' To Chicago	Vng VRS8011, VngE PPT12002
How Long Blues	Vng VRS8011, VngE PPT12002
I Want A Little Girl	Vng VRS8011, VngE PPT12002
Sent For You Yesterday	Vng VRS8011, VngE PPT12002
Boogie Woogie	Vng VRS8011, VngE PPT12002
How You Want Your Lovin' Done	Vng VRS8011, VngE PPT12002
Leave Me	Vng VRS8011, VngE PPT12002

LISTEN TO THE BLUES

Jimmy Rushing (vo) acc. Emmett Berry (tpt); Lawrence Brown (tbn); Rudy Powell (clt, alt); Buddy Tate (ten); Pete Johnson (p); Freddie Greene (g); Walter Page (bs); Jo Jones (d).

New York City—August 16, 1955

See See Rider	Vng VRS8505, VngE PPT12016
It's Hard To Laugh Or Smile	Vng VRS8505, VngE PPT12016
Every Day	Vng VRS8505, VngE PPT12016
Evenin'	Vng VRS8505
Good Morning Blues	Vng VRS8505, VngE PPT12016
Roll 'Em Pete	Vng VRS8505
Don't Cry Baby	Vng VRS8505
Take Me Back, Baby	Vng VRS8505, VngE PPT12016
Rock And Roll	Vng VRS8505, VngE PPT12016

JO JONES SPECIAL
Rushing out.

Same date

| *Caravan* | Vng VRS8503, VngE PPL11002 |

SIR CHARLES THOMPSON

SIR CHARLES THOMPSON SEXTET

Joe Newman (tpt); Benny Powell (tbn); Pete Brown (alt); Sir Charles Thompson (p); Gene Ramey (bs); Osie Johnson (d).

New York City—December 30, 1953

Bop This	Vng VRS8003
Memories Of You	Vng VRS8003
For The Ears	Vng VRS8003
Oh Joe!	Vng VRS8003

SIR CHARLES THOMPSON QUARTET

Sir Charles Thompson (p); Freddie Greene (g); Walter Page (bs); Jo Jones (d).

New York City—January 22, 1954

Swingtime In The Rockies	Vng VRS8006, VngE PPT12007
Honeysuckle Rose	Vng VRS8006, VngE PPT12007
These Foolish Things	Vng VRS8006, VngE PPT12007
Sweet Georgia Brown	Vng VRS8006, VngE PPT12007

JOE TURNER

JOE TURNER SINGS KANSAS CITY JAZZ

Joe Turner (vo) acc. Joe Newman (tpt); Lawrence Brown (tbn); Pete Brown (alt); Frank Wess (ten); Pete Johnson (p); Freddie Greene (g); Walter Page (bs); Cliff Leeman (d).

New York City—March 6, 1956

Cherry Red	Atl LP1234, LonE LTZ–K15053
Roll 'Em Pete	Atl LP1234, LonE LTZ–K15053
Low Down Dog	Atl LP1234, LonE LTZ–K15053
How Long Blues	Atl LP1234, LonE LTZ–K15053
Piney Brown Blues	Atl LP1234, LonE LTZ–K15053

Omit Newman and Wess.

Same date

Morning Glories	Atl LP1234, LonE LTZ–K15053

Joe Turner (vo) acc. Jimmy Nottingham (tpt); Lawrence Brown (tbn); Pete Brown (alt); Seldon Powell (ten); Pete Johnson (p); Freddie Greene (g); Walter Page (bs); Cliff Leeman (d).

New York City—March 7, 1956

I Want A Little Girl	Atl LP1234, LonE LTZ–K15053
Wee Baby Blues	Atl LP1234, LonE LTZ–K15053
You're Driving Me Crazy	Atl LP1234, LonE LTZ–K15053
St. Louis Blues	Atl LP1234, LonE LTZ–K15053

EARL WARREN

EARL WARREN AND HIS ORCHESTRA

Ed Lewis, Harry Edison, Joe Newman, Al Killian (tpt); Dicky Wells, Eli Robinson, Lewis Taylor, Ted Donnelly (tbn); Earl Warren, Jimmy Powell (alt); Lester Young, Buddy Tate (ten); Rudy Rutherford (bar); Clyde Hart (p); Freddie Greene (g); Rodney Richardson (bs); Jo Jones (d).

New York City—April 18, 1944

5440	*Empty Hearted*	Svy 507
5441	*Circus In Rhythm*	Svy 539
5442	unknown title	unissued
5443	*Tush*	Svy 507, 539

FRANK WESS

FRANK WESS QUINTET

Frank Wess (ten, fl); Benny Powell (tbn); Jimmy Jones (p); Oscar Pettiford (bs); Osie Johnson (d).

New York City—May 8, 1954

Frankosis	Cmd FL20031, AtlE LP1
You're My Thrill	Cmd FL20031, AtlE LP1
Basie Ain't Here	Cmd FL20031, AtlE LP1

Henry Coker (tbn) replaces Powell.

Same date

Some Other Spring	Cmd FL20031, AtlE LP1
Wess Point	Cmd FL20031, AtlE LP1
Mishawaka	Cmd FL20031, AtlE LP1
Flute Song	Cmd FL20031, AtlE LP1

FRANK WESS SEXTET

Joe Wilder (tpt); Henry Coker, Urbie Green (tbn); Frank Wess (ten, fl); Jimmy Jones (p); Oscar Pettiford (bs); Osie Johnson (d).

New York City—May, 1954

Pretty Eyes	Cmd FL20032
Wess Of The Moon	Cmd FL20032
I'll Be Around	Cmd FL20032
Danny's Delight	Cmd FL20032
All My Life	Cmd FL20032
Romance	Cmd FL20032
Frankly The Blues	Cmd FL20032

NORTH, SOUTH, EAST . . . WESS

Henry Coker, Bennie Powell (tbn); Frank Foster, Frank Wess (ten); Kenny Burrell (g); Eddie Jones (bs); Kenny Clarke (d).

New York City—Spring, 1956

What D'Ya Say?	Svy MG12072
Dill Pickles	Svy MG12072

Dancing On The Ceiling	Svy MG12072
Hard Sock Dance	Svy MG12072
Salvation	Svy MG12072
Lazy Sal	Svy MG12072

ERNIE WILKINS

FLUTES AND REEDS

Ernie Wilkins (alt, arr); Frank Wess, Jerome Richardson (ten, fl); Hank Jones (p); Eddie Jones (bs); Kenny Clarke (d).

New York City—August, 1955

Shorty George	Svy MG12022, LonE LTZ–C15016
Bouncing With Boots	Svy MG12022, LonE LTZ–C15016
That's A Woman	Svy MG12022, LonE LTZ–C15016
Doin' The Thing	Svy MG12022, LonE LTZ–C15016
Blues In A Cold Water Flat	Svy MG12022, LonE LTZ–C15016
Stereophonic	Svy MG12022, LonE LTZ–C15016

TOP BRASS

Joe Wilder, Ernie Royal, Donald Byrd, Ray Copeland, Idrees Suliman (tpt); Hank Jones (p); Wendell Marshall (bs); Kenny Clarke (d); Ernie Wilkins (arr).

New York City—November, 1955

58 Market Street	Svy MG12044, LonE LTZ–C15013
Trick Or Treat	Svy MG12044, LonE LTZ–C15013
Speedway	Svy MG12044, LonE LTZ–C15013
Dot's What	Svy MG12044, LonE LTZ–C15013
Top Brass	Svy MG12044, LonE LTZ–C15013
Ballad Medley	Svy MG12044, LonE LTZ–C15013

LESTER YOUNG

LESTER YOUNG AND HIS BAND

Vic Dickenson (tbn); Lester Young (ten); Dodo Marmarosa (p); Freddie Greene (g); Red Callender (bs); Henry " Tucker " Green (d).

Hollywood—December, 1945

123A	*D.B. Blues*	Ald 123, Esq 10–067, VgE LAE12016
123B	*Lester Blows Again*	Ald 123, Esq 10–067, VgE LAE12016
124A	*These Foolish Things**	Ald 124, Esq 10–164
124B	*Jumpin' At Mesner's*	Ald 124, Esq 10–164

*Omit Vic Dickenson.

Howard McGhee (tpt); Vic Dickenson (tbn); Willie Smith (alt); Lester Young (ten); Wesley Jones (p); Curtis Counce (bs); Johnny Otis (d).

	It's Only A Paper Moon	Ald 127, Esq 10–098
	After You've Gone*	Ald 127, MldscE 1034, VgE LAE12016
	Lover Come Back To Me	Ald 128, Esq 10–098
	Jammin' With Lester	Ald 128

*Lester Young with rhythm only.

LESTER YOUNG QUINTET

Lester Young (ten); Joe Albany (p); Irving Ashby (g); Red Callender (bs); Chico Hamilton (d).

Hollywood—August, 1946

	New Lester Leaps In	Ald 137, Esq 10–088, VgE LAE12016
	You're Driving Me Crazy	Ald 137, VgE LAE12016
	She's Funny That Way	Ald 138, VgE LAE12016
	Lester's Be Bop Boogie	Ald 138, Esq 10–164, VgE LAE12016

LESTER YOUNG AND HIS BAND

Shorts McConnell (tpt); Lester Young (ten); Dense Thornton (p); Fred Lacey (g); Rodney Richardson (bs); Lyndell Marshall (d).

New York City—February 18, 1947

46	*Sunday*	Ald 162
	S.M. Blues	Ald 162
	Jumpin' With Symphony Sid*	Ald 163, Esq 10–123
49	*No Eyes Blues**	Ald 163, MldscE 1034
50	*Sax-O-Be-Bop*	Ald 164, Esq 10–252, VgE EPV1127
51	*On The Sunny Side Of The Street**	Ald 164, Esq 10–252
	Just Cooling*	Ald 3057, VgE EPV1127

*Omit McConnell on these tracks.

LESTER YOUNG SEXTET

Lester Young (ten); Gene DiNovi (p); Chuck Wayne (g); Curley Russell (bs); Tiny Kahn (d).

New York City—November, 1947

1020	*Tea For Two*	VgE LAE12016
1021	*East Of The Sun*	Ald 3016, VgE LAE12016
1022	*Sheik Of Araby*	Ald 3016, VgE LAE12016
1023	*Something To Remember You By*	Ald 3057, VgE LAE12016

Shorts McConnell (tpt); Lester Young (ten); Dense Thornton (p); Fred Lacey (g); Tex Briscoe (bs); Roy Haynes (d).

Chicago—December 29, 1947

AL141	*I'm Confessin'*	Ald 212, Esq 10–123, VgE LAE12016
	Easy Does It	Ald 212
123	*One O'clock Jump*	Ald 200, VgE EPV1127
124	*Jumpin' At The Woodside*	Ald 200, VgE EPV1127

Probably from December 29, 1947 session.

Movin' With Lester	Ald 3257
Lester Smooths It Out	Ald 3257

THE JAZZ GIANTS '56

Roy Eldridge (tpt); Vic Dickenson (tbn); Lester Young (ten); Teddy Wilson (p); Freddie Greene (g); Gene Ramey (bs); Jo Jones (d).

New York City—January 21, 1956

I Guess I'll Have To Change My Plans	Norgran LP1056, CoE 33CX10054
I Didn't Know What Time It Was	Norgran LP1056, CoE 33CX10054
Gigantic Blues	Norgran LP1056, CoE 33CX10054
This Year's Kisses	Norgran LP1056, CoE 33CX10054
You Can Depend On Me	Norgran LP1056, CoE 33CX10054

DICKY WELLS

DICKY WELLS AND HIS ORCHESTRA

Bill Coleman (tpt); Dicky Wells (tbn); Lester Young (ten); Ellis Larkins (p); Freddie Greene (g); Al Hall (bs); Jo Jones (d).

New York City—December 21, 1943

T19003	*I Got Rhythm*	Sig 90002
T19004	*I'm Fer It Too*	Sig 90002
T1920	*Linger Awhile*	Sig 28115
T1921	*Hello Babe*	Sig 28115

ABBREVIATIONS

A list of record label abbreviations used in the foregoing discography. All record companies are American unless otherwise stated.

Ald	Aladdin	Mer	Mercury
ARS	American Record Society	MerE	Mercury (British)
Atl	Atlantic	Norgran	
AtlE	Atlantic (British)	OK	Okeh
BN	Blue Note	PaE	Parlophone (British)
BrE	Brunswick (British)	PhiE	Phillips (British)
Clef		PJ	Pacific Jazz
Cmd	Commodore	Sig	Signature
CoE	Columbia (British)	Storyville	
De	Decca	Svy	Savoy
Debut		" V " D	" V " Disc
EmA	EmArCy	Verve	
EmAE	EmArCy (British)	Vg	Vogue (French)
Epic		VgE	Vogue (British)
HMV	HMV (British)	Vi	RCA Victor
Jazztone		Vng	Vanguard
Key	Keynote	VngE	Vanguard (British)
LonE	London (British)	Vo	Vocalian

A list of instrument abbreviations used in the discography.

alt	alto saxophone	fr-h	french horn
arr	arranger	g	guitar
bar	baritone saxophone	p	piano
bs	bass	tbn	trombone
clt	clarinet	ten	tenor saxophone
d	drums	tpt	trumpet
fl	flute	vo	vocal

ACKNOWLEDGMENTS

In compiling this discography I have used information from a number of sources. I would like to express my grateful thanks to the following for their invaluable help:

Albert J. McCarthy and Dave Carey of "Jazz Directory" (published by Cassell & Co. Ltd.); Charles Delauney of "Hot Discography" (published in New York by "Criterion"); Derek Coller of the "Discophile" magazine; Jorgen Grunnet Jepsen and Ernie Edwards; Edgar Jackson; Guy Kopelowicz; Kurt Mohr and Anthony Rotante of "Record Research".

ALUN MORGAN.